STATE
AND
LOCAL
POLITICS

EIGHTH EDITION

STATE
AND
LOCAL
POLITICS

DAVID R. BERMAN

M.E. Sharpe
Armonk, New York
London, England

Editions 1–5 published by Allyn and Bacon, Inc.;
editions 6 and 7 published by Wm. C. Brown Communications, Inc.

Library of Congress Cataloging-in-Publication Data

Berman, David R.
State and local politics / David R. Berman.— 8th ed.
p.   cm.
Includes bibliographical references and index.
ISBN 1-56324-767-4 (alk. paper)
1. State governments—United States.
1. Local government—United States.
I. Title.
JK2408.B47   1996
320.973—dc20   —dc20
[320.973]   96-19264
CIP
Printed in the United States of America

The paper used in this publication meets the minimum requirements of
American National Standard for Information Sciences—
Permanence of Paper for Printed Library Materials,
ANSI Z 39.48-1984.

BM (c)   10   9   8   7   6   5   4   3   2   1
BM (p)   10   9   8   7   6   5   4   3   2   1

To Susan, Wendy, and Max

CONTENTS

☆ ☆ ☆

LIST OF TABLES, FIGURES, AND BOXES

TABLES

PREFACE

In the first edition of this book, which appeared in 1975, I set out to present a clear, concise, and current analysis of the broad environment in which state and local governments function, the nature of political activity at these levels, and what state and local governments have done or have failed to do in important areas of public policy. My goals were to explain the role of state and local governments in the federal system and how and why political life varied from one state to another and from one locality to another. These have continued to be my objectives through seven revised editions.

In this edition, as in the past, I have drawn upon a wide variety of scholarly journals and books and government documents. I have sought to examine broad theoretical questions, as well as to explain and evaluate the operation of state and local governments. At times, the text takes a critical view of the performance of state and local governments. While one may, indeed, take considerable pride in state and local governments in the United States, one should also be aware of fiscal and other constraints on their activities and note that problems of corruption, slow or poorly performing institutions, and political accountability are still found at these levels. State and local governments, moreover, continue to face a number of policy problems, for example, in educating children, reforming the welfare system, protecting the environment, and fighting crime.

In this edition, I have reintroduced a political systems model in chapter 1 to sharpen the book's overall focus. In several of the chapters, boxed inserts have been added that show the experiences or observations of practitioners or that focus on particular issues or developments. Much of the material has been rewritten or rearranged to improve clarity. As an aid to students, important terms and concepts have been highlighted in the text. The book is up-to-date in its reference to such matters as the drive toward devolution in the federal system; court decisions regarding the taking of property, affirmative action, and minority-majority districts; and movements to limit terms and to reform schools and the welfare system. New material has been added to each chapter, reflecting current developments and studies.

The text is divided into four parts. Part One, consisting of the first two chapters, offers an overview of the basic characteristics of state and local political systems and of the broader intergovernmental systems in which these units function. Chapter 1 looks at general influences (intergovernmental, economic, social, and cultural) on state and local governments; the dynamics of state and local political systems (for example, patterns of participation, influence, and policymaking); and at broad trends affecting these units. Chapter 2 offers considerable detail on the basic nature of the federal system and the legal, financial, and political relations among federal, state, and local governments.

Part Two of the book is devoted to politics at the state level. This section begins with a chapter on constitutional foundations that brings together material regarding the status of state governments under the United States Constitution, the nature of state constitutions, and legal provisions affecting citizen participation (suffrage and direct democracy). The second chapter in Part Two is devoted to political parties, interest groups, the mass media, and problems of conduct and political accountability. The remaining chapters in Part Two offer an updated account of state legislatures, the governor and administration, and state courts and the system of justice.

Part Three is concerned with local-level politics. Chapter 8 sets the tone with a discussion of different types of communities, different types of local governments, and various problems of governing metropolitan areas. Chapter 9 focuses on local political systems and explores questions about the concentration of political power in local communities. The official local government policymakers and the distribution of local services are examined in chapter 10.

Part Four of the text is devoted to problems and policies. It shows state and local governments in action: raising and spending money; attempting to resolve difficult human and financial problems in the areas of education and welfare; making decisions that affect the quality of the environment, the supply and cost of energy, and the manner in which land is used; and, in the field of law enforcement, enacting laws defining criminal conduct, enforcing these laws, and operating correctional systems.

PART ONE

★ ★ ★

STATE AND LOCAL POLITICS

1

☆　☆　☆

STATE AND LOCAL POLITICS: AN OVERVIEW

State and local officials, some have suggested, strive to "satisfy the irritating without irritating the satisfied."[1] Whatever their performance in this regard, these levels of government are important. What happens in state capitols and city halls is often vital to the quality of life in the United States. Understanding politics at these levels also goes a long way toward understanding "who gets what, when, and how" in this country.[2]

This book offers a blend of approaches to the study of state and local politics. Following tradition, the text describes these levels in terms of their roles within the federal system, their legal base and governmental structure, their interest groups and political parties, and their basic governmental activities. Drawing on research, the book also considers such matters as the social, economic, and cultural forces that help explain why politics in one part of the country is different from another; the desires, values, and expectations of individuals that have political repercussions; and the behavior of public officials—especially the factors that help explain the decisions they make. In addition, it gives considerable space to an analysis of major problems in public policy confronting state and local governments.

In looking at what state and local officials do, why they do it, how they do it, and with what effect, it is useful to think of them as functioning in a broader political system such as outlined in figure 1–1. Essentially, state and local

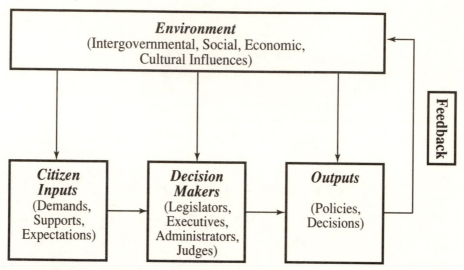

FIGURE 1-1 Political Systems Model

officials respond to inputs of various types, which they convert into policy decisions or outputs.[3] The inputs consist of demands for action and, as explained below, citizen supports and expectations. The outputs or policies may be classified in various ways, depending, for example, on their intent, how many people are directly affected, and the amount of conflict they create (see box 1–1).

The outputs can have several effects. They may, for example, settle a demand or controversy, be challenged by a disappointed group, or give rise to related demands. All this activity takes place in a broad and ever-changing environment consisting of a complex set of intergovernmental, social, economic, and cultural factors. Such factors condition every stage of the input-output process. They both help set the character of state and local politics and help distinguish the politics of one state or locality from another.

This introductory chapter begins with an overview of the broad environment in which state and local officials function. We then look at the dynamics of the political system. The remainder of the chapter presents an overview of major environmental changes affecting politics and public policy at the state and local levels. The basic conditions, processes, relationships, and developments outlined here are elaborated on more fully in later chapters.

THE ENVIRONMENT

INTERGOVERNMENTAL FACTORS

State and local governments function within a broad intergovernmental, economic, social, and cultural environment. The intergovernmental aspect

---

BOX 1–1 TYPES OF POLICIES

There is probably no universally acceptable way to classify the types of policies produced on the state and local levels. Some—such as those embodied in welfare, education, and highway programs—provide direct benefits to specific groups or the general public and involve large expenditures of public funds. Others—such as crime control or environmental protection—impose regulations on behavior but require only a relatively small outlay of public funds. At times, lawmakers have felt free to ignore questions of revenue limitations and, to please important constituents, have distributed benefits among various groups or geographical areas. In formulating such *distributive policies*, legislators engage in logrolling, that is, supporting each other's projects. Such decisions generally have had low public visibility and have been relatively free from conflict because benefits can be given out without disturbing the benefits given to others. Often more controversial have been *regulatory policies* that, though they typically cost the government relatively little, impose restrictions on the activities of some individuals or groups to protect others or the general public. Here one finds conflicts between environmental, consumer, or labor groups, on one hand, and business groups on the other. Even more controversial are *redistributive polices*, involving the transfer of resources as government is asked to come to the aid of the have-nots. These involve large classes of people and political party struggles. Historically, *developmental policies* intended to encourage economic growth, such as luring businesses by offering tax deductions, have enjoyed widespread support. In recent years, however, such policies and, indeed, the idea that growth is good, have become more controversial.

---

involves relationships between governments at different levels (federal-state, federal-local, and state-local) and at the same level (state-state, local-local). What state officials do is often conditioned by what is done by national officials, by officials in other states, and by officials in local units within their own state. Local officials, likewise, find their problems and authority affected by national, state, and other local policymakers.

Interest groups help link national, state, and local politics. Inability to secure its objectives on one level of government often prompts a group to take its cause to another level. Civil rights groups representing black Americans, for example, found resistance to their demands for an end to discrimination in housing, education, and employment on the state and local levels, so they shifted their attention to Congress and the federal courts. Several civil rights victories on the national level in the 1960s, however, brought intensified efforts by opponents to limit or negate their impact on the state and local levels. More recently, pro-life and pro-choice forces have taken their battle over abortion from the states to the federal courts and Congress and back to the states again.

Political party and election activity also helps draw the various strata of government together. The national political parties have the base of their strength in state and local organizations. For example, during his long tenure as mayor of Chicago, the late Richard Daley was a powerful force, not only in Illinois local and state politics but also in the national politics of the Democratic Party. At election time, state and local campaigns often influence and are influenced by national campaigns and issues. Often, if a party's national candidates do well, so do its candidates in the states and localities.[4]

Legal and fiscal factors, finally, bring the various levels of government into close relationships with each other. The United States Constitution, as interpreted largely by the United States Supreme Court, determines the allocation of governmental authority between the national and state governments and imposes limitations on all levels of government. State constitutions, laws, and judicial decisions further allocate authority between state and local governments and impose additional limitations on both levels. All strata of government have a common financial source—the people of the United States—and are in competition for the tax dollar. The fiscal ties between the various levels of government are complex. Money raised by one level is frequently transmitted to another, with various types of restrictions on how that money may be spent.

Politics on all levels is interrelated, and the nation may well be becoming increasingly uniform with the development of a national economy and culture. The nature of politics, however, continues to vary from state to state. There are differences among the states, for example, in the level of citizen participation and the number of competing interest groups. There are also differences in the extent to which state governments innovate in the development of new programs and follow what may be considered liberal or conservative courses of policy. Some of the differences show up in easily recognizable patterns. Southern states, for example, have traditionally been lower in the level of citizen participation than have states in other regions. In general, the most innovative and liberal states (for example, those most supportive of civil rights legislation, regulations to protect consumers, and educational and other social service programs) are in nonsouthern, coastal, or Great Lakes states such as New York, Massachusetts, California, Oregon, and Wisconsin.[5]

ECONOMIC FACTORS

In looking for factors that help explain why politics is different in one jurisdiction than another, attention must be given to economic, social, and cultural conditions. Economic conditions are important, in part, because the way people make their living has a large influence on the nature of an area's political activity. An area may be dominated by a single economic activity, such as farming, mining, manufacturing, or retailing. Groups or individuals prominent in an industry important to an area's employment level and general prosperity have at least considerable potential influence in an area's political life. Often, however, there are conflicts between economic interests, for example, between rival companies or industries or when groups such as labor unions and those concerned with the physical environment challenge the dominant industries.

In addition to the number and diversity of economic interests within an area, scholars have emphasized the importance of a state's or locality's level of economic development. In determining economic development, we look at such factors as the rate of industrialization, population size, urbanization, and personal income. Generally, as a state becomes more industrialized, it becomes more heavily populated and urbanized, and the income of its citizens improves. Along with increases in wealth come higher levels of education, a greater tendency for citizens to participate in politics, a higher degree of party competition, and a richer tax base to support public programs. In general, it appears that highly industrialized and urbanized states have a more competitive party system, more citizen participation (for example, larger voting turnout), and a higher level of governmental expenditures for such functions as health, education, and welfare.[6]

There are, however, several exceptions to these generalities. Relatively poor states like Alabama and Oklahoma, for example, have had large expenditures for certain types of public assistance programs.[7] Data on voting turnout (see table 1–1) suggest that many of the states where participation has been lowest (largely in the South and Southwest) are indeed among the least urbanized and economically developed. However, so are many of the states that rank unusually high in citizen turnout—Idaho, Montana, North Dakota, South Dakota, and Utah. Political culture and formal or informal limits on the opportunity to vote perhaps have played a more important role than urbanization and economic factors in explaining variations in voting turnout. Similarly, one finds that such factors as differences in political leadership and political party strength help explain why states with comparable economies often arrive at quite different policy decisions, for example, in regard to welfare spending.

SOCIAL FACTORS

We find other important dimensions of state and local politics by looking into the social characteristics of the populations within an area and the distribution of different types of people throughout a state or locality. Ethnic,

TABLE 1–1   Voter Turnout by State in Presidential Elections:
              1960–1992

States Consistently Below the National Average	States Consistently at Least 5% Above the National Average
Arizona	Connecticut
Arkansas	Idaho
Florida	Iowa
Georgia	Minnesota
Hawaii	Montana
Kentucky	North Dakota
Maryland	Oregon
Nevada	South Dakota
North Carolina	Utah
South Carolina	Washington
Tennessee	Wisconsin
Texas	
Virginia	

Source: Statistical Abstract of the United States and Current Population Reports (Washington, D.C.: Government Printing Office, various years).

racial, and religious differences have long been particularly important factors in state and local politics.[8] Ethnic politics have played an important role in northeastern states such as Massachusetts for many years. In these areas, party slates of candidates for state and local offices are commonly balanced with Yankee, Irish, and Italian names, and Catholic versus Protestant conflicts often take place over issues such as parochial schools, birth control, and abortion. Elsewhere, the religious factor has been evident in the activities of particular subcultures such as Mormons in the West and the Baptists in the South. Throughout the "Bible Belt" of the South and Midwest, conservative Protestant majorities have long made their influence felt on "morality" policies such as those regarding liquor and gambling.[9]

Race relations have been especially important in the politics of several southern states and are of increasing importance in other parts of the country where large numbers of blacks have migrated. Over the past several years, sharp gains have been made in the number of blacks voting and holding office. Contributing to this have been the various national voting rights acts of the 1960s, which made it possible virtually to triple black registration, and a growing awareness of black pride and power.

The increase in black officeholders has, in some areas, created a sense of normalcy about blacks holding such positions and has engendered considerable pride in the black community. The increase has also been important in sensitizing white officials about black problems and, in some cases, has brought about more equitable policies.[10]

Blacks represent over 20 percent of the total electorate in seven southern or border states (Alabama, Georgia, Louisiana, Maryland, Mississippi, North Carolina, and South Carolina). Black electoral power is particularly evident in large cities like Washington, D.C., Newark, New Jersey, and Atlanta, Georgia, which have black majorities, and in cities like Baltimore, Detroit, and St. Louis, where blacks constitute more than 40 percent of the total population. The concentration of blacks in large cities has provided them with at least great potential influence in several local, state legislative, and congressional races in strategic states like New York, California, Pennsylvania, Illinois, Ohio, and Michigan.

Spanish-speaking Americans—largely Mexican but also Puerto Rican, Cuban, and Central and South American—have also become more politically active and significant. People with Spanish heritage constitute 10 percent of the population, some 27 million people, and a relatively young and rapidly growing segment of the population. They are an especially important part of local, state, and congressional constituencies in Arizona, California, Colorado, Florida, Illinois, New Mexico, and Texas. To increase their influence, Hispanic groups have been active in registering and mobilizing Hispanic voters (who, with the principal exception of Cubans, tend to be Democrats), recruiting candidates, and bringing about reforms in the electoral system to improve Hispanic representation.

Like the Spanish-origin population, the Asian and Pacific population is concentrated in a few states, most noticeably Hawaii and California. In Hawaii, 62 percent of the population is Asian or Pacific Islander. Democrats in Hawaii have historically drawn upon the support of Japanese American and other ethnic groups in defeating Republicans, whose base of support has been in the smaller white population. The situation is, however, somewhat fluid. In any given election we are likely to find voting groups of Filipinos, Japanese, whites, Chinese, and Hawaiians. From election to election, however, the groups form different winning coalitions.[11]

The American Indian, Eskimo, and Aleut populations are important in Alaska, where they constitute around 14 percent of the population. Indian groups have been especially significant in New Mexico, Oklahoma, South Dakota, Arizona, and Montana, where they comprise from 4 to 7 percent of the population. In these states difficulties center on the efforts of states and localities to tax Indians and regulate activities such as casino gambling on the reservations, and the efforts of tribal leaders and their representatives in legislatures and local councils to secure more assistance from the state and local governments.

Frequently, throughout the nation, the mass migration of people with differing characteristics into an area has brought about changes in that area's politics.[12] In Arizona, for example, an early migration from Texas set the stage for the dominance of conservative Democrats in state politics. This dominance was upset by a later migration from the Midwest, which developed a two-party system, if not Republican dominance.[13] Partisan divisions in border states like Maryland, Kentucky, West Virginia, and Missouri were largely established by the settlement of migrants from the states of the Confederacy in the southern portions of these states and the settlement of Yankees in their northern portions.

Similarly, the difference between liberal northern California and conservative southern California largely stems from different sources of immigration into the two regions. A more cosmopolitan and urban migration from the northeastern part of the country settled the San Francisco area, while large numbers of the migrants to the Los Angeles area came from the rural, Protestant Midwest.[14] More recently, Anglos in California and other states have reacted to the changing ethnic composition of their populations produced by the influx of many Hispanics and Asian immigrants. Migration has produced antiforeign sentiments and demands on the state level, for example, for making English the official language of the state.

The distribution of a state's population also has significance in understanding its politics. In many states, factors such as accessibility to water and urbanization have concentrated much of the population into one or two large cities. Chicago, New York City, Denver, and Atlanta, for example, have contained a large percentage of their states' total population. Many conflicts in state politics, for example, questions concerning representation in state legislatures or the distribution of state aid to local governments, have set the big cities against the "down staters" or the rest of the population in suburban and rural areas. Sometimes conflicts take on regional splits of a rural-urban nature. People in southwestern Kansas, essentially a sparsely settled area of ranchers and farmers, for example, have been unhappy about the way the urban-dominated legislature allocates funds for schools and roads. In the early 1990s, they were warm to the idea of having their counties, seven in all, secede from Kansas and form a new state along with other rural areas in neighboring states.

Conflict in local politics often occurs between neighborhoods or different sections of a city that are composed of people with different lifestyles and conflicting aspirations. Ethnic and racial groups representing different parts of a city also may struggle for control of city hall, as one group tries to replace or succeed another in power. An example of an *ethnic succession conflict* took place in Boston during the closing decades of the nineteenth century when Yankee (native) control of local politics was successfully challenged by Irish Catholics. Currently, the growing numbers of Hispanics and blacks in many communities have brought about similar conflicts for control over local governmental institutions.

CULTURAL FACTORS

Several years ago, historian W. J. Cash observed that every now and then a journalist or a professor will assert that the South is simply a geographical division of the United States. Nobody, Cash wrote, has ever paid much attention to this observation, and rightly so, because there was in the South "a complex of established relationships and habits of thought, sentiments, prejudices, standards, and values, and associations of ideas," shared by most people, that distinguishes the area from others.[15]

Despite the many differences among people in a region, state, or locality, these political areas are commonly thought of as having a dominant political culture somewhat along the lines indicated by Cash. The term *political culture* refers to widely shared and long held values, beliefs, and attitudes that condition political behavior. The political culture of a given area affects the way its citizens and public officials perceive conditions, structure institutions, and solve problems.

Some of the basic values that were dominant at one time within a given jurisdiction are reflected in the basic laws that set governmental authority, structure, and basic procedures. Many of the older state constitutions, for example, reflect the values prominent when they were written by placing considerable emphasis on legislative supremacy and popular control of government. Other constitutions, however, reflect what has been called the "managerial tradition," which places emphasis on streamlined and efficient government headed by a strong governor.[16] On the local level, many communities have demonstrated a preference for a businesslike, "good government" approach by adopting charters (the local equivalent of a constitution) providing for a council-manager form of government along with nonpartisan elections held at large and independently of other elections. Other cities, particularly the larger ones, have opted for structures quite different from those outlined above.

Much of the research on cultural regions in the United States is based on what is known as the "Doctrine of First Effective Settlement."[17] By this it is meant that the first European or white population to have settled a given area in the United States, be it a town, state, or region, had a long-term impact on the future development, including political development, of the area. Much, indeed, can often be told about the politics of a given area by reference to the area's "founding fathers" and the institutions and practices they left behind. At the same time it is also clear that political cultures do change. Change may come about as the result of dramatic events, broad-scale political movements that cause people to reexamine their political attitudes, or the migration of people into an area who hold different political attitudes from those already residing there.

Political cultures in states and localities represent, in part, the lingering impact of major events such as the Civil War or the Great Depression of the 1930s. Social and political movements have also left their imprint on the culture of various areas of the country. One example is the Populist movement, which took root in rural southern and plains states in the 1890s. Farmers played a particularly prominent role in this movement. Bent on reform, they decided to "raise less corn and more hell." The movement led to the establishment of commissions to regulate the rates and services of railroads and other large enterprises, and the passage of antitrust legislation designed to break up monopolies and curb collusion among businesses. Populists also championed the rights of a growing class of industrial laborers and campaigned for measures such as the initiative and referendum, which would open the political process so government would respond to the interests of "the people" rather than to those of the corporations—or alternatively, to interests of "the little fellers" rather than "the Rockefellers."

On the heels of the Populist movement came the Progressive movement, which reached its peak during the last decades of the nineteenth century and the first two decades of the twentieth century. Unlike the Populists, the Progressives were led for the most part by white, middle-class city dwellers. The Progressives, however, championed reforms earlier advocated by the Populists on economic regulation, protection of workers, and democratizing the political system. On the state level, the Progressive influence became particularly evident in New York, Wisconsin, California, and Oregon. On the local level, the Progressive movement took the form of the "municipal reform movement" directed in large part against local "boss rule."

Scholars also consider historical migration patterns important in understanding the culture of the American states. Research on migration patterns conducted by political scientist Daniel Elazar has led to a widely used classification of three types of political culture, which, he feels, exist in various parts of the country.[18] One type is an individualistic culture in which political participation is looked on as a means of improving one's social and economic position, and politics takes the character of bargaining among individuals and groups motivated by their own self-interests rather than any perception of the common good. A certain amount of governmental corruption is expected and even tolerated by the public. Politics to people with this cultural background is a specialized business "better left to those willing to soil themselves by engaging in it." The individualistic political system is perhaps best represented by the traditional big-city political machines discussed in later chapters. Government, from this cultural perspective, functions to provide only certain minimal services and, for the most part, stays out of the social and economic realms.

Elazar's moralistic culture is, in many ways, the direct opposite of the individualistic one. The moralistic culture places emphasis on the importance of the common good and the implementation of certain shared principles. All citizens have a duty to become involved in political activity, to sacrifice their time and efforts as good citizens committed to the general welfare. Government officials likewise are expected to place the public good above the interests of specific groups, political parties, or their own personal interest. People in this culture look at government in a positive fashion and feel it is justified in intervening in private affairs for the common good. The public bureaucracy is expected to be professionally competent, hired on the basis of merit, and to pursue the interest of all.

Elazar's third culture is a traditionalistic one in which an elite takes a dominant role in government and exercises authority in a somewhat paternalistic manner. Government functions to maintain the existing social order. Active participation in politics is limited to those who hold leading social positions—the positions themselves are often inherited through family connections. Elitism leaves little room for political parties—they are less important than personal and family connections—and conservatism limits the role of the bureaucracy.

Elazar traces the origin of the moralistic culture to the Puritans of New England. Their Yankee descendants carried the culture westward, touching the northern parts of midwestern states, all the way to Oregon, Washington, and California. Individualistic culture began in the settlement in the Middle Atlantic area of many different ethnic and religious groups from eastern and southern Europe and Ireland. This pluralism developed in a greater acceptance of individualism in much of New York, New Jersey, Pennsylvania, Delaware, and Maryland. The culture spread westward into the central parts of midwestern states such as Ohio, Indiana, and Illinois, where it continues to be the dominant political culture. Traditionalistic culture, according to Elazar, developed with the settlement of southern states and a cotton-plantation-centered economy.

Even though the influence of these patterns of settlement has undoubtedly lessened over the years, some research suggests that these cultural influences continue to be important. States identified as predominantly moralistic, for example, do appear to have higher rates of citizen participation (for example, voting turnout), higher tax efforts, and larger bureaucracies than those found in other states.[19]

Dynamics of the System

While environmental forces greatly condition what state and local officials do, our understanding of politics at these levels also requires consideration of such system characteristics as the level of political participation, who participates, citizen supports and expectations, the openness of the system, and how policy is made.

Participation in Politics

Participation in state and local politics, as in national politics, takes several forms. Individuals, for example, contact policymakers to give campaign contributions, to ask for particular personal favors, or to complain about a policy or service. Other activity is collective as people become active in political party, campaign, or interest group organizations.

At one time it was commonly assumed that party and campaign activity was largely undertaken for material gains or rewards such as employment should a person's party or candidate secure office. There has, however, been a decline in patronage over the last several decades. Because of this decline and perhaps more fundamental changes in society, people who undertake political activity are commonly assumed to be more concerned about particular candidates, issues, and causes. Moreover, it has become clear that political organizations may attract people simply by the social or psychological benefits they offer, such as fraternity, prestige, and a sense of accomplishment.[20]

Extensive political activity, however, is normally limited to a relatively small number of people. Better than half of the adult population may fail to vote, even in national elections. Only about 3 percent of the adult population is active in a political party, and only about 10 percent makes 90 percent of all campaign contributions. Moreover, most of the organized groups making demands on government are actually run by only a small fraction of their memberships.

Who are the most active? Much of our knowledge is based on voter studies. Studies demonstrate that the most important factors affecting voting participation are age and education. Participation tends to increase with increases in age and education. More generally, education and wealth (which is highly associated with education) are important political resources giving those who have them an important advantage in political influence. Wealth offers individuals a greater opportunity to run for office and to secure influence through campaign contributions. Education gives citizens greater knowledge of where to take their grievances and how to express them.

Nonparticipation is related not only to a lack of political resources but also to a lack of motivation. The motivational meaning of nonparticipation, however, has long been debated. Some have argued that voter apathy indicates alienation from government—the feeling that "my opinion doesn't count for much because other people really run the show" or that "my vote is futile because the system does not respond to people like me." Recent surveys suggest that as many as 50 percent of the American people have shared this view.[21] Other observers have attributed nonparticipation to laziness. Former California Governor Jerry Brown has suggested that, rather than laziness, nonparticipation results from the citizen's studied conclusion "that whatever we are doing isn't worth commenting on one way or another."[22] Some observers, finally, look on nonparticipation as an indication of satisfaction with the status quo. From this perspective, participation is primarily a method of protest—if people are unhappy, they will become involved by voting and other means to bring about change. The lack of interest in participation, thus, suggests that people see no need for change.

In the final analysis, it may be that there is no single explanation for the failure to vote.[23] Some may be alienated from the system, having no sense of civic duty or feeling their involvement will not change things for the better. This attitude may be particularly characteristic of those with limited income and education. Others, however, may be relatively content and simply see no reason to become involved. For them, voting is a matter of utility, that is, something they will undertake when it appears useful or effective to do so. Many of those who vote on a regular basis, on the other hand, do so out of a sense of civic duty.

How do state and local governments measure up on voter participation? One finds, in general, that turnout is much lower in state and local elections than might be expected and lower than in national elections. National elections generally draw from 20 to 30 percent more voters. The net effect of this difference is that the composition of the state and local electorate is likely to be less representative of the population than the presidential electorate, thereby giving greater weight to the affluent and others who are more likely to vote.[24] In other words, because of the generally lower turnout, the state and local electorate is likely to be more conservative than the national electorate, perhaps making those levels of government less disposed toward redistributive policies such as welfare that benefit lower-income people.[25]

Voting participation rates, however, also vary among states and localities. These may, as suggested earlier, reflect differences in political culture. One, for example, can expect to find the sense of civic duty higher in moralistic states and, thus, a higher level of voting in these places. The existence of variation in the composition of the electorate among the states also means there may be rather sharp differences in the class composition of the electorate and, as a consequence, certain policies. Research suggests, for example, that states where the poor participate at the greatest rate (states with the highest turnout) are likely to have the highest welfare benefits.[26] In a broader study of democracy in the states, political scientist Kim Quaile Hill has found sharp variations not only in turnout rates but in restrictions on the right to vote and the amount of choice given voters, that is, among competing political parties. By his measures, states with moralistic cultures and high levels of economic development are more democratic than others and also more likely to have extensive civil rights policies and generous assistance programs for the poor.[27]

SUPPORTS AND EXPECTATIONS

Regardless of the extent of active citizen participation, governments on all levels need citizen support (even if in the form of tacit approval through nonparticipation) if they are to continue functioning without forcing their decisions on people.[28] The term *support* in this context refers to predispositions to regard the governmental system as legitimate and to comply voluntarily with the official decisions. Supportive attitudes are needed for the government itself, for the particular governmental officials in power, and for particular governmental programs or policies.

Favorable public attitudes may be produced by manipulating public opinion, as most public officials attempt to do to some extent.[29] Attitudes are also conditioned by *political socialization,* that is, the process by which people are brought into society and taught to share its goals and values. Essential in the socialization process are the politically relevant beliefs and attitudes an individual inherits from family, learns from friends or peer groups, and derives from formal education.

Supportive attitudes, of course, may also be produced through satisfactory policy performances. What is a satisfactory policy performance, in turn, depends largely on citizen expectations of what a particular unit of government should be doing and how it should be performing its functions. In governmental services and functions, Americans appear to have definite notions about what each level of government should be doing. Polls suggest, for example, that citizens see the national government playing the dominant role in national defense and an important role in general economic policies, social justice and civil rights (helping minorities and protecting constitutional freedoms), environmental protection, social security, and the provision of social programs for the poor, disadvantaged, and handicapped. People have viewed state governments as playing important roles in such areas as building roads, hospitals, and recreational facilities and in providing education and, in conjunction with the federal government, welfare services. For local governments, citizens have looked for important decisions in regard to urban development, police protection, education (a function they share with the state), and the provision of services such as fire protection, water, sewage disposal, and street cleaning. These views have been relatively stable, though surveys conducted in the mid-1990s show the public more inclined to give the states a greater role in regard to welfare and environmental protection and to reduce the federal role in these areas.[30]

In addition to performing certain governmental tasks, state and local governments are expected to fulfill other functions. Public expectations of this nature may vary from place to place. A study by Professors Oliver Williams and Charles Adrian suggests, for example, that city governments may be looked on by citizens primarily in one of four ways: (1) as instruments of community growth, (2) as providers of life's amenities, (3) as caretakers, and/or simply (4) as arbiters of conflicting interests.[31] In the first role, the city government's prime mission is to expand the population and wealth of the community, an objective commonly shared by merchants, newspaper editors, and chambers of commerce. In the second role, governments are expected primarily to make the community a pleasant place in which to live (that is, to give a great deal of attention to schools and parks and keeping polluting industries out of the area). But a city government as caretaker is expected to provide only essential services (for example, police and fire protection) and to strive to keep taxes low. As an arbiter of conflicting interests, the city is looked on as an umpire with no other mission than to resolve conflicts arising in the community.

Other studies suggest that citizen approval relates not only to how well governments perform expected functions but also to how these functions are performed. For example, governments are evaluated by citizens for their efficiency, honesty, the character of their most prominent officials, and the attitudes accompanying the provision of services. Governments on all levels appear to be publicly evaluated by such standards.[32]

HOW CLOSE TO THE PEOPLE?

One long cherished American belief is the idea that small units of government are preferable to larger units because smaller units are closer and more responsive to the people. We, however, are still left with the questions: Do people feel closer to their state and local governments than to the national government? Do they follow state and local politics more than national politics? Do they participate more in state and local elections than in national elections? How do citizens evaluate state and local governments in comparison with the national government?

The extent to which citizens identify with and feel attached to their states and localities, as one might expect, varies from area to area. Identification with the state, for example, appears particularly strong in Texas. The sometimes fierce pride people take in being Texans may have something to do with the fact that for nine years (1836–1845) Texas was a sovereign nation with its own president, congress, navy, and diplomatic corps. Curiously, while Texans appear unusual in the extent to which they identify with their state, they also appear to have an unusually negative view of government in general. On the other hand, people in California and New York do not identify with their states as strongly as they do in Texas, but are far more inclined to have a positive view of their state government.[33]

On a national basis, research indicates that people are likely to identify far more strongly with the nation than with the state and locality in which they reside. Indeed, state and local identifications and loyalties may be less important to many people than their ties to religious, racial, or professional groups. Increased mobility has undoubtedly been a major contributing factor in the relative lack of identification with state and local governments. Close to one-fifth of the nation's population, or over forty million people, moves to a different location, often out of state, at least once each year. The effect of this movement has been most pronounced on the local level. Overall, one result of increased mobility may be, as political scientist Norton E. Long has written, that "local citizenship has for most, though not all, lost any special privileges or significance."[34]

Research findings also suggest that citizens are better informed about national than about state and local politics and, as suggested above, more likely to vote in national elections.[35] State politics appears to suffer as a top priority item for most people because it is seen to be neither as immediate as local politics (which involves the provision of direct and very visible services such as police protection, refuse collection, or street repair) nor as glamorous and important as national and international affairs.

In general, those who follow state politics the most closely tend to do so almost exclusively of other levels and tend to be supportive of state governments. The people most attentive and supportive are those persons raised in small towns or rural areas, who currently live outside metropolitan areas, who have lived in a state for the longest periods, and who are from the southern part of the country. The latter finding undoubtedly reflects the unique historical role played by the states in southern politics. In the Northeast, one often finds a more cosmopolitan influence and, not surprisingly, fewer people who give first or second priority to state politics. Similarly, the higher a person's educational attainment and class identification, the broader his or her outlook and the less likely he or she is to be concerned exclusively with state politics at the expense of politics on other levels.

Indications of citizens' opinions of various state and local institutions and policies are given in various chapters of this book. One general measure of what citizens feel about various levels of government has been their response to the question: From which level of government do you feel you get the most or least for your money—federal, state or local? Response has varied over the years, but the general trend has been against federal government. In 1989 (the first year the question was asked), 36 percent thought the federal government gave them the least for the money. In 1990, it was 41 percent and in 1994 it was 46 percent. Table 1–2, reflecting the 1994 survey on which level gave least for the money, indicates that males, people between thirty-five and forty-four, college graduates, wealthier citizens, and those holding higher-status jobs have been particularly critical of the federal government. People in lower-income brackets have been unusually critical of state and local governments. The survey also suggests that people in the North, Midwest, and South tend to be more critical of local governments than they are of state governments, while the opposite is true among people in the Northeast and West.

In more positive terms, survey information suggests that the various levels of government have different clienteles. The preference for federal spending has been particularly strong among people over sixty-five and those retired (probably because of Social Security), nonwhites, and those with relatively low levels of education and income. The preference for local spending has been particularly high among those in managerial positions, middle-aged

TABLE 1–2   From Which Level of Government Do You Feel You
Get the *Least* for Your Money—Federal, State, or Local?
(in percent)

	Federal	State	Local	Don't Know/ No Answer
Total public	46.1	21.2	19.3	13.3
Male	51.9	20.3	16.6	11.2
Female	40.7	22.1	21.9	15.4
Total head of household	47.2	21.1	18.8	12.8
Male head	54.7	19.1	16.5	9.7
Female head	40.8	22.8	20.8	15.5
Under 35 years of age	44.1	19.7	21.8	14.4
18–24	39.2	22.9	18.2	19.7
25–34	46.7	18.0	23.6	11.6
35–44	55.0	19.9	18.7	6.5
45–65	47.2	22.7	17.6	12.5
Over 65	37.5	24.1	17.7	20.7
High school incomplete	35.6	20.8	22.0	21.5
High school graduate	44.2	19.8	20.9	15.1
College incomplete	48.0	26.0	18.8	7.3
College graduate	58.5	20.1	13.3	8.1
Household income				
Under $15K	32.5	24.1	25.8	17.6
$15–24.9K	41.8	19.0	21.0	18.2
$25K+	53.4	21.0	17.5	8.1
$25–29.9K	50.9	19.7	15.5	13.8
$30–39.9K	50.9	21.4	18.7	9.1
$40K+	55.7	21.2	17.3	5.9
Own	49.6	20.4	18.3	11.7
Rent	40.9	23.0	20.8	15.3
White	46.7	20.9	19.2	13.2
Black	41.7	23.8	23.9	10.6

(continued)

TABLE 1-2 (*continued*)

	Federal	State	Local	Don't Know/ No Answer
Employed	51.3	21.5	18.3	8.9
Employed female	45.4	23.0	20.5	11.1
Not employed	38.0	20.7	21.0	20.4
Nonemployed female	36.1	20.9	23.4	19.6
Professional/manager/owner	56.0	18.6	15.7	9.7
White collar/sales/clerical	58.0	20.2	18.3	3.5
Blue collar	42.7	24.6	21.7	11.0
Retired	42.8	20.7	16.1	20.4
Married	49.1	20.6	19.7	10.6
Not married	42.1	22.0	18.7	17.2
Household size				
1–2 people	46.6	20.8	18.9	13.7
3–4 people	42.9	22.0	22.7	12.4
5+ people	49.8	34.8	10.4	4.9
Children in household under 18	48.5	19.6	22.0	9.9
No children	43.7	22.3	17.8	16.2
Northeast	43.9	29.0	14.9	12.2
North	52.0	17.3	21.4	9.3
South	45.2	15.9	26.6	12.3
West	43.3	27.9	7.4	21.4
Nonmetro	44.2	20.6	25.7	9.5
Metro: 50,000 and over				
Fringe	41.9	24.8	15.5	17.9
Central city	52.0	18.7	15.9	13.4

Source: U.S. Advisory Commission on Intergovernmental Relations, *Changing Public Attitudes on Government and Taxes* (Washington, D.C.: Government Printing Office, 1995), p. 12.

citizens, and those who are relatively well educated and wealthy. These relationships help explain the finding that Republicans have an usually strong attachment to local government. Understandably, one finds people between eighteen and thirty-four, a bracket that includes many of those in state-supported colleges, relatively high in ranking state governments as giving the most for their money.[36]

Citizen support for state and local governments can be expected to vary by time and place. Measuring citizen attitudes on which level of government gives them the most for their money provides only a relative indication of citizen support rather than an absolute one and, as indicated above, is not the only or perhaps even the most important means by which these levels are publicly evaluated. Few Americans appear willing to abolish state and local governments, even though many may feel that these levels give them less for their taxes than the national government. Other functions performed or thought to be performed by these levels (such as avoiding the concentration of power in the national government and allowing diversity in meeting local problems) and tradition are factors leading to their support.

At the same time, it is difficult to deny that some states and many localities have been dominated by one party or group that has offered the voters few choices and has been less than responsive to minority groups or interests. State and local governments in general have been closer in participation and responsiveness to some people than to others. Given the relatively upper-class composition of the state and local electorate, these levels, particularly the latter, appear less disposed than the federal government toward polices that benefit the less affluent.

POWER AND PROCESS

The most basic question to be asked about a political system is: Who governs? Most analysts assume that the answer to that question goes a long way toward explaining who benefits from what governments do or fail to do. In considering the question of who governs, political scientists commonly regard political systems as being either elitist, pluralistic, or democratic in nature. In the first system, as identified in the traditionalistic culture, political systems are dominated by a small group of the population, for example, major business leaders, and may or may not include the official officeholders. *Pluralistic systems*, on the other hand, reflect the activity of many groups or interests, none of which controls all aspects of public policy. As later chapters suggest, observers differ over whether local systems are elitist or pluralistic, a disagreement that reflects, in part, different methodologies in studying how power is dispersed. In general, however, big-city governments seem pluralistic, sometimes hyperpluralistic, and state political systems have been developing in that same direction. Some groups, however, particularly those representing major economic interests, may be more influential than others.

The theme that state and local officials are also tied into public opinion, at least in a general sense, and thus can be said to be democratic in substance as well as procedure, finds some support in the literature. This linkage was indicated in an important study by political scientists Robert Erikson, Gerald

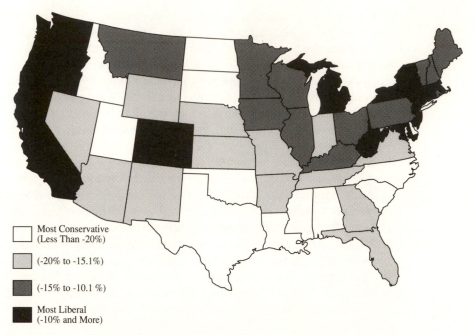

Most Conservative
(Less Than -20%)

(-20% to -15.1%)

(-15% to -10.1 %)

Most Liberal
(-10% and More)

FIGURE 1-2   Map of State Ideology (Percentage Liberal Minus
Percentage Conservative)

Source: Robert S. Erikson, Gerald C. Wright, and John P. McIver, *Statehouse Democracy: Public Opinion
and Policy in the American States* (New York: Cambridge University Press, 1993), p. 18. Reprinted with
permission of Cambridge University Press.

C. Wright, and John P. McIver.[37] Examining public opinion survey information, the authors were able to identify ideological (liberal-conservative) divisions among the states (see figure 1–2). Further investigation indicated that
the ideology affects the policy positions of political parties and, through this,
the direction of public policy in the various states. Thus, the more conservative
the outlook of the public, the more conservative the parties, and the more
conservative the direction of state policy.

Citizens, through their action or inaction, appear willing to give those who
hold state or local office considerable discretion to make decisions. The input
of the general citizenry is not in the number of decisions they make but in their
importance, for example, who governs, for how long, and major issues of
public policy.[38] The public, in effect, gives government officials an opportunity to experiment with policies but reserves the right to remove those officials
from office if things go wrong. This concept, perhaps best labeled *potential
democracy*, contrasts with the ideas of traditional democracy, wherein the
public is assumed to make its will known before action is taken rather than

retrospectively. The notion of potential democracy also conflicts with the assumptions behind the concept of *participatory democracy*—that the general public is interested in and informed about governmental affairs and is willing and able to get involved in shaping public policy.

Under the various interpretations outlined above, the official decision makers have been looked upon as agents of a governing elite, umpires in disputes among groups interests, or the instruments of the people. Perhaps most accurately, one can portray them as individuals whose behavior is conditioned to some extent, at least at certain times, by all these and several other forces, not the least of which are their own personal values.

Often those who come to power have their own idea of what reforms are necessary and initiate new laws or programs in the absence of demands that they do so. Demands for new policies or the modification of an existing policy may also arise from a problem discovered by an administrator in the course of attempting to implement a law. At other times, an administrator or legislator may seek to experiment with an idea he or she has picked up in a professional journal or while attending a convention with counterparts in another jurisdiction. In addition to these "inputs from within" or "internal demands" (coming from those in office) are external demands from various sources. Some come from public officials on other levels of government. Federal administrators, for example, call upon state and local officials to devise clean air standards that comply with federal regulations, and federal judges order local school boards to devise school desegregation plans. Citizen views on policy matters are expressed through personal contacts with decision makers, letters, petitions, elections, court suits, lobbying, and sometimes violent demonstrations. Under normal conditions, however, as suggested earlier, public officials deal with several small specialized publics that have a particular interest in a matter before a legislative body or in a particular program.

Much policymaking on the state and local levels, particularly in recent years, has been characterized by conflict. Some of this comes over rival economic interests or concerns. Some also reflects matters of social status or prestige among groups. People are spurred into political action to prevent a loss of personal prestige, to maintain a dominant lifestyle, or, in a more limited way, simply to maintain their way of life. Scholars have found concern with threats to cherished values or a way of life involved in opposition to the Equal Rights Amendment, the use of "progressive" textbooks in the schools, and the "English as an official language movement" and other controversies discussed in later chapters. Much of the conflict in local politics we discuss in the following pages concerns turf protection, that is, efforts to keep undesirable people, activities, or facilities out of one's neighborhood. With a mixture of economic and social objectives, neighborhood groups mobilize against LULUS (Locally Unwanted Land Uses) such as public housing units, waste dumps, or halfway houses. Proposals to locate such facilities give rise to the NIMBY (Not In My Backyard) syndrome. For the nervous politician, it's often a case of NIMTOF (Not In My Term of Office).

How good are state and local officials as policymakers? A prominent state lawmaker once noted: "Most successful candidates for the state legislature can do two things well: ask strangers for their vote and ask relatives and friends for money."[39] Policymaking, on the other hand, he suggested, is a far more difficult activity. City council people, as we note in chapter 10, rate themselves far better in terms of responding to constituent needs and demands than in devising plans and policies. They are, from this perspective much stronger as representative bodies than they are as governing bodies. Certainly, state and local officials have been confronted with a variety of long-standing and difficult policy problems such as crime, poverty, and environmental deterioration for which remedies have been elusive.

TRENDS AND PROBLEMS

Governmental institutions at the state and local levels and the broad environment in which they function are constantly changing. Broad-scale economic changes, for example, have forced many state and local officials to cope with the aftereffects of plant closings and massive local unemployment. Many of the forces at work are international in nature as states and localities are being increasingly caught up in a globalized economy (see box 1–2).

We find other important forces conditioning the politics, problems, and policies of state and local officials by examining population data, changes in the pattern of intergovernmental relations and in the nature of the political demands made on these levels of government.

POPULATION TRENDS

There are now some 262 million Americans. This figure represents an increase of about thirty-eight million since 1980 and fifty-eight million since 1970. With population growth comes a variety of problems, traffic congestion and pollution among them. Throughout much of the period since 1970 the birthrate has been low—only slightly above 2.0 children, or zero population growth—though it has increased somewhat in recent years. A low rate has several effects on governmental politics and programs. Lower birthrates, for example, have reduced the need for teachers and new schools. At the same time, because older people are becoming relatively more numerous in the population, greater emphasis is placed on the medical, economic, and other problems of the aged. As the baby boom generation (the relatively large number of people born between 1946 and 1964) heads toward retirement,

---

BOX 1–2 STATES, LOCALITIES, AND THE GLOBAL ECONOMY

In this increasingly globalized economy, many state and local officials, working with members of Congress and local business leaders, have taken it upon themselves to do what they can to protect industries in their home areas from foreign competition and to prevent these same industries from moving to nations where wages are lower. Many states and some cities and counties actively encourage foreign tourism, solicit foreign investments into their economies, and try to develop foreign markets for the products of firms located at home. States and localities advertise in the international media, send trade missions of government and business leaders to foreign countries, and have opened some two hundred foreign offices in twenty-two countries around the world with the goal of expanding trade and tourism.

---

these pressures will increase dramatically, adding pressures in states like Florida, which already have relatively large elderly populations.

Governmental officials, chambers of commerce, and other influential groups within state and local politics have long equated population growth with economic development, prosperity, and progress. However, rapid growth and urban crowding have also been seen to cause a number of problems, such as demands for schools, hospitals, and better housing and transportation systems; strains on public power sources and sanitation systems; air pollution; and crime. Some states and many suburban areas have attempted in recent years to keep growth to a minimum. Emphasis has sometimes been placed on attracting big-spending tourists and clean (nonpolluting) industries while avoiding permanent, low-income residents.

Although the overall population may be holding steady, growth continues in many areas, largely because of population shifts. In recent years, many Americans have migrated to the Sun Belt (southern and western) region of the country. Many migrants have been attracted by job opportunities offered by industries that have relocated in the South and West. Industry has found labor and fuel costs to be lower in these regions than in others. Other migrants, especially those nearing retirement age, have been attracted by the warmer climate and relatively low cost of living in the South and West. Recent losses have been dramatic in older eastern cities hard hit by plant closings and in the Farm Belt region of the Midwest.

Sun Belt states, of course, also have had their problems. Many of them have experienced a large growth in per capita income, but many also have continuing problems with high unemployment and economic stagnation. Thus, although southern states have had a larger growth in per capita income than any other region, the South is still the poorest region in the nation. Other parts of the Sun Belt face severe problems such as water shortages that threaten continued development or the need to increase revenues dramatically to accommodate new demands for governmental services. Difficulties such as these, together with the efforts of officials in the northern and eastern states to revitalize their areas, have given some credence to the slogan: "The North will rise again."

The relative distribution of population between metropolitan and nonmetropolitan areas is also of considerable importance in state and local politics. Around 80 percent of the population lives in Metropolitan Statistical Areas (MSAs) identified by the federal Office of Management and Budget. An MSA is a recognized population center of fifty thousand people or more, consisting of a city (or cities) and the surrounding suburbs and other outlying areas that are socially and economically integrated with each other. Metropolitan areas generally have been growing in population. Most of the growth has been in the South and West.

The implications of these trends are explored in later chapters. We note here, however, that problems such as inadequate public facilities, pollution, crime, and slum conditions are prominent in much of the country. In many cities there are large aggregations of homeless people and what appears to be a permanent underclass, held down by poor education, lack of job skills, and unstable family conditions. A number of urban places are also characterized by a flourishing underground economy built around drugs, vice, gambling, stolen goods, and other criminal activity. To many observers, these problems are not the exclusive concern of local governments directly involved but will increasingly require the joint efforts of national, state, and local governments.

INTERGOVERNMENTAL TRENDS

State and local governments in the United States have considerably more freedom from national governmental control than have subnational governments in many other countries. They are valued because they help disperse governmental powers and allow a certain amount of flexibility in meeting local problems. Implicit in the theory of federalism are the ideas that no one level of government should have all governmental powers and that only problems that are truly national should be handled by the national government, while those that are unique to a given area or allow diversity should be handled by state and local governments.

Nevertheless, there are certain deficiencies to a federal system. Although dispersing governmental powers on a geographical basis acts as a check on overcentralization, it may also lead to confusion, inefficiency, and a wide diversity in the protections afforded citizens of the United States. Should each state be permitted to regulate the local activities of national companies or to set its own requirements on railroad trains that travel in interstate commerce?

Should each state be the judge of whether a woman should have an abortion? Should each local community make the final decision as to whether children are to be bused to schools to achieve racial integration?

Questions concerning what types of diversity are permissible have constantly come before the United States Supreme Court. In several cases, the Court has concluded in favor of uniformity and the protection of individual rights under the Constitution and against diversity. In the long run, it may be argued, nearly all our problems are truly national in nature and the rights of individuals must be uniformly recognized no matter where they happen to live.

The problem of balancing governmental centralization and decentralization will undoubtedly continue to be an important one. This problem has characterized not only national-state relations, but also state-local relations and, in recent years, proposals to establish metropolitan governments above or out of existing local governments. Centralization (vesting governmental authority in a larger unit) can result in advantages such as providing public services more efficiently, increasing professionalism, removing overlapping and unfair tax burdens, and providing uniform rights and benefits. Decentralization, on the other hand, can allow unique solutions to unique local problems; can avoid the dominance of a large, alien, and impersonal bureaucracy; and can provide greater opportunities for increased citizen participation.

The past several years have seen an on-again, off-again movement of the federal level to devolve more authority back to state and local governments. The call for a "New Federalism," which embodied this concept, originated in the Nixon White House in the late 1960s and was expanded upon by the Reagan Administration in the 1980s. The central goal of New Federalism for both presidents was to return more authority and responsibility from the national government to state and local governments. The heart of the new approach in the Nixon years was giving states more discretion in federal grant programs by turning to more flexible block grants and a no-strings-attached general revenue-sharing program. Under President Reagan, the goal of decentralization was taken to require a complete return of responsibilities to state governments for a number of domestic programs, such as welfare, largely financed by federal funds.

The Republican capture of Congress in 1994, for the first time in forty years, once again brought demands for downsizing the federal government and for greater devolution of authority. In what some have called "Newt Federalism" (after House Speaker Newt Gingrich) the Republicans have sought to turn many federal programs, including welfare, over to the states. Others have worried that should this happen, the states will ignore the poor and engage in a "race to the bottom" to see who can offer the lowest benefits. Many local officials have been concerned that proposed large cuts in federal spending will have devastating effects on their local economies and budgets.

While the current thrust of federal-state relations is one of greater decentralization or devolution of authority, the emerging pattern of state-local relations is in many respects one of greater centralization at the state level. Legislative reapportionment, the increased difficulties of local governments in dealing with their problems, and requirements attached to federal programs have brought about an increased interest by state officials in urban affairs and in matters that have been traditionally handled on the local level. States have assumed more responsibilities in areas like education and land-use planning, once considered the nearly exclusive concern of local governments. Through improvements in staffing, state legislatures have increased their institutional capabilities to become involved in these matters. Critics of these centralizing trends see the states doing, at best, a spotty job in helping their localities, and, in the long run, the danger of inaction and overload at the state level. The lobbying effort by local governments at the state level has always been of great importance to local officials. In this era of "fend for yourself federalism" at the national level it has become even more important.

DEMANDS AND PERFORMANCE

Generally, the broader political environment has not been a good one for any level of government—national, state, or local—over the past several decades. Though states and localities have sometimes looked good when compared to the national government, they have been given low evaluations by citizens. Gallup poll data in the mid-1980s, for example, showed that only 23 percent of the public rated the honesty and ethical standards of United States senators as high or very high. Comparable percentages for elected state officials and for elected local officials were 15 percent and 18 percent, respectively. Of twenty-five occupational groups rated in terms of honesty and ethical standards, state and local officials outranked only labor union leaders (13 percent), people in advertising (10 percent), people who sell insurance (10 percent), and people who sell automobiles (5 percent). In a 1994 ranking of twenty-six occupations, local officeholders were ranked 14th on the list, while state officeholders were ranked 21st. Congressmen were rated 25th, just above the perennial loser, car salespeople.[40]

Since the 1970s, there has been a widespread feeling, in the words of Peter Drucker, "that government is big rather than strong; that it is fat and flabby rather than powerful; that it costs a great deal but does not achieve much."[41] In the late 1970s, this type of thinking was reflected in a "taxpayers' revolt," most dramatically illustrated in June 1978, when the voters of California chose to reduce their property taxes by adopting Proposition Thirteen as an amendment to their state constitution. Proposition Thirteen placed a cap on property tax rates and limited the ability of state and local governments to raise revenue through other means. To Howard Jarvis, coauthor of the amendment, its adoption constituted a warning to public officials: "To ignore us is political suicide. We the people are still the boss."[42] That the people are still the boss has continued to be felt in the mid-1990s with popular adoption of term limitations on legislators and more restraints on the ability of state and local officials to raise and spend revenues.

Although resources may be wanting, or at best unpredictable, the demands on state and local governments have, if anything, increased. Studies suggest, for example, that there has been a severe eroding of the nation's infrastructure—the network of roads, bridges, mass transit facilities, dams, water and sewer systems, and other public facilities—vital to the country's commerce and well-being. The deterioration of vital public facilities is the result of long-term neglect and underinvestment. Along with this development has been a rapid increase in the number of groups seeking governmental assistance. In addition to the more traditional economic groups (business, labor, agriculture), state and local governments have been confronted with demands of minority racial groups and ethnic groups, women, the young, old, the poor, environmentalists, consumer advocates, and even public employees themselves. We look at these problems and developments in the following chapters.

ENDNOTES

1. Quoted by William Endicott, "The Trouble with State Legislatures," *Arizona Republic* (1 April 1984): 5. Article copyrighted by *Los Angeles Times*, 1984.

2. Harold D. Lasswell, *Politics: Who Gets What, When and How* (New York: McGraw-Hill, 1936).

3. On political systems see, generally: Robert A. Dahl, *Modern Political Analysis* (Englewood Cliffs, N.J.: Prentice Hall, 1963); and David Easton, *A Systems Analysis of Political Life* (New York: John Wiley and Sons, 1965).

4. On the relations between national and state elections see, for example: John E. Chubb, "Institutions, the Economy, and the Dynamics of State Elections," *American Political Science Review* 82 (March 1988): 134–154; Laura L. Vertz, John P. Frendreis, and James L. Gibson, "Nationalization of the Electorate in the United States," *American Political Science Review* 81 (September 1987): 962–966; and William Claggett, William Flanigan, and Nancy Zingale, "Nationalization of the American Electorate," *American Political Science Review* 78 (March 1984): 77–91.

5. The most innovative states, according to a pioneering analysis of eighty-eight different programs by Jack L. Walker some time ago, are New York, Massachusetts, and California. See: Jack L. Walker, "The Diffusion of Innovations among the American States," *American Political Science Review* 63 (September 1969): 880–899. The notion that innovativeness is an enduring trait one can associate with the various states has been a controversial one. See: Virginia Gray, "Innovation in the States: A Diffusion Study," *American Political Science Review* 67 (December 1973): 1174–1193. Compare this with Robert L. Savage, "Policy Innovativeness as a Trait

of American States," *The Journal of Politics* 40 (February 1978): 212–224. On liberalism, see David Klingman and William W. Lammers, "The 'General Policy Liberalism' Factor in American State Politics," *American Journal of Political Science* 28 (August 1984): 598–610.

6. See: Thomas R. Dye, *Politics, Economics and the Public: Policy Outcomes in the American States* (Chicago: Rand McNally, 1966). A case for the importance of political factors such as party competition over economic ones is found in Sarah McCally Morehouse, *State Politics, Parties, and Policy* (New York: Holt, Rinehart and Winston, 1981).

7. See: Ira Sharkansky, *The Maligned States: Policy Accomplishments, Problems, and Opportunities* (New York: McGraw-Hill, 1972), pp. 39, 42–43.

8. See, for example: Michael Novak, *The Rise of the Unmeltable Ethnics: Politics and Culture in the Seventies* (New York: Macmillan, 1972); Nathan Glazer and Daniel P. Moynihan, *Beyond the Melting Pot: The Negroes, Puerto Ricans, Jews, Italians and Irish of New York City*, rev. ed. (Cambridge, Mass.: M.I.T. Press, 1970); and Raymond E. Wolfinger, "The Development and Persistence of Ethnic Voting," *American Political Science Review* 59 (December 1965): 896–908.

9. See: John D. Hutcheson Jr. and George A. Taylor, "Religious Variables, Political System Characteristics, and Policy Outputs in the American States," *American Journal of Political Science* 17 (May 1973): 414–421; David Fairbanks, "Religious Forces and 'Morality' Policies in the American States," *Western Political Science Quarterly* 30 (September 1977): 411–417; and David R. Morgan and Kenneth J. Meier, "Politics and Morality: The Effect of Religion on Referenda Voting," *Social Science Quarterly* 61 (June 1980): 144–148.

10. See, generally: Leonard A. Cole, *Blacks in Power: A Comparative Study of Black and White Elected Officials* (Princeton: Princeton University Press, 1976). See also: Kenneth J. Meier and Robert E. England, "Black Representation and Educational Policy: Are They Related?" *American Political Science Review* 78 (June 1984): 392–416.

11. See discussion by Michael Haas, "Comparing Paradigms of Ethnic Politics in the United States: The Case of Hawaii," *Western Political Science Quarterly* 40 (1987): 647–672.

12. Research on migration in the 1970s and 1980s suggests that in the short run at least, a person who moves into an "incongruent" environment (one dominated by a party with which he or she does not identify) is more likely to adapt by becoming a political independent than by changing his or her party identification. Yet, while identification is not likely to change or to be slow to change, newcomers are likely to vote for candidates of the dominant party upon their arrival. See: Thad Brown, *Migration and Politics: The Impact of Population Mobility on American Voting Behavior* (Chapel Hill: University of North Carolina Press, 1988).

13. David R. Berman, "Regime and Party Change: The Arizona Pattern," in Maureen Moakley, ed., *Party Realignment in the American States* (Columbus: Ohio State University Press, 1992), pp. 35–55.

14. See: Raymond E. Wolfinger and Fred I. Greenstein, "Comparing Political Regions: The Case of California," *American Political Science Review* 63 (March 1969): 74–85.

15. W.J. Cash, *The Mind of the South* (New York: Alfred A. Knopf, 1941), p. 2.

16. See: Daniel J. Elazar, "The Principles and Traditions Underlying State Constitutions," *Publius: The Journal of Federalism* 12 (Winter 1982): 11–25.

17. See: Wilbur Zelinsky, *The Cultural Geography of the United States* (Englewood Cliffs, N.J.: Prentice Hall, 1973), pp. 23ff.; and the discussion in Raymond D. Gastil, *Cultural Regions of the United States* (Seattle: University of Washington Press, 1975), pp. 27–28.

18. The most recent edition of this work is: Daniel J. Elazar, *American Federalism: A View from the States*, 3rd ed. (New York: Harper and Row, 1984).

19. Ira Sharkansky, "The Utility of Elazar's Political Culture," *Polity* 2 (Fall 1969): 66–83. See also: Erick Herzik, "The Legal-Formal Structuring of State Politics: A Cultural Explanation," *Western Political Quarterly* 38 (September 1985): 413–423; Charles A. Johnson, "Political Culture in American States," *American Journal of Political Science* 20 (August 1976): 491–509; and John Kincaid, "Political Cultures in the American Compound Republic," *Publius* 10 (Spring 1980): 1–15. For a critical assessment of the theory underlying the cultural measurements see: David R. Berman, "Political Culture, Issues and the Electorate: Evidence from the Progressive Era," *Western Political Quarterly* 41 (January 1988): 169–180.

20. James Q. Wilson, *Political Organizations* (New York: Basic Books, 1973). See also: Penny M. Miller, Malcolm E. Jewell, and Lee Sigelman, "Reconsidering a Typology of Incentives among Campaign Activists: A Research Note," *Western Political Quarterly* 40 (1987): 519–526.

21. The perceived futility of voting may account for low turnout among disadvantaged minorities. See: Frances Fox Piven and Richard A. Cloward, *Why Americans Don't Vote* (New York: Pantheon Books, 1988).

22. Quoted by George Will, "Cool-Hand Jerry," *Newsweek* (10 November 1975): 3.

23. See: Lynn Ragsdale and Jerry G. Rusk, "Who Are Nonvoters? Profiles from the 1990 Senate Elections," *American Journal of Political Science* 37 (August 1993): 721–746.

24. See: Howard D. Hamilton, "The Municipal Voter: Voting and Non-Voting in City Elections," *American Political Science Review* 65 (December 1971): 1135–1140, quote at p. 1140.

25. See, on local governments: Paul Peterson, *City Limits* (Chicago: University of Chicago Press, 1981).

26. For a study linking participation differences and policy outputs at the state level see: Kim Quaile Hill and Jan E. Leighley, "The Policy Consequences of Class Bias in State Electorates," *American Journal of Political Science* 36 (May 1992): 351–365.

27. Kim Quaile Hill, *Democracy in the Fifty States* (Lincoln: University of Nebraska Press, 1994).

28. Easton, *A Systems Analysis*.

29. See: Murray Edelman, *Politics as Symbolic Action: Mass Arousal and Quiescence* (Chicago: Markham Publishing, 1971).

30. See: Everett F. Cataldo, "Orientations toward State and Local Government: The Salience of Subnational Politics," in James A. Riedel, ed., *New Perspectives in State and Local Politics* (Waltham, Mass.: Xerox College Publishing, 1971), pp. 101–121. See also poll conducted by Hart and Tetter for Council for Excellence in Government, as reported in "The Dimming American Dream," *State Legislatures* (July/August 1995): 7.

31. Oliver P. Williams and Charles R. Adrian, *Four Cities: A Study in Comparative Policy Making* (Philadelphia: University of Pennsylvania Press, 1973).
32. Cataldo, "Subnational Politics."
33. Alan Rosenthal and Maureen Moakley, eds., *The Political Life of the American States* (New York: Praeger, 1984).
34. Norton Long, "The City as Underdeveloped Country," *Public Administration Review* 32 (January/February 1972): 57–62, quote at p. 57.
35. Pioneering research in this area is found in M. Kent Jennings and Harmon Ziegler, "The Salience of American State Politics," *American Political Science Review* 64 (June 1970): 523–535.
36. See: Advisory Commission on Intergovernmental Relations, *Changing Public Attitudes on Government and Taxes* (Washington, D.C.: Government Printing Office, 1991), p. 21.
37. Gerald C. Wright Jr., Robert S. Erickson, and John P. McIver, "Public Opinion and Policy Liberalism in the American States," *American Journal of Political Science* 31 (November 1987): 980–1001. See also: Robert S. Erikson, Gerald C. Wright, and John P. McIver, *Statehouse Democracy: Public Opinion and Policy in the American States* (New York: Cambridge University Press, 1993).
38. See: E.E. Schattschneider, *The Semi-Sovereign People* (New York: Holt, Rinehart and Winston, 1960).
39. Tom Loftus, *The Art of Legislative Politics* (Washington, D.C.: Congressional Quarterly Press, 1994), p. 9.
40. Leslie McAneny and David W. Moore, "Annual Honesty & Ethics Poll: Congress and the Media Sink in Public Esteem," *The Gallup Poll Monthly* (October 1994).
41. Peter F. Drucker, "The Sickness of Government," *The Public Interest* (Winter 1969): 3.
42. Quoted in *Intergovernmental Perspective* (Winter 1979): 7.

2

☆ ☆ ☆

THE INTERGOVERNMENTAL ENVIRONMENT

A former governor was once quoted as saying: "There is no faster way to clear out a room than to begin talking about federalism."[1] Yet, as indicated in chapter 1, the relations among various levels of government form an important part of the setting for state and local politics and, therefore, merit extended attention. The first sections of this chapter consider various theories on the role of state governments in the federal system, the pattern of federal aid regulation, and the political influence of state and local governments on national policy. The concluding two sections touch on other sets of intergovernmental relations: state-local and "horizontal federalism," that is, relations among states and among local governments.

FEDERALISM: FROM COMPETITION TO COOPERATION

The Articles of Confederation, in effect from 1781 to 1789, gave this country its first national constitution. The Articles created what amounted to a league of state governments, each of which retained its own sovereignty (governmental powers). The independent states established their own monetary systems and frequently enacted tariffs against goods produced in other states. Coming to the aid of the many farmers who had fallen into debt, some states delayed foreclosures on farm mortgages and issued paper money, making it possible to pay off debts with cheaper dollars. In Massachusetts, such action was stimulated by an armed insurrection by debt-ridden farmers in 1786–1787, known as Shays's Rebellion.

The framers of the United States Constitution faced several problems caused by the existence of nearly autonomous state governments. A few held the states responsible for so much economic and political turmoil that they favored abolishing these units of government.[2] Others defended the states. Most agreed, however, that at a minimum, a stronger national government was needed to provide a common defense, protect property rights, and help develop an integrated national economy. The constitutional document produced in 1787 reflected these concerns. Under the Constitution, for example, Congress was given broad powers to regulate commerce among the states, the exclusive right to coin money, the authority to establish a uniform system of weights and measures, and power to protect patents and copyrights. Among other matters, states were prohibited from passing laws impairing the obligation of contracts, a provision that was to take on considerable importance in checking the ability of state governments to regulate economic activity (chapter 3).

The ratification of the United States Constitution in 1787, however, did not settle disputes over the basic nature of the relationship between the national government and the states. Throughout the nation's history, "states' rights" has served as a rallying cry for those who oppose what they see as federal governmental incursions on the power and prerogatives of the states. Sometimes the idea of states' rights has been championed by those who perceive state governments as being better disposed to their interests or who simply oppose particular federal programs. People may be for states' rights on one issue and against states' rights on another, depending how the issues affect their interests or policy preferences.

Yet, while states' rights has often been a political football used for all kinds of purposes, proponents and opponents of this position have also based their views on more involved theories of federalism. Three common viewpoints on the topic have been compact theory, dual federalism, and cooperative federalism.

COMPACT THEORY

The earliest constitutional argument used by the supporters of states' rights—prominent among whom were John C. Calhoun of South Carolina (1782–1850) and other critics of national policies regarding slavery and trade— was that sovereignty was absolute and indivisible, and ultimately rested with the states. The Union was but a compact among sovereign states, as it had been under the Articles of Confederation, and not one established directly by the people. Congress, therefore, was restricted to the powers expressly delegated to it in the Constitution, and the power to interpret the Constitution resided in the states, not with the United States Supreme Court. The individual states could interpose their authority between the national government and the people of the states to veto or nullify any national legislation they found to be invalid. If necessary, they could secede or withdraw from the Union.

Most contemporary scholars dispute the claims of the compact theorists and maintain that the United States Constitution drastically altered the national-state relations established under the Articles of Confederation. Direct contact was made between the national government and the people by allowing voters to select members of the national House of Representatives and by making the laws of Congress apply directly to individuals. The people meeting in conventions, rather than state legislatures, ratified the Constitution. The people, moreover, were made the source of authority for the new Constitution in its Preamble. The sovereignty article contained in the Articles of Confederation was omitted, and the Supremacy Clause served to ensure the dominance of the United States laws, treaties, and Constitution over the activities of the states.

The actual test of the nature of the Union came in the Civil War. After the war, in *Texas* v. *White*,[3] the Supreme Court sustained what had been decided on the battlefield in declaring that Texas had never left the Union and indeed could not have, because the relationship was indissoluble.

DUAL FEDERALISM

Following the Civil War, the defenders of states' rights moved from the compact theory, and the argument that full sovereignty rested in the states, to the concept of dual federalism. Under dual federalism, the states and the national government have separate spheres of authority and each is supreme in its own sphere. The sphere of state authority is protected by the Tenth Amendment to the Constitution.[4] Because all governmental authority is distributed among the national and state governments, the expansion of the authority of one diminishes the authority of the other, in a zero-sum manner (see figure 2–1).

During the heyday of dual federalism, the tasks of dividing up the functions of government between the state and national levels and protecting the constitutional sphere of authority of each fell to the Supreme Court. From the 1890s to the late 1930s, the Supreme Court, as "umpire of the federal system," used its authority to limit congressional action on the grounds that it conflicted with the authority the Constitution had given to the states. At other times, the Court concluded that certain activities of the states were invalid because they were the type that could be dealt with only by Congress.

Since the late 1930s, the Court has generally championed the doctrine of national supremacy and has upheld the extension of national authority without much consideration to the limiting effects of dual federalism or the Tenth

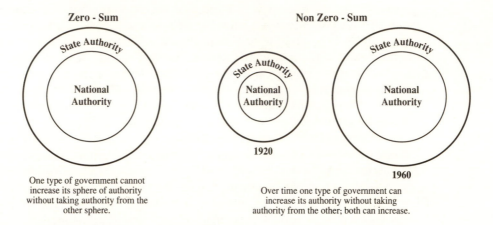

FIGURE 2–1 National-State Relations

Amendment. Recently, however, a more conservative Court has reminded the national government that under some conditions, at least, it is limited by state sovereignty. A significant ruling in this regard came in the 1995 case of *United States* v. *Lopez* in which the Court, by a 5–4 decision, invalidated a federal law that barred the possession of guns near school grounds. The Court concluded that Congress had moved into an area of regulation reserved for the states. Several groups have been encouraged by this and other decisions to challenge federal authority on other matters. The concept of dual federalism, moreover, continues to influence how many people, including prominent politicians, view federal-state relations.

COOPERATIVE FEDERALISM

Dual federalism represents a formal, legalistic approach to federal-state relations, centering on the question of which level of government has authority to undertake particular responsibilities. Under the concept of "cooperative federalism," on the other hand, the emphasis is on the need to combine governmental resources to solve particular problems. The pragmatic question is: How can the federal, state, and local governments best pool their efforts to combat various problems such as the need for improved transportation, educational systems, or crime fighting efforts? Attention is directed at the problem to be addressed, rather than the formal division of authority. Federal, state, and local governments, more broadly, are not looked upon as competitors, none of which can grow without taking authority from the other. Rather, it is assumed that the activities of federal, state, and local governments can and should all be doing more at the same time—the relationship is not zero-sum. From this perspective the growth of the national government since the 1930s has not diminished the states; they, too, have been doing more than ever before, though not as much by themselves.

In looking at the history of the republic one finds a strong tradition of the federal, state, and local governments sharing responsibilities. As political scientist Morton Grodzins once noted, the federal system actually resembles a marble cake in which federal, state, and local activities run together, rather than a layer cake where these activities are separated.[5] Thomas Anton, another student of federalism, notes that one consequence of power sharing by federal, state, and local governments is that relationships among governments are unstable. The fact that governments share authority for a variety of services means that governmental organizations frequently bump into one another. "With each bump," Anton writes, "an opportunity is provided to challenge or affirm existing understandings regarding who should do what, on whose budget."[6]

The stresses and strains of two world wars, the severity of the Depression of the 1930s, and increasing problems in areas such as transportation, income security, crime, health, and education over the last several decades have played major roles in bringing the various levels of government into closer collaboration.[7] During the 1960s, observers noted that each of the various levels of government had something special to contribute to the partnership: the federal government had the money, the states had the legal authority, and the local governments had the problems.

As the pattern of cooperative federalism emerged in earnest during the 1930s, Congress, rather than the Supreme Court, assumed the role of umpire of the federal system. That is, with the advent of cooperative federalism, the responsibilities of state and local governments began to vary with congressional decisions as to which levels would participate in specific programs and the nature of that participation (see table 2–1). The chief congressional tool of cooperative federalism has been the system of federal aid, discussed below.[8]

CONTINUING DISPUTES

Programs are now commonly undertaken within the cooperative framework. Indeed, one can find truly intergovernmental programs such as the Medicaid health program for the poor, where all levels of government (federal, state, and local) are involved, but no single level fully dominates the process.[9] Yet, despite numerous programs of a cooperative nature, many people continue to view national-state relations as essentially competitive in nature or, ideally, as being along dual federalistic lines. As part of his "New Federalism" program, for example, President Reagan in his 1982 State of the Union address proposed to give the states control over some forty programs

TABLE 2–1   Differences between Dual and Cooperative Federalism

Dual Federalism	Cooperative Federalism
National-state competition over control of functions	Shared responsibilities among various levels in performing functions
Focus on states' rights	Focus on common problems
Legalistic approach to intergovernmental relations	Pragmatic approach to intergovernmental relations
Supreme Court acts as umpire of the federal system	Congress acts as umpire of the federal system
Zero-sum relationship	Non-zero-sum relationship

then being administered by the federal government. Under Reagan's proposal, the programs would continue to be financed by the federal government out of a special trust fund established for that purpose for a four-year period. After that, however, states would have to support the programs out of their own revenue sources. Reagan also proposed that the states and the national government swap responsibility for certain functions. The president proposed that the states start paying for the Aid to Families with Dependent Children (AFDC) welfare program and the food stamp program. The federal government, in exchange, would pick up the total cost of the Medicaid program.

State governors, acting through their national associations, were favorable to the notion of "sorting out" governmental responsibilities between the two levels, but were reluctant to undertake full responsibility for the much criticized AFDC program. Rather, the governors argued, the federal government should assume full responsibility for all welfare programs—AFDC, food stamps, and Medicaid—while the states should handle the funding for functions like education and highways. The notion of federalizing welfare found little support in the Reagan White House.

While the "sorting out" negotiations failed in the Reagan years, state and local governments were forced into a new era of "fend-for-yourself" federalism in which they became less reliant on federal funds and more reliant on their own financial resources (see box 2–1).[10] The pendulum shifted back somewhat in 1992 with the election of Democrat Bill Clinton, who spoke favorably of re-creating federal-state-local partnerships in various areas of policy and increased federal assistance such as that intended to revitalize urban areas.

The Republican takeover of Congress in 1994, for the first time in forty years, once again shook the intergovernmental world. Since then, Congress has been bent on both cutting federal spending and devolving more authority

---

BOX 2–1 FEND-FOR-YOURSELF FEDERALISM

"When compared with the states of other major democratic federations—Australia, Canada and West Germany—American state governments operate in a fairly harsh and politically risky fend-for-yourself fiscal environment. While the long road to stronger state revenue systems in the United States has been paved with the political bones of former governors, state officials in the other major federations have been more successful in enlisting the help of their central governments in raising revenue."

Source: John Shannon, "The Return to Fend-for-Yourself Federalism: The Reagan Mark," *Intergovernmental Perspective* (Summer/Fall 1987): 34.

---

to the states. Reducing the power of the federal government and passing more decision-making authority back to the states was part of the "Contract with America" Republican House members campaigned on in the 1994 elections. Since 1994, the Republicans have sought to turn many federal programs into block grants over which states will have considerable discretion. While a shift to the states appeared to have popular backing, some observers wondered if the states are really ready for new responsibilities, that is, if they are better qualified to administer various social programs and can do so more efficiently.

THE POLITICS OF FEDERAL AID AND REGULATION

FEDERAL ASSISTANCE

The national government funnels the money it collects back to states and localities in different ways. In 1994 federal spending affecting states and localities amounted to more than $1.3 trillion—nearly $5,000 for every person in the country. Over half of this money came as direct payments to individuals under Social Security, Medicare, and other programs. Additional funds were spent on salaries and wages for postal, defense, and other employees and for the procurement of various commodities such as military equipment. About 16 percent of the federal spending came in the form of grants that went directly to state and local officials. A list of states that have benefited particularly well from federal spending is presented in table 2–2. Many of the most prominent on this list—Alaska, Maryland, New Mexico, and Virginia—benefit from having major military installations.

Federal spending has been vital to the health of many local economies. Understandably, members of congressional delegations and state and local

TABLE 2–2   States Ranking Highest in Federal Spending per Capita

Rank	State	Amount per Capita
1	Alaska	$7,656
2	Maryland	7,306
3	Virginia	7,004
4	New Mexico	6,816
5	Hawaii	6,449
6	North Dakota	6,127
7	Missouri	6,019
8	Massachusetts	5,856
9	Rhode Island	5,489
10	Montana	5,418

Source: United States Department of Commerce, Economics and Statistics Administration, Bureau of the Census, *Federal Expenditures by State for Fiscal Year 1994* (Washington, D.C.: Government Printing Office, 1995).

officials have sought to secure their share of the funds. Public officials in the Graybelt, for example, were alarmed by studies conducted in the late 1970s that suggested that northern and eastern states were not doing as well as southern and western states in regard to receiving federal dollars.[11] A Coalition of Northeast Governors resolved to pressure for greater regional equity in the allocation of federal spending. Partly because of that pressure, northern and eastern states have received a larger share of the federal spending.

The bulk of direct federal aid payments to state and local governments has consisted of categorical grants-in-aid, block grants, and, from 1972 to 1986, general revenue sharing. Categorical grants-in-aid programs have provided most of the funds. Some of the grants have been of a developmental nature intended to help states and localities undertake various construction projects, such as a hospital or airport, or pursue other programs that help improve local economies, such as slum clearance. Other grants, such as for special education programs aimed at handicapped children or for aid to dependent children, have been of a redistributive nature in that they give funds supplied by taxpayers to people in need. The various programs have their own particular requirements and financial arrangements. A majority are "project grants" requiring that a state or local government apply for funds (usually at the nearest federal regional office) for a specific program and wait for approval. Most programs call for matching of state or local funds and require detailed reports to federal agencies. Most also authorize federal agencies to approve plans, audit expenditures, and impose various regulations.

Block grants carry many of the restrictions of the categorical grants but provide funds for broad functions and allow states and localities to develop their specific program needs. An example of this type of federal aid program, the Community Development Block Grant, is discussed in chapter 14. Under the general revenue-sharing program, which was eliminated as part of a broader effort to cut back federal expenditures, funds were distributed to states and localities on an automatic basis with only a few restrictions placed on how the money could be spent.

Federal aid through the categorical and block grant programs usually goes directly to state governments, where it is either spent or redistributed to local governments. From the 1930s to the early 1980s several federal programs channeled funds directly to local governments without significant involvement of the state legislatures or governors. During the 1980s this federal-local partnership was virtually ended by the Reagan Administration, which sought to increase the ability of state governments to control federal spending within their states.

In 1950 total direct federal aid stood at a little over $2 billion. Increases, particularly in highway and urban development programs, raised the total to around $11 billion in 1965. The continued growth of established programs and the addition of several new social programs raised the total to around $78 billion in 1978. By 1995, the total spent on federal aid had gone to $228 billion. Although the total amount of federal aid has grown over the years, when the amount is adjusted for inflation, aid reached its peak in "constant dollars" in 1978. Since that year, federal aid has also generally declined as a percentage of state and local expenditures, from around 27 percent to 17 percent in 1989, before rising to around 20 percent currently. Compared to the late 1970s, state and local governments generally have been raising a larger percentage of the funds they spend, being less dependent on federal grants. As table 2–3 illustrates, much of the money spent on grants is consumed by Medicaid (providing medical services to the poor), highway planning and construction through highway trust funds, and the welfare program Aid to Families with Dependent Children (AFDC). Medicaid has been by far the most expensive federal grant, providing more than $310 per capita in 1994. Medicaid, highway planning and construction, and welfare have accounted for about half of all federal grant spending in recent years.

Debates over the necessity and merits of federal aid have long characterized politics in Washington. Much of the attention has been focused on the categorical grants, of which there are now some six hundred in existence. No doubt, over the years, categorical grants have enabled state and local governments to accomplish more than they would have been able to do otherwise. The system of aid has also helped foster minimum national standards in such areas as welfare and has redistributed wealth from richer areas to poorer ones. Through requirements attached to grants (for example, that personnel paid by the grant be selected on the basis of merit), the system has helped improve the caliber of state and local administration.

TABLE 2–3   Major Federal Grants to State and Local
             Governments, FY 1994

Program	Amount per Capita
Medicaid	$310.4
Highway trust funds	70.48
Aid for dependent children	62.96
Housing assistance	50.21
Child nutrition	25.84
Education for disadvantaged	25.81
Federal Transit Administration	14.89
Community development	13.82
State employment services	12.66
Job training	12.50
Social services block grant	10.52
Waste treatment works	7.46

Source: United States Department of Commerce, Economics and Statistics Administration, Bureau of the Census, *Federal Expenditures by State for Fiscal Year 1994* (Washington, D.C.: Government Printing Office, 1995).

At the same time, since the 1970s the grant system has been faulted for being too complex, cumbersome, and unpredictable; for distorting state and local program priorities; and for impairing the control of state and local elected officials. Congress has developed grant programs in a piecemeal fashion to deal with specific problems. Both it and potential applicants have found it difficult to keep track of all the programs. It has been hard to obtain an overall view of how the entire system is operating and to coordinate the decisions of the various granting agencies.

The problem of securing information on and applying for federal programs has necessitated the appointment of federal coordinators, the assistance of congressional delegations, and the aid of national organizations. In an effort to overcome the information problem, most state governments and some local ones employ staffs to deal with the intricacies of federal aid. In some areas, state, county, and city governments share a federal aid coordinator on a cooperative basis. Following application, the process has been characterized by red tape, uncertainty, and delay as regional officials channel the request according to their own procedures. They often check back and forth with the Washington agency and wait until it works out interagency squabbles. If funding is authorized, it may be allocated on a stop-and-go basis, causing state and local officials to renege on promises.

Although state and local officials have had considerable influence in shaping federal programs and may reject certain types of programs, the aid system tends to inhibit program flexibility and encourage certain types of expenditures to the detriment of others. Priorities are locked into federal programs, and state and local officials see little reason to pour money into activities that are not federally assisted. State and local officials, to get the most for their taxpayers' money, may neglect projects that are not listed in the catalogue of federal aid or that require more matching funds than other projects. There is no doubt, for example, that the federal highway program has fostered dependence on the automobile at the expense of other means of transportation. Without some form of block grant that gives greater flexibility in spending federal money, state and local officials are encouraged to secure new categorical grants or to broaden older ones to adjust to changing demands or priorities.

Categorical grants have also contributed to the tying together of the various levels of government on a function-by-function basis. This has shifted responsibility to administrators at different levels of government and has lessened overall general policy control by elected state and local officials. Perhaps the most meaningful interaction under the categorical aid system has been that among administrators at different levels of government engaged in common activities. For example, there may well be closer ties among the United States Bureau of Public Roads, state highway departments, and city public works directors than among these officials and governmental officials on their same level. This "functional federalism" or "picket fence federalism" has facilitated intergovernmental cooperation in the performance of certain functions, but has made it more difficult to coordinate the different functions performed in a given state or locality.[12]

Block grants and general revenue sharing have been championed by those who see the need to give state and local officials more control over the spending of federal funds. Revenue sharing carries the added bonus for some in that it gives elected state and local officials major control over the distribution of federal funds, rather than, as in the grant system, giving that control to administrators at different levels of government. From a different perspective, however, it has been argued that potentially controversial programs such as welfare assistance are best entrusted to administrators or policy professionals who are somewhat isolated from state and local politics.[13]

REGULATIONS, CONTROLS, AND MANDATES

State and local governments have long been subject to various types of regulations and controls adopted by the federal government.[14] Some of these, as suggested above, have come as a condition of accepting federal aid. All grants, for example, are subject to certain crosscutting requirements such as one that bars the use of federal funds to support programs that discriminate against racial minorities.

In other situations, state and local governments have been subject to crossover sanctions. This refers to a situation in which state and local governments stand to lose federal aid unless they adopt certain policies that are only indirectly related, if related at all, to the aid program in question. In 1974, for example, Congress used the threat of withholding federal highway funds to encourage states to adopt a fifty-five-mile-per-hour speed limit. Ten years later, at the urging of such groups as Mothers Against Drunk Driving (MADD), Congress passed the National Minimum Drinking Age law that authorized the secretary of transportation to withhold highway funds from any state that failed to raise its drinking age to twenty-one by 1987. Though several states resisted—some brought unsuccessful court suits challenging the authority of Congress—they also feared losing federal highway aid (5 to 10 percent of what they had coming). The drinking age became twenty-one throughout the nation as the twenty-nine states that had lower drinking ages passed the appropriate laws.

Another broad area of some controversy in recent years has concerned the ability of the federal government to order state and local governments to comply with certain policies under the threat of civil and criminal penalties. The issue was raised in 1976 when the United States Supreme Court in the case of *National League of Cities* v. *Usery* declared that the commerce clause did not permit Congress to extend minimum-wage and maximum-hour regulations under the federal Fair Labor Standards Act to state and local employees who were engaged in the "traditional functions" of these levels of government.[15] The question of what functions were traditional ones was left undefined. The suit was brought by state and local officials who were concerned, in large part, over the fiscal consequences of the regulations. The majority of the justices in the 5–4 decision apparently felt that in this case Congress had infringed on the rights of the state and local governments.

The 1976 decision was expected to signify a trend toward more decentralization of legal authority down to the state and local levels. This did not happen, however, as several challenges to federal legislation based on the criteria in the *National League of Cities* case proved unsuccessful in the late 1970s and early 1980s. Finally, in the case of *Garcia* v. *San Antonio Metropolitan Transit District* (1985) the Supreme Court, in another close 5–4 decision, held that the "traditional function" test was unworkable and that the question of extending the Fair Labor Standards Act to state and local employees was to be answered by Congress rather than the courts.[16] The *National League of Cities* decision was thus overruled and Congress, at least for the time being, was given a blank check on such matters. States and localities, as a consequence, have been forced to comply with a number of regulatory mandates, some of which, as in the area of environmental protection, have required the expenditure of large amounts of state and local funds. One estimate made in 1992 is that state and local governments were spending up to 24 percent of their budgets to make up for unfunded federal mandates.

Since the mid-1970s costly federal mandates have occurred in policy areas such as air and water quality, solid waste, hazardous waste, transportation standards, labor management, health care, courts, and corrections. Recent examples of congressional legislation creating unfunded mandates are the Americans with Disabilities Act, the Safe Drinking Water Act, and the National Voter Registration Act. Mandating allows federal officials both to claim credit for acting on a variety of issues and, by shifting much of the burden for paying for these programs onto state and local governments, to reduce pressures on the federal budget. As a National Governors' Association official put it: "The idea is that they get the credit, we get the bills."[17] In 1990 the National Conference of State Legislatures complained: "It makes no sense to create 50 new fiscal crises in the states in the course of resolving the federal budget crisis."[18]

In 1995 Congress took a step to make federal mandating more difficult. This came as a result of an intensive lobbying effort by state and local officials and their organizations. It was also greatly facilitated by the election of a Republican Congress. Mandate reform had been part of the House Republicans' "Contract with America." The legislation, however, is at best only the first step toward reform. It makes it more difficult for the federal government to adopt future unfunded mandates; however, it does not apply to existing mandates. The law also exempts large categories of legislation from coverage, for example, civil rights mandates and mandates associated with major entitlement programs. Even where it does apply, the requirement of full federal funding can be waived by a majority vote of the Senate or House.[19] Drawing on the experience of similar legislation in the states, some authorities doubt that the federal mandate law will be very effective.[20]

STATE AND LOCAL INFLUENCE ON NATIONAL POLICY

While state and local officials may appear from the above discussion to be at the mercy of federal officials, volumes of research indicate state and local officials, working individually or through associations, are not altogether powerless in influencing the development of federal policies affecting them and the implementation of those policies.[21] State and local officials normally have had an input in the development of federal policies, though some administrations and climates of opinion have been more favorable than others. Moreover, as one observer has noted, a federal grant-in-aid "is the product of a political bargaining process, not just in Washington where the grant is created, but also at the state and local levels where it is executed."[22]

BUILT-IN INFLUENCES

The influence of state and local governments is built into the national political system. Perhaps the leading role in representing the particular interests of various areas of the country is played by congressional delegations. Members of Congress represent states and localities, and while they have considerable discretion in many matters of public policy, they are expected to serve the interests of their constituents. The ability of members of Congress to promote the interests of their states depends in part on the individual state's population. The larger the state, the more congressional delegates it has working on its behalf. Their influence may also depend in large part on the degree of party competition within the state. Where party competition is weak, as in the South, the system may produce relatively cohesive congressional delegations and, equally important, enable congressional delegates by virtue of the seniority rule to secure committee chairmanships and other positions of influence. States where party competition is weak tend to be among the least populated, but these advantages may make up for what they lose in numbers.

Members of Congress, on some issues at least, differ according to the nature of the districts from which they are elected.[23] Those from districts dominated by large cities, for example, tend to be favorable to housing and welfare programs. Those from rural areas, on the other hand, are generally united in opposition to housing and welfare programs. In contrast to their big-city colleagues, congressional delegates from rural areas are also likely to oppose spending for mass transit and efforts to control the sale of handguns. Suburban members of Congress are closer than their rural counterparts to the positions of big-city members on these and many other questions. Given this disposition, large cities have been at least potentially better off in Congress since 1964, when the Supreme Court required that the House of Representatives be apportioned on a one-person, one-vote basis.[24] This decision shifted control of the House from rural to suburban representatives. While the change may have helped urban areas generally, the continued shrinking of central cities, and the high concentration of the poor and nonwhite in them, appears to have had the effect of reducing the impact of big-city delegations in the House.

Federal judges and administrators may be less disposed than congressional delegates toward giving priority to local, state, or regional concerns. The selection of federal judges and administrators is less directly influenced by state and local politics. Judges and administrators, moreover, are expected to base their decisions on what are considered "nonpolitical" legal and professional criteria. Yet, as several chapters of this book indicate, state and local officials are not altogether powerless in influencing (if not frustrating) the policies set forth by federal courts and federal administrators. This is perhaps most evident in the discussion of the school desegregation cases and the federal environmental protection laws.

Another built-in influence of state governments on national policy is in the process of amending the United States Constitution. Under the Constitution, amendments may be proposed by two methods: (1) a two-thirds vote of both houses of Congress, or (2) a national constitutional convention called by Congress on application of two-thirds of the state legislatures. Amendments may be ratified by the legislatures of three-fourths of the states or by special conventions in three-fourths of the states. Thus far, only the first method, the congressional initiative one, has been used to propose constitutional amendments, and all amendments but one have been ratified by state legislatures. The method of ratification is determined by Congress. In the matter of repealing Prohibition, it was felt that this could be more easily accomplished by special conventions in the states than by state legislatures.

From time to time states have petitioned Congress to hold a constitutional convention to develop an amendment on a particular subject. In recent years, for example, several states have called for a constitutional convention that would propose an amendment to require the national government to balance its budget. Past efforts to bring about constitutional change in this manner have failed to secure the approval of the required number of states. The chief value of this exercise has been in generating publicity and informal pressure for a particular cause. Because there is little law on the subject, it is not known how delegates to such a convention would be selected, what rules would govern their procedures, or, indeed, if the delegates can be limited to the matters specified in the state petitions.

State legislatures play a more determinative role in the amending process by passing on the amendments proposed by a Congress. The requirement that these must be approved in at least three-fourths of the states gives a minority of the states with only about 20 percent of the national population considerable clout in the amending process. In political terms, the requirement means that activists in a relatively small number of jurisdictions are in a good position to defeat proposals that are generally favored on a national level.

A prominent example of this and of the politics of constitutional revision is seen in the failure of the proposed Equal Rights Amendment to secure ratification by thirty-eight states before the deadline of 30 June 1982.[25] The proposed amendment, which contained a guarantee that "equality of rights under the law shall not be denied or abridged by the United States or any state on account of sex," was passed by Congress in 1972. Thirty-four states had ratified the amendment by 1975, but by that time a conservative reaction set in and no further progress was made after Indiana ratified in 1977.

Stop-ERA forces were particularly effective in most southern states, a few western states (Nevada, Utah, and Arizona), and in some large midwestern states, the most pivotal of which was Illinois, where supporters went so far as to go on a prolonged hunger strike and to shackle themselves together at the door to the state senate. The movement had, in the opinion of some observers, suffered because many people associated it with unconventional or radical causes and saw it threatening privileges enjoyed by women. Some opponents saw the ERA at odds with traditional social roles of women as housewives and mothers. The proposal received strong opposition from fundamentalist religious bodies who feared that it would destroy family values. Some opponents of ERA suggested that rather than seeking a constitutional amendment, activists should seek to eliminate sex discrimination on a state-by-state basis— a course of action that ERA supporters declared would take until the year 3000 to complete.

In a more indirect fashion than constitutional amendment, state legislatures influence national policy by playing their idealized function of testing out ideas and programs for possible adoption on the national level. In this role, the states have tried out no-fault insurance, bans on throwaway bottles and cans, and, more recently, welfare-to-work programs (where recipients "pay back" benefits by doing public service jobs) and health care reforms.

Often national action has resulted not only because of the merits of a state-initiated program but also because individual state action has caused disparities or confusion. In the area of business regulation, for example, state laws such as those requiring specific labeling on products have resulted in so much diversity that national companies have called for national uniform action to get away from the "fifty-headed monster." The alternative, uniform state laws, is difficult to achieve because of the need to secure the cooperation of fifty different jurisdictions and because of the various compromises needed to steer measures through state legislatures.

LOBBYING ACTIVITY

State and local officials, as the previous discussion suggests, have had strong motivations for influencing national policies and have often taken the opportunity to do so. They have attempted to overturn unpopular United States Supreme Court decisions, secure the adoption or modification of federal programs, and influence Congress or national administrators toward the approval of specific projects for their home territories. Sometimes state and local governmental officials have had a common objective in influencing national policy. At other times there have been disputes over the directions of that policy and fierce competition among state or local governments for particular favors.

To supplement the work of individual members of Congress, several states and large counties and cities have established "outposts of influence and intelligence" in Washington to keep up with the latest federal activities of interest to their jurisdictions.[26] On occasion, those who work on behalf of specific states, counties, and cities in Washington are aided by special delegations that include prominent citizens as well as public officials. These delegations make the rounds in Washington, seeking high-level political and administrative contacts to influence decisions regarding such matters as the funding of programs, the awarding of grants and contracts, and the interpretation of rules and regulations. The importance of such decisions to a governor's or mayor's ability to deliver services and thus win reelection often casts these officials in the role of foreign ambassadors in Washington. To some extent governors and mayors use their relations with the federal government as presidents use foreign relations—to increase their political support back home.[27]

State and local officials also make use of national organizations in their intergovernmental activity. Such organizations do not represent the interests of specific states or localities, but the interests of states or units of local government such as cities or counties in general. Chief among the organizations that in one way or another represent the views of state and local officials on matters of federal policy are the National Governors' Association (formerly the Governors' Conference), the National Association of Counties, the National League of Cities, the United States Conference of Mayors (USCM), and the National Association of Towns and Townships (NATaT).[28] Such organizations commonly describe themselves as "public interest groups" and collectively are known as the "intergovernmental lobby."[29]

These groups provide structures through which state and local officials can network, exchange ideas and information, and both shape and respond to changes in public policy. They also help educate people in Washington about the roles and activities of state and local governments in the federal system, define problems affecting state and local governments, and help shape the federal policy agenda.

On policy matters the public interest groups have generally stressed the interdependency of American governmental units and lobbied for a greater federal role as a partner in various programs. Following the relaxation in international tensions in the late 1980s, they called for increased financial help from a "peace dividend"—the allocation of defense budget savings toward education and other domestic needs. The public interest groups, however, have also been concerned about court decisions such as the *Garcia* case mentioned earlier, which have eroded state and local protections against the expansion of congressional authority. They contend that the Tenth Amendment to the United States Constitution is a major substantive limit on national power and should be so viewed by the courts.

Groups representing state and local officials undertake research on policy issues, try to get their message out through the media, testify at formal hearings, contact individual congresspeople, work with administrators such as those in the Department of Housing and Urban Development (HUD) in developing rules and regulations, and on occasion file court suits. Prominent state and local officials, for example mayors or governors, often represent their organizations' positions. They have often enjoyed considerable success (see box 2–2). Few people—lobbyists, lawmakers, or informed observers—however, view public interest groups as having anywhere near the clout enjoyed by well-financed private groups who seek access and influence through such

---

BOX 2–2 INFLUENCE OF THE LOCAL LOBBY

"When cities advise us on foreign relations, we treat them as we would any other constituent, noting their concerns. But if they tell us that the housing program in St. Louis is not working because of the way HUD is administering it, then we get right into it."

Source: Christopher Bond, "How Much Does Federalism Matter in the U.S. Senate?" *Intergovernmental Perspective* (Spring 1990): 38.

---

means as campaign contributions. State and local groups rely primarily on the quality of their presentations and the provision of information.

Since the late 1970s the state and local lobby in Washington has met difficult barriers because, for political and economic reasons, the federal government has cut back on its role as an intergovernmental partner. In the Reagan White House, cutbacks in grant programs aiding state and local governments were seen as a matter of "defunding the left" and of reducing subsidies for selfish special interest groups. State and local officials, for their part, do not look upon themselves as special pleaders for some narrow interests but as representatives of semisovereign governments that provide the bulk of domestic services in this country and thus should be heard in Washington.[30]

STATE-LOCAL RELATIONS AND HORIZONTAL FEDERALISM

NATURE OF THE STATE-LOCAL RELATIONSHIP

Courts commonly view local governments as the "legal creatures" of their states. As such, they may exercise only those powers given to them. Moreover, because of the inferior legal status of municipalities, counties, and other units of local government, states have virtually unlimited ability to intervene in local affairs by stipulating various rules and requirements and by mandating the performance of certain functions.

State legislators, regardless of the nature of their constituencies, ideologies, or party identification, have been generally reluctant to relinquish control over local governments. Attitudes concerning state-local relations seem to be very much a product of Miles's Law: "Where you stand depends on where you sit." From where they sit, local officials usually see more local autonomy to be a good thing. From where they sit, state legislators, regardless of party, ideology, or type of constituency they represent, tend to see more local autonomy as something that might bring undesirable results.[31]

Although state officials have allowed a bit more local discretion, such as in regard to revenue sources, in recent years, they have also assumed responsibilities in areas like land use and education, once considered to be of concern only to local governments. Local governments in all parts of the country have also found themselves increasingly dependent on state financial aid (grants and shared revenues) to support their activities (see chapter 11).

Perhaps most infuriating to local officials in recent years has been the tendency of state governments to rely on their legislative and regulatory authority to compel local units to assume responsibilities for services and to absorb the resulting costs. Just as the federal government has responded to its budget difficulties by passing off expenditures to the states, states have responded to their economic problems by requiring localities to assume the costs of various programs. Local reaction to this, however, has forced some changes. Most states, for example, now require the preparation of fiscal notes, which alert legislators to the costs they are imposing on local governments by mandating particular programs. Several states use the note process in conjunction with a program to repay local governments for the cost of complying with mandates. Mandate reimbursement laws and the publicity given to the mandate problem appear to have helped reduce the number of mandates. Yet, as one expert on the subject has concluded: "the experience of the states is that, despite the stringency of the anti-mandate legislation, when a state legislature has a will to pass an unfunded mandate, a way will ultimately present itself."[32]

Also of some concern to local officials are state mandates of a preemptory or "thou shall not" nature. Prohibitions of this type frequently reflect the desire of a particular group to avoid local authority or to minimize, if not avoid completely, local governmental taxation or regulation. Local officials, for example, have continually to guard against state legislation that would exempt certain business from local sales and other taxes.

In recent years, efforts to circumvent local authority have been especially intense on control over smoking, rents, and guns. Tobacco companies have encouraged the move away from city and county nonsmoking ordinances in favor of state legislation on the subject. Commonly, states have preempted local action through the passage of statewide clean air bills. Because of industry pressure, statewide regulations are often less demanding than the local ordinances they replaced. Those opposed to rent controls have also lobbied at the state level, seeking to prohibit local action. Landlord associations have had considerable success in this regard. Thanks in large part to the National Rifle Association, some thirty states also prohibit local gun control ordinances.[33]

Much of the day-to-day involvement of state government in local affairs comes through a rather elaborate system of state administrative supervision and assistance. This system developed on a function-by-function basis; for example, a state department of education was given the authority to implement legislative directives regarding education on the local level and a state department of welfare was charged to ensure that state policy was being implemented by county or city welfare officials.[34]

Several states now also have agencies with more general responsibilities in regard to local governments. Nearly every state has an office of community or local affairs to provide technical assistance in areas such as local finance and planning. These services particularly benefit the smaller municipalities lacking well-developed professional staffs. Community or local affairs agencies also serve as a means of communication between state and local governments. One study has suggested that officials in these agencies "usually consider themselves as intermediaries between state and local governments, the advocates of the state point of view in dealing with local officials, and the advocates of the local point of view in dealing with state officials."[35]

Other state officials attempt to promote interlocal cooperation, to coordinate state and federal grants to localities, and to ensure that local units obey state laws, particularly in regard to budgetary and financial matters. On the whole, the emphasis in state-local administrative relations has been as much or more on assisting local units rather than supervising them. Indeed, state administrators depend a great deal on the cooperation of local administrators in implementing programs. State agencies also commonly depend on the help of local administrators in securing support for their programs in the legislature. On the other hand, local officials are not hesitant to contact those officials on the state level regarding activities in which they have a common interest. Often, local officials or groups representing them are involved in the formation of state regulations affecting localities.[36]

LIMITS ON STATE CONTROL

Although local governments are the "legal creatures" of their states, the actual degree of state control varies from place to place. New England states, for example, have a relatively strong tradition of favoring local autonomy. There has been an equally strong tradition in southern states in favor of state centralization. In all states, however, the extent of state control is limited by several factors, one of which is the practical difficulty of supervising the host of local governments, often numbering in the thousands, scattered within their boundaries. State involvement is also limited by popular belief in the right of "local home rule" that, while receiving little recognition in law, has functioned much like the slogan of "states' rights" in being used to oppose state infringements on local prerogatives. As noted previously, state control has been further minimized or circumvented at times by the ability of local governments to go directly to the national government for assistance that state governments are unwilling or unable to provide.

A final limitation on state control stems from the political influence of local governments in their states' political systems. This influence is evidenced, in part, by the tendency of state legislators to safeguard the interests of the local areas they represent. Legislators, for example, are on guard to make sure that the communities they represent receive their share of state road funds. The interests of local units are further protected and advanced by various groups. Given the importance of state officials in determining the environment in which local officials must operate, it comes as no surprise that some of the most active pressure groups in state politics are those representing local officials. State legislators and administrators frequently find themselves concerned with organizations representing county officials and school district administrators, as well as with specific local occupational groups, such as teachers and police officers.

The only organizations that can claim to be speaking for all or nearly all the cities are state municipal leagues (or leagues of cities). State municipal leagues are found in nearly every state, usually located in or close to the state capital. They are unique pressure groups in that they are given support by one level of government to influence another level. The primary concern of the leagues has traditionally been to secure favorable state action to ease the financial problems of the cities and to upgrade local governmental authority and administration. The emphasis, it might be said, has been as much on making it possible for local governments to deal with various problems as on the problems themselves. The leagues, especially those with a heterogeneous membership from central city, suburban, and rural areas, have found it difficult to address issues like reapportionment or certain metropolitan area problems, such as whether a local income tax should be levied at the place of residence or employment.[37]

Historically, most state-local conflicts have occurred between the states and their largest cities. State relations with small towns, rural communities, and, more recently, suburbs have been relatively good. Despite the dominant legal position of the states, disputes among states and their large cities have often paralleled those among the states and the national government. In both sets of relationships, disputes have arisen over the distribution of legal authority. Disputes have also focused on whether certain matters should be handled uniformly or on the basis of local needs. City officials have been alarmed at times by centralizing tendencies on the state level and the failure of state legislatures to respond to their needs.[38] From time to time, they have even threatened to secede from their states.[39] For example, in the early 1970s, then-Mayor John V. Lindsay of New York City called on the national government to charter a number of "national cities" so that his city, which has a budget larger than that of the State of New York, and other large cities could escape the "servitude" imposed by state governments.[40]

State-local relations are characterized by state-imposed limitations on local discretion and by high levels of state involvement in what might be called local affairs. From the local point of view, the more discretion or less central-ization, the better. Yet, as noted in several places in the above discussion, state involvement is not always unwelcome to local officials. Local officials com-monly see not only the need for enhanced authority or discretion but also the need for involvement in the form of state assistance, for example, of a technical or financial nature, in jointly addressing a problem. In other words, in the real world, states are evaluated by both the amount of discretion and the amount of assistance they give local units. The optimum situation for local units would be state policies which give them both high levels of discretion and high levels of assistance. The worst of all possible worlds would be low levels of discretion and low levels of assistance.

The recurrent disputes between the two levels of government over the proper level of state assistance and over the relative merits of centralization and decentralization are not likely to abate in the immediate future. Fortu-nately, a number of states have, in recent years, established state-local panels or commissions as forums for the discussion of such problems.[41]

HORIZONTAL FEDERALISM

In addition to the pattern of vertical federalism (national-state-local rela-tions) there is an important and active pattern of horizontal federalism that takes place among states and among local units. Much of the interaction among state governments is competitive. In several national political conflicts, such as those involving the distribution of federal aid programs or the regu-lation of oil and natural gas prices, various states or regions are pitted against each other. Competition is also sometimes found in rather fierce struggles involving the location of industrial plants or other major business enterprises. In their efforts to lure industry away from other states or to influence the choice of a location for a new branch plant, state officials compete with each other in offering a variety of tax reductions and other incentives to businesses. Competition of this nature, however, may be wasteful. It is somewhat doubt-ful that this "smokestack chasing" does much more than depress the general level of state taxation on corporations. Factors other than tax incentives, such as the quality of an area's labor force, public facilities, and lifestyle, appear to have much more to do with a firm's decision on where to locate. Thus, tax reductions may be given to encourage decisions that would have been made anyway.[42] The principal beneficiaries of the incentive "arms race" as currently conducted have been corporations and their stockholders. If the competition among the states were placed more directly on matters of equal if not more importance to business, such as the quality of the infrastructure, educational system, and environment, every citizen would benefit.[43]

Along with competition, relations among state governments are frequently cooperative. Some of this cooperation comes through groups like the

Governors' Association and through formal compacts and agreements among states to perform various functions (see the next chapter). Some states also tend to borrow legislative and administrative innovations developed by other states.[44] State officials often compare themselves to other states in their own league. They find it useful to learn what other states with roughly the same socioeconomic characteristics are doing about a given problem. In addition to gathering basic information, a sponsor of a particular proposal may be anxious to demonstrate that the proposed change has not produced the problems its opponents predict. The sponsor may also be eager to demonstrate that the proposed legislation has been widely adopted throughout the country and may argue that his or her state should not be the last to get on the bandwagon.

Governmental information and experiences are disseminated among the states in a number of ways, some of the most important of which are the publications and conferences sponsored by the organizations affiliated with the Council of State Governments. Established in 1933, the council is managed by a board made up of representatives from each of the fifty states. The council acts as secretariat for several groups of state officials, including the Governors' Association, the Conference of Chief Justices, the National Association of Attorneys General, and the National Legislative Conference for legislators and legislative staff. Many of these organizations, like the Governors' Association, provide a forum for state officials with common responsibilities to discuss mutual problems and to make their position known on matters of national policy. The National Conference of Commissioners on Uniform State Laws, also affiliated with the council, has endeavored with only limited success to tackle the problem of diversity in laws and regulations among the states on such matters as marriage and divorce, traffic, and business activity.

Local governments are likewise tied together by formal and informal contacts among officials and activities of national associations. Some of the most troublesome aspects of interlocal relations occur in metropolitan areas—a subject discussed in chapter 8.

ENDNOTES

1. U.S. Senator and former Virginia Governor Charles Robb, quoted by Steven D. Gold, "The State of State-Local Relations," *State Legislatures* (August 1988): 17–20, at 17.
2. Merrill Jensen, *The Making of the American Constitution* (New York: D. Van Nostrand, 1964).
3. 7 Wallace 70 (1869).
4. The Tenth Amendment reads: "The powers not delegated to the United States by the Constitution, nor prohibited by it to the States, are reserved to the States respectively, or to the people."
5. Morton Grodzins, *The American System: A New View of Governments in the United States* (Chicago: Rand McNally, 1966).

6. Thomas J. Anton, *American Federalism and Public Policy: How the System Works* (New York: Random House, 1989), p. 102.

7. See: Edward S. Corwin, "The Passing of Dual Federalism," *Virginia Law Review* 36 (February 1950): 1–24.

8. For a further breakdown of the various phases of federal-state relations see: Deil S. Wright, "Intergovernmental Relations: An Analytical Overview," *The Annals* 416 (November 1974): 1–16.

9. See: Saundra K. Schneider, "Intergovernmental Influences on Medicaid Program Expenditures," *Public Administration Review* (July / August 1988): 756–763.

10. See: John Shannon, "The Return to Fend-for-Yourself Federalism: The Reagan Mark," *Intergovernmental Perspective* (Summer / Fall 1987): 34–37.

11. See: Carol S. Weissert, "Restraint and Reappraisal," *Intergovernmental Perspective* (Winter 1977): 19–22.

12. On picket fence federalism see: Deil S. Wright, *Understanding Intergovernmental Relations* (Belmont, Calif.: Wadsworth, 1978).

13. Paul E. Peterson, Barry G. Rabe, and Kenneth K. Wong, *When Federalism Works* (Washington, D.C.: The Brookings Institution, 1986).

14. For background and details see: U.S. Advisory Commission on Intergovernmental Relations, *Regulatory Federalism: Policy, Process, Impact and Reform* (Washington, D.C.: Government Printing Office, 1984); and Joseph Zimmerman, *Federal Preemptions: The Silent Revolution* (Ames: Iowa State University Press, 1991).

15. 426 U.S. 851 (1976).

16. 469 U.S. 528 (1985).

17. Quoted by Neal Peirce, "Angry States Left with Tab for Social Services," Washington Post Syndication, August 1989.

18. Statement by National Conference of State Legislatures, quoted by John L. Larkin, "Budget Proposals Incur Wrath of States, Cities," *PA Times* 13 (September 1990): 1.

19. For commentary on the legislation see: Timothy J. Conlan et al., "The Politics of Mandate Reform," and John Novinson, "Unfunded Mandates: A Closed Chapter?" *Public Management* (July 1995): 17–19; and Timothy J. Conlan, James D. Riggle, and Donna E. Schwartz, "Deregulating Federalism? The Politics of Mandate Reform in the 104th Congress," *Publius: The Journal of Federalism* 25:3 (Summer 1995): 23–39.

20. Janet M. Kelly, "Lessons from the States on Unfunded Mandates," *National Civic Review* (Spring 1995): 133–139.

21. See, for example: Michael J. Rich, "Distributive Politics and the Allocation of Federal Grants," *American Political Science Review* 83 (March 1989): 193–213; Richard P. Nathan, "State and Local Governments under Federal Grants: Toward a Predictive Theory," *Political Science Quarterly* 98 (Spring 1983): 47–57; Christopher Hamilton and Donald T. Wells, *Federalism, Power, and Political Economy: A New Theory of Federalism's Impact on American Life* (Englewood Cliffs, N.J.: Prentice Hall, 1990); and William T. Gormley Jr., "Food Fights: Regulatory Enforcement in a Federal System," *Public Administration Review* 52 (May / June 1992): 271–280.

22. Nathan, "State and Local Governments under Federal Grants," pp. 47–57.

23. See: Richard Lehne, "Representation in Congress: A Projection for 1972," *National Civic Review* (July 1971): 372–376. Several studies have shown, however, that on

questions concerning aid to large cities, party affiliation is more predictive of how a member of Congress will vote than is the nature of his or her constituency, that is, whether it is a large city, a suburb, or a rural area. Democrats, especially those from the North, are far more likely than Republicans to support urban programs. See: Demetrios Caraley, "Congressional Politics and Urban Aid: A 1978 Postscript," *Political Science Quarterly* 93 (Fall 1978): 411–419. Voting patterns of rural representatives are, as might be expected, favorable to small-town America. See: David Saffell, "Congressional Representation of Rural and Small-Town Interests, 1981–1990," *National Civic Review* (Spring 1993): 157–167.

24. *Wessberry* v. *Sanders*, 376 U.S. 1 (1964).

25. See, generally: Val Burris, "Who Opposed the ERA? An Analysis of the Social Bases of Antifeminism," *Social Science Quarterly* (June 1983): 305–317; David W. Brady and Kent L. Tedin, "Ladies in Pink: Religion and Political Ideology in the Anti-ERA Movement," *Social Science Quarterly* (March 1976): 564–575; Kent L. Tedin et al., "Social Background and Political Differences between Pro- and Anti-ERA Activists," *American Politics Quarterly* (July 1976): 395–408; and Mark R. Daniels et al., "The ERA Won—At Least in the Opinion Polls," *PS* (Fall 1982): 578–584. A book-length study on the subject is: Janet K. Boles, *The Politics of the Equal Rights Amendment* (New York: Longman, 1979).

26. James K. Freeland, "Marble Cake and the Man in Washington," *State Government Administrator* (September 1967): 14–15. See also: Jacqueline Calmes, "444 North Capital Street: Where State Lobbyists Are Learning Coalition Politics," *Governing* (February 1988): 17–21. On activities of small cities in regard to lobbying, see: Rochelle L. Stanfield, "Small Cities Are on the Prowl for Help in Washington," *National Journal* (7 November 1978): 45–62.

27. Dennis O. Grady, "Gubernatorial Behavior in State-Federal Relations," *Western Political Quarterly* 40 (June 1987): 305–318.

28. To round out the discussion of the state-local lobby, mention should also be made of the Advisory Commission on Intergovernmental Relations (ACIR). This agency was created by Congress in 1959 as a permanent agency to monitor the operation of the federal system, to conduct studies, and to recommend improvements. ACIR is a bipartisan body of twenty-six members who serve two-year terms. Nine of the members represent the national government, fourteen represent state and local government officials, and three represent the public at large. See: Deil S. Wright, "The Advisory Commission on Intergovernmental Relations: Unique Features and Policy Orientation," *Public Administration Review* 25 (September 1965): 193–202; and "ACIR and the Federal System, 1959–1989," Symposium, *Intergovernmental Perspective* 15 (Fall 1989).

29. For recent accounts on the intergovernmental lobby see: Nicole Achs, "Clout," *American City & County* (May 1992): 79–81; R. Allen Hays, "Intergovernmental Lobbying: Toward an Understanding of Issue Priorities," *Western Political Quarterly* 44 (December 1991): 1081–1098; Jonathan Walters, "Lobbying for the Good Old Days," *Governing* (June 1991): 33–37; Charles H. Levine and James A. Thurber, "Reagan and the Intergovernmental Lobby: Iron Triangles, Cozy Subsystems and Political Conflict," in Allan J. Cigler and Burdett A. Loomis, eds., *Interest Group*

Politics, 2nd ed. (Washington, D.C.: CQ Press, 1986), pp. 202–220; and B.J. Reed, "The Changing Role of Local Advocacy in National Politics," *Journal of Urban Affairs* 5 (Fall 1983): 287–298. More in-depth studies are found in Suzanne Farkas, *Urban Lobbying: Mayors in the Federal Arena* (New York: New York University Press, 1970); Glen E. Brooks, *When Governors Convene: The National Governors' Conference in National Politics* (Baltimore: John Hopkins University Press, 1962); and Donald Haider, *When Governments Come to Washington: Governors, Mayors and Intergovernmental Lobbying* (New York: The Free Press, 1974).

30. David B. Walker, "Intergovernmental Relations and the Well-Governed City: Cooperation, Confrontation, Clarification," *National Civic Review* (March/April 1986): 65–87, at 83.

31. David R. Berman, Lawrence L. Martin, and Laura Kajfez, "County Home Rule: Does Where You Stand Depend on Where You Sit?" *State and Local Review* 17 (Spring 1985): 232–234. See also: Rufus E. Miles, "The Origin and Meaning of Miles' Law," *Public Administration Review* 38 (September/October 1978): 399–403.

32. Kelly, "Lessons from the States on Unfunded Mandates," p. 136.

33. See, generally, the review in David R. Berman, "States and Their Local Governments: Mandates, Finances, Problems," *The Municipal Year Book* (Washington, D.C.: International City Management Association, 1991), pp. 76–81.

34. See, generally: Charles R. Adrian, *State and Local Governments,* 3rd ed. (New York: McGraw-Hill, 1972), pp. 89–98.

35. *State Planning: New Roles in Hard Times* (Lexington, Ky.: Council of State Governments, 1976), pp. 9–10.

36. See: Glenn Abney and Thomas A. Henderson, "An Exchange Model of Intergovernmental Relations: State Legislators and Local Officials," *Social Science Quarterly* (March 1979): 720–731; and Glenn Abney and Thomas P. Lauth, "The Governor as Chief Administrator," *Public Administration Review* (January/February 1983): 40–49.

37. David R. Berman, "Speaking for the Cities: A Study of State Municipal Leagues," *Public Affairs Bulletin* no. 6 (1970).

38. See, generally: David R. Berman, "State-Local Relations: Patterns, Politics, and Partnerships," *The Municipal Year Book* (Washington, D.C.: International City/County Management Association, 1995), pp. 55–65.

39. See, generally: W. Brooke Graves, *American Intergovernmental Relations* (New York: Charles Scribner's Sons, 1964), pp. 695–736.

40. Remarks by Mayor John V. Lindsay, reprinted in Robert L. Morlan, ed., *Capital, Courthouse, and City Hall,* 5th ed. (Boston: Houghton Mifflin, 1977), pp. 38–39.

41. Several states have little Advisory Commissions on Intergovernmental Relations (ACIRs) or comparable organizations to provide a forum for discussing intergovernmental issues and devising solutions. Such bodies may also conduct research, analyze problems, and make recommendations to the legislature and governor on intergovernmental matters. The range of activities depends on the size of their budgets and staff. Membership is typically open to various state as well as local officials. See, generally: Advisory Commission on Intergovernmental Relations, *State-Local Relations Organizations: The ACIR Counterparts* (Washington, D.C.: Government Printing Office, February 1991); Deborah D. Roberts, "Carving out Their

Niche: State *Advisory Commissions on Intergovernmental Relations," Public Administration Review* (November/December 1989): 576–580; and Andree E. Reeves, "State ACIRs: Elements of Success," *Intergovernmental Perspective* (Summer 1991): 12–13, 24.

42. See: Bernard L. Weinstein, "Tax Incentives for Growth," *Society* (March/April 1977): 73–75; and Carol Steinbach, "Economic Development in the States," *State Legislatures* (March 1979): 7–11.

43. Dennis O. Grady, "State Economic Development Incentives: Why Do States Compete?" *State and Local Review* (Fall 1987): 86–94.

44. Jack L. Walker, "The Diffusion of Innovations among the American States," *American Political Science Review* 63 (September 1969): 880–899.

PART TWO

★ ★ ★

STATE POLITICS

3

★ ★ ★

CONSTITUTIONAL FOUNDATIONS

While drafting the Massachusetts Constitution in 1779, John Adams wrote of the goal of "a government of laws, and not of men." Through subsequent years, political life in Massachusetts and other states has been shaped and limited by formal rules affecting governmental power, structure, and citizen participation. Some of the most fundamental of these are found in the United States Constitution. Others are found in state constitutions. This chapter examines the general nature and significance of these documents. It concludes with a discussion of suffrage, direct democracy, and popular control of government in the states.

STATE POWERS UNDER THE UNITED STATES CONSTITUTION

GENERAL POWERS AND LIMITATIONS

The United States Constitution delegates certain powers to the national government and prohibits the states from some types of activities. Nowhere does the Constitution outline what the states may do. Their powers are residual or reserved. This is to say that the states can do anything that they are not prohibited from doing or anything that has not been delegated exclusively to the national government.

Among the reserved powers of the states are those to tax, spend, and regulate intrastate commerce (commercial activities within a state). Through a general *state police power*, the states may also act to promote or maintain the health, safety, welfare, and morals of their citizens. In addition, states exercise certain powers at the deference of Congress, such as control over elections and those involved in the implementation of national programs. Local governments as agents of the states have similar powers subject to the same limitations.

The greatest overall limit on the scope of state and local activity is the *supremacy clause* in Article VI of the Constitution, which reads: "This constitution, and all the laws of the United States which shall be made in pursuance thereof; and all treaties . . . made under the authority of the United States shall be the supreme law of the land." If a court finds a state or local law in conflict with the United States Constitution, national laws, or treaties entered into by the national government, it is null and void.

The Judiciary Act of 1789, shaped by the first Congress, made the supremacy clause effective by bringing state courts into the federal judicial system. Section 2 of that act granted an appeal to federal courts from state courts when a "federal question" involving an act of Congress, a United States treaty, or the Constitution had to be resolved. In so doing, Congress fostered uniformity within the federal system by establishing the United States Supreme Court as the arbiter of conflicts between the national and state governments and as the final interpreter of the Constitution.

The United States Supreme Court has often used its power of review to check state and local action. It did so in its early years to advance national supremacy and the development of a national economy. For much of the period since the 1940s, the Court has more often been concerned with issues of civil liberties and rights and, though often changing direction, has frequently used its power to protect the rights of racial, religious, and political minorities and of people accused of crime and from what it considered unfair state and local practices. In addition, the court has generally given a liberal interpretation to the powers of the national government enumerated in Article I, Section 8, of the Constitution. The enumerated powers have been given an added dimension by the doctrine of *implied powers*, under which Congress is not limited to those powers expressly delegated but is able to take "necessary and proper" action to carry out its enumerated powers.[1]

The United States Supreme Court constantly interprets and reinterprets the Constitution. It has also experienced changes in composition and leadership that have resulted in different attitudes toward the powers of state and local governments. The Supreme Court headed by Chief Justice Warren Burger and largely composed of justices nominated by President Nixon, for example, was generally less restrictive of state and local activity than was the preceding Court headed by Earl Warren. The current Court under Chief Justice William Rehnquist and appointees of Presidents Reagan and Bush has, as indicated in chapter 2, often been even more willing to limit the scope of national powers and to give states more leeway in making policy.

Despite some variation by different courts, over the years certain broad constitutional constraints have been placed on the ability of states and localities to regulate economic activity, interfere with civil liberties, and conduct relations with other states. We consider these on the following pages.

REGULATION OF ECONOMIC ACTIVITY

One finds a wide variety of regulations on economic activity on the state and local levels. These include laws regarding the sanitary conditions under which foods and drugs are produced; the labeling, grading, and selling of products; occupational and business licensing; the rates and services of public utilities like electric power and natural gas companies; the financial conditions of banks and other lending institutions; the selling of insurance and securities within a state; and a host of laws affecting land use and environmental matters.

Before the Civil War, the ability of states to regulate economic activity was limited by Article I, Section 10, which prohibited state action "impairing the obligation of contracts." This clause, as interpreted by the courts, was a major defense against state regulations that, among other things, interfered in private contracts (such as those involving debts) and interfered with corporate charters, licenses, or franchises the state had granted. Today, the due process clause of the Fourteenth Amendment has taken the place of the contract clause as a defense against state interference with private property rights. The clause generally requires procedural due process, meaning laws must be enforced in a fair manner. This may be interpreted to mean that a businessperson charged with false advertising, for example, has a right to a hearing to defend himself or herself. The clause may also be used to challenge the constitutionality of a law itself on the grounds that it is unfair or unjust, regardless of how it is specifically applied. When such a case arises, the term *substantive due process* is employed. Along with due process arguments, much of the current debate over the protection of property rights from federal as well as state and local regulations now revolves around the *takings clause* in the Fifth Amendment to the United States Constitution (see box 3–1).

The power of the states and localities to regulate general economic activity also has been limited to a considerable extent by the development of what is a national police power somewhat similar to but superior to the states' police power. Courts have interpreted the power of Congress to regulate commerce "among the several states" to relate not only to buying and selling but all forms of transportation and to the movement of people from state to state. Even activities within a single state may be regulated if they have a substantial impact on interstate commerce. The United States Supreme Court employed

BOX 3–1 PROPERTY RIGHTS: THE TAKINGS ISSUE

One provision of the United States Constitution of some concern to state and local governments in recent years is a clause in the Fifth Amendment prohibiting governments (by judicial interpretation, state and local as well as the federal government) from taking private property for public use without just compensation to the owner. The Supreme Court has in some cases interpreted the clause to limit the ability of local governments to enforce environmental, land use, and other types of regulations. In *Lucas* v. *South Carolina Coastal Council* (1992), for example, the Supreme Court upheld a claim that a state environmental protection law prohibiting a developer from constructing homes on his property constituted a taking without just compensation.

In another case, *Dolan* v. *City of Tigard* (1994), the Court concluded that the Oregon city's requirement that a property owner dedicate 10 percent of her property for flood-plain protection and other public purposes in exchange for a building permit amounted to an unconstitutional taking. The Court ruled that such restrictions on land use must meet a two-part test: there must be a reasonable relationship between the proposed use and the need for improvements, and the restrictions on land use must be "roughly proportional" to the burdens the use might place on public resources (see chapter 14). Chief Justice Rehnquist, speaking for the Court majority, declared that property rights are as important a part of the Bill of Rights as freedom of speech and religion or the protection against unreasonable searches and seizures.

In several parts of the country, state courts have also come to the rescue of property owners by relying on broad takings clauses in state constitutions. Further relief has been sought through the adoption of state and federal legislation. Critics of these trends argue that property owners should be subject to reasonable regulations for the benefit of the community as a whole and that the takings movement's attack on government regulations threatens needed land-use controls, progress made on the environmental front, and public health and safety.

this broad interpretation of the power to uphold the provisions of the 1964 Civil Rights Act, which forbade discrimination on the basis of race, religion, or national origin in places of public accommodations.[2]

Whether the courts will find that Congress has a specific power to regulate commerce is difficult to predict (see the discussion of the *Usery, Garcia,* and *Lopez* cases in chapter 2). It is clear, however, that when Congress has acted in a lawful manner to regulate commerce, all state and local laws in conflict must give way. In several policy areas, such as automobile emission standards, Congress has preempted the field, leaving no room for state and local action. Even in the absence of congressional legislation, courts may invalidate state and local laws on the grounds that the laws interfere with the flow of interstate commerce. Thus, some years ago, the Supreme Court concluded that Arizona could not impose a limit on the length of passenger and freight cars traveling in interstate commerce, and Illinois could not require that trucks traveling in interstate commerce be equipped with certain types of mudguards.[3]

More recently, federal courts have ruled that state laws banning the importation of solid wastes from other states violate the commerce clause. Garbage, according to these rulings, is a commodity like any other, and banning its shipment across state lines is restricting the free flow of interstate trade. States that have run out of landfill space or find it cheaper to dispose of solid wastes in a neighboring state have welcomed the decisions. Other states have complained about becoming dumping grounds and have continued to seek ways around the rulings. In a related type of case in 1992, the Supreme Court invalidated an effort by the state of Alabama to discourage the importation of hazardous wastes by imposing a special tax on the disposal of out-of-state hazardous wastes. The tax was considered discriminatory and an unconstitutional barrier to interstate trade.

A definite answer to the question of just exactly what types of economic activity states and localities may legally regulate cannot be given. Perhaps a more relevant question concerns the extent to which states and localities are willing and able to regulate economic activity. Some observers have been concerned, for example, over the extent to which states and localities are willing to offend economically important industries and perhaps risk damage to their economies by enforcing environmental protection laws (chapter 13).

CIVIL LIBERTIES AND RIGHTS

Historically, state and local governments have taken a multitude of actions that affect the civil liberties or rights of people within their jurisdictions.[4] The adoption of constitutionally questionable laws of this nature, such as those passed in the 1950s banning Communists from employment or participating in political activity, appear largely related to the cultural roots of the states, in this example, to a traditionalistic political culture.[5]

The key vehicle for the protection of civil liberties and rights has been the Fourteenth Amendment to the United States Constitution, which provides that no state shall "deprive any person of life, liberty, or property, without due process of law; nor deny to any person within its jurisdiction the equal protection of the laws." Over the years, the United States Supreme Court has held that the due process clause of this amendment incorporates many of the guarantees found in the Bill of Rights to the United States Constitution and protects them against state and local action. Thus, today states and local governments, as well as the national government, function within the limits imposed by the First Amendment's guarantees of freedom of speech, religion, press, and assembly. State legislatures and courts also must live up to the constitutional standards, as interpreted by the Supreme Court, of the Fourth, Fifth, Sixth, Seventh, and Eighth Amendments to the United States Constitution, which largely relate to the rights of those suspected or convicted of a crime.

The incorporation of many of the freedoms contained in the Bill of Rights into the Fourteenth Amendment has led to a nationalization of the protection of civil rights and a vastly increased role for both the federal courts and Congress in setting standards to guide the behavior of state and local authorities. Specific decisions under the due process clause have also caused considerable controversy both nationally and locally. One example is the 1962 case of *Engle* v. *Vitale*.[6] In this case, the Supreme Court invalidated a New York law under which a state board of regents had composed a prayer and had required that it be said aloud in public schools by each class in the presence of a teacher at the beginning of every school day. The Court concluded that government had no business writing prayers, even nondenominational ones. Controversy erupted again in 1992 with a 5–4 Supreme Court decision in *Lee* v. *Weisman* that public schools cannot include nondenominational prayers in graduation ceremonies.

A most controversial Supreme Court decision was *Roe* v. *Wade*[7] in 1973, a decision in which the Court ruled that state governments cannot prohibit abortions during the first three months of pregnancy and only under certain circumstances thereafter. In 1989, after years of political conflict over the matter, the Court, in *Webster* v. *Reproductive Health Services*, indicated that it would give state governments more discretion in regulating abortions (see box 3–2). In a subsequent decision, *Planned Parenthood of Southeastern Pennsylvania* v. *Casey*, in 1992, the Court allowed further restrictions on abortions but refused, by a narrow 5–4 vote, to overturn *Roe* v. *Wade*.

Under the equal protection clause of the Fourteenth Amendment, states may classify persons or things for the purpose of regulation or carrying out a program, but the classification cannot be unreasonable or arbitrary. In other words, state laws cannot discriminate against people, groups, or businesses unless there is a reasonable basis or justification for the discrimination. Two of the most significant Supreme Court decisions affecting state and local governments in recent years, *Brown* v. *Board of Education of Topeka, Kansas*[8] and *Reynolds* v. *Sims*,[9] were decided on the basis of the equal protection clause. The *Brown* case signaled the beginning of the effort to end racial discrimination in public schools. The *Reynolds* case required state legislatures to be reapportioned on a one-person, one-vote basis, ending discrimination against voters in urban and suburban areas and in favor of those from rural areas. Both cases are discussed in considerable detail elsewhere in this text. In recent years, as later pages also note, the Court has moved away from the approval of "race conscious" remedies by voiding plans for school desegregation, restricting affirmative action programs (see box 3–3), and making it more difficult to carve up election districts to ensure representation for minorities.

BOX 3–2 ABORTION: THE LEGISLATOR'S VIEW

Recent Supreme Court decisions have had the effect of stimulating more activity by pro-life forces at the state level to reduce further the scope of the *Roe* decision. Pro-choice leaders, not altogether happy with this development, have argued: "We don't have a fundamental right if we have to defend it in fifty states year after year." They prefer federal legislation that prevents states from interfering with the right to choose. Pro-life leaders, in contrast, would like federal laws or a constitutional amendment giving states more complete freedom to regulate or prohibit abortions.

Clearly, many state legislators would rather not deal with the issue at all. As one former Wisconsin lawmaker remembers: "When it came to the issue of abortion, the members of the legislature were not the generals. We were the soldiers in the line of fire. Regardless of how you voted, you were going to make a slew of single-issue voters mad. If you even said kind words about compromise, you became suspect by your own side—a potential traitor." Some, perhaps many, state legislators feel uncomfortable dealing with such questions as abortion, which are debated as moral absolutes. In explaining the difficulty of addressing the abortion issue, a legislative leader in Indiana noted: "We are so used to dealing in shades of gray that we don't like it when we have to see in black and white." Another added that when it came to abortion, "I don't know the right thing to do. . . . I don't have an innate feeling one way or another. I watch other people that do know and say to myself, 'Gee, that must be nice.' "

Sources: David Shribman, "Abortion-Rights Activists, Fearing More Setbacks in the States, Hope to Make the Issue National Again," *The Wall Street Journal* (20 March 1991): 22; Tom Loftus, *The Art of Legislative Politics* (Washington, D.C.: CQ Press, 1994), p. 77; and Rob Gurwitt, "Abortion: The Issue Politicians Wish Would Go Away," *Governing* (January 1990): 50–56.

INTERSTATE RELATIONS

Four provisions of the Constitution were intended to regulate relationships among the states. Article IV provides that: (1) each state give "full faith and credit" to the "public acts, records, and judicial proceedings of every other state"; (2) citizens of each state be "entitled to all privileges and immunities of citizens in the several states"; and (3) persons charged with a crime who flee to another state be returned to the state having jurisdiction over the crime. Article I, Section 10, provides for and regulates interstate compacts and agreements.

The full faith and credit clause applies to civil judgments in regard to rights under wills, contracts, and deeds. It does not apply to criminal proceedings. A most difficult area in the application of the clause has been divorce. A divorce granted by a state to two of its residents will be recognized by other

---

BOX 3–3 THE EROSION OF AFFIRMATIVE ACTION

In 1978 the United States Supreme Court upheld the general principle of giving special consideration to minorities, though in this case it found that a set-aside program for minorities in a medical school was too rigid (*Bakke* v. *University of California*). Subsequent decisions upheld affirmative action programs for hiring and promotion and a federal program requiring that 10 percent of public works contracts go to minority-controlled companies. In 1989, however, the Court voided a city of Richmond practice of awarding 30 percent of the city's work to minority companies. In May 1995, it let stand a lower court decision that had rejected a University of Maryland program that reserved scholarships for black students. California and other states followed up by moving to end affirmative action in admissions and hiring at universities. Other legislatures moved to end minority set-asides in public works programs. By the end of the year, many had considered legislation to abolish "preferential treatment" based on gender, sexual orientation, or ethnicity, as well as on race.

---

states even though they may not recognize the grounds on which the divorce was granted. A man or woman who establishes residence in another state for the purposes of obtaining a noncontested divorce, however, may find that the divorce will not be recognized in his or her home state. The recognition of same-sex marriages has also become controversial in recent years.

The general intent of the privileges and immunities clause is to prevent discrimination within a state against citizens of other states. Thus, a citizen from one state can purchase property in another state and use the other state's highways. There is, however, no clear definition of privileges and immunities. Out-of-staters, for example, do not enjoy the political rights of residents in regard to voting in local elections, and they often have to pay more to go to a state university or even to obtain a hunting license.

The purpose of the interstate rendition clause is to make it impossible for a criminal to avoid prosecution by fleeing to another state. The Constitution requires that governors return such fugitives. The courts, however, have interpreted this as being up to the discretion of the governors. Governors have on occasion refused to return fugitives, especially when extradition would have resulted in unusual punishment, such as work in a chain gang. Under an act of Congress, when certain felonies are involved, federal officials can pursue and return a fugitive who has fled across state lines or out of the country.

The final area of interstate relations covered by the Constitution is that of interstate compacts. An interstate compact is a formal agreement between two or more states. Under the Constitution, a state is prohibited from entering into a compact or agreement with another state or foreign government without the consent of Congress. The original intent was to restrict the states for fear they would threaten the stability of the Union by making military or economic alliances with each other or with foreign countries.

Since the 1920s, the device has been looked on as a means through which states could cooperatively settle mutual problems that otherwise would have to involve the federal government. Congress has encouraged such use by consenting to agreements in advance and by allowing many relatively minor agreements to be made without the formality of consent. Currently there are some 120 active agreements among the states.

Through the compact device, state governments have formed research and planning bodies to study regional problems, technical commissions to allocate water supplies from interstate rivers, and joint educational programs. Perhaps the most well-known compact agency is the Port Authority of New York and New Jersey (formerly known as the Port Authority of New York), created jointly by the states of New York and New Jersey to construct and operate bridges, highways, and airports linking the two states in the New York metropolitan area.

The compact device has been used primarily to tackle specific and rather technical problems concerning two or more states. Compacting states have been reluctant to delegate broad governing powers to compact agencies. Moreover, interstate compacts and agreements, though increasingly used, have not prevented the involvement of the national government in regional problems. Much of this involvement has come from acts of Congress that have brought the states and the national government together in regional agencies having the authority to coordinate plans for the economic development of certain areas like Appalachia or to guide the multipurpose development of river basins. Two unique federal-interstate compacts have also been developed to manage the water resources of the Delaware and Susquehanna rivers. In these two instances, at least, the device has become another instrument of cooperative federalism rather than a means of avoiding national governmental involvement.[10]

STATE CONSTITUTIONS

State constitutions, like ordinary state laws, are subordinate to the Constitution and laws of the United States government, and may be invalidated in the event of a legal conflict with these documents. State constitutions, however, are the fundamental laws of the states and, as such, may be used by state courts to invalidate the actions of state legislators, governors, or administrators. These basic documents are constantly interpreted and reinterpreted by the highest state courts, which, like the United States Supreme Court, act as a "continuous constitutional convention." State attorneys general also play an important role in constitutional interpretation as they are often required by law to give advisory opinions on the constitutional validity of proposed legislation and administrative regulations.

Over the years, state courts have developed a rather complex body of state constitutional law.[11] As indicated below, in some instances this law has given citizens certain rights and guarantees not provided by the federal courts. Indeed, over the last several years, the inclination of the United States Supreme Court to retreat from a zealous concern with civil liberty cases has encouraged a movement toward the resolution of basic conflicts of this nature in state courts under the provisions of state constitutional law. The thinking of state court judges about constitutional rights continues to be greatly influenced by the United States Supreme Court, that is, they tend to go no further than the High Court in protecting constitutional rights. In certain exceptional circumstances, however, state courts have looked upon United States Supreme Court interpretations of the federal Constitution as requiring only minimal standards (for example, for criminal justice procedures), which can be expanded upon by state constitutions and laws.

Since the 1930s, when the United States Supreme Court began its current policy of avoiding, when possible, controversies involving governmental regulation of business, much of the law on this subject has also been based on state court interpretations of state constitutions. State courts have rejected legislation regulating business on the basis of state constitutional doctrines relating to equal protection of the laws, due process, and the principles that limit the amount of legislative power that can be delegated to administrative agencies.

The following discussion examines the general characteristics and contents of state constitutions and the politics of changing them.

GENERAL CHARACTERISTICS

State governments have had considerable experience in writing state constitutions. Thirty states have had more than one constitution, and most state constitutions have been subject to several amendments. Compared to the United States Constitution, which has about sixty-seven hundred words and has been amended only twenty-seven times in 180 years, most state constitutions are detailed, lengthy, and contain a number of amendments. The average state constitution is more than three times as long as the federal Constitution. The Louisiana Constitution of 1921, which was replaced by a new constitution in 1974, contained over two hundred fifty thousand words. Only a few states have fewer than ten thousand words in their constitutions. Constitutions effective in nineteen states have been amended one hundred times or more. Many remain difficult to read. As one jurist has noted, some state constitutions "have all the literary quality of the Yellow Pages."[12]

Several factors account for the relatively great length and detail of state constitutions. A broad historical factor accounting for this condition was the loss of popular confidence in state legislatures from the end of the Civil War to the early 1900s—a period in which forty-two states adopted or revised their constitutions. Those who wrote or revised their state's basic documents felt that extensive and detailed regulations were necessary to prevent the corruption and mismanagement that characterized the era. State constitutions adopted before or after this period contain fewer restrictions on the powers and procedures of state legislatures and, overall, are briefer and more confined to fundamentals.

Another fundamental factor accounting for length and detail is that, partly in reaction to the era of corruption and mismanagement, state constitutions have been relatively easy to change through the amendment process, especially when compared to the United States Constitution. Ease of amendment (the methods are described below) has encouraged various groups to put matters in the constitution, for safer keeping, that otherwise could be enacted simply by statute. Further contributing to this tendency has been the frequent failure in the states to make the distinction between constitutional and statutory law. Like the United States Constitution, state constitutions should be concerned with basic and enduring fundamentals of government. Other matters should be taken care of by simple legislation. By this criterion, Louisiana should not have amended its constitution to declare Huey Long's birthday a legal holiday, and South Dakota should not have adopted a constitutional authorization for a twine and cordage plant at the state penitentiary.

A final reason has been the failure of state constitutions to grow, as has the federal Constitution, through judicial interpretation. While state courts have been active in interpreting state constitutions, they have found their scope of interpretation considerably narrowed by the detailed nature of many of the documents. Faced with this detail, they are more likely to find an act of the state legislature in conflict with a state constitution than the Supreme Court of the United States is to invalidate an act of Congress or of a state legislature under the United States Constitution. There is also a greater possibility that a negative state court decision will be overridden by a constitutional amendment. When this happens, of course, the constitution becomes even longer and more detailed, and perpetuates the cycle.

CONTENTS

Within a typical state constitution, as in the United States Constitution, one finds a preamble, a Bill of Rights, an outline of the structure of state government, and a section of methods for changing the constitution.[13] Other provisions of state constitutions (which are not found in detail, if at all, in the United States Constitution) relate to matters concerning governmental finance, local government, civil service, voting and elections, the regulation of corporations, and public education, health, and welfare programs. One may also find obsolete provisions in state constitutions, such as those on Civil War pensions and prohibitions on granting titles of nobility, as well as antiquated or complex wording that leads only to legal confusion and inconsistencies.

Preambles commonly contain a statement of the purpose of the government and indicate that its source of authority is "the people." The Bill of Rights found in state constitutions (sometimes called the Declaration of Rights) contains many of the same rights guaranteed in the Bill of Rights to the United States Constitution. Portions of the national Bill of Rights, as explained previously, have been made applicable to state action via the Fourteenth Amendment. As a result, for example, the United States Constitution and a state constitution may both guarantee the equal protection of the laws and due process of law. This duality frequently gives those whose rights may have been infringed upon the option of taking their case to either state or federal courts, or both if necessary.

State governments may also place in their constitutions guarantees not found in the United States Constitution. For instance, several states have added *right to work* statements to their Bills of Rights. These provisions forbid union membership as a condition for securing or holding a job. Twenty-eight states have equal rights provisions in their constitutions similar to the Equal Rights Amendment that was proposed to the United States Constitution. During the late 1970s and early 1980s, proponents of the national ERA drew on the fact that courts have not interpreted state ERAs in a radical way (for example, to invalidate rape laws, legitimize homosexual marriages, or take away the right of women to be supported by their husbands) to counter arguments that a national ERA would have these effects.[14] Other rights not found in the United States Constitution range from the "right to play bingo" to the "right to individual dignity" and, in one constitution, the "right to revolution."

All state constitutions have adopted the principle of the separation of powers along legislative, executive, and judicial lines. The only deviant in basic structure among the states is Nebraska's unicameral, or one-house, legislature. Under state constitutions, the legislatures have general rather than enumerated powers. They look to their constitutions for limitations on their powers (for example, as found in the Bill of Rights) rather than specific authorizations to pass laws.

State constitutions generally fragment authority. The executive authority under most state constitutions is divided among several officials directly elected by the voters. In addition to the governor, these officials commonly include a lieutenant governor, attorney general, secretary of state, state treasurer, state superintendent of instruction, and several boards or commissions. Judicial functions and powers are likewise commonly distributed among a number of independently established courts that have been difficult to integrate into a unified court system.

Updating and streamlining state governments has, of necessity, placed great emphasis on state constitutional revision. Among the objectives have been to remove some of the limitations on the legislature, to strengthen the administrative position of the governor, and to eliminate barriers to the modernization of local governments. A more general goal has been to produce documents that are brief, flexible, easily read, and confined to fundamentals.

THE POLITICS OF CHANGE

State constitutions can be changed through the amendment process. They also can be completely replaced with a new constitution. In all states except Delaware, voters must approve amendments or new constitutions.

Most constitutional amendments have been initiated by state legislatures, which are authorized to do so in every state. Another method of making amendments is through the constitutional initiative found in seventeen states. This device allows private citizens to place a proposed constitutional amendment on the ballot. Though it has been of some value to groups lacking influence in the state legislature, it is less likely to succeed than an amendment sponsored by the legislature.

Constitutional conventions are the oldest method of change through which amendments can be developed or an entirely new document written. The state legislatures usually initiate the conventions. In some states the legislature is compelled at certain times to ask the voters whether or not they would like to have a convention. If the voters approve the call for a constitutional convention, delegates are selected in a manner determined by the legislature. Generally they are elected from state legislative districts on a partisan ballot.

Most state constitutional conventions have been limited by the legislature to revising only specific areas in the documents. Legislators have been uneasy about what a constitutional convention might do if it were allowed to rewrite as it saw fit. Limited constitutional conventions have been particularly popular in older states where vested interests are more deeply rooted in state constitutions.

State constitutional conventions are organized much in the same way as state legislatures. Organizational sessions are held to select the convention's president or chairperson, who in turn usually has the power to appoint committees. The committees, aided by professional staffs and consultants, consider different sections of the constitution to be revised and may hold open hearings. Recommendations are then submitted by the committee for debate and action by the entire convention.

Research indicates that while few delegates appreciate any distinction between constitutional and statutory lawmaking, their perception of their role is somewhat different from that of state legislators. Convention delegates tend to see themselves as trustees of the public interest at large rather than as the representatives of specific areas, parties, or interests. This perception is no doubt related to the fact that the convention is a one-shot affair and delegates do not stand for reelection.[15] Other research indicates, however, that while delegates to constitutional conventions may initially consider themselves as statesmen for the public interest, they may come away from conventions thinking that such proceedings are as political as anything else.[16] Certainly, framers of new constitutions face the possibility that what they have done will offend particular interests who will seek to have the document voted down.[17]

A common conflict experienced by delegates to constitutional conventions has been between reformers and defenders of the status quo.[18] Party politics has played a role in several state constitutional conventions, such as in the 1967 New York convention and the 1961–1962 Michigan convention. In the New York convention and the Illinois convention of 1969–1970, serious splits occurred between delegates from large urban areas (especially New York City and Chicago) and those from the rest of the state. Urban-rural conflicts have been frequent in the several conventions held to consider the apportionment of state legislatures. Among other politically divisive issues have been those of state aid to parochial schools, tax exemption, legislative salaries, and those relating to the powers of local government.[19]

State constitutions, through the amending process, are very susceptible to changes in public opinion. One scholar has suggested that because state constitutions rest so heavily on popular sentiment, minorities in the states and localities need the security of the United States Constitution and laws to protect them from politically dominant majorities.[20] Others find, however, that the record of change through amendment is not all that alarming. Amendments having to do with basic constitutional protections are relatively infrequent—amounting to only about 5 percent of the proposals and some 7 percent of the adoptions. There have, moreover, been about as many individual and minority rights-expanding changes as rights-reducing changes.[21]

SUFFRAGE AND DIRECT DEMOCRACY

The first state constitutions formed in the early 1800s placed considerable emphasis on legislative supremacy. Along with this, the early documents reflected the notion that a system of frequent legislative elections was an essential safeguard—as essential if not more so than a Bill of Rights—against tyranny. Annual elections, it was felt, would make state legislators the "people's agents." Those who abused their powers or failed to do their duty as representatives would, it was assumed, simply fail to be reelected.[22]

In terms of active voting participation in state politics, however, the constitutional framers had in mind only a small percentage of the population. Through the years, suffrage has steadily expanded. Some of this liberalization began on the state level, but much of it has resulted from amendments to the United States Constitution, from Supreme Court decisions, and from acts of Congress. Reflecting the Populist and Progressive movements, however, several states and localities have something the national government does not have: provisions for the exercise of direct democracy.

DEVELOPMENT OF VOTING RIGHTS

At the time of adoption of the United States Constitution, states restricted suffrage to adult white males who, in some states, also had to meet certain religious and property-holding qualifications. Religious and property-holding requirements were swept away under the influence of Jeffersonian and Jacksonian democracy.[23] Amendments to the Constitution were later added to prohibit the states from denying the vote on the basis of race (Fifteenth Amendment, 1870), gender (Nineteenth Amendment, 1920), and to those eighteen years of age or older (Twenty-sixth Amendment, 1971).

Enforcement of the Fifteenth Amendment's ban against discrimination on the basis of race has been the most difficult. Early implementation efforts were resisted especially in southern states by social, economic, and physical pressures against voting by blacks and by regulations and practices sanctioned by state law. Among the latter were: (1) the "white primary," which excluded blacks in several southern states from voting in the Democratic Party primary, leaving them with no effective choice among candidates because the nominees of the Democratic Party were usually unopposed in the general election; (2) the poll tax, which discouraged poor whites as well as blacks from voting; and (3) a literacy test requirement, which was primarily aimed at blacks, particularly in those states where it was mandatory for all those whose grandfathers could not vote before the adoption of the Fifteenth Amendment (affecting only blacks, of course).

United States Supreme Court decisions eliminated the white primary and the grandfather requirements attached to the literacy test. The adoption of the Twenty-fourth Amendment to the United States Constitution in 1964 ended the use of the poll tax in presidential and congressional elections. Subsequent decisions by the Supreme Court ended use of the poll tax in state and local elections. The literacy test first became subject to federal law under the 1964 Civil Rights Act. Congress in this legislation required that states accept a sixth-grade education as meeting the literacy requirement unless illiteracy could be otherwise proven. The act also required election officials to give the tests in writing (to provide evidence of actual failure) and prohibited using minor errors as a basis for declaring illiteracy.

The 1965 Voting Rights Act went even further in limiting discrimination in the application of the literacy test. This act authorized national officials to suspend the literacy test and directly register voters if the test was found discriminatory. In the first twenty-two months following the passage of the 1965 legislation, black registration increased nearly 80 percent. Studies conducted in 1968, however, disclosed that states requiring passage of literacy tests still generally had lower registration and turnout than states without these requirements. Literacy tests were having a particularly adverse effect on the registration of blacks and Hispanics. Faced with these continuing problems, Congress amended the Voting Rights Act in 1970 to ban the use of such tests as prerequisites for voting.

The Voting Rights Act of 1965, as amended and extended in 1970, 1975, and 1982, contains several other restrictions on the power of state and local officials in regard to suffrage and elections. The act, for example, confines residency requirements for voting in presidential elections to thirty days and establishes uniform standards for absentee registration and balloting in presidential elections. Provisions added in 1975 require that voter information material and ballots be printed in a language other than English in political jurisdictions in which 5 percent or more of the population is illiterate in English.[24] As implemented, this provision requires more than five hundred cities and counties in thirty states to hold elections in more than one language.

Another section of the act requires that jurisdictions (cities, counties, or states) with a history of voting discrimination submit proposed changes affecting voting rights (including redistricting or changing county boundaries) to the United States Department of Justice (or the United States District Court for the District of Columbia) for approval. This "preclearance" requirement applies primarily to several southern states.

In recent years the Voting Rights Act has been used not so much to remove barriers to minority voting as to attack practices that dilute the voting strength of minorities. A common reaction to the elimination of the literacy test and other barriers to the vote in several states was the adoption of practices such as using at-large elections in majority white districts to weaken the voting strength of minorities. The Justice Department has drawn upon the Voting Rights Act to require that states, particularly those subject to preclearance, devise majority minority districts in which minorities, voting as a bloc, can elect minority lawmakers. The creation of such districts has facilitated the election of minorities to state and congressional offices. Recent United States Supreme Court decisions, however, have cast doubt on the validity of this practice (chapter 5).

All in all, the Voting Rights Act has been one of the most effective pieces of civil rights legislation ever passed by Congress. As noted in chapter 1, the act, along with massive voter registration drives, has greatly increased the voting participation of blacks and the number of black officeholders, especially in southern states.[25]

As a result of congressional and court action and constitutional amendments, the requirements for voting are now basically uniform among the
states. State governments commonly require: (1) United States citizenship; (2)
a certain minimum residency in the state, county, or precinct (but lengthy
residency requirements such as residency in the state for one year and in a
county for three months are unconstitutional for all elections);[26] (3) voter
registration (though states may be in legal trouble if they attempt to close
registration more than fifty days before an election); and (4) a minimum age
(now uniformly eighteen). State governments may disqualify those who have
been declared insane, convicted of a felony,[27] dishonorably discharged from
the armed forces, or have tried to overthrow the United States government.

PARTICIPATION AND THE ELECTION SYSTEM

Even though state governments have included (or have been forced to
include) more voters in the election process, they have retained considerable
authority or control over the administration of the election system. Choices
open to the states in regard to the election system may encourage or discourage participation and may condition the outcome of an election.[28]

The scheduling of elections, for example, affects the level of voter participation. Some states attempt to insulate the election of their officials from the
election of national officials by scheduling state elections in odd-numbered
years. Many other states schedule their own elections to coincide with congressional but not presidential elections. Even though measures designed to
reduce the impact of national elections may have a worthy objective, they do
tend to reduce the level of voter participation.

The ballot form may also affect political participation. Some states make
the voters' task in selecting candidates relatively simple by allowing them to
vote a straight party ticket with a single vote. States that use an office ballot,
under which each office must be voted on separately, not only make the
voters' task more difficult but also encourage split-ticket voting and a falloff
in voting for offices toward the end of the ballot. Falloff is particularly great
among lower socioeconomic groups.[29] Parties with a lead in registered voters
may be expected to favor a system in which all candidates of a party can be
chosen with a single vote. Minority parties may be expected to favor a ballot
that encourages split-ticket voting.

Over the years, the type of voter registration system adopted by the states
has had the greatest impact on voter participation. Even though from 80 to 90
percent of those registered actually do vote, it is not uncommon to find that
from 40 to 50 percent of those eligible fail to register. Historically, some states
have made registration difficult by setting registration deadlines months in
advance of election day and making potential voters sign up at designated

locations that are open for a limited number of hours at inconvenient times, or so distant that citizens must make lengthy trips to them. Laws have also required complicated identification procedures and the "purging" or removal of voters from registration lists because they failed to vote in a previous election. Cumbersome state registration practices in the 1970s may have depressed voter participation by as much as 9 percent.[30]

In the 1970s some states began to supplement the traditional system of personal registration, requiring individuals to appear before a duly designated registrar, with a system of registration by mail. Early studies suggested, however, that the use of the mail registration system did not necessarily lead to unusually high levels of voter turnout and that mail registration probably had much less to do with participation than other factors such as voter interest in specific candidates or issues.[31]

As another reform, an increasing number of states adopted motor-voter registration laws, which authorized state motor vehicle department employees to hand out voter registration materials to people renewing or first receiving driver licenses. The process appeared cost-effective, costing but a fraction of what it would have cost to use deputy registrars, and particularly effective in reaching potential voters, such as young people, who are otherwise hard to reach.[32]

The success of state motor-voter laws encouraged the introduction of federal legislation to do the same thing on a national basis. Congress responded with the National Voter Registration Act (NVRA) in 1993. The act, which became effective in January 1995, requires, among other matters, that states make registration available at motor vehicle departments, various social service agencies, and through the mail. States that had liberal registration laws, for example, allowed registration on election day or, in the case of North Dakota, did not require voters to register, were exempt from the law. Several states challenged the law on the grounds that it infringed upon states' rights, but, thus far, the suits have not been successful. As might have been predicted from the experience of the states, the immediate effect of the act was to swell the voting rolls—more than five million citizens registered to vote in the first eight months after the act went into effect. Ultimately, registration could improve to four out of five adult Americans, compared to the current three out of five.

Analysis, drawing on the state experience with similar reforms, suggests that most of the voter increase had to do with motor-voter programs allowing people to register when getting a driving permit, rather than with other reforms required by the NVRA, such as mail-in and welfare agency-based registration or limitations on the purging of voter rolls.[33] Thus far, there has been little evidence of benefit for a particular party. Republicans have generally feared such reform would benefit the Democrats. Because Democrats have made the same assumption, the battles in Congress and state capitols over registration reform have been highly partisan.

By and large, governments have gone beyond eliminating barriers to voting to actively encouraging voting. Along with more liberal registration systems, states have made it easier to vote by adopting early voting systems (giving voters several days in which to vote) and voting by mail.[34] Because of these changes, the failure to vote now appears to be far more a matter of choice and personal circumstance than institutional barriers

DEVICES OF DIRECT DEMOCRACY

Through devices of direct democracy, citizens make their own laws rather than have laws made for them by elected representatives. One example of direct democracy is the New England town meeting, discussed in chapter 8. Other examples are the initiative and referendum, which allow voters directly to determine policy issues. The devices were largely the product of the Populist and Progressive movements, serving as means through which corporate control of state legislatures could be circumvented.[35]

Many politicians in the late nineteenth century and early twentieth century viewed the initiative and referendum as radical because they conflicted with the older notion of representative democracy, in which citizens have little more to do than choose lawmakers. Historically related to the adoption of the initiative and referendum is the recall device, which allows voters to remove an official from office prior to the expiration of his or her term. It has been valued as a way of keeping officials from straying from public opinion and punishing those who do so.

The initiative, found in twenty-four states, may be used to enact laws or amend the state constitution. Under state law, a specified number of qualified voters must sign a petition containing a statement of the law or proposed constitutional amendment. The proposal is then submitted to the voters for their approval or rejection at the next regular election or at a special election. The proposal goes into effect if approved by at least 50 percent of the voters. In some states the initiative device functions indirectly. In this process, once a petition is filed, the state legislature has a certain amount of time to consider the measure. If the legislature fails to act or changes the proposal in a manner unacceptable to its sponsors, the measure is then placed on the ballot for voter approval or rejection.

The direct initiative has been used most often in western states, including California, Washington, Colorado, Oregon, North Dakota, Oklahoma, and Arizona. In these states, it has long been a regular feature of state politics. In other states, the device has never been used to any great extent or was used extensively only in the years immediately following its adoption.[36]

There are three types of referenda: the compulsory referendum, the optional referendum, and the petition (or protest) referendum. The compulsory referendum is used when, by law, certain propositions, such as a constitutional amendment or a bond issue, must be submitted to a popular vote. The optional referendum is employed when the legislature voluntarily submits a question, usually a highly controversial issue, to a popular vote. The legislature may or may not be bound by the vote. With the protest petition or protest referendum, a specific number of voters through a petition may force a measure passed by the legislature to be submitted to a popular vote. For example, a political party may petition to have a redistricting plan adopted by the other party submitted to the voters in hopes that they will reject it.

The recall is a device permitting voters to remove public officials from office before their terms expire. In some states, the recall can be used for any state and local official, whether appointed or elected. In others the recall is confined to elective offices only, and judges may be exempted. The recall requires a petition supported by a certain number of signatures of qualified voters, the number depending on state law and the office involved. If the petition meets the requirements of state law, the voters are asked whether or not they want to keep the official in office. In some states the voters decide between the challenged official and a candidate who would be his or her successor.

Recalls aimed at local officials have been common, especially in recent years (see chapter 9). Because of the large number of signatures required, statewide recall drives very rarely qualify for the ballot. The only governor to be removed from office by the recall process was the governor of North Dakota in 1921. In 1987 a recall election for the governor of Arizona was canceled because the legislature impeached the individual involved and removed him from office prior to the scheduled recall vote. From time to time, recall campaigns have been put together for state legislative seats. On some occasions they have been used effectively for these positions. In 1983, for example, the recall was used in Michigan to remove two state senators who had favored tax increases. Their removal shifted the balance of power in the senate.

Although actual state recall elections are rare, threats to recall legislators and governors have become more common in recent years. What little research has been done on the subject suggests that incumbents who lose recall elections usually do so because of some action they have taken, such as voting for a tax increase, that converts a significant number of their original supporters into opponents.[37]

The three devices of direct democracy provide a safety valve with which the voters can bypass legislative inaction, challenge governmental policies, and rid themselves of unsatisfactory elected officials. However the devices present some difficulties. Some of these have to do with voter behavior. Unless well-known personalities or major issues are involved, elections of this nature do not draw much public attention or participation. On initiative and referendum measures the voters are often faced with many technical questions about which they have been given little information. Many citizens simply skip over the propositions and confine their electoral involvement to the selection of candidates listed at the top of the ballot. In any given election, 10 to 25 percent of

---

BOX 3–4 VOTERS AND BALLOT ISSUES

"In major candidate races, the majority of voters consistently vote along party lines. Moreover, 'swing' voters respond to specific images of the candidates they receive from television news and commercials. These images generally have a profound impact on the outcome of candidate races.

"By contrast, a ballot measure is an abstraction: words printed on paper few voters read. Furthermore, the essence of the issue that voters are being asked to decide is often subject to broad debate and confusion. . . . Voter volatility is more pronounced in ballot issue campaigns. On issues, voters generally do not rely on political party anchors or human imagery in their decision making. In addition, they filter conflicting interpretations of the issue and its ramifications. The result can be a wild roller-coaster ride. Major shifts in voter preferences, which might take weeks to develop in a candidate campaign, can occur virtually overnight in a ballot measure campaign."

Source: Paul Mandabach, "Strategic Nuances," *Campaigns & Elections* (September 1995): 19.

---

the voters may fail to express their preference on one or more of the propositions. Falloff in voting is particularly likely among the less well educated.[38]

Even those who do vote, however, may not make a well-informed decision. Those who have not studied the issues before entering the voting booth often have difficulty, based on the technical and legalistic manner in which the propositions are written, deciding what the actual nature and significance of the choices involve. Voters may be misled by the wording of propositions. In still other cases, they may be misinformed prior to the election by an advertising blitz conducted by those on one side of the issue. In situations where they hear both sides of a controversy during an election campaign, a sizable number of voters may switch from one side to another, based in large part on the quality of the media campaigns directed at them, and, in effect, remain undecided down to the time of the election (see box 3–4).

Voter instability and confusion are likely to characterize hotly contested propositions involving important but somewhat complex issues, such as nuclear energy or insurance reform. At that, voters can simplify the problem of securing information and vote as if they were informed through the shortcut of taking voting cues from relatively well-informed people or groups who share the same interests and values.[39]

Along with problems involving voter turnout and informed decision making, the devices of direct democracy pose certain problems for the groups who would use them. Citizens' groups seeking to place proposals on the ballot often encounter problems in securing the specified number of signatures. Most states require that the total be equal to a certain percentage (from 5 to 10) of the number of ballots cast at the last general election. As the number of voters has increased over the years, so, too, has the total number of signatures required. In a large state, the requirements can come close to half a million signatures. Technicalities of the law often provide opponents of change with an opportunity to challenge success-fully the validity of signatures. Groups have to allow for this by collecting many more signatures than they really need. Not surprisingly, given the obstacles, of the hundreds of initiative petitions circulated in recent years only 15 to 20 percent actually make it to the ballot.[40]

Success with the instruments of direct democracy requires, first of all, enough organizational strength to collect the necessary number of signatures. For groups lacking a ready organization or network of volunteers, there is the option of hiring a signature-gathering firm, though this can cost anywhere from $2 to $5 per signature. Success very often also requires a considerable expenditure of funds to support a campaign in regard to a proposed measure. Polling, media production, and other campaign activities are often provided under contract by private firms that specialize in such matters.[41]

Under a 1978 Supreme Court ruling, corporations, political organizations, and individuals may spend as much as they please on initiative and referendum campaigns. (This is contrary, as noted below, to elections in which candidates are involved.) Considerable sums may be spent. For example, in California in 1982, the National Rifle Association and other opponents of a stringent gun control measure pumped $1 million into a campaign that successfully defeated the measure. Six years later, roughly $100 million was spent in another California initiative campaign involving the highly complex topic of insurance reform.[42]

Generally, most of the funds spent in initiative and referendum campaigns in recent years have been raised by business-backed committees that have been trying to defeat various measures, such as those relating to environmen-tal and consumer protection, increases in corporate taxation, or calling for a ban on disposable bottles. Studies suggest that the side that spends the most money on such campaigns is likely to be successful 57 percent of the time.[43]

Despite the obstacles just mentioned, devices of direct democracy have been used by all types of groups for all types of purposes (see box 3–5). During the early 1970s, the devices were commonly used by environmental and consumer advocates to bypass recalcitrant state legislatures.[44] The most dra-matic use of the initiative and referendum in the late 1970s was to consider taxing and spending limitations, such as Proposition Thirteen in California.

In the late 1980s groups used the initiative process to secure adoption of controversial measures declaring English to be the official language of partic-ular states. In a number of states with large Spanish-speaking populations—Arizona, California, Colorado, and Florida—such proposals were rejected in the state legislatures, but were later approved in popular balloting.

BOX 3–5   SECURING PUBLIC SUPPORT: SOME UNUSUAL PROPOSITIONS

Voters commonly turn down proposals on the ballot to raise taxes. One exception to this pattern occurred in Michigan in 1994 because of the way lawmakers framed the question. In this case the voters were not asked to vote yes or no on whether they wanted new taxes but to choose, in effect, between an increase in the sales tax or an increase in the income tax. They chose to rely on the sales tax. For the previous several years, on a simple yes or no vote, Michigan voters had refused to take this course of action.

Voters in Washington in 1995 were asked to pass on an initiative that would have legalized Las Vegas-style gambling on some Indian reservations. As part of the promotion, supporters promised to pay every person who voted in the election an annual share of 10 percent of the profits from slot machines, estimated to be about $100 for each voter. Critics considered the offer an outright bribe, though on a mass scale. Supporters said they were simply sharing the revenue with people, even those who did not vote for the measure. Despite the inducement, voters overwhelmingly rejected the measure.

Voters, ignoring elite opinion in these and other states, apparently looked upon English proficiency as a highly important symbol of national identity. Many viewed bilingualism, on the other hand, as implying a disrespect for American culture and threatening political cohesion and stability.[45] Consistent with the "English Only" vote was the decision of California voters in 1994 in favor Proposition 187, which cut off nonemergency health, social services, and education for undocumented aliens.

Among the major reforms coming via the initiative route in the early 1990s was the effort, largely successful, to limit the number of terms members of Congress and state legislators can serve (though the United States Supreme Court has invalidated state term limits on members of Congress). Controversy has also erupted over antigay rights measures that have appeared on the ballot—one being adopted in Colorado in 1992 (though later invalidated by the courts). Overall, studies indicate that the statewide initiative process has been about equally useful to conservative and liberal causes—though conservatives appear to have been more active in recent years.

LIMITS ON POPULAR CONTROL

The right to vote and to otherwise participate in the political system is, of course, fundamental in a democracy. There is no guarantee, however, that government will be conducted according to majority rule. As indicated earlier in this chapter, the majority cannot infringe upon the constitutionally protected rights of minorities. In actual practice, moreover, what government does may have less to do with the demands of the "people" as such than with the functioning of the party and interest group system and the activities of newspapers and television stations. We discuss these in the following chapter.

ENDNOTES

1. See: *McCulloch* v. *Maryland,* 4 Wheaton 316 (1819).
2. *Heart of Atlanta Motel* v. *United States,* 379 U.S. 241 (1964).
3. See: *Southern Pacific Co.* v. *Arizona,* 325 U.S. 761 (1945); and *Bibb* v. *Navajo Freight Lines,* 359 U.S. 520 (1959).
4. "Civil liberties" generally refers to the protection of certain liberties, such as speech and religion, from governmental interference. "Civil rights" usually means protection of particular groups of people, for example, blacks or women, from discrimination by government or by private parties.
5. James L. Gibson, "Pluralism, Federalism and the Protection of Civil Liberties," *Western Political Quarterly* 43 (September 1990): 511–533.
6. 370 U.S. 421 (1962).
7. 410 U.S. 113 (1973).
8. 347 U.S. 483 (1954).
9. 377 U.S. 533 (1964).
10. See, generally: Advisory Commission on Intergovernmental Relations, *Multistate Regionalism* (Washington, D.C.: Government Printing Office, 1972). See also: Martha Derthick, *Between State and Nation: Regional Organizations of the United States* (Washington, D.C.: The Brookings Institution, 1974); Marian E. Ridgeway, *Interstate Compacts* (Carbondale: Southern Illinois University Press, 1971); Weldon V. Barton, *Interstate Compacts in the Political Process* (Chapel Hill: University of North Carolina Press, 1967); Susan Welsh and Cal Clark, "Interstate Compacts and National Integration: An Empirical Assessment of Some Trends," *Western Political Quarterly* 26 (September 1973): 475–484; Richard C. Kearney and John J. Stucker, "Interstate Compacts and the Management of Low Level Radioactive Wastes," *Public Administration Review* (January/February 1985): 210–220; and Patricia Florestano, "Past and Present Utilization of Interstate Compacts in the United States," *Publius* 24 (Fall 1994): 13–25.
11. See: Ronald K.L. Collins, "Rebirth of Reliance on State Constitutions," *National Law Journal* (12 March 1984): 25–32; and Note, "Development of the Law—The Interpretation of State Constitutional Rights," *Harvard Law Review* 95 (1982): 1324.
12. Oregon Supreme Court Justice Hans A. Linde, quoted by Elder Witt, "State Supreme Courts: Tilting the Balance toward Change," *Governing* (August 1988): 30–38.
13. On the content of state constitutions, see: *Model State Constitution,* 6th ed. (New York: National Municipal League, 1968); and Robert B. Dishman, *State Constitutions: The Shape of the Document* (New York: National Municipal League, 1960); John Kincaid, ed., "State Constitutions in a Federal System," *Annals of the American Academy of Political and Social Science* (March 1988): entire issue; and Bradley D. McGraw, ed., *Developments in State Constitutional Law* (St. Paul: West Publishing, 1985).

14. See: "Equal Rights Provisions: The Experience under State Constitutions," *California Law Review* 65 (1977): 1086, 1088–1089.

15. See: Robert S. Friedman and Sybil L. Stokes, "The Role of the Constitution-Maker as Representative," *Midwest Journal of Political Science* 9 (May 1965): 148–166.

16. See: Wayne R. Swanson, Sean A. Kelleher, and Arthur English, "Socialization of Constitution-Makers: Political Experience, Role Conflict, and Attitude Change," *The Journal of Politics* 34 (February 1972): 183–198.

17. See: Arthur English and John J. Carroll, "Constitutional Reform in Arkansas: The 1979–1980 Convention," *National Civic Review* (May 1982): 240–250, 257.

18. See: Elmer E. Cornwall, Jay S. Goodman, and Wayne R. Swanson, *Constitutional Conventions: The Politics of Revision* (New York: National Municipal League, 1974).

19. See: *Thirty Years of State Constitution-Making* (New York: National Municipal League, 1970), pp. 75–76.

20. H. Kermit L. Hall, "The Legacy of 19th-Century Bills of Rights," *Intergovernmental Perspective* (Fall 1991): 15–17.

21. Janice C. May, "Amending State Bills of Rights: Do Voters Reduce Rights?" *Intergovernmental Perspective* (Fall 1991): 45–48.

22. Bayrd Still, "An Interpretation of the Statehood Process, 1800 to 1850," *Mississippi Historical Review* 23 (September 1936): 189–204.

23. Property-holding requirements for certain types of elections, such as bond elections, survived until recent years.

24. The legislation affects seven language groups: Native American, Alaskan native, Chinese, Filipino, Japanese, Korean, and Spanish.

25. See, for example: Richard L. Engstrom, "The Voting Rights Act: Disenfranchisement, Dilution, and Alternative Election Systems," *PS: Political Science & Politics* (December 1994): 685–688; and Chandler Davidson and Bernard Grofman, eds., *Quiet Revolution in the South: The Impact of the Voting Rights Act 1965–1990* (Princeton: Princeton University Press, 1994).

26. See: *Dunn v. Blumstein*, 405 U.S. 330 (1972).

27. About half of the states automatically restore voting rights to felons who have completed their sentences.

28. See, generally: Richard J. Carlson, ed., *Issues of Electoral Reform* (New York: National Municipal League, 1974).

29. See, for example: Donald G. Zauderer, "Consequences of Ballot Reform: The Ohio Experience," *National Civic Review* (November 1972): 505–507, 520.

30. Raymond E. Wolfinger and Steven J. Rosenstone, *Who Votes?* (New Haven: Yale University Press, 1980), pp. 78–79.

31. See: *State Voter Registration by Mail* (Lexington, Ky.: Council of State Governments, 1976).

32. Amy E. Young, "In the States," *Common Cause Magazine* (Fall 1992): 37.

33. Stephen Knack, "Does 'Motor Voter' Work? Evidence from State-level Data," *The Journal of Politics* 57 (August 1995): 796–811.

34. Voting by mail has been found to reduce the costs of election administration as well as to increase the level of participation. Questions have been raised, however, concerning the integrity of the ballot because of the lack of secrecy and the possibility

of fraud. See: Randy H. Hamilton, "American All-Mail Balloting: A Decade's Experience," *Public Administration Review* 48 (September/October 1988): 3–14; and Glen W. Sparrow, "The Use of the Mail for Voting: Can It Produce Greater Participation for Lower Costs?" *State and Local Government Review* 17 (Spring 1985): 225–231.

35. See, for example: David R. Berman, *Reformers, Corporations, and the Electorate* (Niwot, Colo.: University Press of Colorado, 1992).

36. See: Charles M. Price, "The Initiative: A Comparative State Analysis and Reassessment of a Western Phenomenon," *Western Political Quarterly* 28 (June 1975): 243–262; and Hugh A. Bone and Robert C. Benedict, "Perspectives on Direct Legislation: Washington State's Experience, 1914–1973," *Western Political Quarterly* 28 (June 1975): 330–351.

37. Charles Press and Lawrence Sych, "Participation in State Recall Elections," paper prepared for the Annual Meeting of the American Political Science Association, 1987.

38. David B. Magleby, *Direct Legislation: Voting on Ballot Propositions in the United States* (Baltimore: Johns Hopkins University Press, 1984).

39. On the information problem, see: James H. Kuklinski, Daniel S. Metlay, and W.D. Kay, "Citizen Knowledge and Choices on the Complex Issue of Nuclear Energy," *American Journal of Political Science* 26 (November 1982): 616–642; and Arthur Lupia, "Shortcuts versus Encyclopedias: Information and Voting Behavior in California Insurance Reform Elections," *American Political Science Review* 88 (March 1994): 63–76.

40. Richard L. Arnold, "Increasing Use of Initiatives," *Campaigns & Elections* (June 1995): 19.

41. David B. Magleby, "Taking the Initiative: Direct Legislation and Direct Democracy in the 1980s," *PS: Political Science & Politics* (Summer 1988): 600–611.

42. Amy F. Young, "The Changing Nature of Initiative Campaigns," *Common Cause Magazine* (July/August 1989): 43.

43. David D. Schmidt, "Corporate Funds Fuel Initiative Campaigns," *Public Administration Times* (October 1982): 1, 4.

44. For an account of the use of the initiative for environmental protection, see: Carl E. Lutrin and Allen K. Settle, "The Public and Ecology: The Role of Initiatives in California's Environmental Politics," *Western Political Quarterly* 28 (June 1975): 352–371.

45. Jack Citrin, Beth Reingold, Evelyn Walters, and Donald P. Green, "The 'Official English' Movement and the Symbolic Politics of Language in the United States," *Western Political Quarterly* 43 (September 1990): 536–559.

4

☆ ☆ ☆

PARTIES, GROUPS, AND INFLUENCE

"Politics," a distinguished statesman once noted, "are almost as exciting as war, and quite as dangerous. In war you can only be killed once, but in politics many times."[1] Politics in the states, as elsewhere, involves recurring, often intense, and seemingly life-threatening struggles among competing individuals and groups. This chapter focuses on central participants in the process of conflict and accommodation—political parties and interest groups—and on the broad role played by the mass media in the political system. It concludes with a consideration of problems that have evolved out of "politics as usual" in regard to ethical behavior and public accountability.

POLITICAL PARTIES IN STATE POLITICS

THE LEGAL CONTEXT

Until the early twentieth century, legislatures and courts considered political parties to be private associations and, as such, not subject to governmental regulation. This view changed in reaction to the era of boss rule and corruption in the early 1900s and with the ability of Progressives to secure legislation regulating party organization, nominations, finance, and campaign activities. The Progressive assault on political parties was most pronounced in the western part of the country. In states like California, it helped create a still-functioning system of candidate- or issue-centered politics rather than one of partisan politics.[2]

Other restrictions on political parties have come from acts of Congress or United States Supreme Court decisions on voting and elections. In a 1944 decision voiding the white primary as a violation of the Fifteenth Amendment, the Supreme Court concluded that parties were not simply private organizations but performed important public functions and, thus, in regard to primaries, could be regulated in the public interest.[3]

Another more recent example of Supreme Court activity that may have a considerable effect on political parties has to do with the practice of political patronage, that is, using political party affiliation as a condition for holding public office. The Supreme Court has indicated that it will examine closely cases where state and local officials refuse to hire or decide to dismiss employees solely on the basis of their political affiliation.[4] Courts have found such actions violate the First and Fourteenth Amendments. To pass the test of constitutionality, a case must be made that party affiliation is an appropriate requirement for effective job performance. Some critics of recent Court decisions in this area contend that patronage helps to ensure that the government runs smoothly. They also argue that it is vital to the maintenance of viable political parties, which, in turn, are necessary for responsible government.

Whatever their overall merits in the political system, parties are heavily regulated by state governments as well as by the federal government. The states, for example, impose their own requirements as to what a political party must do to have its candidates' names printed on the election ballot. Often candidates' names are automatically placed on the ballot if their party received a certain percentage of the total vote in the last election. New parties may have to meet more rigorous requirements, such as securing thousands of names from various parts of the state on a petition. As noted below, state law may also broadly outline the organization of political parties and place limitations on their campaign activities, especially in regard to finance.

Another area of state law affecting political party activity concerns making nominations for office. The earliest method of securing a nomination for state legislative and administrative posts, including that of governor, was to get the endorsement of a *political caucus,* an informal meeting of political leaders in the legislature. The caucus method gave way to the convention system, dominated by party officials such as county chairs, in the early nineteenth century. Beginning in the late nineteenth century, the convention method was slowly replaced by state law with the direct primary, through which ordinary voters from the general public make the nominations.

Currently, the *closed primary* is the most commonly used type of direct primary. It is found in more than forty states. This type of primary limits participation to those who have registered as party members. People who register as independents have no primary in which to vote. Nine states allow voters to receive the ballots of all parties holding primary elections. In some of these *open primary* states, the law restricts voters to participating in the primary of only one party. Washington and Alaska use a "blanket" primary in which a voter is able, just as in regular elections, to split the vote, choosing his or her favorite nominee for each office regardless of party.

Louisiana's "open elections," or *unitary primary*, also allows voters to choose by office from among all the candidates running for a position, though in this system they are not identified on the ballot by party. The candidate for an office who receives the majority of votes cast in the primary election is automatically elected to office. This eliminates the need for a general election. If no candidate for an office receives a majority of the votes, a runoff is held between the top two vote getters and the winner of this contest takes office. For several years, California had a unique cross-file system (abolished in 1959) under which a candidate could file his or her name in more than one primary and could win the nomination of both parties. During the 1940s and 1950s, Republican candidates thus were often able to win their primary and that of the Democratic Party, and run unopposed in the general election.[5]

With the movement from caucuses to conventions to primaries, the nomination process has become more democratic. In many places, the only opportunity for voters to make a choice among candidates is to vote in the primary of the dominant political party. Primaries have also helped reformers within a party to defy party officials by directly appealing to the voters. On the other hand, primaries usually attract only a small percentage of the eligible voters. Because those who do vote tend to be more ideologically inclined, that is, unusually conservative or liberal, the nominee may be far more extreme than others who identify with the party and than people in the general electorate. Primaries have also made campaigns more expensive, giving an advantage to those with access to funds.[6]

Another problem with primaries is that they often bring out internal party divisions and cause bitter public disputes that not only embarrass the party but also make it more difficult to unite party members behind the eventual nominee. Several supporters of a defeated candidate may refuse to support the primary winner in the general election. This appears to be particularly true of those most actively involved in the campaign of the defeated candidate and those with relatively low levels of party identification and relatively strong ideological orientations.[7]

Party officials also worry about the possibility of primary "raiding"—a situation in which members of one political party vote in another party's primary. The fear is that voters from the other party will attempt to secure the worst possible nominee, who could easily be defeated in the general election. The extent to which this happens, however, is difficult to determine. In some elections many people may participate in the other party's primary. However,

BOX 4–1   THE RUNOFF: IS IT FAIR?

Several southern states provide for a runoff, or second primary, if no candidate receives a majority of the votes cast in the first primary. The runoff, held between the two leading vote getters, is intended to ensure that the winning candidate receives a majority of the vote. There is some evidence that the system has hurt black candidates, which some claim was the real intent behind adopting the system in the first place. One study suggests that the average candidate who has the most votes in the first round is likely to win the runoff primary 70 percent of the time. Black candidates who lead in the first round, however, are likely to win only 50 percent of the time. One can find examples where blacks who led in the first primary contest because whites scattered their votes among a number of white candidates lost to a single white candidate in the runoff because the latter picked up most of the support that went to those who were eliminated from the race. This type of outcome, however, is not inevitable. Much depends, for example, on the margin of victory enjoyed in the first primary.

See: Charles S. Bullock III and Loch K. Johnson, *Runoff Elections in the United States* (Chapel Hill: University of North Carolina Press, 1992); Alexander P. Lamis, "The Runoff Primary Controversy: Implications for Southern Politics," *PS* (Fall 1984): 782–787; and Joseph Stewart Jr., James F. Sheffield Jr., and Margaret E. Ellis, "The Mechanisms of Runoff Primary 'Disadvantage,'" *Social Science Quarterly* 76 (December 1995): 807–822.

it may well be that they actually vote for the candidate they like best rather than the one who would be easiest to defeat in the general election.

Aside from the general use of the direct primary (of either the closed or open variety), the various states also provide for special nominating procedures. Minnesota and Nebraska hold nonpartisan primaries (that is, those that do not identify candidates by party label) to select candidates for the state legislature. The convention system is still used in a few states, for example, New York and Connecticut, to make nominations for some offices. Some states also use runoff primaries, though their use has been controversial (see box 4–1).

PARTY ORGANIZATION AND ACTIVITIES

The major political parties in this country are highly decentralized. National organizations have little control over state and local organizations. The latter generally place priority on capturing state and local offices and may ignore or even publicly disassociate themselves from an unpopular presidential nominee of their party.

Just as national political parties are loose confederations of state political parties, state political parties are usually loose confederations of city and county political organizations. Indeed, for a considerable period of party history, the most influential party leaders were the bosses or machines found on the local level. Today, local parties are still active in large cities as diverse as Chicago, Detroit, Los Angeles, Houston, and Nashville, performing the functions traditionally carried out by parties, such as conducting voter registration drives, doing door-to-door campaigning, raising funds, canvassing by telephone, and recruiting volunteers.[8] Yet the style of local campaigning has changed since the turn of the century, and, in most cities, the type of local "political machine" in existence in that era, whose strength was based on immigrant votes, patronage, and "honest graft," has all but vanished. (See chapter 9.)

At the bottom of the typical party structure are precinct committeemen, committeewomen, or precinct captains, usually chosen in primary elections. Precincts are voting districts established by law. In recent years, there has generally been little interest in precinct committee work and little interest among party members in precinct committee member elections. Precinct positions created by state law often go unfilled. When there is a contest for a precinct position, only a few hundred votes may be cast and the candidate whose name appears first on the ballot will enjoy a great advantage. Above the precinct level, state law may provide for party committees for each district or unit from which public officials are elected, for example, ward (city council district), city, state legislative, county, congressional district, and state central committees. Ward and city committees are not frequently found in small municipalities.

Generally, each committee is selected by a convention or meeting of the committees just under it in the organizational structure. For example, the state central committee is selected by the congressional district committee members, and the congressional district committee members are selected by county committeemen and committeewomen.

Committees above the precinct level raise money, organize and conduct campaigns, handle patronage assignments, and recruit candidates for state and local offices. The state central committee also voices the party position on public issues and organizes the state convention of party officials. State conventions are used to frame the party's platform. The chief value of these general statements on policy issues is for use in the campaign to appeal to different groups of voters. Often the platforms are simply statements of the gubernatorial candidate's campaign pledges.[9] In addition to platform duties, state conventions nominate and elect state party leaders, endorse candidates for statewide offices, and designate the national committee members. In presidential election years, state conventions may also select delegates to the national nominating conventions—though this function is now largely performed through direct primaries—and choose individuals whose names will appear on the ballot as presidential electors.

Box 4–2 The Potential of the Party Chair's Job

As one United States senator, who had been state chairman of his party, told an interviewer: "It was clear to me from the beginning that the chairmanship had a great deal of potential as a launching pad. I had an opportunity to develop party contacts and make friendships throughout the state, and I had the resources of the headquarters, meager though they were, to consolidate my position. One year I made twenty fund-raising speeches to various counties, and I visited every county in the state. I organized two state conventions, over which I presided. I appointed several party groups or committees, which pleased a lot of people. Most important, however, every two or three months I put out a newsletter which was primarily a report on my activities in behalf of the party. By the time I had decided to run for sure, I was one of the best-known party leaders in the state."

Source: Robert J. Huckshorn, *Party Leadership in the States* (Amherst: University of Massachusetts Press, 1976), pp. 122–125.

By all indications, there is considerable turnover in the position of state chairperson. The average tenure is only about three years in office.[10] During their careers, state chairpersons have held a variety of appointive public offices and other party positions. At times, the state office has functioned as a stepping-stone to elective office (see box 4–2).

The job of state party chairperson varies a great deal. Some chairs are "political agents" of the governor; that is, they are selected by the governor and work closely with that official. Others belong to the same political party as the governor but may be classified as "in-party independents" because they were not chosen by the governor and have a power base of their own in, for example, the party organization. A third type of party chairperson is the out-party independent. In this case, the state chairperson's party does not control the governorship, and because of this, the chairperson of the party may, and commonly does, function as spokesperson for the out party.[11]

State party organizations commonly offer financial assistance and services (such as polling and campaign seminars) to candidates for state and congressional seats. Republican organizations have had considerably larger budgets than Democratic organizations and, as a consequence, have been more active than their opponents in offering contributions and services.[12] Part of the disparity in budgets and activities stems from the greater amount of aid state Republican Party organizations receive from their national party.[13]

Since the 1960s, however, both Democratic and Republican party organizations have been strengthened. Both have improved their ability to raise funds and mobilize voters, for example, through get-out-the-vote campaigns.[14] Many state organizations have built a significant presence in their jurisdictions by undertaking such activities, conducting "generic" campaigns for Democrats or Republicans generally, and targeting the takeover of particular seats, for example, in state legislatures. Party organizations have heightened their activities even though voter loyalty to the parties has decreased.

At the same time, party organizations in recent years have lost ground to organizations such as Political Action Committees (PACs) in terms of overall influence in the political process. Party organizations also suffer when compared to what, ideally, they might be doing. A centralized and cohesive state party organization might be expected to: (1) recruit candidates and nominate them in conventions and/or officially designate their choices in primaries; (2) offer candidates for all or nearly all state and county offices; (3) coordinate campaigns for the entire party slate; (4) raise funds for the entire ticket on a year-round basis; (5) be involved through the state party chairperson in working with the party's legislative leaders and governor on matters of policy and patronage; and (6) have a degree of permanence in being able to resist successfully attempts at being taken over by a particular candidate or group.[15]

Few state political organizations have all or most of these elements of strength. The primary system has diluted the party organization's control over recruitment and nominations. It is not uncommon for an antiparty or reform candidate to enter a primary and win it without the official organization's support (or despite its opposition). Parties in a dozen states do endorse candidates before the primary, and some have been able to have these endorsements made clear or designated on the ballot. Parties using this system have retained or gained some control over nominations. Yet, only a few state party organizations fall into this category.[16]

Some state parties fail to offer candidates for more than a few offices. Indeed, like the Republican Party in the South before the 1960s, the party's goal may not be winning elections at all, but rather sharing national patronage should the party capture the White House. Other state party organizations exist in name only, as individuals running under the same partisan label in effect declare themselves and run independent campaigns for votes and money. Decisions regarding policy and patronage are often made without the involvement of the state organization. Members of a party who serve in the legislature may find the state organizations too liberal or conservative for their tastes.

Public Support

In their relations with general party members, both party officials and candidates of a given party are faced with the rather unpleasant fact that they cannot always depend on the support of those who identify themselves as Democrats or

Republicans. A person becomes a member of a political party simply by declaring himself or herself to be a member and, in a closed primary state, by registering as one. Party members incur no obligations by virtue of their membership. Many may not even vote for some of the candidates of their party.

Evidence suggests that there may be considerably more party voting in elections to state legislatures than there is in "top of the ticket" contests for president, Congress, or governor. The reason for this is that voters generally have less knowledge about the candidates for state legislative seats and other positions than they do about the more glamorous offices, and thus are more dependent on the "party cue" provided them.[17]

On the whole, political parties within states where the major parties are relatively competitive (two-party states) attract the same types of groups that are attracted to the respective parties on a national basis. Currently, Democrats are more likely than Republicans to attract older voters (fifty or over); religious, racial, and ethnic minorities; people who live in cities; and people with limited education, income, and occupational skills. Republican candidates appear to do better among WASPs (white Anglo-Saxon Protestants), those in high-income brackets, those with college educations, those in business and professional occupations, and those Protestants who belong to fundamentalist religions. Recently, the two parties have differed in terms of gender appeal, with Democrats doing better among women than men, and Republicans doing better among men than women.

The coalition of interests behind the various parties differs over time and by candidate. Indeed, behind the ups and downs in the fortunes of a given political party are shifts of groups toward and away from its candidates. Parties and their candidates try to appeal to the same groups and attempt to make their appeal as broad as possible. As a consequence, parties at election time may appear to be nonideological organizations whose basic stands on the issues seem to offer the voters little, if any, choice. As discussed below, however, one cannot assume there are no differences between Democrats and Republicans or that a change in control of government from one party to another will not make a difference in the direction of public policy.

Although the Democratic and Republican parties do, in general, give voters a meaningful choice among candidates and issues, the public has shown signs of weakening attachment to the two major parties in recent decades. This change, called *dealignment*, has been evident in: (1) the growth in the number of political independents who are not aligned with any party; (2) an increase in the number of people voting for independent or third-party candidates; and (3) an increase in split-ticket voting, that is, individuals voting for candidates of one party for some offices and candidates of another party for other offices. Split-ticket voting, in turn, has contributed to *divided government* on the state level as, increasingly, one major party controls the governorship while the opposite major party controls one or both houses of the legislature.

Party Competition

Political scientists use a variety of measures of party competition in the states, that is, the extent to which control of state government is likely to be dominated by a particular political party, either Democratic or Republican. The results vary with the types of contests examined and the number of years over which competition is measured. Looking at various measures, there has been agreement that competition has been particularly strong in a scattered groups of states such as North Dakota, Washington, and New Jersey and particularly low in several southern states.[18]

While for much of our history Democrats and Republicans have competed strongly for dominance at the national level, it has not been uncommon for one or the other of these parties to dominate state politics for relatively long periods of time. As a Republican candidate for governor once trumpeted: "Iowa will go Democratic when Hell goes Methodist."[19]

Parts of the Midwest have had a strong Republican tradition. The most clearly identified one-party states, however, have been a half dozen or so Democratic ones in the South. The pattern of Democratic dominance developed as a result of the Civil War, although it did not extend to mountain areas in Tennessee, North Carolina, or Virginia, where the economy was not based on cotton or the use of slaves. Democratic dominance in the South, moreover, has been strongly challenged over the last several decades by the Republican Party. Observers have attributed this change to the economic development of the region bringing more diversity of interests, and to an increased migration of people from other states into the area.[20] Republican gains have been primarily with white voters. Republicans appear to have made their greatest gains among whites in areas where there is a particularly high concentration of blacks.[21] The Democrats, on the other hand, have greatly benefited from the increase in black registration. Skillful Democratic politicians have been able to build winning coalitions of blacks and middle- and lower-middle-class whites.

One effect of increased party competition in the South has been that the Republican primary for major offices has become far more competitive. In terms of the general election, Republican candidates in the South, like candidates of minority parties elsewhere, have frequently been able to win state-wide contests because these races are based more on the images of particular candidates than on party identification. Moreover, once a member of a minority party is elected, even out of unusual circumstances, he or she acquires the same type of advantage enjoyed by other incumbents when it comes to reelection.[22] Outside the South, one finds that increased immigration from the Midwest, the conversion of former Democrats, and a growing conservative electorate has also meant a realignment of voters in the Mountain West, especially in presidential elections, toward the Republican Party.[23]

Third parties have emerged from time to time in the states to champion certain issues or interests neglected by the major parties. All in all, support for third parties appears to be strongest in the western states and weakest in southern states. Support also seems strongest in the larger states and those with the highest levels of education.[24]

One example of a important third party from the past is the liberal Farmer-Labor Party (FLP), which during much of the period between 1920 and 1944 held the balance of power between Democrats and Republicans in Minnesota. In 1944, the FLP merged with the state's Democratic Party.[25] In recent years, the state of New York has had three third or minor parties: Liberal, Conservative, and Right to Life (opposed to abortions). In this state, third parties benefit from a state law that allows cross-endorsements, that is, parties to nominate candidates already nominated by other parties. Thus, commonly, the Liberal Party nominates the choice of the Democratic Party for a particular office, while the Conservative and Right to Life parties nominate the Republican candidate. Because of the cross-endorsement system, third parties are in a position to withhold or contribute votes to the candidates of the major parties. In a close race these votes could be important. Because of this, third parties may be able to use their endorsement as a bargaining chip with the major parties or candidates, for example, to influence their stand on issues like abortion.[26]

Although third parties may be important participants in state politics, they do face several difficult obstacles in this regard. They have to compete with the strong attachment many feel to the two major parties, the "winner take all" nature of the election system, and the definite prospect that if a third party has anything to offer, its programs and following will be swallowed up by one of the two major political parties. The use of single-member districts for the election of nearly all political candidates creates a "winner take all" situation in which votes cast for losing candidates do not count. Voters may well feel that unless their ballots are cast for Republican or Democratic candidates, their votes will be wasted. It is likewise difficult to attract financial support for campaign activity without a good chance of victory. Another obstacle facing third parties is simply getting on the ballot. Although states have been relatively willing to leave room for candidates to run as independents for president, they have made qualifying as a political party that can nominate candidates for other offices rather difficult. State law, for example, may require a new party to secure a large number of signatures from various sections of the state on a petition before its candidates' names can even appear on the ballot. The laws governing access to the ballot are made by legislators who belong to the major parties and are not eager to have competition.

PARTY CONTROL

While many would contend that there isn't much difference between Democrats and Republicans, research suggests that the major political parties generally do provide voters some choice along liberal-conservative lines, though the range of the differences between the parties varies from state to state. In any given state one is likely to find that Republican voters and leaders are more conservative than Democratic voters and leaders. Both parties, however, are also deeply influenced by the climate of public opinion in the various states—that is, both parties are more conservative in states where public opinion is more conservative and more liberal in states where public opinion is more liberal. Thus, in the conservative South, the Democratic Party is not as conservative as the Republican Party but is more conservative than the Democratic Party in the more liberal areas of the country such as the Northeast.[27]

Conceding that the parties reflect different ideologies and the aspirations of different coalitions of interests, does this mean that there will be sharp differences in the direction of governmental policy if control of government shifts from Republican to Democrat or Democrat to Republican? Since the mid-1960s, several studies have been made by political scientists on this question.[28] Some scholars have sided with political scientist Thomas Dye in claiming that the party system itself as well as public policy outcomes (for example, the amount spent on education) are dependent on levels of economic development. Generally, how much a state spends does have more to do with the amount of wealth in a state than with what party is in power. On the other hand, disputes over the allocation of funds are likely to be highly partisan in nature. This is especially true on social welfare issues, where Democrats, reflecting a different constituent interest, are more favorably inclined than are Republicans. More generally, in two-party states, Republicans in the electorate and in office tend to be less supportive than Democrats in regard to regulating business, advancing the goals of organized labor, or supporting governmental expenditures for programs like housing, education, and medical care.[29]

In a growing number of states, the significance of party control has become more difficult to assess because the parties share control of the government. As figure 4–1 indicates, since the 1940s there has been a steep decline in the number of states with unified governments, that is, where one party controls the office of governor and both houses of the legislature.

The decline of unified government in the South has much to do with the growth of a two-party system as Republicans have made inroads on the dominance of the Democratic Party. Outside the South, however, research conducted by political scientist Morris P. Fiorina suggests that much of the long-term decline in unified government has been due to a loss of Republican control in state legislatures (the 1994 election, in which Republicans made large gains, was not included in his study). Fiorina argues that the Republican loss has been associated with the growth of professionalism in the state legislatures, that is, with the growth in legislative pay, staff, and, perhaps most

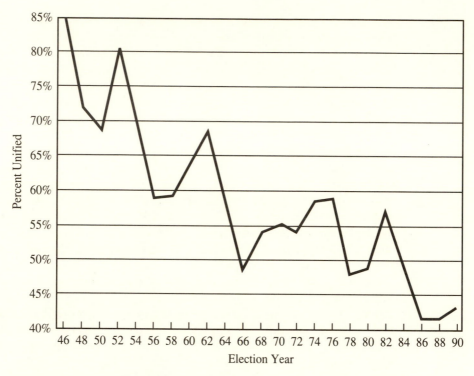

FIGURE 4–1 Unified State Governments

Source: Morris Fiorina, *Divided Government* (New York: Macmillan, 1992), p. 25. Copyright © 1992 by Allyn and Bacon. Reprinted/adapted by permission.

important in this context, the length of time legislators must spend on the job. Fiorina argues that the idea of becoming a full-time legislator has been more attractive to Democrats than Republicans because Republicans generally have more lucrative career opportunities.[30]

The significance of divided government at the state level is not altogether clear. Certainly it can heighten the likelihood of conflict and gridlock, though this is not always the case.

INTEREST GROUP AND MEDIA ACTIVITIES

INTEREST GROUP CHARACTERISTICS

Several years ago, a Montana legislative lobbyist boasted to a reporter: "Give me a case of Scotch, a case of gin, one blond, and one brunette, and I can take any liberal!"[31] The notion that state officials are overwhelmed and corrupted by selfish interest groups has been a common one. It is also a distortion of reality, although problems growing out of the play of interest groups do exist.

Interest group activity is a time-honored form of participation in the political process. The right to belong to a politically active organization is not only consistent with the constitutional guarantee to assemble peaceably "and to petition the government for a redress of grievances" but also perhaps the only way to influence public officials in an effective manner.

Unlike political parties, interest groups do not run candidates for office, though they may indeed actively support or oppose the candidates offered by the parties. Interest groups are not concerned with running the government or with more than a narrow range of policies of particular interest to their members. They are more homogeneous than political parties in that the members have a shared characteristic, such as an occupation, goal, race, or experience. Interest groups are freer from governmental regulation of their activities than political parties are.

Some groups are structured to stay abreast of the flow of decisions by being organized on the national, state, and local levels. The United States Chamber of Commerce, for example, represents a federation of more than three thousand state and local chambers of commerce and trade associations. Similarly, there are state and local affiliates of the national labor organizations and farm groups. Most national groups are organized on a federal basis, and the state and local affiliates operate without much national direction or control on matters of state and local policy.

While interest group power on the national level is thinned out by the vast number of groups that must compete for influence, it may be relatively concentrated in states because one or a few groups represent the dominant economic interest or activity. It is important to note, however, that "control" by an economically dominant interest is not always exercised and, indeed, is most often attempted on issues related only to immediate well-being or self-interest. It should also be noted that because of economic development and increased migration, many states have become far more pluralistic in recent years. As a consequence, there has been an increase in the number of interest groups at the state level and a drastic reduction in the ability of any one group or set of groups to dominate public policy.[32]

LOBBYING

The most regulated area of interest group activity is lobbying. The fear of special interest influence has prompted about half the states to require that legislative lobbyists register and disclose the names of their employers, the amounts of money they are spending on lobbying activity, and the purposes of their lobbying effort. Some states also prohibit lawmakers from accepting gifts from lobbyists. In Wisconsin the law prohibits legislators from accepting anything of value, be it a meal or a paid vacation, from lobbyists. Much lobbying in the states continues to be of a social nature, as lobbyists wine and dine lawmakers.

State laws on lobbying are for the most part ineffective. As one observer discovered some time ago, lobbying laws are "imprecise in language, selective and uncertain in their application, and dotted with internal contradictions."[33] Often, laws are unclear about what constitutes lobbying and who qualifies as a lobbyist. The laws often apply only to full-time lobbyists. Although there are professional, full-time lobbyists on the state level, most of those who lobby can claim to be part-time amateurs.

Table 4–1 ranks the states in terms of how stringently they have tried to regulate lobbying. The author examined how various states ranked in regard to twenty-two lobbying regulation requirements. These covered how broadly or narrowly "lobbyist" is defined, disclosure items, and the provisions for enforcement of the laws. New Jersey, Washington, and Wisconsin were the most stringent, while Arkansas was the least stringent (three states were not included in the study). Political culture appears to have more to do than any other factor in explaining the order in which the states are ranked, with moralistic states, as expected, being particularly likely to adopt rigorous regulations.

Contrary to popular belief, few lawyers and former legislators are found among state lobbyists. While professional lobbyists—some with many clients—are indeed active, most lobbyists are nonprofessionals. Lobbyists do not appear to be partisan but are willing to work with whatever party is in power. Lobbyists with whom a legislator is likely to be in frequent contact are often looked on as allies. A legislator from a farm area, for example, is very likely to get along well with the lobbyist representing the Dairy Association. Lobbyists may be depended on to supply information and other services to a legislator and, indeed, are often sought out by legislators to support bills they want to see become laws.

Lobbyists have different styles or methods of attempting to influence legislators. Some are "contact men" who use personal acquaintances and friendships with individual legislators and personal presentation of arguments. The "informant," on the other hand, relies on prepared information presented in public through more formal channels such as legislative hearings. The essence of the lobbyist's job is to round up the natural support for his or her cause; the lobbyist seldom attempts to convert the opposition through threats, bribery, or just conversation.[34] While money is an asset to lobbyists, other resources are also important. To a considerable extent, lobbyists rely on their expertise as to how the legislative process works and how to influence key players. Perhaps more fundamentally, they also rely on the information they supply and the willingness of legislators to trust them.[35]

TABLE 4–1   States Ranked by Stringency of State Lobbying Regulation (0 = weakest / 18 = strongest)[a]

State	Score	State	Score
1. New Jersey	18	25. Texas	10
2. Washington	18	26. Alabama	8
3. Wisconsin	18	27. Florida	8
4. California	17	28. Louisiana	8
5. Maryland	17	29. Georgia	7
6. Massachusetts	17	30. Mississippi	7
7. Connecticut	16	31. Nevada	7
8. Hawaii	16	32. Ohio	7
9. Colorado	15	33. South Carolina	7
10. Minnesota	15	34. West Virginia	7
11. Nebraska	15	35. Utah	6
12. Alaska	14	36. Missouri	5
13. Oregon	14	37. North Dakota	5
14. Indiana	13	38. Tennessee	5
15. Maine	13	39. Kentucky	4
16. New York	13	40. New Hampshire	4
17. Arizona	11	41. New Mexico	4
18. Idaho	11	42. Delaware	3
19. Kansas	11	43. North Carolina	3
20. Pennsylvania	11	44. Illinois	2
21. Iowa	10	45. Vermont	2
22. Michigan	10	46. Wyoming	2
23. Oklahoma	10	47. Arkansas	0
24. Rhode Island	10		

Source: Cynthia Opheim, "Explaining the Differences in State Lobby Regulation," *Western Political Quarterly* 44 (June, 1991): 409. Reprinted by permission of the author and *Political Research Quarterly*, the University of Utah, copyright holder.

[a]Data for Montana, South Dakota, and Virginia were unavailable.

There is, however, reason to believe that lobbying may be more corrupt on the state level than on the national level. For one thing, state politics is less visible to citizens than is national politics, and in the absence of scrutiny, practices like bribery can be more prevalent. Second, state legislatures meet less often and for shorter periods than Congress. Because of this and the relatively amateur status of the legislators, there is less likely to be an esprit de corps or a set of informal rules that would guard against corrupt behavior. Finally, state legislators make less money than members of Congress and may perceive a greater need to receive payment for their services to an interest group or individual.[36]

OTHER TARGETS AND TECHNIQUES

Groups are also concerned with influencing administrators, judges, political parties, and, not of least importance, their own members and the public at large. Administrators become important because they commonly have much discretion in developing rules and regulations and implementing policy directives. At times the relationship between a group and an administrative agency is that of a friendly clientele: for example, the relationship between a farm group and a state agricultural agency. The clientele group may be depended on to support the agency's requests for appropriations or program expansion. At other times, as between a poverty group and a welfare administrator, the relationship may be basically antagonistic. As chapter 6 indicates, interest group demands on the courts are no less important, though far less visible and far more formally expressed.

Groups may be concerned with political parties whose platforms they try to influence and whose candidates may well appreciate the group's endorsement and campaign contributions. In an effort to secure the adoption of particular policies, interest group leaders also enter into temporary alliances with other groups to maximize the strength of their effort. Allies on one issue may be opponents on another issue. Other groups and organizations also have been called on to exert indirect pressure on policymakers. In the 1970s, for example, groups working for the adoption of the Equal Rights Amendment urged other organizations not to hold their national conventions in states where the legislatures had refused to ratify the amendment. Although some fifty national organizations agreed to boycott these states, the economic impact and ultimate political effects of the boycotts were uncertain. Boycotts may be more successful when directed at a single state, as in the boycott of Arizona as a meeting place by several national associations in the mid-1980s because of the state's refusal to adopt a holiday honoring slain civil rights leader Martin Luther King Jr.

Often a group will supplement its "inside" direct lobbying activity with "outside" or grassroots activity aimed at convincing policymakers there is widespread support for their cause. Sometimes group leaders rely on mobilizing group members into action. State Municipal Leagues, for example, often encourage mayors and other officials who belong to the organization to contact state lawmakers directly on a pending issue. Group members may be encouraged to write, fax, or phone lawmakers or drop in on them for a personal visit. On some issues people in several groups or on several mailing lists might be mobilized to exert pressure on lawmakers as part of a well-planned and orchestrated demonstration of broad public support.

At times, a group may take its case to the public through the media. Some groups conduct regular public relations campaigns to build up a favorable public image, for example, of the important role played by public school teachers in preparing children for success in life or of the importance of a particular industry to the economy of the state. Generally favorable public images are cultivated to prevent threats to the interests of the group or as a bank of goodwill to be drawn upon if a particular group needs public support in dealing with public officials.

Public protest activity is another means by which groups make their demands and grievances known. Public demonstrations, sit-ins, picketing, marches, and rioting have been used by groups with little or no hope that communication through more conventional channels will be effective. In recent years, these techniques have been employed by racial, poverty, and antinuclear groups. Protest activity is designed to generate favorable or sympathetic media coverage, promote group cohesion, and secure the support of groups that do enjoy access to decision makers. Disruptive politics may well lead to reform, though sometimes more symbolic than real, to satisfy the sympathetic third parties. Disruptive politics may sometimes create a backlash against the demonstrating group.[37]

INFLUENCE IN STATE POLITICS

How important are interest groups in state politics? Which groups are most important or influential?

In answer to the first question a group of political scientists have collaborated to classify the various states according to the overall impact of interest groups in the state political system. As indicated in table 4–2, interest groups are considered a dominant force in Alabama, Florida, Louisiana, New Mexico, Nevada, South Carolina, and West Virginia. On the other end of the scale are five states (Delaware, Minnesota, Rhode Island, South Dakota, and Vermont) where interest groups are considered relatively subordinate actors in state politics to, for example, political parties, governors, or legislators. Political scientists have long looked at state political systems as being essentially either interest group based or political party based.

State officials come in contact with a variety of lobbyists. Nationwide, one frequently finds lobbyists representing business interests (for example, private utilities, banks, insurance companies), local governmental units, universities and colleges, and labor associations. Other groups often prominent at the state level are those representing the professions, especially where administrative and regulatory matters affecting them are involved; permanent reform-minded groups such as the League of Women Voters and the citizens' lobby Common Cause; and *ad hoc* groups formed to achieve specific goals (such as abortion law reform or penal reform). Important roles have been played in recent years by groups organized to protect the consumer, the environment, and the interests of women and the elderly. Historically, religious organizations have been influential in highly controversial areas of state

TABLE 4–2   Classification of the Fifty States According to the
Overall Impact of Interest Groups with Indication of
Recent Changes

States Where the Overall Impact of Interest Groups Is:

Dominant (7)	Dominant/ Comple- mentary (21)	Comple- mentary (17)	Comple- mentary/ Subordinate (5)	Sub- ordi- nate (0)
Alabama	Arizona	Colorado	Delaware	
Florida	Arkansas	*Connecticut* <	Minnesota	
Louisiana	> *Alaska*	Indiana	Rhode Island	
New Mexico	California	Maine	> *South Dakota*	
Nevada <	Georgia	Maryland	Vermont	
South Carolina	Hawaii	Massachusetts		
West Virginia	Idaho	Michigan		
	Illinois <	Missouri		
	Iowa <	New Hampshire		
	Kansas <	New Jersey		
	Kentucky	New York		
	> *Mississippi*	North Carolina		
	Montana	North Dakota		
	Nebraska	Pennsylvania		
	Ohio	> *Utah*		
	Oklahoma	> *Washington*		
	Oregon	Wisconsin		
	> *Tennessee*			
	Texas			
	Virginia			
	Wyoming			

Source: Prepared by Clive S. Thomas and Ronald J. Hrebenar. Reprinted with permission of Congressional Quarterly Press.

< = moved up one category since 1989.   > = moved down one category since 1989.

policy concerning church-state relations (prayers in school and aid to parochial schools), regulation of moral conduct (prostitution, gambling, and liquor control), and so-called family matters (birth control, abortion, and gay rights).[38]

Research suggests that state legislators more frequently consider business groups as "powerful" than any other type of group.[39] The nature and effectiveness of specific interest groups, however, vary with each state and, more importantly, with the particular issues within each state. In regard to organized labor, the traditional business adversary, union members constitute a particularly large segment of the labor force in states like New York, Michigan, and Pennsylvania, yet they are relatively scarce in a number of southern and western states. Many of the states in the latter category discourage unionization through "right to work" laws that prohibit union membership as a condition for securing or retaining a job.

Over the years, certain important economic interests have acquired a reputation of having dominant positions in state politics.[40] Maine, for instance, was at one time considered to be dominated by the "Big Three": power, lumber, and manufacturing concerns. This dominance was exemplified in the absence of effective state water pollution regulations.[41] In Texas, power has been seen to rest in the hands of the oil industry, in Delaware, in the hands of Du Pont, and in Montana, in the hands of the copper industry. The Wyoming cattle industry, working through the Wyoming Stock Growers Association, has historically been viewed as dominant in that state's economic and political life, though more recently it has shared its prominence with the mineral industry, which in turn has been challenged by environmentalists on a number of issues.[42]

While generalizations are dangerous, the effectiveness of an interest group appears strongly related to:

1. What it represents—the dominant economic interests in an area and economic groups representing businesspeople, farmers, and laborers are generally held to have greater access than groups, for example, representing consumers and poor people.
2. Whether the group is on the offensive or defensive—it is generally easier to prevent something from happening than to make it happen.
3. The size, wealth, and cohesion of the group and the amount of information and services it can supply to decision makers.
4. Most importantly, the status of the group in the eyes of the decision makers—whether they share the same group interest.

THE MASS MEDIA

Newspapers, television stations, and radio stations must also be looked on as influential participants in state politics. (Their role in local politics is discussed in chapter 9.) This influence is partly manifested from their function as interest groups having a stake in various areas of public policy. State policies affecting the ability to gather and publish information have been of particular importance to the mass media. The media, for example, have long pushed for the adoption of open meeting and open record laws (discussed in the following section). The media have called for "shield laws" that protect newspeople who refuse to reveal their confidential sources of information to public officials or juries. The media have also fought the imposition of "gag rules" forbidding prosecutors, defense lawyers, and police from talking to reporters about a pending case. On these latter issues, courts and legislative bodies have had difficulty in weighing the criteria necessary for a free press and the requirements essential for a fair trial.

The most basic function of the media—that of informing the public on political affairs—has been subject to considerable controversy. One complaint of particular importance to our discussion here has been that television and radio stations and newspapers do not give the public enough information on state affairs. In some states, part of this problem may be that the state capital is located in a small or medium-sized city, distant from the state's major newspapers and television stations. However, even when the state house is only a few blocks away, the major media frequently appear to regard state affairs as less newsworthy than national or local affairs. Newspaper editors and television news directors frequently argue that there is little public demand for more information on state government. Some research suggests, however, that such a demand does indeed exist.[43]

More controversial than the debate over the extent of coverage are questions concerning the nature and effects of what coverage is given to state politics. Many have criticized media coverage of state campaigns for paying more attention to the horserace aspects of the contests (who is winning and why) than to issues. There is also some indication in the literature that the press treats men and women differently in certain contests. For example, the issues raised by women running for governor appear to receive less attention in the press than do those raised by male candidates for governor.[44]

More generally, the media have been accused of bias in their coverage of state government, being either too negative or too supportive of those in power. One study, based on an analysis of the contents of ninety-four newspapers, found that the extent of critical reporting varies greatly from newspaper to newspaper.[45] Much of the critical reporting that does occur has less to do with governmental policies than with the performance of individuals, for example, the honesty, integrity, or competence of particular state officials. In general, however, the study found that newspaper reporting on political affairs is primarily neutral, containing neither criticism nor praise of public officials, policies, or institutions. Though some papers seeking to find the whole truth behind a story do, from time to time, engage in investigative reporting and occasionally interject criticisms into the news they report, a more common practice is merely to pass along to their readers the information contained in governmental handouts or press releases. The study did suggest, however, that negative reporting is influential, in that readers of highly critical papers were more likely than others to be distrustful of government.

In assessing the impact of the media, some researchers have operated on the theory that people are highly selective as to what messages they receive from television, newspapers, and elsewhere, and thus "screen out" information that conflicts with their preexisting beliefs. The bulk of more current research, however, indicates that the media do influence attitudes. Television, which has become the chief source of political information for most people, has had a particular ability to shape and change opinion.

To some extent the influence of newspapers may rest on their ability to dominate the news market. Far greater competition among those who supply news occurs on a statewide basis than in a local community. But in some states, such as New Hampshire, there may be only one newspaper with statewide circulation and no major television station as a competitor. As the ability of a single publisher to dominate the news market increases, one might expect to find the publisher increasingly able not only to control the news but also to deter people from running for office, to influence how candidates handle issues, and to decide who will be elected.[46] As one governor was heard to say: "Never argue with a person who buys ink by the barrel." Another has added: "Never screw up on a slow news day."[47]

ETHICAL BEHAVIOR AND PUBLIC ACCOUNTABILITY

"An honest politician is one who, when he is bought, stays bought." Many Americans agree with this sentiment of Senator Simon Cameron expressed in 1894. Problems of illegal conduct at the state and local levels have captured headlines in recent years. There has been a growth in federal indictments and convictions of state and local officials on federal corruption charges. In 1970, thirty-six state and local officials faced federal indictment. In 1991, 357 did so. Charges range from bribery, to extorting money from contractors, to kickback schemes. Part of the increase may be due to the fact that there are more laws to violate than in 1970 and more zealous prosecutors.

Some indictments and convictions have been the result of sting operations in which undercover law enforcement agents induce others to commit crimes and then arrest them. Sting operations on the state and local levels involving elected officials were encouraged by the success of the Federal Bureau of Investigations' "ABSCAM" operation in 1978–1979, which targeted corruption in Congress. A FBI sting operation in South Carolina in the late 1980s led to indictments of state legislators for taking bribes for their help in pushing a bill to legalize parimutuel betting. About the same time, a sting operation in 1991 conducted by the Phoenix, Arizona, Police Department led to the indictment of several Arizona state legislators for allegedly accepting bribes from an undercover agent posing as a gaming consultant looking for help in getting support for casino gambling in the state.

Concern over the influence of special interests and the possible betrayal of the public trust by governmental officials has led to restrictions on political activity. Some of these, as noted earlier, have had to do with lobbying activity. States have also adopted laws and regulations concerning campaign finance, conflicts of interest, and open meetings of governmental bodies or agencies (these rules are commonly known as *Sunshine Laws*).

CAMPAIGN FINANCE

Anyone who campaigns for political office is likely to attach considerable importance to the building of a sizable campaign fund. While the candidate who spends the most money does not necessarily win a primary or a general election, a candidate needs at least a minimum amount to get in the running.

This minimum amount, moreover, has grown because campaigns have become more expensive. A candidate for governor of a large state may need more than $2 million to conduct a primary and a general election campaign. Candidates for the state legislature from urban districts can expect to spend $5,000 to $50,000. At times, expenses go way beyond these figures. In Florida, for example, a candidate spent $10 million running for governor in 1990 and still lost the race. A race for the state senate in the same election cost one candidate nearly $400,000.[48]

Much of the campaign money, especially in statewide races, now goes for the "three Ps"—polling, packaging, and promotion. For major contests, use of professional pollsters, direct mail specialists, and media experts has replaced personal appearances and reliance on party and volunteer workers. Candidates for statewide office often rely heavily on expensive television advertising.

One effect of the increased sophistication and costs of state campaigns has been the emergence of wealthy candidates who can at least help supply some of their own expenses—especially the important start-up costs. Although laws commonly limit contributions, there are no restrictions on how much an individual may spend out of his or her own income to run for office. The situation presents some profound problems for the political system. As one state legislator has noted: "When the average-income person can't afford to run for office, our democratic process is suffering. We're becoming an elitist form of government in which only the well-to-do or retirees will be candidates."[49]

Unless an individual candidate is independently wealthy, he or she must rely on contributions. For seed money to get their campaigns going, candidates often rely on contributions from relatives and friends. Once a candidate has won the primary, he or she can also turn to his or her party for support. How much support they are likely to receive in legislative races depends in large part on whether the party to which they belong is a majority or minority in the legislature. In the first case, the primary goal of the state party organization is likely to be one of ensuring that incumbents be reelected, and incumbents in the most difficulty are likely to receive the most support. When the party is in the minority, party officials are likely to put resources in races where they have the best chance to unseat or replace incumbents who belong to the other party. An incumbent member of their own party is likely to be given less attention.[50]

Along with party sources, candidates for office receive contributions from Political Action Committees (PACs). PACs, of which there are some twelve thousand nationwide, represent various occupational groups or ideological causes. The number of PACs at the state level has risen dramatically in recent years.[51] Many PACs operate on a national basis. Because of this, an increasing proportion of the money that goes into campaigns comes from outside the affected states. Indeed, some funds come from PACs formed by corporations based in whole or in part in other countries.[52]

Finally, in addition to friends and relatives, party sources and PACs, candidates for state office secure contributions from a broader range of politically interested individuals. These contributors, who supply much of the money spent on state campaigns, are likely to be relatively wealthy and well-educated people who give on a regular basis.[53]

What is the effect of campaign contributions? One effect of the system of special interest contributions (from groups or individuals who are not old friends or relatives) has been to facilitate the reelection of incumbents. Wanting to be on the safe side, groups are far more likely to give funds to incumbents than those challenging incumbents. Reliance on special interest contributors has also raised fears of a government of "checkbook democracy," in which successful lawmakers are obligated to those who contribute large sums of money.

Those who make large contributions are, indeed, likely to receive both access to the successful candidates they supported and, at least, the opportunity to influence their decisions. Yet, contributors may, in fact, be limited in the types of policies they can influence. As a member of the New Jersey legislature has noted, contributors generally have little influence "on matters at the core of a member's personal beliefs, such as abortion, or involve the vital interests of his constituency, such as funding of local infrastructure." On the other hand, money can have greater influence on issues about which legislators have no strong personal or constituency interest, such as laws regarding banking, utilities, insurance, or the regulation of the professions.[54] One can find, for example, strong indicators that donations from the alcohol industry might have something to do with how legislators voted on measures such as extending tavern hours.[55] Some time ago a government study estimated that 15 percent of the money for state and local campaigns comes from individuals in illegal gambling and racketeering enterprises who seek to purchase protection.[56]

Fear of special interest influence and corruption has prompted the states to adopt several types of regulations on campaign finance. Most impose limits on how much money may be spent by candidates, committees working on a candidate's behalf, or both. Courts, however, may question the legality of expenditure limits unless they are required as a condition of accepting public funding. States also impose limits on the sources and size of contributions. Some states prohibit corporations, unions, those who hold public contracts or licenses from state agencies, and state employees from contributing. Some also prohibit contributions from outside the state.

The size of the contribution may also be limited, though often there is no limit on how many times the maximum contribution can be made, for example, to different committees working for the same candidate. Some states get around this by placing limits on the total amount that can be contributed per election. A single contributor, however, may still make a contribution that exceeds the limits by funneling funds through a number of other people, each of whom stays within the limits of the law. The states, finally, require candidates to appoint a campaign treasurer to keep track of funds, to bring the sources of support and expenditures out into the open, and to make public reports during the campaign and/or at its conclusion. States are moving toward requiring disclosure of campaign expenditures several days before an election so that voters can take the information into account when they make their decisions.

State laws regarding campaign finance vary greatly. Some laws place limits only on primaries and others cover both primaries and general elections. Some laws apply only to campaign expenditures, others only to the source of funds, and still others to both. Sanctions for the violation of the laws range from simple public disclosure to criminal penalties. The record of enforcement of campaign finance laws has been less than impressive.[57]

Some state governments have played a more positive role in regard to campaign finance. To encourage a shift away from reliance on a few big contributors, some states allow tax deductions or credits on state income taxes for small contributions to candidates, political parties, or campaign committees. Some states follow the federal practice of allowing taxpayers to allocate one or two dollars as a contribution to a party or to a general campaign account in their state income tax returns. Most of these programs are used to help support only statewide campaigns for governor and other offices. As a condition of accepting state support, candidates must agree to limit their spending.

In most of these states, political contributions are made without increasing the contributor's tax liability. Participation rates have varied greatly among the states. In New Jersey, Michigan, and Rhode Island, the rate of taxpayer participation has been as great or greater than the rate of participation (about 28 percent) in the national program. On the whole, however, only two of every ten taxpayers have been willing to shift one dollar of their taxes to campaign support programs and only two or three out of one hundred have been willing to do so when it increases their tax liability. Existing programs have been criticized because they generally do not help finance primary campaigns. More troublesome has been the finding that public aid has not been at a high enough level to significantly reduce reliance on "fat cat" contributors.[58] There has been a tendency, however, for public funding programs to help minority political parties and, in some places at least, to increase the competitiveness of elections.[59]

CONFLICTS OF INTEREST

Once in office, public officials may find it possible to use their positions to advance their own economic interests. Payoffs may be received by officials for their support in securing or thwarting new policies. Of course, bribery of a public official is illegal, but the distinction between a bribe and a legal campaign contribution is often difficult to make. The determination of what constitutes an illegal conflict of interest may also be controversial. Broadly, a conflict of interest occurs in those situations in which a public official uses his or her office to secure private and especially material gain. For example, a legislator may work for approval of legislation that benefits a company with which he or she is associated. In the legislative setting, possible conflicts of interest can be expected because the legislators usually also have full-time private jobs. Many legislators and other public officials, moreover, have investment holdings that may be affected by government activities.

Some states specifically prohibit legislators from voting on matters in which they or their families have a financial interest. More broadly, many states and localities have financial disclosure laws requiring candidates for office and those in office to file detailed statements revealing the sources of their income. In some areas of the country, the laws apply to nonelected high-level administrative officials as well as elected officeholders and to the immediate families of candidates or officeholders. Some people have objected to disclosure laws as an invasion of privacy and feel that this "invasion" deters well-qualified people from public service.

State laws and regulations commonly prohibit legislators and other public officials on the local as well as state levels from accepting employment or gifts conflicting with their public responsibilities. Some states have conflict-of-interest laws with "no-cup-of-coffee" provisions that ban officials from accepting anything of value from lobbyists or private citizens. Other laws prohibit public officials from using confidential information related to their employment for personal profit, representing private parties in proceedings against the state or local government or before a regulatory body, and selling goods or services to the state or local government.

OPEN MEETINGS AND RECORDS

Open meeting laws and laws requiring public records to be open for inspection are intended to reduce secrecy in government and to make it more difficult for officials to make clandestine bargains or hide their mistakes. Open meetings are generally required whenever a collective decision, commitment, or promise is made by a legislative body, subcommittee of a legislative body, or other governmental agency. Exceptions are made for personnel matters involving specific individuals. The open meeting requirement may apply to executive and legislative activities at both state and local levels. While few have championed secrecy, many have argued that the effects of the open meeting laws have not been all positive. The laws, it has been argued, have somewhat hamstrung officials, making them far less candid in public, and, in some cases, have led to more secrecy as officials hold private, informal meetings in which the actual decisions are made.

ENDNOTES

1. Winston Churchill, 1920.
2. Martin Shefter, "Regional Receptivity to Reform: The Legacy of the Progressive Era," *Political Science Quarterly* 98 (Fall 1983): 459–483.
3. *Smith* v. *Allwright,* 321 U.S. 649 (1944).
4. *Branti* v. *Finkel,* 100 S.Ct. 1287 (1980).
5. George S. Blair, *American State Legislatures: Structure and Process* (New York: Harper and Row, 1967), p. 69.
6. Sarah M. Morehouse, "Money versus Party Effort: Nominating for Governor," *American Journal of Political Science* 34 (August 1990): 706–724.
7. See, generally: Donald Bruce Johnson and James R. Gibson, "The Divisive Primary Revisited: Party Activists in Iowa," *American Political Science Review* 68 (March 1974): 67–77; Patrick J. Kenney and Tom W. Rice, "The Effect of Primary Divisiveness in Gubernatorial and Senatorial Elections," *The Journal of Politics* 46 (August 1984): 904–915; and Penny M. Miller, Malcolm E. Jewell, and Lee Sigelman, "Divisive Primaries and Party Activists: Kentucky, 1979 and 1983," *The Journal of Politics* 50 (May 1988): 459–470.
8. William Crotty, ed., *Political Parties in Local Areas* (Knoxville: University of Tennessee Press, 1986).
9. Robert J. Huckshorn, *Party Leadership in the States* (Amherst: University of Massachusetts Press, 1976), pp. 122–125.
10. *Ibid.,* p. 38.
11. *Ibid.*
12. Timothy Conlan, Ann Martino, and Robert Dilger, "State Parties in the 1980s: Adaptation, Resurgence and Continuing Constraints," *National Civic Review* (July/August 1985): 303–309.
13. Timothy Conlan, Ann Martino, and Robert Dilger, "State Parties in the 1980s," *Intergovernmental Perspective* (Fall 1984): 6–13.
14. See: Cornelius P. Cotter, James L. Gibson, John F. Bibby, and Robert Huckshorn, *Party Organization in American Politics* (New York: Praeger, co-published with the

Eagleton Institute of Politics, 1984). A study sponsored by the U.S. Advisory Commission on Intergovernmental Relations reached similar conclusions. See overview by Conlan, Martino, and Dilger, "State Parties in the 1980s: Adaptation, Resurgence and Continuing Constraints."

15. See, generally: David M. Olson, "Attributes of State Political Parties: An Exploration of Theory and Data," in James A. Reidel, ed., *New Perspectives in State and Local Politics* (Waltham, Mass.: Xerox College Publishing, 1971), pp. 123–157.

16. See: Morehouse, "Money versus Party Effort." See also: Malcolm E. Jewell, "State Party Endorsements of Gubernatorial Candidates Declining in Effectiveness," *Comparative State Politics* 16 (June 1995): 7–13; and David Soherr-Hadwiger, "New Mexico's Modified Pre-Primary Nominating Convention," *Comparative State Politics* 15 (June 1994): 1–7, in which the argument is made that the system has not significantly reduced the number of candidates or contributed much to party vitality.

17. See, for example: Richard Murray and Arnold Vedlitz, "Party Voting in Lower-Level Electoral Contests," *Social Science Quarterly* 59 (March 1979): 752–757.

18. See discussion by Thomas M. Holbrook and Emily Van Dunk, "Electoral Competition in the American States," *American Political Science Review* 87 (December 1993): 955–962.

19. "Slow Down: You're in Iowa," *Newsweek* (13 February 1984): 14.

20. See, for example: Jack Bass and Walter DeVries, *The Transformation of Southern Politics* (New York: Basic Books, 1976).

21. Micheal W. Giles and Kaenan Hertz, "Racial Threat and Partisan Identification," *American Political Science Review* 88 (June 1994): 317–326.

22. "Winning the Vote," *National Journal* (17 August 1985): 1918. See also: Merle Black and Earl Black, "Republican Party Development in the South: The Rise of the Contested Primary," *Social Science Quarterly* 57 (December 1976): 574–578.

23. The Mountain West includes: Arizona, Colorado, Idaho, Montana, Nevada, New Mexico, Utah, Wyoming. On political change in this region see: Peter F. Galderisi et al., eds., *The Politics of Realignment: Party Change in the Mountain West* (Boulder, Colo.: Westview Press, 1987).

24. For an account of third- or minor-party activity and electoral support, see: Euel Elliott, Gerald S. Gryski, and Bruce Reed, "Minor Party Support in State Legislative Elections," *State and Local Government Review* (Fall 1990): 123–131.

25. Millard L. Gieske, *Minnesota Farmer-Laborism: The Third-Party Alternative* (Minneapolis: University of Minnesota Press, 1979).

26. Robert J. Spitzer, "A Political Party Is Born: Single-Issue Advocacy and the New York State Election Law," *National Civic Review* (July/August 1984): 321–328.

27. Robert S. Erikson, Gerald C. Wright, and John P. McIver, *Statehouse Democracy: Public Opinion and Policy in the American States* (New York: Cambridge University Press, 1993).

28. See review by Thomas R. Dye: "Party and Policy in the States," *The Journal of Politics* 46 (1984): 1097–1115. See also: Sarah M. Morehouse, *State Politics, Parties and Policy* (New York: Holt, Rinehart and Winston, 1980). A recent useful empirical study is James C. Garand, "Partisan Change and Shifting Expenditure Priorities in the American States," *American Politics Quarterly* 13 (October 1985): 355–391.

29. See, for example: Kenneth Janda et al., "Legislative Politics in Indiana," in James B.

Kessler, ed., *Empirical Studies in Indiana Politics* (Bloomington: Indiana University Press, 1970), p. 32.

30. Morris P. Fiorina, "Divided Government in the American States: A Byproduct of Legislative Professionalism?" *American Political Science Review* 88 (June 1994): 304–316.
31. John Gunther, *Inside U.S.A.* (New York: Harper and Brothers, 1947), p. 47.
32. See: Clive S. Thomas and Ronald J. Hrebenar, "Changes in the Number and Types of Interest Groups and Lobbies Active in the States," *Comparative State Politics Newsletter* (April 1988): 32–36. On change in western states, see: Clive S. Thomas and Ronald J. Hrebenar, "Comparative Interest Group Politics in the American West," *The Journal of State Government* (September/October 1986): 124–136; and Ronald J. Hrebenar and Clive S. Thomas, eds., *Interest Group Politics in the American West* (Salt Lake City: University of Utah Press, 1987).
33. Edgar Lane, *Lobbying and the Law* (Berkeley and Los Angeles: University of California Press, 1964), p. 177.
34. L. Harmon Zeigler and Hendrik Van Dalen, "Interest Groups in the States," in Herbert Jacob and Kenneth N. Vines, eds., *Politics in the American States*, 2nd ed. (Boston: Little, Brown, 1971), pp. 122–160.
35. Alan Rosenthal, *The Third House: Lobbyists and Lobbying in the States* (Washington, D.C.: CQ Press, 1993).
36. Lester Milbrath, *The Washington Lobbyists* (Chicago: Rand McNally, 1963), pp. 302–303.
37. Michael Lipsky, "Protest as a Political Resource," *American Political Science Review* 62 (December 1968): 1144–1158.
38. See: David Fairbanks, "Religious Forces and 'Morality' Policies in the American States," *Western Political Science Quarterly* 30 (September 1977): 411–417. On the new religious right, see: Clyde Wilcox, *God's Warriors: The Christian Right in Twentieth-Century America* (Baltimore: Johns Hopkins University Press, 1991).
39. Wayne L. Francis, "A Profile of Legislator Perceptions of Interest Group Behavior Relating to Legislative Issues in the States," *Western Political Quarterly* 24 (December 1971): 702–712.
40. See: Zeigler and Van Dalen, "Interest Groups," pp. 126–140.
41. See: Duane Lockard, *New England State Politics* (Princeton: Princeton University Press, 1959).
42. T.A. Larson, *Wyoming: A Bicentennial History* (New York: W.W. Norton, 1977).
43. William T. Gormley Jr., "Television Coverage of State Government," *Public Opinion Quarterly* 42 (Fall 1978): 354–359.
44. Kim Fridkin Khan, "The Distorted Mirror: Press Coverage of Women Candidates for Statewide Office," *The Journal of Politics* 56 (February 1994): 154–173.
45. Arthur H. Miller, Edie N. Goldenberg, and Lutz Erbring, "Type-Set Politics: Impact of Newspapers on Public Confidence," *American Political Science Review* 73 (March 1979): 67–84.'
46. See: Eric Veblen, *The Manchester Union Leader in New Hampshire Elections* (Hanover, N.H.: The University Press of New England, 1975).
47. Thad L. Beyle and Robert Hueffner, "Quips and Quotes from Old Governors to New," *Public Administration Review* (May/June 1983): 268–270, at 268.

48. T.K. Weterell, speaker of the Florida House, "Florida Takes the Big Money out of Political Campaigns," *State Legislatures* (August 1991): 44.

49. Representative Robert Jones, North Carolina, quoted by Sandra Singer, "The Arms Race of Campaign Financing," *State Legislatures* (July 1988): 24–28, at 24–25.

50. Joel A. Thompson, William Cassie, and Malcolm E. Jewell, "A Sacred Cow or Just a Lot of Bull? Party and PAC Money in State Legislative Elections," *Political Research Quarterly* 47 (March 1994): 223–237.

51. See: James D. King and Helenan S. Robin, "PACS and Campaign Finance in National and State Elections," *Comparative State Politics* 16 (August 1995): 32–44; Anthony Gierzynski and David Breaux, "Money and Votes in State Legislative Elections," *Legislative Studies Quarterly* 16 (1991): 203–218; and Gary Moncrief, "The Increase in Campaign Expenditures in State Legislative Elections: A Comparison of Four Northwestern States," *Western Political Quarterly* 45 (1992): 549–558.

52. Timothy J. Conlan, "Federalism and American Politics: New Relations in a Changing System," *Intergovernmental Perspective* (Winter 1985): 32–45. On foreign corporations see: Jean Cobb, "Political Currency," *Common Cause Magazine* (January/ February 1990): 28–30.

53. Ruth Jones and Anne Hopkins, "State Campaign Fund Raising: Targets and Response," *The Journal of Politics* 47 (1985): 433–449.

54. Bill Schluter, Republican member of the New Jersey Assembly, "Contributions Don't Affect Votes? Don't You Believe It," *Governing* (August 1990): 98.

55. Amy E. Young, "In the States," *Common Cause Magazine* (March/April 1991): 43.

56. National Advisory Commission on Criminal Justice Standards and Goals, *A National Strategy to Reduce Crime* (Washington, D.C.: Government Printing Office, 1973), p. 99.

57. Robert J. Huckshorn, "Who Gave It? Who Got It?: The Enforcement of Campaign Finance Laws in the States," *The Journal of Politics* 47 (August 1985): 774–789. See also: James S. Fay, "State Campaign Finance Laws: The Issue of Enforcement," *National Civic Review* (December 1973): 603–607.

58. Jack L. Noragon, "Political Finance and Political Reform: The Experience with State Income Tax Checkoffs," *American Political Science Review* 75 (September 1981): 667–687.

59. Ruth S. Jones, "State Public Campaign Finance: Implications for Partisan Politics," *American Journal of Political Science* 25 (May 1981): 342–361. See also: Patrick D. Donnay and Graham P. Ramsden, "Public Financing of Legislative Elections: Lessons from Minnesota," *Legislative Studies Quarterly* 20 (August 1995): 351–364; and Kenneth R. Mayer and John M. Wood, "The Impact of Public Financing on Electoral Competitiveness: Evidence from Wisconsin, 1964–1990," *Legislative Studies Quarterly* 20 (February 1995): 69–88.

5

☆ ☆ ☆

STATE LEGISLATIVE POLITICS

State legislatures are major focal points of state politics. Their activity or lack of activity is of direct concern to governors, administrators, judges, political parties, interest groups, and politically active citizens. State legislatures, as one authority has put it, "are the guts of democracy, where battle is waged and ultimately where consensus gets built."[1]

State legislatures have become, if anything, more important in recent years as they have assumed more responsibilities. With this, they have also become more representative of the general population, better paid and more stable bodies, and far better equipped in terms of professional staff support to perform their functions.

The early 1990s, however, brought some negative reactions to the professionalization of state legislatures and a demand for a return to a simpler "citizen legislature" model. This demand has been represented by the *term limitations movement*.

This chapter begins with a discussion of state legislative institutions and proceeds to examine the characteristics of individual legislators, the environment in which they work, the lawmaking process, legislative behavior, and, finally, some comments on how the public has evaluated the legislatures.

LEGISLATIVE STRUCTURE

Every state but Nebraska has two legislative bodies. Both houses may be referred to as the legislature, the general assembly, the legislative assembly,

119

or, in Massachusetts, the general court. The upper state house is uniformly called the senate, whereas the lower house may be known as the house of representatives, the assembly, or the house of delegates.

The size of state senates ranges from sixty-seven in Minnesota to twenty in Alaska and Nevada. Alaska and Nevada also have the smallest state lower house, with forty members each. Several states have more than one hundred members in their lower house. In a majority of the states, members of the lower house are elected for two-year terms and members of the upper house are elected for four-year terms. All house members are up for election at the same time. In about half the states, senators serve staggered terms—that is, half of the senate is up for reelection every two years. By having staggered terms, states ensure there will be some continuity in legislative membership from session to session.

APPORTIONMENT AND DISTRICTING

Legislative apportionment refers to the process of determining the number of representatives that a geographical unit or election district may send to a legislative body. Two basic principles have been used to determine the apportionment of seats in state legislatures: population and area. When population is used, each election district is cut up to have substantially the same number of people, or, if a district has more people than others, it is given proportionately more representatives. When area or geography is used, the emphasis is on giving equal representation to specific units, regardless of differences in their populations.

Up to the mid-1960s, representatives from rural areas generally dominated state legislatures. Laws in most states based representation in at least one house of the legislature on area rather than population. Voters in each county, for example, would select the same number of state senators, regardless of the population disparities among the counties. Often, representatives from metropolitan areas where more than half of the population lived would have no more than 20 percent of the senate seats. While plans often gave urban counties more representatives in the lower state houses, they also commonly guaranteed each county at least one representative and placed a limit on the number of representatives any one county could have.

The net effect of these and related practices was to preserve rural domination of state legislatures at the expense of the rapidly growing urban areas. Critics regarded rural-dominated state legislatures as insensitive to the needs of urban areas. They looked at state legislatures as the domain of "small-town" thinkers, isolated from the problems and aspirations of the majority of the state's population, and both unable and unwilling to respond to the needs of the great majority of their people. Large-city politicians argued that because of malapportionment at the state level, they had to appeal directly to the national government for assistance in meeting their problems.

The United States Supreme Court in the 1964 case of *Reynolds* v. *Sims*[2] ruled that both houses of a state legislature must be apportioned on a population basis. The decision eventually led to the reapportionment of every state legislature in the nation along the population principle. It brought an end to rural dominance. In most states, the result of reapportionment was to shift the locus of political power from rural to suburban areas rather than to large cities. Indeed, considering population trends, large cities might actually have become overrepresented in malapportioned state legislatures if reapportionment had not come about.

The "reapportionment revolution" of the 1960s helped usher in a new era in state government by giving representation to new groups and by stimulating concern with reforming and streamlining state government along a variety of dimensions. In regard to policy, reapportionment appears to have brought about a greater attention in state legislatures to problems of urban areas and increased spending for education, welfare, health, and hospitals.[3]

Redistricting—the carving up of new districts after each ten-year census on the basis of population—continues to provoke legislative struggles. In most states, legislatures have the responsibility of creating new district lines every ten years, using the national census to adjust to population changes within the state.[4] In addition to legislative districting, state legislatures also redraw congressional districts to reflect population changes since the last census and to adjust to possible changes in the number of representatives.

Legislative districting is a highly personal problem for state legislators. Quite understandably, legislators are reluctant to tamper with the district boundaries from which they were elected. They view the districting job first of all from the standpoint of their own self-preservation. Beyond this, legislators strive to avoid changes that would adversely affect a colleague (for example, force incumbents to run against each other, unless, of course, the likely loser happens to belong to a rival political party) and to maximize party and area interests. Considering the political difficulties in redistricting, several states have placed the task in the hands of special boards or commissions. There is no assurance, however, that these bodies will not divide politically on the question of redistricting. In such situations the courts have had to step in and devise districting plans.

The most important issues in recent years have concerned specific districting arrangements. Courts have generally insisted upon no greater than a 10 percent deviation in the size of legislative districts (although sparsely settled states may give each county at least one representative, regardless of their population). While creating districts that are relatively equal in population is no great problem, how the district lines are drawn may give rise to charges of discrimination. There is a good possibility that even though districts may be roughly equal in population, the legislature has drawn or gerrymandered them in such a way that racial, ethnic, or political minorities secure little if any

FIGURE 5–1   Oklahoma House of Representatives Districts (Based on 1990 Census)

Source: The Oklahoma Department of Libraries. Reproduced with permission.

representation. A plan may distribute a minority vote among several districts so that it cannot secure any representation at all. Or it may concentrate the minority vote in one district where it is overwhelmed by the vote of those with opposite characteristics. *Gerrymandering*—the drawing of district lines to the advantage of one partisan or demographic group over another—is a common practice. State districting maps commonly contain a number of distinct shapes with unusual forms and sizes that reflect these considerations as well as the population criteria (see figure 5–1).

The courts have not been greatly concerned about problems of political gerrymandering, that is, the drawing of district lines by Democrats to discriminate against Republicans, or vice versa.[5] As far back as 1960, however, the High Court showed that legislatures would not have a free hand in drawing district lines where racial discrimination was evident.[6]

At one time, the courts approved plans calling for affirmative or benign gerrymandering, that is, carving out districts to create seats for specific minorities, as being compatible with the federal Voting Rights Act. With the High Court's blessing, the United States Department of Justice used the act to encourage states to create "majority minority" districts so as to facilitate the election of blacks, Hispanics, and other minorities. In recent years, however, a more conservative Supreme Court has indicated that such "racially conscious" plans may violate the equal protection clause of the Constitution. The Court has been particularly skeptical when race clearly has been the predominant consideration in drawing district lines. Odd or bizarre-looking districts that are hard to justify other than on the grounds that they are packed with members of a particular race or ethnic group are particularly likely to be invalidated by the Court.[7]

Currently the states are free to choose between single-member and multi-member districts.[8] Although little empirical research has been done on the subject of districting, each type of district is thought to have distinct advantages and disadvantages. The single-member district system makes fewer demands on voters because they have fewer candidates to become familiar with and choose among. The system may also encourage the selection of legislators more familiar with the voters and more responsive to their problems. Minorities, in particular, may find it easier to secure representation, although, as mentioned above, gerrymandering may prevent this. On the other hand, critics argue, single-member districts encourage the selection of legislators with essentially parochial outlooks who see their mission to be one of promoting the interests of a very small segment of the population rather than the interests of the broader community or of the state. Multimember districts of a countywide basis may reduce these dangers but bring with them increased election costs and the increased possibility that minorities (political as well as racial) will be overwhelmed in the broader electorate and fail to secure representation.

Bicameralism and Unicameralism

Back in the 1960s, the one-person, one-vote rule refocused attention on the historic disputes between proponents of bicameralism and unicameralism. Reformers argued that the chief function performed by having two houses was the representation of both area and population. Now that both houses must be based on the same principle, they contended, bicameralism owed its continued existence largely to inertia and tradition. Picking up on this theme, practitioners like Jesse Unruh, former speaker of the California Assembly, argued that bicameral systems "are costly and inefficient anachronisms which thwart the popular will, cater to private interests, and hobble responsible decision making, until they are no longer responsive to the needs of the people they are supposed to serve."[9]

Those favoring unicameralism continue to argue that having only one house would enhance legislative responsibility, would reduce the influence of pressure groups, promote economy and efficiency, and, coupled with other reforms, produce better legislative personnel. With one house, there would be no more buck-passing (blaming the other house or a conference committee for the failure to take action or for the action taken). Time could be saved by eliminating the conference stage and avoiding duplicate hearings and procedures. Money could be saved by speeding the process and, because the adoption of the plan would normally bring a severe reduction in legislative offices, bring savings in the form of legislative salaries. The influence of interest groups would be diminished because there would be fewer points of access and because the public's attention would be better focused on a smaller legislative body. The legislature would become not only more visible but also more prestigious, increasing competition for office and thus enhancing the chances of securing the cream of the crop.

There is no way to verify some of the claims for unicameralism. The experience of Nebraska with unicameralism is inconclusive on these points.[10] Theoretically, a small, unicameral legislature may be more conducive to a system wherein the legislature sits primarily as an operating board whose chief task is to render services as quickly and as efficiently as possible. This type of legislative body is widely popular in city governments, particularly those under the council-manager form, where emphasis is placed on the need to provide services in a businesslike manner. A two-house legislature, or at least a large, one-house legislature, is more conducive to a system in which the legislature plays a more deliberative function and is expected to represent a highly heterogeneous population. Defenders of bicameralism argue, moreover, that even though both houses must be based on the same population principle, two houses perform a valuable checks-and-balances function, thus preventing hasty legislation.

The strongest practical obstacle to unicameralism, as one might expect, has been the reluctance of state legislators to abolish their own offices. Few major interest groups, moreover, have seen any particular benefit in unicameralism and have left the difficult task of securing legislative support to groups of civic-minded citizens with only limited resources. Without legislative support, the most viable method of reform is found in the constitutional initiative, but this exists in only about one-quarter of the states and, as noted in chapter 3, is sometimes difficult to use.

THE LEGISLATORS

QUALIFICATIONS

State constitutions set the qualifications for membership in state legislatures. These relate to age, citizenship, and residence. The age requirement is usually higher for members of the senate, with twenty-five years of age being the most common, and is frequently as low as age twenty-one for the lower house. Some states, in keeping with changes in suffrage qualifications, have reduced the minimum age for legislative service to eighteen. Candidates must be United States citizens and have resided in their state and county for a specific period before becoming eligible for public office. In the event of a challenge to eligibility, each house sits as the judge of the qualifications of its members.

BOX 5–1   VOTERS AND LEGISLATIVE PAY RAISES

Legislative salaries went from an average of $1,500 in 1950 to over $18,000 in the 1980s. Public opposition to increases, however, has stymied salary hikes in recent years. Voter approval of increases is required in some states, and voters have overwhelmingly rejected such proposals. Even where voter approval is not needed, legislators are timid about proposing them because salary increases are unpopular and may come back to haunt legislators who vote for them. To some extent, however, legislators have maneuvered around this opposition by increasing per diem amounts, travel allowances, expense accounts, or pension benefits.

In addition to the minimum legal requirements, candidates for the state legislature must meet more informal but more vital qualifications. It is useful to have the characteristics of *availability*—to have a family, be connected with an organized religion, own a home, be of pleasing physical appearance, and have a scandal-free past. It is also helpful, if not absolutely necessary, to have deep roots in the community and not be tied down by a job or financial concerns.

The latter point has been especially important because legislative salaries have traditionally been low, though there is considerable variation in the amount of compensation. The current range is from New Hampshire, where each legislator receives only $200 plus mileage every two years, to New York, where the annual salary is $57,500.[11]

The notion that state legislators should not be paid a great deal, like the notion of term limitations, reflects, in part, the idea that no one should make a living passing laws. Rather, this function should be a public responsibility performed without motives of personal gain. Raising the salary, it is argued, would encourage the creation of a professional class of lawmakers rather than "citizen legislators" and would attract only greedier legislators, not more dedicated ones. However, the fact is that at least 75 percent of the potential state legislators have been effectively disqualified from serving because they cannot afford to serve. Salaries are seldom adequate to meet the costs of getting elected or to make up for the long absences from businesses and other places of employment (see box 5–1).

RECRUITMENT AND LENGTH OF SERVICE

State legislative candidates are recruited in various ways. Many are self-recruited. They declare themselves to be candidates and enter primaries without the encouragement or consent of party officials. In areas where party organizations are strong, candidates who decide to run on their own take the time to secure the support of party officials. On some occasions, party officials take the initiative in recruiting candidates. At times they talk individuals into running out of party loyalty, even when the chances of victory are dim, in the hope of improving the party's prospects in a future election. Party officials may also turn to individuals who are not actively identified with the party but are expected to make good candidates because they enjoy high social status and prestige. Interest groups may also recruit candidates and are often in a position to provide the necessary financial support.[12]

Perhaps as many as half of all legislative candidates are unopposed in their primaries. Lack of opposition is especially likely when an incumbent chooses to stand for renomination or when the chances of a member of the minority party to gain victory in the general election appear slim. Many candidates are also unopposed in the general election because the minority party may be so weak or have so little expectation for success that it does not enter candidates.[13]

Throughout most of the nation's history, state legislatures have been characterized by rapid turnover among members. Members of state legislatures have been likely to remain in office for a much shorter period than members of Congress.[14] Often, from one-third to one-half of a legislative body is composed of new members. Compared to Congress, state legislatures have had a more transient and less experienced membership. Effective control in many state legislatures appears to have been concentrated in the hands of the relatively few legislators who do return on a regular basis.

As might be expected, turnover rates are higher in states where legislators have the shortest terms and thus must face more frequent elections. Even more important, turnover rates are also higher in states where legislative compensation is relatively low. While some legislators fail to secure reelection, many more decline to run for reelection in large part because they feel they cannot afford to continue serving.

Some evidence suggests that over the long run, the turnover rate in state legislatures is lessening. That is, even though state legislators still do not serve as long as members of Congress, they are, nevertheless, serving longer than they did in the past.[15] In recent years, this has had less to do with an increase in the ability of incumbents to get reelected than with an increase in the attractiveness of the job and, thus, an increase in the willingness of incumbents to come back for further terms. Legislators, over the years, have increased their responsibility, visibility, prestige, staff resources, and, though it might still be considered low in many states, compensation.

Yet, just as state legislatures have become more attractive and professional in nature, there has been a countermovement away from the professional model back toward an amateur citizen legislature norm. Heading this drive has been an effort felt in nearly every state to set limits on the number of terms members of the legislature can serve (see box 5–2). The reform's popularity

---

BOX 5–2   TERM LIMITS: PROS AND CONS

Backers of term limits for state legislators argue for a return to the concept of the *citizen legislator*, who serves only for a limited period, rather than a *professional legislator*, who makes a lifetime career out of legislative service. After long years of service, reformers argue, legislators tend to become out of touch with the needs of the public. By creating more open seats (ones in which no incumbent is running), term limits are expected to raise the level of competition for office, bring in people who are more responsive to the voters and who are willing to bring about necessary changes.

Arguments against limitations include that they interfere with the right of people to vote for whomever they want, that they throw the good legislators out with the bad, and that a "citizen legislature" filled with amateurs is likely to be a weak institution even more under the control of interest groups and less able to check the power of governors. Opponents also argue that the reform is not needed because citizens are really not all that powerless in getting rid of incumbents—they do not need to be protected against themselves through a "stop me before I vote" measure—and because of this and other factors, turnover rates are actually rather high. Some also contend that term reform is less likely to bring about meaningful change than other reforms, such as those involving campaign finance, and, by itself, will only produce different players playing the same game.

---

reflects a general dissatisfaction with the job performance of incumbent lawmakers. Since 1990, twenty states have adopted term limitations for state legislators. Some laws call for lifetime bans, others restrict the number of consecutive terms a member can serve. In nineteen states term limits came through voter action. Utah is the only state where legislators limited their own terms by statute. Other than having access to the initiative process, states with term limits tend to be among those that have traditionally ranked high in terms of innovating new policies.[16]

While the effects of term limits are not as yet altogether clear, it does appear that some legislators, being no longer able to plan on an extended legislative career, have decided to resign and move on to other pursuits, including higher offices. In many states, however, turnover rates have been historically high and are unlikely to be changed by new restrictions. What is likely to change the most is that leadership positions will be assumed by less experienced and, possibly, less effective legislators.[17]

SOCIAL AND PERSONAL CHARACTERISTICS

One result of the formal and informal qualifications and the recruitment process for state legislative seats is that the typical state legislature is not a cross section of the state's population. Hispanics, blacks, and women, for

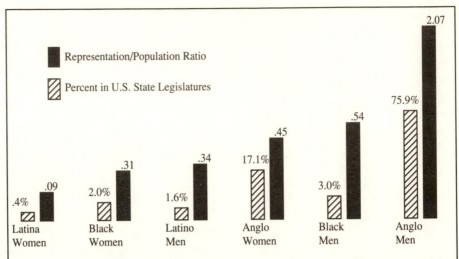

Note: The number of Asian/Pacific Islander legislators was not available. The figure for Anglo men was derived by subtracting the number of female, black, and Latino male legislators from the total number of legislators in 1993.

FIGURE 5–2   U.S. Legislatures, 1993. Ethnic and Gender Percentages and Representation/Population Ratios

Source: Wilma Rule, "Why Women Should Be Included in the Voting Rights Act," *National Civic Review 84* (Fall-Winter 1995): 360. Reprinted with permission. Copyright © 1995 National Civic League Press. All rights reserved.

example, are generally not represented in legislatures in proportion to their numbers in the state's population, though the representation of each of these groups is on the rise. As figure 5–2 illustrates, Anglo males continue to dominate state legislatures. They hold better than 75 percent of the seats. If each group in the figure were represented in state legislatures in the same percentages as they are present in the general population, each would have a representation/population ratio of 1. As the figure indicates, Anglo men, with a representative/population ratio of 2.07, are about twice as numerous in state legislatures as they are in the general population. All other groups are underrepresented. Most severely underrepresented are Latino (Hispanic) women and black women.

Evidence suggests the relative scarcity of women in legislatures is not due primarily to voter bias—female candidates now do about as well as male candidates—but to the scarcity of female candidates.[18] Research suggests, moreover, that gender does matter. On some issues—abortion being one—gender is related to how legislators vote, with women being more opposed to controls than are men.[19] More generally, women have made an impact on state legislatures by encouraging the consideration of legislation dealing with women, children, and families.[20]

On the whole, state legislators are better educated, wealthier, and of higher social status than the general public they serve. Available evidence indicates that the vast majority of state legislators are lawyers, farmers, or those engaged in some form of business activity (including insurance and real estate). Nationally, the most frequent occupational background is that of a lawyer. The percentage of legislators who are lawyers, however, has dropped from about 22 percent in 1976 to about 17 percent currently. Observers attribute the drop to the growing demands of the legislative job. It has become increasingly difficult to be both a full-time legislator, meeting virtually year-round, and a successful lawyer. Because of the increased demands of the job, a growing number of legislators are retirees and, though they often have trouble making ends meet, people with no other jobs.[21]

A study by James Barber focused on the political significance of personality in the recruitment and adaptation of legislators.[22] Barber interviewed first-term members of the Connecticut House of Representatives to determine their attitudes toward their roles in the legislature, their motivations for seeking election, and their willingness to return to office. Four legislative types were categorized from the findings: Spectator, Advertiser, Reluctant, and Lawmaker. The Spectator is willing to sit by as a passive bystander and enjoy watching the legislative show. While willing to serve several terms, he or she usually has no further political ambition beyond that seat in the legislature. The Spectator is characterized as a person "of modest achievement, limited skills, and restricted ambitions, political or otherwise."[23] The Spectator comes from a small town in which competition for political office is slight and tends to spend much energy on fellowship activities or social gatherings, leaving little time for increasing his or her competence in legislative matters.

The Advertiser category is composed of lawyers, businesspeople, and professionals who go into politics with the intention of getting something out of the venture, such as public recognition or business contacts. Legislative service to this group is a means, not an end, and is not looked on as a long-term commitment. The Advertiser is an active legislator who seeks the limelight and brings an infusion of conflict into the legislature. The third category is that of the Reluctant. These legislators give the impression that they are serving under protest. They do not want to run for office, but are drafted or forced into it by friends. The Reluctants are somewhat bewildered by the legislature and have little desire to serve more than two terms. They tend to retreat from the more active part of the legislative process and become concerned with formal rules and procedures. The final category, that of the Lawmaker, is

---

BOX 5–3   CITIZENS IN CHARGE: THE NEW HAMPSHIRE LEGISLATURE

"The New Hampshire legislature is of and by the people. There is one member for roughly 2,300 residents; my constituents are more likely to see me filling my gas tank or at the general store than on the evening news. We answer our own mail; we write our own speeches. . . . For the most part, the legislature is dominated by retirees (the average age is around 60), peppered with a follower of the Reverend Sun Myung Moon and three husband-and-wife teams, with relatively few working men or women. Low legislative wages keep all but a score of lawyers from serving—one reason the legislature is able to work quickly, if not always rationally." The New Hampshire House has four hundred members who receive $100 annually.

Source: Steven R. Maviglio, member of the New Hampshire House, *Governing* (February 1990): 70.

---

composed of those who devote an unusual amount of time and energy to the formulation and production of legislation. The Lawmakers are ranked high in activity and willingness to return for three or more terms.

VARIATIONS IN CAREER PATTERNS AND OPPORTUNITIES

The term limit movement seems destined to generally weaken the status of state legislatures. Yet, one can also expect to continue to see variations from state to state in the overall professionalism of the legislative body, that is, in regard to such factors as the time in session, compensation, and staff resources. A professionalization index, based on the extent to which legislatures in the various states resemble Congress on these dimensions, is shown in table 5–1. At the top of the list we find larger states such as New York and California, though Alaska is also ranked relatively high. On the bottom and, in many respects closer to the citizen legislature model, are New Hampshire (see box 5–3) and several states in the sparsely settled West.

State legislatures differ in regard to compensation, staffing, traditions, organization, and other characteristics. Given this variation, there is a tendency for different types of legislative bodies to attract and, to some extent, accommodate the needs of different types of legislators. The type of legislator typically found in a particular legislative body varies, for example, with whether that body can be described as a career legislature, a springboard legislature, or a dead-end legislature. The lower state houses of New York, California, and Connecticut may serve as examples. In New York, house members tend to anticipate long years of service. To accommodate this desire, both pay and staff resources are relatively high. With legislative careers in

TABLE 5–1   Professionalization Levels of State Legislatures

Rank	State	Level	Rank	State	Level
1	New York	.659	26	Louisiana	.185
2	Michigan	.653	27	Oregon	.183
3	California	.625	28	South Carolina	.178
4	Massachusetts	.614	29	Virginia	.170
5	Pennsylvania	.336	30	Maine	.161
6	Ohio	.329	31	Mississippi	.160
7	Alaska	.311	32	Nevada	.160
8	Illinois	.302	33	Alabama	.158
9	Colorado	.300	34	Kansas	.152
10	Missouri	.287	35	Rhode Island	.148
11	Hawaii	.276	36	Vermont	.145
12	Wisconsin	.270	37	Indiana	.139
13	Florida	.255	38	Tennessee	.135
14	New Jersey	.255	39	Georgia	.133
15	Arizona	.250	40	West Virginia	.125
16	Oklahoma	.250	41	Idaho	.119
17	Connecticut	.233	42	Montana	.110
18	Washington	.230	43	Arkansas	.105
19	Iowa	.225	44	Kentucky	.101
20	Texas	.210	45	New Mexico	.098
21	Maryland	.204	46	South Dakota	.083
22	North Carolina	.203	47	Utah	.082
23	Minnesota	.199	48	North Dakota	.075
24	Delaware	.192	49	Wyoming	.056
25	Nebraska	.186	50	New Hampshire	.042

Source: Peverill Squire, "Legislative Professionalization and Membership Diversity in State Legislatures," *Legislative Studies Quarterly* 17 (February 1992): 72. Copyright © 1992 by The Comparative Legislative Research Center. Reprinted with permission of author and *Legislative Studies Quarterly.*

mind, emphasis is placed on seniority (years of continuous service) as a criterion for advancement. In California, on the other hand, there has been a greater tendency for members to use house seats as a springboard to other political offices. Highly visible committee positions are prized. These and other positions are distributed with little regard for seniority. Bypassing seniority makes it easier for relative newcomers to gain the visibility needed to move on to other positions. The Connecticut house, finally, does not appear to be particularly attractive to either those who wish to make a legislative career (the workload is heavy but the resources are light) or those who wish to start climbing the political ladder. A relatively large number of its members look at the position as a dead end and return to private life after serving a year or two.[24]

The Working Environment

Legislative Sessions

Until the late 1960s, most state legislatures met in biennial sessions (every other year). The number of days in which the legislatures could meet in regular session was usually limited (for example, to sixty days) by state constitutions. These limitations were reinforced by legal provisions that cut off legislative pay after the specified number of days had passed. Apparently it was felt that the longer state legislatures met, the more damage they were likely to do.

Since the "reapportionment revolution" and the renewed interest in state government that began in the late 1960s, restrictions on the frequency and length of legislative sessions have been liberalized. Currently, thirty-four state legislatures meet annually,[25] compared to only six in 1949. Several states in recent years have also eliminated restrictions on the number of days the legislature can meet.

Most state legislative regular sessions begin in January and end two or three months later. Following each regular session, the legislature may be called into a special session. This may be done at the call of the governor, who may restrict the session to special areas of concern. In some states, the legislature, by a large vote (greater than a majority), may compel the governor to call a special session on a given topic chosen by the legislature. Normally, special sessions are devoted to issues like tax reform and reapportionment that would prove too time-consuming during the regular session.

Parties and Factions

Within state legislatures, the major actors are political parties and factions, presiding officers, committees, and legislative staffs.

In two-party states, decisions as to who will fill the various offices in the legislature are made on a partisan basis. The first step in organizing the legislature in these states is the calling of a *party caucus*—a meeting of all the members of a particular party in the legislature—to decide on nominees for presiding officer and other legislative offices. Those supported by the numerically dominant party are elected on a straight party vote. When a legislative body is divided on a relatively equal basis among members of different political parties, one may also expect that party membership differences will also be reflected on policy matters. In one-party states, decisions on legislative organization and policy matters are made by factional voting involving a split

---

BOX 5-4 SPEAKER DU JOUR

In those situations in which the parties have an equal number of members in the house or senate, the legislators may find it difficult to break a tie vote on organizational matters. This problem occurred in Indiana in 1988 after voters elected fifty Republicans and fifty Democrats to the House of Representatives. With the body evenly split and no one willing to break the partisan deadlock, party leaders agreed to an experiment in which a Democrat and a Republican alternated being speaker. In addition to "a speaker du jour," the agreement provided for two partisans for just about every position, for example, a Democratic and Republican majority leader, and gave each committee a Democratic and Republican chair. The experiment resulted in chaos. It was ended when one of the Democratic members switched to the Republican side.

---

within the dominant party or alliances that cuts across party lines. Factions may be organized around ideological differences, such as liberals versus conservatives, area interests, or personalities.

In most states there are floor leaders (majority and minority) for the various parties or factions. As in Congress, the majority leader often assists the presiding officer in planning strategy. If the executive branch is headed by the majority leader's party, the majority leader manages the governor's bills on the floor. Most state legislatures have one or more leadership committees, such as policy and steering committees, that are headed by party or factional leaders and are concerned with guiding pending legislation through the legislature. The dominant party caucus and the leaders elected out of this caucus may effectively control the work of the legislature. Often, however, severe splits within the dominant party along personal or ideological lines weaken the leaders and prevent unified action (see box 5-4).

PRESIDING OFFICERS

The speaker of the house is the presiding officer in the lower state legislative body. The house speaker is a member of that body and is elected by the dominant party or faction. The speaker's powers are comparable to those of the Speaker of the House in the United States House of Representatives in that he or she may recognize who can speak on the floor, make rulings on procedural questions, and appoint committees and refer measures to them.

More than thirty states designate the lieutenant governor as presiding officer in the senate. Like the vice president of the United States, who presides in the United States Senate, the lieutenant governor is not a member of the state senate, does not participate in its debates, and votes only in the event of a tie on the floor. The lieutenant governor usually has less control over appointment of committees or interpreting rules than does the speaker of the house. A president pro tem is elected out of the senate to preside over it when the lieutenant governor is unavailable. Where there is no lieutenant governor, the senate elects its own presiding officer, usually called the president of the senate, with powers like those of the speaker in the lower house.

The choice of a presiding officer is important because of the power (usually shared with party or factional leaders) he or she has over the functioning of the legislature. At times, the fate of legislation can be determined by the manner in which the presiding officer interprets the legislative body's rules of procedure. The presiding officer has considerable opportunity to be arbitrary in interpreting rules and procedures because of the low public visibility of the legislative process and because the legislators themselves usually have little knowledge of the rules.[26] Presiding officers may also determine the fate of legislation by their choice of what committee or committees will consider a bill. When the presiding officer has a choice of committees, he or she may select one that can be expected to be hostile to the bill or one that can be expected to be favorably disposed.

COMMITTEES

Like Congress, state legislatures make use of standing (permanent) legislative committees that have jurisdiction in such areas as education, highways, and commerce.[27] Some states have joint standing committees composed of members of both houses. The joint committee approach avoids the repetition of hearings and separate deliberations by committees in each house.

Committee members may owe their appointments to the decisions growing out of a party or factional caucus or a committee on committees. Appointments may also be made by party or factional leaders and/or the presiding officer.[28] Indeed, when there is an intensive campaign for the position of presiding officer, candidates are likely to use the promise of committee assignments as bargaining weapons to build a winning coalition.[29] However chosen, state legislators are less likely than congressional members to secure appointment to the same committees year after year. Furthermore, as noted earlier, committee chair positions do not necessarily go to senior members.

Committee assignments also frequently reflect an effort to preserve a party representation roughly proportionate to the one in the legislature (for example, if Republicans have 60 percent of the legislative seats, they receive 60 percent of the committee seats and all the chairmanships) and to achieve some type of geographic balance. Committee assignments are also related to the interests of individual legislators. Many committees are made up of people who have a personal interest in the subjects considered by the committees— for example, bankers sit on banking committees and insurance executives sit on insurance committees. To be sure, these appointments bring considerable expertise to the committee's work but they also invite a conflict of interest and preferential treatment for certain lobbyists.[30]

One long-term trend in state legislatures has been to reduce the number of standing committees. This reduction has eliminated many archaic committees and much of the overlapping jurisdictional problems created by a large number of committees. There has also been a trend toward the use of interim committees. Interim committees work between legislative sessions, using this time to make more thorough investigations of problems than are possible during the regular session.

Overall, however, committees in the state legislatures do not play as important a role as those in Congress. Though improvements have been made, most lack the time, staff, and experience found at the national level. Committees in state legislatures, as noted above, may well be dominated by the leaders who appoint them. In fact, some committees exist basically in name only and seldom meet. Those that do meet are far more likely than congressional committees to find their recommendations rejected on the floor, although, as discussed later, important variations do exist among committees in this regard.

LEGISLATIVE STAFF

For much of the nation's history, people elected to state legislatures have had to rely heavily on their own resources in securing office space, secretarial help, and professional staff assistance.[31] Among the oldest forms of assistance are a central secretarial pool and a bill-drafting service, the latter of particular importance to nonlawyer legislators. At the turn of the century, many states created legislative reference services, which often developed as a part of a state library or archive to provide information, make research reports, and maintain legislative records. Although most states still have legislative reference services, several of them also have legislative councils of professional staff members who perform informational functions similar to those provided by legislative reference services and, in addition, prepare an annual legislative program. Unlike the legislative reference service, the professional staffs of legislative councils (also known by various other names) are under the direct control of the entire legislature, a small bipartisan group of legislators, or the dominant party or its leaders.

In recent years, there has been an increase in the number of professional members who are assigned to such general or central legislative staffs. Also, more professional members have been assigned to standing legislative committees, to the staffs of individual legislators (especially legislative leaders), and to special committees or legislative offices concerned with matters such as budget review, administrative oversight, and program evaluation. In addition to acting as a source of information and advice (see below), legislative staffs help form a network of contacts that aid in integrating the activities of committees, legislative leaders, both houses of the legislature, the executive branch, and private citizens.[32]

LEGISLATIVE FUNCTIONS: THE LAWMAKING PROCESS

State legislatures perform a variety of functions. Among these are:

1. *executive functions*, such as confirming or rejecting gubernatorial appointments;
2. *investigative functions*, both to unearth data for legislation and to examine the activities of administrative agencies;
3. *judicial functions*, such as determining the qualifications of their own members and exercising the power of impeachment; and
4. *intergovernmental functions*, such as making decisions relating to the proposal and ratification of amendments to the United States Constitution, considering interstate compacts and agreements, passing legislation affecting local levels of government, and deciding whether or not to participate in federal programs.

By far the most noteworthy function of state legislatures is the making of statutory law. The legislative process in the states is much like that at the national level. The bill or legislative proposal is formulated, introduced into each house, referred to committees that may hold hearings, passed by a majority in both houses, sent to a conference committee to iron out any differences in the way the measure passed the two houses, and finally sent to the governor, who either signs or vetoes the measure.

ORIGINS OF LEGISLATION

Today (as we discuss more fully in chapter 6), the source of most major legislation is the governor. In some states, a legislative council may prepare the legislative program in accordance with the governor, the recommendations of legislative leaders, or both. Other sources of legislation are interest groups, committees, and individual legislators.

The origins of a bill may materially influence its fate. Top priority is normally given to those programs developed by the governor or put together in the dominant party's caucus. In other cases, the fate of a legislative proposal may be influenced by the reputation of its sponsor. As one scholar has noted: "On matters not directly affecting their major concerns, busy legislators are usually quite willing to let themselves be guided by the judgment of colleagues whom they consider intelligent, informed, and reliable."[33]

REFERRAL AND COMMITTEE ACTION

In an effort to coordinate the business of the legislature, most states require that bills be introduced by a specified date early in the legislative session. In most cases, bills are referred by a presiding officer to a standing committee.[34] Several legislatures have placed legal barriers to the ability of committees to pigeonhole (put aside and ignore) bills referred to them. About one-third of the states require committees to report all bills, favorably or unfavorably. This may be avoided, however, by reporting on a number of bills near the end of the legislative session so that there is little or no time to take action on them. In states where committees do not have to report all bills, committees can be discharged from considering legislation by a petition signed by a majority of members. This device is effectively limited, however, by the fear of offending committee chairpersons, who may retaliate against any legislation sponsored by those who sign the petition.

The workloads of standing committees and the extent to which they screen and modify the bills referred to them vary greatly.[35] Differences of this nature may be found within a given state legislature and among the standing committees of different state legislatures. Some legislative committees report favorably on the bulk of bills referred to them, while others report favorably on only one-quarter of the bills referred to them. The same type of variation may be found in regard to the willingness of committees to modify (for example, rewrite or amend) bills referred to them. Committees that take a passive approach to their responsibilities (for example, those that rank relatively low in screening or rewriting bills) are generally sensitive to the wishes of the sponsors of bills, but their recommendations are more likely to be modified or rejected when considered by the entire legislative body.

LEGISLATIVE ACTION

Committee reports are normally placed on a calendar to wait their turn for floor consideration. Many states now use a consent calendar, which allows noncontroversial bills to be placed on the agenda for unanimous passage without debate. A few states have groups similar to the Rules Committee of the United States House of Representatives that determine what bills to call up, when to call them up, and how they are to be considered. In some states a rules committee, policy committee, majority leader, or party caucus may refuse to allow a committee's recommendations to go to the floor for a vote.

As in Congress, the legislative body may meet as a committee of the whole, where it has more freedom in debate and no record of votes is taken. Discussion and debate on the floor in most legislatures are more restricted than in Congress. Voting usually is done by roll call and may require an absolute majority—a majority of the total membership, not simply those who are voting. In several states each bill must be read aloud in full before final passage.

State legislatures, like Congress, make use of *conference committees* to iron out differences between the two houses on particular pieces of legislation. Conference committees, sometimes called "the third house," regularly resolve controversial legislation in some states. The committees are composed of both house and senate members. Members may act as trustees of their respective houses, with considerable discretion in working out a bill, or may be, in effect, the agents of party leaders in the respective houses who must approve of the compromise.[36]

In any given legislative session, thousands of bills may be introduced. Only about one-third of these are eventually adopted, though there is a wide variation among the states: some approve nearly three out of four proposals, whereas others approve fewer than one out of ten.[37] Much of the adopted legislation is noncontroversial (such as minor adjustments in past legislation) and is disposed of without much commotion or publicity. For some legislation, the legislators engage in logrolling, or supporting projects and programs that benefit other members' parts of the state in return for their support.

When conflict does exist, bargains and compromises may be made to build a coalition large enough to secure the passage of legislation or defeat a legislative proposal. Different kinds of issues create different types of conflict groupings that may be between political parties, factions cutting across party lines, regional interests, or pressure groups. According to a survey of legislators in every state conducted by political scientist Wayne Francis, partisan conflict is highest in states over such issues as election laws and legislative apportionment. Apportionment is also seen to provoke regional conflicts, as do questions involving local governments. Conflict among pressure groups appears more noticeably on policies regarding labor, business, liquor, civil rights, gambling, and taxation. Factional conflict occurs in many of the same areas where there is interest group conflict and also in policies affecting apportionment (particularly in one-party states).[38]

FOLLOWING UP ON LEGISLATION

The lawmaking process does not end once a legislature passes an act and the governor signs it into law. Many legislative policies and programs are lost or subverted in the administrative process. Legislators have long been considered deficient in reviewing the manner in which laws are administered—in checking for waste and dishonesty and in ensuring that laws are being implemented as intended (though the legislature's intent or policy goals are commonly difficult to determine).

In recent years, state legislatures have taken steps to improve the performance of their administrative oversight function. Fearing the danger of a "runaway bureaucracy," several states have taken measures that allow the legislature to review and, in some cases, veto administrative rules and regulations so that they do not go into effect. In several states, these actions are taken by legislative resolutions that cannot be reviewed by the governor and thus made subject to the chief executive's veto power.

Along with the addition of this *legislative veto* as a control over agencies, several states now have what are called *sunset laws*. These laws require certain agencies (most generally, those with regulatory responsibilities) to justify their existence every so many years. Agencies that fail to convince legislatures that they should be reauthorized automatically go out of business (go down like the sunset). Professional staffs, often in legislative audit offices, have been assigned the task of making independent evaluations of the agencies and passing along their findings to the legislature.

Use of sunset laws has thus far not resulted in the massive termination of agencies and the corresponding reduction in state budgets many of its advocates foresaw. Between 1976 and 1981, some fifteen hundred agencies were reviewed under sunset legislation and about one of every five agencies reviewed was terminated. Many of those terminated were small and obscure agencies or minor licensing boards. Many agencies and programs that have survived the sunset process were modified in one way or another by the experience; for example, public members were added to boards or changes were made in administrative procedures to improve their operation and efficiency. Nevertheless, disappointment in the effectiveness of the sunset mechanism, the costs of undertaking reviews, and intensive lobbying by various vested groups have prompted several states to abandon the exercise.[39]

LEGISLATIVE BEHAVIOR

GENERAL FACTORS AFFECTING BEHAVIOR

In attempting to assess the behavior of state legislators, one must consider a wide variety of factors. Some theorists see legislators and other politicians as primarily interested in securing election or reelection for their own private ends, such as prestige.[40] From this perspective, legislators are more concerned with gaining favorable popular recognition, for example, through providing favors and taking popular stands on issues, rather than with actual legislating.

Legislators may indeed be motivated by their perceptions of what is in their own political self-interest. This, however, does not appear to be their only motivation. As mentioned earlier, some legislators serve only reluctantly and have no desire to stand for reelection or election to a higher office. Presumably some legislators (and perhaps all legislators at least part of the time) do have policy and other goals that are not related in their own minds to their success with the voters. Also, many appear to be guided in their behavior by their ideology or private political philosophy.[41] On some issues, such as abortion, the lawmaker's gender and religion may also matter—males and fundamentalists being more likely than women and nonfundamentalists to oppose abortion.

In the real political world, however, individual legislators find themselves subject to various external, institutional, and situational factors that may condition their behavior. External factors include the pressures exerted on legislators by interest groups, the public, the governor, the media, and those on other levels of government. Institutional factors that condition legislative behavior include the distribution of power within the legislative body, formal and informal "rules of the game," and variations in leadership, committee arrangements, and legislative staffing. Situational factors relate to matters such as the availability of time and information and the specific nature of the decision to be made.

The importance of staff members in legislative policymaking was discussed earlier, and other important influences on legislative policymaking, the governor and administrators, are discussed in chapter 6. The following discussion centers on how legislative behavior is conditioned by constituency, political party, interest group factors, and other legislators.

CONSTITUENCY INFLUENCE

In theory and perhaps sometimes in practice, a conflict exists between a legislator's role as a representative of his or her constituency and his or her role as a trustee for the constituents. As a *representative* or delegate, the legislator regards his or her role as simply reflecting the wishes of the constituents. As a *trustee*, the legislator feels that he or she has been elected by the voters to exercise independent judgment on issues before the legislature. The dilemma is: "Should I do what is right or what the people back home want me to do?" (see box 5–5). When constituent opinion is set on a particular issue, "doing right" may well be the last thing an individual does as a legislator—as he or she is likely to be voted out of office. A legislator who tries to act as a delegate, on the other hand, may discover that his or her constituents (many of whom did not vote for the legislator and never will) are either divided over the merits of a particular piece of legislation or have no instructions at all on how their representative should vote.

Research suggests that constituent opinion on issues may have much influence on legislative behavior. Legislators do pay attention to policy problems affecting their constituents and to their constituents' views. This is especially true as reelection time nears.[42] They sound out constituent opinion through personal contact and polls. Their idea of what constituents think—more precisely, what those constituents whose support the legislator needs think—conditions their behavior. Sometimes legislators receive clear advance

---

BOX 5–5 THE LEGISLATOR AND THE VOICE OF THE PEOPLE

" . . . I always voted against changing the state's constitution to allow a state lottery because I arrived in the legislature believing that promoting gambling was not a legitimate function of government. If the people wanted this, then they were wrong. . . .

"However, when the people of the state voted to change the constitution to allow a lottery, I felt obligated to vote for a bill that would implement the change. Why? Why, if I felt so strongly against a lottery did I feel after the referendum obligated to work for its implementation? Quite simply, the feeling of being a hired man came over me, and I believed it was my duty to carry out this directive. The debate was over and I lost."

Source: Tom Loftus, *The Art of Legislative Politics* (Washington, D.C.: CQ Press, 1994), p. 4. Loftus is former speaker of the Wisconsin State House.

---

instructions from those they represent. More often, it is a matter of legislators trying to anticipate how constituents might react to a particular decision. Their conclusion as to what is likely to happen or could happen may deter legislators from certain courses of action.

Few legislators in practice actually see any conflict between what they think is right and what they think their constituents want. In some cases, of course, conflicts do arise.[43] On the whole, however, conflict is kept to a minimum by a legislator's political intelligence and by the fact that legislators usually have deep roots in their communities and share their values and goals.[44]

PARTY INFLUENCE

Similarly, legislators seldom see any conflict between their own opinion and that of their political party. The party with which a legislator identifies is also a creature of the particular constituency, likely to be conservative and Republican in suburban areas and more liberal and Democratic in large cities. However, the extent to which legislators of the same political party vote together does vary among the states. Party voting on issues is more evident in the larger urban and industrial states like New York and Pennsylvania, where party alignments are likely to follow urban-rural divisions.

INTEREST GROUP INFLUENCE

Legislators, as noted in the previous chapter, hear from a wide variety of groups. Very often what they hear is simply a statement of a group's position on a particular piece of legislation. Sometimes this is accompanied by a type of pleading known in the South as *poor-mouthing*. As one legislator describes it: "When you contend that you don't have anything, can't get anything, and have no hope for the future, you're poor-mouthing."[45]

Business groups are generally considered to have an important impact on state policy because state legislators view good relations with the business community to be vital to the health of the state's economy. They may, indeed, act to protect the interests of business, even when there is no pressure from outside groups to do so.[46] Although business groups are generally considered by legislators to be the most powerful, educational interests, labor, associations of cities, and other governmental employee organizations are also highly visible to legislators. But again, the actual strength or influence of a group depends largely on its status in the eyes of the legislator—whether or not it represents something important to the legislator's constituency or a cause with which the legislator identifies. A legislator may register a complaint of being pressured when groups not close to him or her attempt to influence his or her vote. Likewise, legislators are most likely to complain about the influence of "special interests" when they fear that groups they oppose are influencing other legislators.[47]

Most contact between lobbyist and legislator takes on the character of cooperation between like-minded individuals, although lobbyists on occasion attempt to influence the opinion of the undecided or opposed. Research conducted by L. Harmon Zeigler suggests that lobbying may cause a legislator to question a previously held opinion, to lean toward the views of the lobbyist, or even to change from one position to another. The first result, however, is far easier to achieve than the last one. Not surprisingly, lobbyists are apt to rate the impact of their efforts to be greater than legislators see it.[48]

STAFF INFLUENCE

Professional staff members perform a variety of functions within the legislature. Perhaps the most important is the fact that they serve as a source of information, without which legislatures would be even more dependent on interest groups and the state executive branch. Staffers also function to distill a large volume of information into a manageable form for legislators. In the absence of this help, legislators may be confronted with "information overload," being swamped by data.

In performing the informational function, the staff enjoys considerable opportunity to suggest policy ideas. Staffers also may shape the nature of policy by defining problems, by suggesting alternate solutions to problems, and by screening the information that reaches the legislators. Yet, while staffers are often close to individual legislators, it should be noted that their influence is likely to be of a supportive nature, that is, suggesting ideas that are in tune with what the legislator already thinks or wants.

THE INFLUENCE OF COLLEAGUES

Another type of influence on a state legislator is that of his or her colleagues. The influence of colleagues is commonly manifested in *cue taking*, a process that occurs when an individual accepts advice on a legislative matter from a fellow legislator who is perceived to be a friend, an expert on a particular policy matter, or a leader. Legislators rely on other legislators for policy advice because no one legislator can possibly be well informed about all the issues on which he or she votes. Advice may also be sought because a legislator is cross-pressured (that is, caught between the demands of two opposing groups) and thus needs additional cues for decision making.[49]

Another aspect of colleague influence grows out of the existence of informal rules of behavior that condition the environment in which legislators work. Research by John Wahlke and Leroy Ferguson on four state legislatures produced some forty rules of the game as perceived by state legislators.[50] The following list presents some of the most commonly mentioned guidelines:

1. Performance of obligations—Keep your word, abide by commitments.
2. Respect for other members' legislative rights—Support another member's local bill if it doesn't affect you or your district; don't railroad bills through; don't appear before a committee other than your own to oppose another member's bill; don't steal another member's bill; respect the rights of a bill's author; and accept the author's amendments to a bill.
3. Impersonality—Don't deal in personalities; don't make personal attacks on other members; oppose the bill, not the sponsor; don't criticize the moral behavior of others.
4. Self-restraint in debate—Don't talk too much; don't speak about subjects on which you're uninformed.
5. Courtesy—Observe common courtesies; be friendly and courteous even if you disagree, and even if you are of an opposite party to your opponent.
6. Openness of aims—Be frank and honest in explaining bills and don't conceal real purpose of bills or amendments.
7. Modesty—Don't be a prima donna, an individualist, an extremist, or a publicity hound; don't talk for the press or the galleries.
8. Integrity—Be honest, a person of integrity and sincerity.
9. Independence of judgment (being independent of outside control)— Don't be subservient to a political organization, a boss, a machine, an interest group, lobbyists, or clients.
10. Personal virtue—Exhibit good conduct, sobriety, and morality.

These and other similar rules of the game are not always honored. If not, a variety of sanctions may be applied. Research suggests that the most common form of sanction is the obstruction of the offender's bills. Others include ostracism (for example, giving the offender the "silent treatment") and loss of patronage, good committee assignments, and other political perquisites.[51]

EVALUATION OF THE LEGISLATURES

State legislatures have been evaluated on the basis of a number of criteria and from a variety of perspectives. Some studies have focused on citizen attitudes in regard to the quality and performance of state legislatures. Other evaluations have been made on the basis of outside study groups.

Studies on citizen attitudes[52] suggest:

1. Only a small percentage of a state's population is interested in or knowledgeable about its state legislature.

2. Those who have opinions generally have been critical of the performance of state legislatures (for example, for wasting time or passing bad legislation), though their feelings may vary over time and by state and, at any given time, citizens may be equally critical of Congress, if not more so.

3. Citizens may evaluate gubernatorial and legislative performance as a whole—that is, when the governor's performance is ranked high, so is that of the legislature, even when the governor is a member of one party and the legislature is dominated by members of the opposite party.

4. Citizens appear to have separate attitudes toward the legislature as an institution (which is rather well supported), the performance of particular legislative bodies (which are likely to be viewed negatively), and the performance of their own legislators, whom they like and return to office even though they disapprove of the legislature of which they are a part.[53]

ENDNOTES

1. Alan Rosenthal, "State Legislatures—Where It's At," *The Political Science Teacher* 4 (Fall 1988): 1.
2. 377 U.S. 533 (1964).
3. H. George Frederickson and Yong Hyo Cho, "Sixties' Reapportionment: Is It Victory or Delusion?" *National Civic Review* (February 1971): 73–78, 85, quote at 78. See also: Douglas G. Feig, "Expenditures in the American States: The Impact of Court-Ordered Legislative Reapportionment," *American Politics Quarterly* 6 (July 1978): 309–325.
4. The exceptions to using federal census data are Massachusetts, which uses a state-conducted census, and Hawaii, which uses registered voter population.
5. The United States Supreme Court has indicated, however, that should an apportionment plan consistently prevent effective participation by a group of partisan voters, that is, actually deny them representation over a period of time (rather than in simply one election), it may well be unconstitutional. See: *Davis* v. *Bandemer*, 106 S. Ct. 2797 (1986).

6. *Gomillion* v. *Lightfoot*, 364 U.S. 339 (1960).

7. See decisions regarding congressional districts in *Shaw* v. *Reno* (1993), in which the Court invalidated use of a congressional district following Interstate 85 across the state for 160 miles to link black voters together; and *Miller* v. *Johnson* (1995), in which the Court upheld a lower court ruling that struck down a majority-black district extending some 250 miles across eastern Georgia.

8. Some lower courts, however, have held that both types of districts may not be used in the same plan because some people would have more legislators working for them than others.

9. Jesse Unruh, "One-House Advocated by Unruh," *National Civic Review* (May 1971): 253–254.

10. Unicameralism has been tested in only a few states and with inconclusive results. The system has worked well in Nebraska, in that the costs of lawmaking have been cut without leading to what might be called "hasty" legislation, and that citizen approval of the legislature's performance is comparable to that of approval rates in other states. Politics in Nebraska, however, seems to be low pressured, and the experiment may not be transferable to larger and more heterogeneous states. Generalization about Nebraska is also difficult because it is distinctive in its use of nonpartisan elections. See, generally: Adam C. Breckenridge, *One House or Two* (Lincoln: University of Nebraska Press, 1958); Richard D. Marvel, "A Member Looks at the Nebraska Unicameral," *State Government* (Summer 1969): 147–155; John P. Senning, *The One House Legislature* (New York: McGraw-Hill, 1937); and John C. Comer, "The Nebraska Nonpartisan Legislature: An Evaluation," *State and Local Review* (September 1980): 98–102.

11. In some states salaries are stipulated in the constitution. In others they are set by statute and or by a special compensation board or commission whose recommendations usually require voter approval. Salaries are highest where they have been set by commissions, second highest where set by statute, and lowest where set in the state constitution. On salary data, see current editions of *The Book of the States*. See also: Elder Witt, "Are Our Governments Paying What It Takes to Keep the Best and the Brightest," *Governing* (December 1988): 30–39.

12. See: Lester G. Seligman, "Political Recruitment and Party Structure," *American Political Science Review* 50 (March 1961): 85–86.

13. Malcolm E. Jewell, *The State Legislature: Politics and Practice* (New York: Random House, 1965), p. 42.

14. See: Alan Rosenthal, "And So They Leave: Legislative Turnover in the States," *State Government* 67 (Summer 1974): 148–152; and Alan Rosenthal, "Turnover in State Legislatures," *American Journal of Political Science* 18 (August 1974): 609–616. See also: James R. Oxendale Jr., "Membership Stability on Standing Committees in Legislative Lower Chambers," *State Government* 54 (1981): 126–129.

15. See: David Ray, "Membership Stability in Three State Legislatures: 1893–1969," *American Political Science Review* 68 (March 1974): 106–112. See also: Karl T. Kurtz, "No Change—For Change," *State Legislatures* (January 1989): 29–30.

16. Jack M. Treadway, "Adoption of Term Limits for State Legislators: An Update," *Comparative State Politics* 16 (June 1995): 1–6.

17. Timothy Hodson, Rich Jones, Karl Kurtz, and Gary Moncrief, "Leaders and Limits: Changing Patterns of State Legislative Leadership under Term Limits," *Spectrum* (Summer 1995): 6–15.

18. Susan Welch, Margery Ambrosius, Janet Clark, and Robert Darcey, "The Effect of Candidate Gender on Electoral Outcomes in State Legislative Races," *Western Political Quarterly* (September 1985): 464–475.

19. See: "Lawmakers' Abortion Votes Are Influenced by Gender," *Governing* (August 1989): 17. This is a report on a survey done by the Center for American Women and Politics at Rutgers University, which showed women were likely to be less opposed than men to abortion.

20. See, for example: Sue Thomas, "The Impact of Women on State Legislative Policies," *The Journal of Politics* 53 (1991): 958–976; and Michelle A. Saint-German, "Does Their Difference Make a Difference? The Impact of Women on Public Policy in the Arizona Legislature," *Social Science Quarterly* 70 (1989): 956–968. Some research suggests, however, that gender differences in regard to legislative activities and priorities are not large. See: Sue Thomas and Susan Welch, "The Impact of Gender on Activities and Priorities of State Legislators," *Western Political Quarterly* 44 (June 1991): 445–456.

21. The percentage of lawyers varies greatly from state to state: for example, it is high (over 40 percent) in New York, Texas, and Virginia, and low (only 2 percent) in Delaware and New Hampshire. In states like Idaho, Montana, North Dakota, and South Dakota, over 25 percent of the legislators have agricultural backgrounds. See: Otis White, "Making Laws Is No Job for Lawyers These Days," *Governing* (June 1994): 27–28.

22. James D. Barber, *The Lawmakers* (New Haven: Yale University Press, 1965).

23. *Ibid.*

24. See: Peverill Squire, "Member Career Opportunities and the Internal Organization of Legislators," *The Journal of Politics* 50 (August 1988): 726–744; and Peverill Squire, "Career Opportunities and Membership Stability in Legislatures," *Legislative Studies Quarterly* 13 (February 1988): 65–82.

25. In most of the states with annual sessions, the legislature is free to discuss or consider any topic it feels necessary. In some states, however, state legislatures devote every other session primarily to budgeting and fiscal matters.

26. Jewell, *The State Legislature,* p. 83.

27. See, generally: Alan Rosenthal, *Legislative Performance in the States: Exploration of Committee Behavior* (New York: The Free Press, 1974).

28. House committees in most states are appointed by the speaker of the house. Senate committees are appointed by the president of the senate, the president pro tem, a committee on committees (a small committee made up of the leaders of a political party), or (in Virginia) elected.

29. Jewell, *The State Legislature,* p. 79

30. *Ibid.*

31. See: *Staff and Services for State Legislatures* (New York: National Municipal League, 1968). On recent trends, see: Brian Weberg, "The Coming of Age for Legislative Staffs," *State Legislatures* (August 1988): 24–27.

32. See, generally: Alan P. Balutis, "The Role of the Staff in the Legislature: The Case of

New York," *Public Administration Review* 35 (July/August 1975): 355–363.

33. John C. Wahlke, "Organization and Procedure," in Alexander Heard, ed., *State Legislatures in American Politics* (Englewood Cliffs, N.J.: Prentice Hall, 1966), p. 145.

34. There is no absolute guarantee that all bills will be referred to a standing committee. Bills may be buried, as in Ohio, in a special reference committee. In some legislatures, important bills may be brought directly to the floor without the benefit of a standing committee's deliberation. See, generally: Rosenthal, *Legislative Performance*, ch. 1.

35. *Ibid.*

36. Royce Hanson, *The Tribune of the People: The Minnesota Legislature and Its Leadership* (Minneapolis: University of Minnesota Press, 1989).

37. William J. Keefe, "The Functions and Powers of State Legislatures," in Heard, ed., *State Legislatures*, p. 39. See also: Alan Rosenthal and Rod Forth, "There Ought to Be a Law," *State Government* (Spring 1978): 81–87.

38. See: Wayne L. Francis, *Legislative Issues in the Fifty States: A Comparative Analysis* (Chicago: Rand McNally, 1967).

39. See: John T. Scholz, "State Regulatory Reform and Federal Regulation," *Policy Studies Review* 1 (1982): 347–359; Donald L. Martin, "Will the Sun Set on Occupational Licensing?" *State Government* (Spring 1980): 63–67; *The Status of Sunset in the States: A Common Cause Report* (Washington, D.C.: Common Cause, 1982); and Richard C. Kearney, "Sunset: A Survey and Analysis of the State Experience," *Public Administration Review* 50 (January/February 1990): 49–63.

40. See: David R. Mayhew, *Congress: The Electoral Connection* (New Haven: Yale University Press, 1974).

41. Articles on the behavior of state legislators include: Robert M. Entman, "The Impact of Ideology on Legislative Behavior and Public Policy in the States," *The Journal of Politics* 45 (1983): 164–182; and David Ray, "The Sources of Voting Cues in Three State Legislatures," *The Journal of Politics* 44 (1982): 1074–1087.

42. See: James H. Kuklinski, "Representativeness and Elections: A Policy Analysis," *American Political Science Review* 72 (March 1978): 165–177.

43. See, for example: Anne H. Hopkins, "Public Opinion and Support for Public Policy in the American States," *American Journal of Political Science* 18 (February 1974): 167–177.

44. See: Helen M. Ingram, Nancy K. Laney, and John R. McCain, *A Policy Approach to Political Representation: Lessons from the Four Corners States* (Baltimore: Johns Hopkins University Press, 1980).

45. John T. Bragg, deputy speaker, Tennessee House of Representatives, "A View from the Commission," *Intergovernmental Perspective* (Summer 1988): 2.

46. See: Margery M. Ambrosius and Susan Welch, "State Legislators' Perceptions of Business and Labor Interests," *Legislative Studies Quarterly* 13 (May 1988): 199–209.

47. See, generally, on lobbying: L. Harmon Zeigler and Hendrik Van Dalen, "Interest Groups in the States," in Herbert Jacob and Kenneth N. Vines, eds., *Politics in the American States*, 2d ed. (Boston: Little, Brown, 1971), pp. 122–160.

48. L. Harmon Zeigler, "The Effects of Lobbying: A Comparative Assessment," *Western Political Quarterly* 22 (March 1969): 122–140.

49. See, generally: James S. Lee, "Toward an Understanding of State Legislative Decision-Making," in Richard H. Leach and Timothy G. O'Rourke, eds., *Dimensions of State and Urban Policy Making* (New York: Macmillan, 1975), pp. 156–175.

50. John C. Wahlke and Leroy C. Ferguson, "Rules of the Game," in Wahlke et al., *The Legislative System: Explorations and Legislative Behavior* (New York: John Wiley & Sons, 1962), pp. 141–169.

51. *Ibid.*

52. See, generally: Samuel C. Patterson, "American State Legislatures and Public Policy," in Herbert Jacob and Kenneth N. Vines, eds., *Politics in the American States*, 3d ed. (Boston: Little, Brown, 1976), pp. 162–165; and Merle Black, David M. Kovenock, and William C. Reynolds, *Political Attitudes in the Nation and States* (Chapel Hill: Institute for Research in Social Science, University of North Carolina, 1974), pp. 174–176. See also: Charles W. Dunn and Samuel K. Gove, "Legislative Reform Vacuum: The Illinois Case," *National Civic Review* (October 1972): 441–446; and Samuel C. Patterson, Ronald D. Hedlund, and G. Robert Boynton, *Representatives and Represented* (New York: John Wiley & Sons, 1975), which is a study of support for the Iowa legislature; and "Statestats: The Poor Public Attitude toward the Legislature," *State Legislatures* (April 1995): 5.

53. See the discussion of citizen attitudes and participation in chapter 1.

6

★ ☆ ☆

GOVERNORS AND ADMINISTRATORS IN STATE POLITICS

The American governor is usually the most visible figure in state politics and often the single most important influence on state policy. Much of the actual work of state government is done by administrative agencies, which are deeply involved in state policy matters. This chapter begins with an overview of the office of governor and the governor's role in regard to policy development and administration. The discussion then turns to the policy roles of administrators and an examination of state personnel systems and problems.

THE OFFICE OF GOVERNOR

DEVELOPMENT OF THE OFFICE

In the colonial period, the governor, usually appointed by the Crown, had a great deal of authority. The governor could call the colonial assembly into session, dissolve it, recommend legislation, and exercise the power of veto. In addition, the governor had full appointive powers, acted as commander-in-chief of the colony's military forces, and served as the head of the highest court within the colony. In time, the governor became a main target of the colonists' dislike of the Crown. This contributed to an emphasis on legislative supremacy in the first state constitutions. In all states but two, New York and Massachusetts, the governor was elected by the legislature rather than the voters. In seven states, the governor was given only a one-year term, and only in New York and Massachusetts did this official have the power to veto legislation.

With the faltering of state legislatures and the growing demands on state governments, the status of governors improved. By the first quarter of the nineteenth century, all governors were popularly elected and their terms and veto powers had been greatly expanded. The new strength of the office, however, was to be diluted in later years under the influence of Jacksonian Democracy and the Progressive movement. Jacksonian Democracy fostered the belief that public officials should be elected rather than appointed and that democracy depended not only on how many people could vote but also on how many offices they could vote for. These beliefs contributed to the adoption of the *long ballot*, which called for the direct election of nearly every executive official. Progressives around the turn of the century continued this trend in the belief that the direct election of officials (even the state printer) would make these officials more accountable to the public and reduce the danger of corruption.

Since the 1960s, the office has become slightly stronger in regard to such legal-institutional characteristics as terms, appointive powers, and budget powers.[1] Governors, in general, enjoy longer terms, greater ability to appoint and remove officials (though these are still limited), and more formal authority over putting together spending and revenue plans. The office also has improved in regard to what are called *enabling resources,* such as staff assistance, access to information, and having time to make decisions, for example, to develop a state budget document.

Too much should not be made, however, of these changes in the strength of the gubernatorial office. In areas like professional staffing, the gains made by gubernatorial offices have been matched by gains made by state legislatures, reducing whatever gains the governor might have made at the expense of the legislature. Governors also have increasingly had to cope with divided government—the fact that one or both of the legislative houses are controlled by the opposition. Governors and legislatures have essentially coequal status and, at any given time and place, may be embroiled in bitter conflict. On the administrative side, compared with the president of the United States, most contemporary governors continue to be "weak" executives in that they have less official authority over the administration of the laws.

There is, of course, considerable variation among governors in the strength of the office and their influence on state policy. An indication of the variation among the states in regard to the enabling and institutional resources of the governors is presented in table 6–1. It suggests that governors in Maryland, West Virginia, Illilnois, Kentucky, Massachusetts, New Mexico, Nebraska, New York, Pennsylvania, and South Dakota enjoy both relatively strong institutional

TABLE 6-1   Gubernatorial Enabling and Institutional Resources,
Contingency Table, 1990–1991

		Enabling Resources		
	Very Strong	Strong	Moderate	Weak
Very Strong		Maryland, West Virginia		
Strong		Illinois, Kentucky, Massachusetts, Nebraska, New Mexico, New York, Pennsylvania, South Dakota	Arkansas, California, Hawaii, Louisiana, Michigan, North Dakota, Ohio, Tennessee, Utah	Georgia, Iowa
Moderate	Vermont	Alaska, Arizona, Connecticut, Delaware, Kansas, Maine, Minnesota, Montana, New Hampshire, New Jersey, North Carolina, Rhode Island, Wyoming	Alabama, Colorado, Florida, Idaho, Missouri, Nevada, Oklahoma, Texas, Virginia, Washington, Wisconsin	Indiana, Oregon
Weak			Mississippi	South Carolina

(left vertical axis label: Institutional Resources)

Source: Robert J. Dilger, "A Comparative Analysis of Gubernatorial Enabling Resources," *State and Local Government Review* (Spring 1995): 125. Reprinted with permission of the author and the Carl Vinson Institute of Government, University of Georgia.

resources and relatively strong enabling resources. On the other hand, the governor of Mississippi has only moderate enabling resources and weak institutional resources, and the governor of South Carolina is weak in both respects.

Though variations in institutional and enabling resources help explain differences in the ability of governors to be effective leaders, research suggests these may not be as important as the personal characteristics of the governors as individuals (for example, their experience in elective office, personalities, and governing style).[2] As with other chief executives, the chief resource of the modern governor is persuasion—the use of charm, reason, solid arguments, and the status of the office to make it difficult for those he or she must deal with to say no.[3] Governors vary greatly in the possession of this power and their ability to use it.

Perhaps more important than formal authority in explaining the overall growing prominence of governors in state politics has been the emergence of a new breed of governors, more professional and reform-minded, and that governors most naturally fill the need for the type of statewide political leadership necessary to tackle increasingly complex problems.[4]

ACTIVITIES AND FUNCTIONS

Survey information suggests that governors spend the largest portion of their time managing state governments, for example, meeting with departmental officials and working on budgeting matters. Working with the legislature, meeting the general public, and ceremonial functions also claim substantial shares of the governors' time. Of all their tasks, however, governors rank working with the legislature as the most difficult and demanding aspect of their job.[5]

In addition to involvement with legislation and administration (discussed below), the governor also serves as chief-of-state and commander-in-chief and makes quasi-judicial decisions on the fate of those accused or convicted of crimes. As chief-of-state, the governor represents the state on important formal occasions and in dealings with other states or the national government. The Washington role has been important to the governor's political career and to the fiscal affairs of his or her state. In recent years, governors also have become visible in representing their states in the international arena—to find foreign markets for locally produced goods or to attract foreign investment into a state.[6]

The governor, as commander-in-chief, has control over the state police (discussed in a later chapter) and the National Guard, except when the president calls the Guard into the service of the national government. Governors have activated the Guard (formerly called the militia), for example, to perform rescue and relief missions in the event of a natural disaster or to enforce the law in cases of civil disorder such as the Detroit ghetto riots in 1967 and the campus disturbances at Kent State University in May 1970. The latter confrontation resulted in the death of four students who had demonstrated against the war in Southeast Asia. In the late 1980s, several governors exerted their control over the Guard to block training assignments of these units in Central America. Congress responded, however, with legislation prohibiting governors from vetoing training exercises on the basis of location.

Quasi-judicial functions are performed by the governor in granting or refusing to grant reprieves (delays in the execution of a criminal sentence), commutations (alteration of a punishment to make it less severe), pardons,

---

Box 6–1 The Governor and the Death Penalty

"In my eight years as governor, I was obliged to consider 59 death-penalty cases. I granted clemency by commuting the sentences of 23 of them to life imprisonment without possibility of parole, far more than any previous governor of California. . . .

"A few of those people went on to leave prison because of changes or loopholes in the law and lead normal, successful, productive lives. One man whose life I spared eventually got out of prison and killed a woman. Even now, twenty-five years later, I still can't decide whether I would have let those 23 prisoners die, if it meant saving the life of that one woman."

Source: Edmund G. ("Pat") Brown, governor of California in the 1960s, with Dick Adler, "Private Mercy,"*Common Cause Magazine* (July/August 1989): 29.

---

and extradition. Quasi-judicial functions, such as determining whether an execution should proceed as scheduled, vest governors with responsibilities that, it appears, many would just as soon not have (see box 6–1).

During the Progressive period in American politics, governors often took the lead on penal reform. Governors, in recent years, however, have often found it wise to take a "get tough" stand on penal matters. Many have found that opposition to the death penalty is an unpopular stand. Liberal use of the pardoning power also may lead to electorally damaging charges that the governor is soft on crime and favors an open-door policy at the penitentiary. On some occasions, governors have also been accused of using their pardoning power in exchange for money or political support. Charges of receiving money for pardoning or commuting sentences, though very rare in the last several decades, were made against the governor of Tennessee in the late 1970s.[7]

CONDITIONS OF THE OFFICE

Qualifications and other conditions of the office of governor, such as terms, removal, succession, and compensation, are spelled out in state constitutions and laws. The essential nature of these provisions can be summarized as follows:[8]

1. *Qualifications.* Governors must be qualified voters, citizens of the United States, of a certain age (usually over thirty), and have lived in their states a certain time (usually five years).

2. *Terms.* Over the last two decades, there has been a sharp increase in the number of governors serving four-year terms. Currently, governors in forty-eight states have four-year terms, compared with only nineteen states in 1960. However, twenty-eight states limit the number of terms a governor can serve to two.

3. *Removal and succession.* In all states except Oregon the governor may be impeached, and in thirteen states the governor may be removed from office by recall. Only one governor has actually been recalled and only four governors have been impeached, convicted, and removed from office (the last one was the governor of Arizona in 1987) in the twentieth century. If a governor should leave office for any reason, he or she is succeeded by the lieutenant governor in thirty-nine states, even though the lieutenant governor may, by virtue of a separate election, be a member of the opposite political party. In states where there is no lieutenant governor, the governor is usually succeeded by a statewide elected official, often the secretary of state, who may also belong to a different political party.

4. *Compensation.* The salary of the governor may be fixed by the state constitution, by statute, or by a special commission. Although salaries have increased in recent years (to an average of around $87,000), they are low in view of the full-time duties of the office and the fact that it may have cost the governor several times that amount to get elected.

Governors, particularly in large states, have several political and administrative aides. These people may include staff members somewhat like those found in the White House Office, those who work with the legislature, those who do liaison work with administrative agencies, and those who function as personal aides to the governor, such as appointment secretaries and press secretaries.

Research shows that governors' professional staff members tend to be in their late thirties (median age is thirty-eight) and well educated, with political experience and ambitions. Most of them participated in election campaigns either for the governor or for some other candidate of the same party. Office or staff positions attract many lawyers—perhaps more than 50 percent of all key staff personnel are lawyers. There are also professional planners, engineers, and political scientists for specific projects and a number of people with journalistic backgrounds for speechwriting and public relations tasks.[9] Looking at trends in the demographics of gubernatorial staffs, one finds a growth in the percentage who are female and in the percentage who have had backgrounds in public administration.

Staff members are generally the personal appointees of the governors. Party leaders and others play a minimal, if any, role in their selection. Staff personnel tend to have intense loyalties to the governor. They are willing to put in long hours of hard work and remain personally anonymous while building the image of the governor. Some research suggests that there is a difference in the way Republican and Democratic governors organize their staffs. Republicans, according to one analysis, have more specialized and larger staffs organized in a more formal and hierarchical manner.[10]

THE GOVERNORS

What types of people have served as governors? What have been their career patterns? Historically, the "average" governor has been white, male, middle-aged, a native of his state, a college graduate, a family man, a veteran, and an attorney by profession.[11]

In career patterns, governors have most often started in state legislatures or in the field of law enforcement; many have served as prosecuting attorneys. Several people have jumped from the state legislature directly to the governorship. Many others have been lieutenant governors or holders of another statewide elective office, such as secretary of state or attorney general, immediately before becoming governor. Although the significance of the different paths people have taken to the office of governor is not altogether clear, experience in state legislative work immediately before becoming governor may be of particular value to governors. With this experience, they come to office with a broad view of the state's current problems, knowledge about how the system works, and familiarity with many of the people, legislators and administrators, with whom they have to work.[12]

Governors in about half the states run together with a lieutenant governor, in some cases in both the primary and general election.[13] Turnover in gubernatorial positions appears to be rather high. Historically, as a group, governors have served fewer years in office than secretaries of state or many other directly elected state officials.[14] Governors in recent years also have been more electorally vulnerable than United States senators. Research suggests that this is because governors receive more media coverage, much of which is negative in nature.[15]

Though incumbent governors still enjoy substantial advantages in getting reelected, voters tend to hold them responsible for bad things that happen "on their watch" (term of office). Rejections of incumbents have sometimes been associated with declining economic conditions and unpopular tax efforts. In gubernatorial elections generally, whether or not an incumbent is involved, the partisan composition of the electorate is usually the strongest influence on outcomes.[16] In some elections, issues such as abortion policy can also weigh heavily with the voters.[17]

Following service as governor, many have run for and been elected to the United States Senate. A number of governors have also been given presidential appointments to cabinet, ambassadorial, or judicial positions. Over much of the nation's history, governors, particularly but not exclusively of large states, have been considered prime candidates for the office of president. The campaigns of former governors Jimmy Carter of Georgia, Ronald Reagan of California, and Bill Clinton of Arkansas have been advanced on the grounds that the managerial experience gained as governor is essential to a successful performance of the job of president. For much of the period following World War II, however, holding a national office such as vice president or membership in the United States Senate has functioned more often than a governorship as the immediate stepping-stone to the White House. The principal advantage of electing these types of officials compared to governors is their "insider's" knowledge of Washington and greater familiarity with national issues, especially foreign policy.

THE GOVERNOR AND STATE POLICY

INVOLVEMENT IN POLICY MATTERS

Under separation-of-powers principles, governors function largely to implement the policy decided on by state legislatures. In actuality, the office of governor has evolved into the central state institution for the initiation of legislative policy. Policy formulation activities of the governor revolve around putting together legislative proposals and attempting to secure their adoption in the legislature. The modern governor is "constantly engaged in exposition, either proposing, explaining, or justifying his programs."[18] In most states, governors spend the bulk of their scheduled time working with legislators and administrators and communicating with the public on matters of public policy.

The involvement of governors in the formulation of public policy results in part because they are elected political figures with promises to keep (for example, tax cuts, welfare shake-ups, or the support of branch colleges) and a constituency to please. State legislatures, moreover, generally lack the time, expertise, and resources to deal with the increasingly complex problems facing them and, like Congress, have become dependent on the recommendations of the executive and, through him or her, professional administrators.

No governor, of course, has the time or the inclination to devote a great amount of attention to every aspect of state policy. Many administrative agencies operate more or less the same way in basic programs, no matter who is governor. Agencies to which the governor pays the closest attention are those concerned with major state functions, those that are currently of political importance, and those of personal interest to him or her. Agencies concerned with highways, education, and welfare fall into the first category and very often into the second category as well. State agencies concerned with economic development are also of frequent interest because of the common role of governors as industrial promoters and recruiters for the state. On some occasions, the governor may take a personal interest in a relatively minor state agency. For example, a governor who is an enthusiastic outdoors person may well become concerned with activities of the department of wildlife and conservation.[19]

In dealing with state legislatures, governors typically use a *selective strategy* in recommending legislation. That is, they propose only a relatively few major measures that appear to have a good chance of being adopted. Governors confine their legislative interests to matters of particular importance to them (much legislation is not) and are aware that an attempt to overwhelm the legislature on a wide range of topics may conflict with the image of legislative independence and cause an adverse reaction.[20]

Influencing the Legislature

Governors outline their legislative program in a "state of the state" message given at the beginning of each legislative session. This message is followed up with specific proposals drafted in a stage agency, which are introduced by one of the governor's spokespeople in the legislature. Governors usually maintain regular contact with legislative leaders while the legislature is in session. Most governors, as a standing rule, have an open-door policy that allows legislators (especially of their own party) to see them almost any time they want. Often, however, much of the liaison burden is placed on staff assistants in the governor's office, most of whom have had previous legislative experience or contact.

Two formal powers available to governors in influencing legislative activity involve special sessions and vetoes. If the governor calls a special session, he or she has control over what will be considered. The legislators must leave their homes and jobs to attend the session. Just by threatening a special session the governor may force action during a regular session. On the other hand, calling a special session may antagonize the legislators and, since the governor puts his or her prestige on the line when a session is held, embarrassment can result if his or her proposals are not accepted.

In most states, every act passed by the legislature must be presented to the governor for acceptance or rejection. If a governor vetoes an act, most states require more than a majority vote of the entire membership of both houses to override the veto. One-fourth of the states give the governor a *pocket veto* under which an act passed at the end of the legislative session must be signed before it can go into effect—if not signed by the governor, it is vetoed. A half-dozen states give the governor the power of executive amendment under which, as an alternative to vetoing an act, he or she can resubmit it to the legislature with the governor's amendments or readopt the legislation in its original form. The executive amendment is a more positive instrument than the traditional veto.

Another type of veto found in the states is the *item veto*. This device, found in one form or another in forty-three states, is used to reject items contained in appropriation bills.[21] In twelve states the governor may reduce as well as eliminate appropriation items. Wisconsin has a unique "partial" system that allows the governor to veto letters and punctuation in budget bills and to make up new words with the letters left over from the vetoed sections. Theoretically, an appropriation for "cattle" could become one for "ale" by striking the *t*s and the *c* in "cattle".[22] In all states item vetoes can be overriden by an extraordinary vote (usually two-thirds) of the legislature.

The item veto gives the governor a greater opportunity to reduce the general level of spending. While some governors have used the item veto for this purpose, perhaps more often governors have used it simply as a means to eliminate or reduce expenditures for programs they oppose. There is little or no evidence, moreover, that the item veto power generally restrains state spending.[23] Governors are often frustrated in using the device because appropriation bills are skillfully written to make it difficult for the governor to ink out appropriations he or she dislikes. To some extent the goal of reducing overall expenditures is also frustrated because legislators, anticipating that the governor will be looking for items to veto, pad the bills with appropriations they would not otherwise include. As with the regular veto, however, a governor can use the threat of an item veto to bargain with legislative leaders or individual legislators.[24]

Governors seldom use the veto, traditional or item. On average, they use the traditional veto on only about 5 percent of the bills passed by the legislature. The legislature overrides only about 6 percent of the vetoed measures. The percentage is low because the governor can usually count on one-third of the legislature to support his or her position (it takes two-thirds for an override) and because many vetoes occur after the legislature has adjourned and has no chance to override them. Gubernatorial vetoes, however, have been more likely to be overridden in recent decades. In the 1940s, for example, less than 2 percent of such vetoes were overridden. The chief reason for this change may be that recent governors have been more likely to be confronted with legislatures that are controlled by the opposite political party.[25]

Among the informal means by which governors can influence legislators are party ties, the judicious use of patronage, and appeals to public opinion. The opportunity for a governor to use his or her party leadership to influence legislation is greatest in a competitive, two-party state where his or her party is cohesive and has a majority in both branches of the legislature. When faced with a legislature dominated by the opposite party, on the other hand, governors are forced to build bipartisan coalitions to secure support for their programs. Beyond this they can rely on their veto power or ability to mobilize public opinion in their favor.

In an ideal (and seldom realized) party situation, the governor may be able to choose the top legislative leaders, play a direct role in the planning of

---

BOX 6–2 A SPECIAL PERK

Governors in some states have had rather unique resources. In Arkansas, for example, governors have had the opportunity to distribute free passes to a popular race track at Hot Springs. Legislators on the good side of the governor have received their share and have passed them on to grateful constituents. Though only worth a dollar each, both the Arkansas press and bemused gubernatorial aides have speculated, only semifacetiously, that the passes have helped account for more gubernatorial bills than any other factor.

Source: Diane D. Blair, *Arkansas Politics & Government* (Lincoln: University of Nebraska Press, 1988), p. 142.

---

legislative strategy, and even control nominations to some extent by getting someone to run in a legislative primary against lawmakers who have not supported him or her. Short of this type of control, the governor may be greatly aided in dealing with the legislature by his or her popularity with the voters and the fact that he or she helped bring many legislators in the party into office on the strength of their vote. Legislators may well see their futures bound to the popularity of a governor who shares the same party identification and thus be more than willing to cooperate with the chief executive. Governors, in turn, sometimes actively campaign on behalf of members of their party seeking seats in the legislature. Though some risk is involved, for example, a loss of prestige in backing losing candidates, it can also be an effective way of gaining influence in the legislature.[26]

Despite limitations on his or her appointive powers, the governor makes some four hundred appointments to regular state positions and has additional opportunities to make scores of other appointments to advisory boards and commissions. Generally, patronage can be more important to a governor than to the president because of the comparatively limited use of the merit system on the state level. Patronage is particularly important in low-income states, where a state job takes on special economic importance. In addition to jobs, governors often have effective if not formal influence over the awarding of contracts and the location of projects such as roads, hospitals, and parks. The location of such projects and patronage decisions are often important to legislators in building up support in their districts. The governor's decisions on these and other matters (see box 6–2) thus can be used to make friends in the legislature.

Most studies give governors high batting averages on securing the acceptance of measures proposed to the legislature, though many proposals may be eventually passed in watered-down form. One study of fourteen states, for example, found that legislatures passed 71 percent of the programs proposed by governors. Success in these states appeared greatest where the governor's party controlled both houses of the legislature and where the governor used the selective strategy described above. Success was also related, but only slightly, to the governor's vote-getting ability (that is, winning by a large margin).[27]

The Governor and Administration

Strengthening the Position of the Governor

Since the turn of the century, there has been a persistent effort to streamline the organizational structure of state government and concentrate executive authority in the governor. Scholars often referred to this effort as the *administrative reform movement*. As indicated in chapter 1, the movement has reflected managerial values as opposed to those centering on legislative supremacy or direct popular control.

The first wave of efforts to achieve administrative reform in the states was stimulated by President William Howard Taft's Commission on Economy and Efficiency, which, from 1910 to 1912, studied the problems of reorganization of the executive branch of the national government. The work of the commission stimulated the first major state reorganization in Illinois under the leadership of Governor Frank Lowden in 1917. Lowden consolidated fifty-four independent agencies into fourteen and placed most of them under the control of the governor. Several states in the 1920s and 1930s followed this example, and by the beginning of World War II, about thirty states had undergone significant reorganizations.

Reorganization efforts were renewed in the 1950s with the creation in some states of Little Hoover Commissions, which were patterned after the National Commission on Organization of the Executive Branch of the Government, chaired by former President Herbert Hoover. Little Hoover Commissions, essentially study and advisory boards, were established in thirty-five states. Some progress was made toward reorganization in states like New Hampshire and New Jersey, but most commissions encountered resistance to their recommendations in the legislatures. Since the reapportionment revolution of the mid-1960s, a new wave of state executive reorganization has taken place.[28]

The principal objective of the administrative reform movements through the years has been to make the transition from a fragmented governmental structure to a structure under the administrative control of the governor. Improving the administrative control of the governor has been taken to involve three basic steps. The first of these is to abolish or relocate agencies, boards, and commissions headed by elected officials other than the governor and other bodies removed from direct gubernatorial control. Under most proposals, only the governor and the lieutenant governor (or a comparable officer) would be vested with direct electoral responsibility. They would be elected on the same ticket. The result of this would be a *short ballot* such as that found on the national level, where the only executive officials directly elected are the president and the vice president. The short ballot is defended on the grounds that it not only fosters administrative efficiency but also relieves what some have felt to be an unfair burden on the electorate.

In the second step, all agencies are grouped together into a small number of departments (from ten to twenty) organized around basic functions and headed by a single administrator subject to gubernatorial appointment and removal. The department heads constitute the governor's cabinet. The governor would be at the head of a rational and streamlined administrative system. Overlapping jurisdictions among agencies would be eliminated, and a clear system of communication and responsibility would be achieved in a hierarchical fashion.

A third step in the reform package is improving the governor's staff resources and providing the governor with the ability to supervise such matters as finance, personnel, and purchasing for the entire administrative system. Reformers envision the type of assistance found in the White House Office and the Office of Management and Budget nationally.

The program of the state reorganization movement is aimed at increasing the coordination of state activity, eliminating waste and inefficiency, and enabling states to tackle more effectively the problems they face. Reorganized state governments are also considered more accountable because the voters are able to hold the governor responsible for what state administrators do or fail to do.

Obstacles to Reorganization

Reformers have had to face three basic obstacles to reorganization: (1) the fear that the voters will lose basic democratic rights and a valuable means of checking governmental action if elective offices are abolished, (2) the fear that reorganization will concentrate too much authority in the hands of the governor, and (3) the belief that certain state functions at least should be "taken out of politics" or removed from gubernatorial control and influence. Opposition to reorganization on these and other grounds has come from voters whose consent is needed for constitutional changes, legislators, political party leaders, interest groups, elected administrative officials, and professional administrators.

The tradition of direct responsibility to the electorate has been particularly difficult to overcome. Voters are accustomed to voting for several state offices and consider them properly elective. Legislators may not wish to see elective offices abolished, especially if the offices in question are held by members of their own political party. Legislators may also see any reorganization that transfers control over administration to the governor as a threat to legislative supremacy, their party's interest, or their ability to influence administrators in the interests of their constituents or favorite groups. The long ballot has been of value to political party officials because it has given them more offices to fill and an opportunity to balance their tickets with representatives of various ethnic groups. Interest groups satisfied with the status quo may see reorganization as threatening their access to administrators and undermining support for their favorite programs. Constitutionally elected officials, of course, may be less than enthusiastic about losing their jobs, and many may be able to draw on a strong personal following to oppose the elimination of their offices.

Administrators who see themselves as professionals are apt to insist that their functions should be separate from "politics," meaning gubernatorial control. Reformers have long argued that the same type of influence should have no role in policy areas like education or those involving technical and quasi-judicial matters such as the regulation of public utilities.

PROGRESS AND CONTINUING PROBLEMS OF CONTROL

Despite political obstacles, there has been a long-range trend toward administrative integration and an upgrading of the formal powers of governors over administration. Most of the recent reorganizations, however, have not affected elected offices and have failed to disturb the status of the better-established boards or commissions.[29]

State governors thus continue to share their executive authority with several directly elected administrative officials. In half of the states, ten or more officials are directly elected by the voters. These include, in addition to the governor, the lieutenant governor, secretary of state, attorney general, treasurer, auditor, controller, superintendent of education, members of various commissions, and numerous other individuals.

In some ways, the governor is in a weaker position in dealing with independent department heads than in dealing with the legislature. The department heads are on the same level as the governor in that they represent a statewide electorate and are responsible only to the voters. The governors, in practice, generally keep at a respectful distance from other elected administrators. Not only are these administrators beyond the governor's control, they may also be members of the opposite political party or rivals within his or her own party for the affections of the electorate.[30]

Since the 1950s, over twenty states have changed their laws to require that the lieutenant governor and governor run on the same ticket. Many of the same states have also taken away the power of the lieutenant governor to preside in the senate. In this situation, the nature of the lieutenant governor's job depends on his or her relationship with the governor. Elsewhere the lieutenant governor is an independent actor. Being a member of a political party that differs from the governor's may mean little, if any, contact with the governor. As a Democratic lieutenant governor once noted about the Republican governor who served at the same time: "I was around the capitol for several months before he actually smiled at me in a hallway and seemed to recognize me."[31] In some states, however, the lieutenant governor, even of the opposite party, has a power base in the legislature. He or she not only frequently presides over the upper house but also in some states, mostly in the South, has the power to appoint legislative committees and to assign bills to committees.

In addition to the high number of independently elected officials, the governors' authority over administration is further limited by restrictions on their powers to appoint and remove administrators. Governors have full appointive powers over only perhaps 16 percent of the top state officials.[32] They often share what authority they have with the state legislature, whose confirmation is needed for appointment or removal, and with various boards and commissions that suggest or screen candidates. Governors often do not have a general power to remove even those they appoint to office. They usually can do so only for "cause," such as incompetence or dishonesty—not because the appointee disagrees with the governor on matters of policy. Because dismissal may require a politically embarrassing hearing, a governor may not even try to remove an administrator he or she finds to be unsatisfactory. Along with these limitations, governors seldom have had an opportunity to make a clean sweep of the bureaucracy during their stay in office because their terms are shorter than those of many administrators.

An important formal control most governors do have over state administration is in regard to budgeting. Under an executive budgeting system, state agencies must clear their spending proposals through the governor or budget official, who in turn submits a single budget request to the state legislature. Before the adoption of the executive budget, administrative agencies took it on themselves to go directly to the legislature to secure funds for their programs.

While executive budgeting has undoubtedly improved the managerial authority of governors, it has not resulted in a systematic and comprehensive review of agency programs. Fragmented government, of course, has meant that some governors have considerably less authority over departmental spending than does the president of the United States. In some states, the governor shares actual control over budget preparation with a civil service appointee, the legislature, and independent department heads through some type of board arrangement. Most governors, moreover, lack anything comparable to the Office of Management and Budget that assists the president in reviewing the budget requests and operations of federal agencies.

In a study of nineteen states some time ago, political scientist Ira

Sharkansky discovered that agencies sought an average of a 24 percent increase over their present budgets.[33] Governors trimmed an average of 14 percent from these proposals. Legislators tended to follow the governor's lead, though there was a range of an 8 percent cut below the governor's recommendations to an increase of 19 percent above his or her recommendations. By and large, state legislatures, because of their amateur, part-time, and fluid composition, and weak committee systems, were seen in no position to make a sophisticated review of agency requests. Because of this, they generally relied on the governor's recommendations.

The study suggested that both governors and legislators are apt to review agency requests less on the basis of programs and more in relation to changes in dollar amounts from the previous year's budget. Agencies that request a great increase over the previous year's budget are likely to encounter considerable resistance from the governor and legislature, especially if state expenditures and debt are already high. At the same time, if a substantial increase in an agency budget is to be made, it usually has to be initiated by the agency itself because governors and legislators seldom will give it more than it requests. The executives and legislators appeared more content in a limited role as reviewers of administrative proposals, preferring to let the agencies initiate and make the case for increases.

All in all, the case may be made that governors, in general, do not dominate the administrative branch of state government. This seems to be due not only to a lack of formal powers but also to the inclination of governors to look upon their role as chief administrator to be one of management rather than one of policy leadership. Within the limitations of their powers, governors do appear to be quite active in attempting to manage the operations of state agencies in the interest of economy and efficiency. Governors, however, appear to be generally less concerned about the substance of agency programs. Perhaps reflecting the values found in the business world and traditional public administration theory, "governors prefer low conflict and efficient management over the active use of administration to affect their own policy goals and objectives."[34]

For whatever reason, survey data indicate that state department heads generally consider the legislature to have far more influence than the governor on the programs and objectives of their departments. In addition to the legislature, the governor has shared influence over the programs offered by state agencies with federal and local administrators, interest groups, and other governmental actors.[35]

ADMINISTRATORS, POLICY, AND THE PUBLIC

Administrative agencies receive the bulk of their authority from legislative statutes. Statutory law may leave little discretion to the administrator, as in the case where only the payment of a fee is required to prompt administrative action. More commonly, however, the administrator is given wide discretion in interpreting such terms as "reasonable," "adequate," or "reputable" in the statute. An agency may also be authorized to use its expertise and powers of investigation to devise standards, such as the qualifications necessary for cab drivers, or to recommend new policies to the legislature. In all these situations, administrators and agencies are deeply involved in policy developments—making, supplementing, modifying, and initiating public policy. Often, the agencies find themselves bogged down in the fine details. As one authority has noted: "Unlike other political arts, such as legislating and policy making, in administration one deals not with the forest but with the trees—plus the bushes, shrubs, thorns, rocks and blades of grass."[36]

At the top of the administrative structure in the various states are "political executives," that is, people who are appointed by the governor to high-level positions and carry such titles as department heads, associate directors, and bureau or division chiefs. These people are part of the governor's management team. Each state also has a number of employees under civil service or merit systems over whom the governor has little direct control. The proportion of state government employees covered by such systems varies from state to state, being somewhat lower in southern states than in other regions of the country.[37]

Political executives are largely middle-aged white males, though there has been a decline in the average age (now forty-eight) and an increase in the percentage of women and minorities in recent years. Administrators also have become increasingly professional as measured by educational attainment. These executives, however, serve for only relatively short periods, with the average time being from three to four years.[38] While political executives come and go, people in the civil service typically enjoy long careers with state governments. Their formal role is one of *neutral competence,* that is, they are not supposed to make policy but to implement the policy objectives of whatever administration happens to be in power in a neutral and competent manner. Within any given agency, however, one is apt to find considerable tension as political executives attempt to gain control over those with civil service protections so that they are acting in accord with the governor's policy directives and, conversely, civil servants strive to protect their independence from politics and their ability to perform in what they see as a professional manner.

Conflict among agency personnel sometimes prompts one official to *blow the whistle* on another and publicly expose what he or she feels are unethical or illegal activities or inefficiencies within the organization, or to bring to the attention of the public policy decisions within the agency that may be dangerous or unwise. Whistle-blowers are given some protection in state law against retaliation for "committing truth."[39] Most administrators, however, are reluctant to blow the whistle on superiors, fearing this could interfere with their careers somewhere down the road (if not being outright fired because they have some protection against this, being passed over for promotion, or being transferred to an undesirable location). Partially for this reason, much whistle-blowing takes the form of informal "bootlegging" of information to newspaper reporters and others who do not reveal the source of their information.

PLAYING POLITICS

The administrative process is part of the broader political process, and one essential function of a major department head is to secure political support for his or her agency. This support is needed to protect the agency's status, appropriations, and authority (usually from the incursions of other agencies) and to promote policies of interest to the agency. Good relations are needed with legislative committees that have authority over the agency's appropriations and program areas. More than one legislature has vested an administrative agency with enormous responsibilities but has failed to provide it with adequate staff, finances, or enforcement powers. To secure these or expand into new areas, administrators lobby state legislatures. In many respects the lobbying activities of administrative agencies in the legislature resemble those of private interest groups. Among the agencies that appear to do the best are those, such as transportation departments, that are in a position to offer legislators services or projects for their districts.[40]

The nature of the political environment in which agencies operate depends on the character and political importance of their functions. If the principal activity is agriculture, farm groups and those with an immediate economic or professional interest in farming constitute the agency's clientele group. Governors, the legislature as a whole, the press, and the general public are directly concerned with the agency only when it is involved in a matter of political importance.

When agency-group relations are close, a group may help the agency in its dealings with the governor or legislature, influence the appointment of key agency personnel, and make direct inputs into administrative policymaking through advisory committees. The ultimate in agency-group cohesion is found in licensing boards for various occupations. These are usually dominated by those already in the profession, who use their authority to limit potential competition.

In the field of business regulation, administrative agencies appear to be involved in a life cycle of relations with their clientele groups. Agencies begin with great energy to tackle a problem and, finding much initial support from other public officials and the general public, proceed to take their law enforcement responsibilities seriously. Within a matter of time, however, public attention to the agency diminishes, and it settles down to routine and peaceful relations with those subject to regulation. Eventually, a clientele relationship develops, and it becomes difficult to distinguish between the objectives of those regulated and those who are supposed to regulate. Both agencies and business have a stake in achieving harmonious relations—the former to secure peaceful compliance and the latter to minimize the controls or secure benefits.[41]

RELATIONS WITH CITIZENS

Administrative relations with groups or individuals may also be characterized by conflict, misunderstanding, and hostility. Court action challenging an agency's authority or procedures is often the ultimate route taken by a discontented group. More generally, citizen complaints concern poor services, discourteous employees, or difficulties in cutting through red tape and other matters that do not seem to merit the time and expense of court action.

One reaction to the occurrence of these types of problems and to the growth of large and complex governmental agencies has been the adoption of the ombudsman concept. An *ombudsman* is a citizens' grievance representative employed by the state to answer inquires and investigate complaints against governmental officials. He or she is independent of any governmental agency. He or she may be able to initiate complaints but generally has no powers other than to publicize and recommend changes in administration. Currently only a handful of states have such an office. Adoption of the idea has been impeded, in part, by legislators who fear competition in handling constituents' complaints and by the natural reluctance of administrators to subject their activities to possible criticism.

PERSONNEL SYSTEMS AND PROBLEMS

Governmental employment on the basis of patronage (or political party affiliation) took root at the state level in the early nineteenth century. The "spoils system," associated with Jacksonian Democracy, led to an almost total turnover in governmental personnel with each change in party control of the governorship. Frequent turnover or rotation in office was defended by Jackson and his followers on the grounds that long tenure in administrative offices led administrators to get out of touch with ordinary people, if not to outright corruption. Spoils defenders disliked the notion of a permanent bureaucracy and disputed the notion that the demands of the work required a highly educated and well-trained elite, in effect, an officeholding class. Spoils, from their perspective, opened the door to governmental employment to ordinary people. For the governor there was the benefit of being surrounded by loyal employees.

On a more basic level, Jackson and others viewed their ability to make appointments as important in building both a personal following and strong political party organizations. Spoils provided a reward for campaign workers and thus an incentive for them to get involved. It also provided a source of party financial support through devices such as making assessments on governmental salaries for party funds, and gave party leaders a large body of public employees for use in campaigns and other party activities.

At the turn of the twentieth century, reformers condemned the spoils approach on the grounds that it brought corruption and incompetent personnel into the public service. The desire to both "throw the rascals out" and develop a politically neutral civil service was a central motivation of the Progressive reformers early in the twentieth century. As so often with political reform, efforts to secure change were given a boost by tragedy, in this case the assassination of President James Garfield in 1881 by a disappointed office seeker. Garfield's assassination intensified efforts to reform personnel systems at the state and local as well as the federal level. The major reform on the state and local levels was the creation of independent, multimembered civil service commissions to hire employees on the basis of merit rather than political affiliation. In addition, employees were to have tenure in their jobs and be protected by law from political pressures.

In recent years, personnel functions have been more commonly regarded as part of overall management, and duties such as recruitment, hiring, and promotion have been assumed in most jurisdictions by personnel directors accountable to the governor. Generally, key policymakers (major departmental and agency heads) are exempt from the classified service on the grounds they must be part of the governor's team and directly accountable to him or her. Many governors, often citing the need to streamline state government and save money, have sought to reduce the number of positions protected under civil service systems and to extend their authority to fire or relocate people holding these positions. To the extent this has happened, government administration has become more politicized.[42] Though, in fact, state employment has not generally diminished, considerable emphasis in state personnel offices has been placed on reducing the size of the state workforce.[43]

Since the early 1970s, state governments have made several other changes in their personnel systems. Chief among these have been: (1) enactment of pay systems in which performance rather than seniority is rewarded (that is, more bonuses than automatic salary increases); (2) creation of different agencies to hear employee grievances (for example, about removal, suspension, or pay) and to administer personnel policies; and, (3) as noted earlier, adoption of measures to protect whistle-blowers (especially those who publicly complain about waste and inefficiency in their agencies) from disciplinary action or dismissal. Drawing on the experience of the states, Congress incorporated these and other measures into a comprehensive civil service reform act passed in 1979 that affected the national bureaucracy.

One reform that has received only modest success in the states is the establishment of executive personnel systems to attract a small cadre of top-quality, high-talented, and high-paid generalists to bring innovation and change into state administration. A model is the Senior Executive Service created by Congress. The notion of such an elite category of administrators, however, has not been popular in the states. Nor has there been much willingness to provide the economic incentives to attract such individuals.[44]

POLITICAL RIGHTS AND EQUAL OPPORTUNITY

Three areas of concern in state personnel systems over the past several years have been the political rights of state employees; equal opportunity in hiring, promotion, and other personnel practices; and collective bargaining in the public sector. These problems are also found on the local level (and are discussed in chapter 10).

One of the most controversial issues of civil service has been the limitations imposed on the political activities of those in the classified service. Rules limiting forms of political activity are found in state legislation and personnel rules. Before 1975, limitations were also imposed under the federal Hatch Act, which applied to state and local employees whose employment was financed in whole or in part by federal loans or grants. Restrictions still in effect in various states prohibit state employees from running for political office, campaigning for or against a political party or candidate, distributing campaign material, marching in a political parade, and actively participating in fund-raising activities for a partisan candidate or political party. Similar prohibitions sometimes exist for nonpartisan campaigns and activity. Generally, the intent of such restrictions is to confine political activity of civil service employees to voting and private discussions.

These rules were designed not to punish public employees but rather to protect them from partisan political pressures and to help maintain the neutrality of the public service. On the other hand, pubic employee groups and others have challenged these restrictions as violating First Amendment freedoms and as creating second-class citizenship for public employees. Survey research suggests that as many as 40 percent of those working for the states under various types of merit plans would increase their political involvement if the restrictions were relaxed. This is particularly true of employees who are female, young, black, and affiliated with social service agencies.[45]

A second problem area concerns equal opportunity in hiring, promotion, and other personnel activities. States, as well as other levels of government and many private businesses, have been required by federal law to eliminate employment discrimination on the basis of race, creed, or sex and to adopt affirmative action practices in relation to women and minority groups. Proponents of equal opportunity have argued that minorities and women have long suffered discrimination in employment and should now be given preferential treatment. Others have countered that employment should be based only on merit and that such preferential treatment constitutes reverse discrimination against white males. In recent years, the United States Supreme Court has tended to lean toward this latter position, thus making it more difficult to justify affirmative action programs.

A related controversy has centered on the notion of comparable worth or, essentially, that there should be equal pay for those doing equal work or work of equivalent difficulty. Critics have argued that under the existing salary systems in most states, women receive less than men for the same work. Others have contended that "comparable worth" is not all that easy to determine and that pay rates are best set by market forces. It has also been contended that implementation of comparable worth standards in the mid-1980s could have cost state governments anywhere from $11 billion to $44 billion—costs equivalent to tax increases from 6 to 24 percent.[46]

Although the record on equal opportunity in the state and local sector falls short of the ideal, it is, by several measurements, better than that of the private sector. In the mid-1980s, white males composed around 58 percent of the private-sector workforce but only 48 percent of state and local employees. Not only are women and minorities better represented in the state and local sector, but the gap between their salaries and those of white males doing comparable work also appears to be less than it is in private employment.[47] Some research suggests that while women are rare in top-level administrative positions in state government, they are not necessarily isolated in male-dominated agencies—though there is some social separation from the "old boys' network" of informal interactions outside the workplace. It may well be, however, that women who do not fit in easily with men are not selected for such positions.[48]

COLLECTIVE ACTIVITY

Another major long-term development in the public service has been the organizing of public employees for purposes of bargaining or meeting and conferring over wages, hours, and working conditions. Close to 50 percent of all state and local government employees are in unions or associations that engage in collective bargaining. Two of the largest organizations are in the field of education: the National Education Association (NEA) and the American Federation of Teachers (AFT), each of which has state and local divisions. Rapid growth has also been experienced by the American Federation of State, County, and Municipal Employees (AFSCME), which is affiliated with the American Federation of Labor and Congress of Industrial Organizations (AFL-CIO), and a number of independent unions, many of which are affiliated with the Assembly of Government Employees. The most intensive unionization in recent years has been at the municipal level, particularly in the nation's largest cities. Unions have also been attracted by the size of the state and local employee group, now at some thirteen million persons. Extensive campaigns have been undertaken since the early 1960s to tap this potential membership. Generally, these efforts have been most successful in states where unionization has been most accepted in the private sector.[49]

A more general factor accounting for the appeal of unionization has been that state and local employees' wages have failed to keep up with the cost of living. Research indicates that public employees have joined unions primarily in an effort to secure increased salaries and fringe benefits (such as sick leave and health insurance) and greater job protection.[50] But in addition to obtaining these material benefits has been the desire for more representation in policymaking activities. Teachers, for example, have been concerned not simply with bargaining on wages and working conditions but also with influencing vital policy matters such as class size and curriculum. A final factor contributing to union organization has been the civil rights movement, which has inspired the numerous publicly employed blacks and other minorities to collective action.

Opponents of unionization have contended that it is not necessary because employees already have the merit system, civil service protections, and governmental employee organizations. It is also argued that unions interfere with management, threaten the civil service traditions (for example, having tenure related to seniority rather than merit), and could obstruct the introduction of technical improvements because they would threaten union-protected jobs.

Since the 1960s, forty states have adopted general public-sector bargaining acts that either require or authorize collective bargaining on both the state and local levels. The common law (judge-made) rule that a sovereign cannot make contracts with his or her employees has been superseded by such legislation. Many states, however, deny their public employees the right to strike either through statute or through common law, which regards strikes as a conspiracy against the public and thus illegal. However, such laws are not effective. Mass jailings, heavy fines, and harsh penalties such as suspension or termination for their violation are impractical and would, if enforced, hurt the employers as much as the striking employees. Teachers, refuse collectors, firefighters, police officers, and others have either bypassed the laws by work slowdowns and massive sick call-ins or have simply defied them. Though public-sector strikes have been relatively rare in recent years, from 1958 through 1976, more than eight thousand work stoppages involving more than four million workers occurred. Teacher unions led all other groups in the number of strikes called during this period.[51]

The turbulence caused by strike activity in the 1970s, particularly as it involved firefighters and police officers, prompted several states to adopt compulsory arbitration or "final-offer selection" legislation to resolve disputes. Police and firefighter contract disputes now commonly go to arbitration. Though settlement by an arbitrator avoids strike activity, it can also be costly to the city. Mayors, faced with heavy financial burdens, have sometimes felt they would have been better off trying to weather a strike. Some observers have argued there is a need to remove no-strike provisions from the law—legislatures in ten states have done so for certain categories of employees, and judicial decisions have had a similar effect in three other states. Reformers argue that the law should extend the same rights to public employees that are enjoyed by those in the private sector. From this perspective, governments should prohibit strikes because of their detrimental effect on the economy or public welfare rather than simply because the employees are in the public sector. Employees of private transit companies and hospitals, for example, can strike, while their counterparts who work for the public cannot.[52]

ENDNOTES

1. See, for example: Thad Beyle, "The Institutionalized Powers of the Governorship: 1965–1985," *Comparative State Politics Newsletter* (February 1988): 23–29.
2. Thad L. Beyle, "Enhancing Executive Leadership in the States," *State and Local Government Review* 27 (Winter 1995): 18–53.
3. On the president's use of persuasion, see: Richard E. Neustadt, *Presidential Power* (New York: John Wiley and Sons, 1960).
4. For a discussion of long-term developments in the office of governor, see: Larry Sabato, *Goodbye to Good-Time Charlie: The American Governor Transformed* (Lexington, Mass.: Lexington Books, 1978). See also: Eric B. Herzik and Brent W. Brown, eds., *Gubernatorial Leadership and State Policy* (Westport, Conn.: Greenwood Press, 1991).
5. Thad L. Beyle, "The Governor as Chief Legislator," *State Government* (Winter 1978): 2–10.
6. See, generally: John Kincaid, "The American Governors in International Affairs," *Publius: The Journal of Federalism* 14 (Fall 1985): 95–114; John M. Kline, "The Expanding International Agenda for State Governments," *State Government* 57 (1984): 2–6; and Dennis O. Grady, "Governors and Economic Development Policy: The Perception of Their Role and the Reality of Their Influence," *Policy Studies Journal* 17 (Summer 1989): 879–894.
7. See: Larry Sabato, "Gubernatorial Clemency: A Time of Trial?" *State Government* (Winter 1980): 40–43.
8. See current editions of the *Book of the States* (Lexington, Ky.: Council of State Governments, annual).
9. See: Donald P. Sprengel, *Gubernatorial Staffs: Functional and Political Profiles* (Iowa City: Institute of Public Affairs, University of Iowa, 1969), reprinted in part in Donald P. Sprengel, ed., *Comparative State Politics: A Reader* (Columbus, Ohio: Charles E. Merrill, 1971), pp. 308–330; and Alan J. Wyner, "Staffing the Governor's Office," *Public Administration Review* (January/February 1970): 17–24.
10. Sprengel, *Gubernatorial Staffs.*
11. See: Samuel R. Solomon, "Governors: 1960–1970," *National Civic Review* (March 1971): 126–146.
12. Sabato, *Goodbye to Good-Time Charlie*, p. 34.
13. Forty-three states have the office of lieutenant governor. In eight states candidates

for governor and lieutenant governor run together in both primary and general elections. In sixteen other states, they run together only in the general election. Candidates for governor and lieutenant governor in the remaining nineteen states are elected on separate ballots. See: Laura M. Zaremba, "Governor and Lieutenant Governor on Same Ballot," *Comparative State Government* 15 (February 1994): 39–40.

14. See: Joseph A. Schlesinger, *How They Became Governor* (East Lansing: Governmental Research Bureau, Michigan State University, 1957).

15. See: Peverill Squire and Christina Fastnow, "Comparing Gubernatorial and Senatorial Elections," *Political Research Quarterly* 47 (September 1994): 705–720; and Kim Fridkin Kahn, "Characteristics of Press Coverage in Senate and Gubernatorial Elections: Information Available to Voters," *Legislative Studies Quarterly* 20 (February 1995): 23–35.

16. Among the works on the topic are: Patrick J. Kenney, "The Effects of State Economic Conditions on the Vote for Governor," *Social Science Quarterly* 64 (1983): 154–162; Thomas M. Holbrook-Provow, "National Factors in Gubernatorial Elections," *American Politics Quarterly* 15 (1987): 471–483; John E. Chubb, "Institutions, the Economy, and the Dynamics of State Elections," *American Political Science Review* 82 (1988): 133–154; Robert M. Stein, "Economic Voting for Governor and U.S. Senator: The Electoral Consequences of Federalism," *The Journal of Politics* 52 (1990): 29–53; Peverill Squire, "Challenger Profile and Gubernatorial Elections," *Western Political Quarterly* 45 (March 1992): 125–142; and Richard G. Niemi, Harold W. Stanley, and Ronald J. Vogel, "State Economies and State Taxes: Do Voters Hold Governors Accountable?" *American Journal of Political Science* 39 (November 1995): 936–957.

17. See: Elizabeth Adell Cook, Ted G. Jelen, and Clyde Wilcox, "Issue Voting in Gubernatorial Elections: Abortion and Post-Webster Politics," *The Journal of Politics* 56 (February 1994): 187–199.

18. Ronald D. Michaelson, "An Analysis of the Chief Executive: How the Governor Uses His Time," *State Government* (Summer 1972): 159.

19. See, generally: Alan J. Wyner, "Gubernatorial Relations with Legislators and Administrators," *State Government* (Summer 1968): 199–203.

20. *Ibid.*

21. Only in the state of Washington does the authority apply to any type of legislation. See: Calvin Bellamy, "Item Veto: Dangerous Constitutional Tinkering," *Public Administration Review* (January/February 1989): 46–51.

22. Tony Hutchison, "Legislating via Veto," *State Legislatures* (January 1989): 20–22.

23. David C. Nice, "The Item Veto and Expenditure Restraint," *The Journal of Politics* 50 (1988): 487–499.

24. Ronald C. Moe, *Prospects for the Item Veto at the Federal Level: Lessons from the States* (National Academy of Public Administration, 1988).

25. Charles W. Wiggins, "Executive Vetoes and Legislative Overrides in the American States," *The Journal of Politics* 42 (1980): 1110–1117.

26. See, for example: Jayne C. Strachan, "Mario Cuomo and New York Legislative Campaigns," *Comparative State Politics* 16 (June 1995): 13–22.

27. Wyner, "Gubernatorial Relations."

28. On reform efforts and obstacles, see: York Wilbern, "Administration in State Gov-

ernments," in *The Forty-Eight States: Their Tasks as Policy Makers and Administrators* (New York: American Assembly, 1955), ch. 5; and A.E. Buck, *The Reorganization of State Governments* (New York: Columbia University Press, 1938). For an examination of reorganization efforts between 1900 and 1975, see: James L. Garnett, *Reorganizing State Government: The Executive Branch* (Boulder, Colo.: Westview Press, 1981). Relevant research is listed in *State Government Reorganization: A Bibliography* (Lexington, Ky.: Council of State Governments, 1979). On more recent developments, see: James K. Conant, "In the Shadow of Wilson and Brownlow: Executive Branch Reorganization in the States, 1965 to 1987," *Public Administration Review* (September/October 1988): 892–902; and James K. Conant, "Executive Branch Reorganization in the States, 1965–1991," in *The Book of the States, 1992–93* (Lexington, Ky.: Council of State Governments, 1992), pp. 64–73.

29. See, generally: George A. Bell, "States Make Progress with Reorganization Plans," *National Civic Review* (March 1972): 115–119; and George A. Bell, "State Administrative Organization Activities," in *The Book of the States, 1976–77* (Lexington, Ky.: Council of State Governments, 1976), pp. 105–112.

30. Wyner, "Gubernatorial Relations."

31. Kathleen Sylvester, "Lieutenant Governors: Giving Up Real Power for Real Opportunity," *Governing* (February 1989): 44–50.

32. See: Deil S. Wright, "Executive Leadership in State Administration," *Midwest Journal of Political Science* 11 (February 1967): 1–26. See also: Thad L. Beyle and Robert Dalton, "Appointment Power: Does It Belong to the Governor," *State Government* (Winter 1981): 2–12.

33. Ira Sharkansky, "Agency Requests, Gubernatorial Support and Budget Success in State Legislatures," *American Political Science Review* 62 (December 1968): 1220–1231, quote at 1231. For an update of this study, see: Joel A. Thompson and Arthur Felts, "Politicians and Professionals: The Influence of State Agency Heads in Budgetary Success," *Western Political Quarterly* 45 (March 1992): 153–168.

34. Glenn Abney and Thomas P. Lauth, "The Governor as Chief Administrator," *Public Administration Review* (January/February 1983): 40–49, at 48.

35. *Ibid.*

36. Charles T. Goodsell, "The Public Administrator as Artisan," *Public Administration Review* 52 (May/June 1992): 246–295, at 246.

37. Dennis L. Dresang, "Public Personnel Reform: A Summary of State Government Activity," *Public Personnel Management* (September/October 1978): 287–294.

38. See, generally: Deil S. Wright, Mary Wagner, and Richard McAnaw, "State Administrators: Their Changing Characteristics," *State Government* (Summer 1977): 152–159; and F. Ted Herbert and Deil S. Wright, "State Administrators: How Professional?" *State Government* 55 (1982): 22–28.

39. See: Tim Barnett, "Overview of State Whistleblower Protection Statutes," *Labor Law Journal* (July 1992): 440–448.

40. Glenn Abney, "Lobbying by the Insiders: Parallels of State Agencies and Interest Groups," *Public Administration Review* (September/October 1988): 911–917.

41. See: Marver H. Bernstein, *Regulating Business by Independent Commission* (Princeton: Princeton University Press, 1955).

42. See: Jonathan Walters, "How Not to Reform Civil Service," *Governing* (November 1992): 30–34.

43. "Downsizing: The Mantra for State Personnel Directors in the '90s," *State Trends* (February/March 1995): 1.

44. Frank P. Sherwood and Lee J. Breyer, "Executive Personnel Systems in the States," *Public Administration Review* (September/October 1987): 410–416.

45. William M. Pearson and David S. Castle, "Liberalizing Restrictions on Political Activities of State Employees: Perceptions of High-Level State Executives," *American Review of Public Administration* 21 (June 1991): 91–103.

46. "Paying for Comparable Worth: Controversial, Moving Ahead,"*Intergovernmental Perspective* 11 (Winter 1985): 23.

47. Nelson C. Dometrius and Lee Sigelman, "Assessing Progress toward Affirmative Action Goals in State and Local Government: A New Benchmark," *Public Administration Review* (May/June 1984): 241–246.

48. See: Gwen Moore, "Gender and Informal Networks in State Government," *Social Science Quarterly* 73 (March 1992): 46–59.

49. Dresang, "Public Personnel Reform."

50. Kenneth S. Warner, Rupert F. Chisholm, and Robert F. Munzenrider, "Motives for Unionization among State Social Service Employees," *Public Personnel Management* (May/June 1978): 181–191.

51. John M. Capozzola, "Public Employee Strikes: Myths and Realities," *National Civic Review* (April 1979): 178–188.

52. See, for example: Sterling D. Speror and John M. Capozzola, *The Urban Community and Its Unionized Bureaucracies: Pressure Politics in Government Labor Relations* (New York: Dunellen, 1973).

7

★ ★ ★

COURTS, JUDGES, AND JUSTICE

The basic function of any court is to interpret and apply the law in order to resolve conflicts. The law involved may be from constitutions or charters, legislative enactments, administrative regulations, or previous judicial decisions. The conflicts may be over the rights and obligations of disputing parties, questions of innocence or guilt, or the validity of official public policies. In this chapter we look at how state courts are equipped to undertake their legal responsibilities and how they actually perform in these areas.

We first look at the broad role played by state courts, particularly the highest state courts, as participants in the political process. The discussion then turns to state court jurisdiction, organization, administration, and to the way judges are selected and removed. The judicial system, particularly in regard to criminal cases, is next considered. The final section comments on judicial decision making.

STATE COURTS IN THE POLITICAL PROCESS

The most obvious function performed by state courts in the political process is the interpretation of constitutions, statutes, and administrative regulations. In exercising the power of *judicial review,* courts not only interpret the law but also may substitute their judgments for those of legislators, executives, and administrators as to what is proper or lawful public policy. Today it is widely recognized that in the performance of the interpretative function, the courts are participating in the policymaking process.[1] Any decision they make promotes one interest or value over another. Even a refusal to become involved in a dispute affects certain interests by supporting the status quo.

This is not to suggest, however, that courts make policy in the same way that legislatures do. Though there are some exceptions, courts generally must wait for cases to come to them and must confine themselves to specific cases and controversies. Legislators, on the other hand, can make public policies of a general nature and of broad application at any time. Interest groups, while having good reason to consider the courts an important target, usually have access to the judiciary only through formal means such as lawsuits and *amicus curiae* briefs.[2] The fact that courts are part of the policymaking process, however, means that the ability to achieve standing (the legal right to bring a case) and other means of access to a court may be every bit as important to a group as its access to legislators or administrators. Unfortunately, the cost of litigation makes securing access more difficult for some groups than others.

ROLE IN REGARD TO STATE AND LOCAL POLICY

One basic function of state courts is to pass judgment on the validity of state legislation. As mentioned in chapter 3, state courts have had to be more severe than federal courts in interpreting state legislation because state constitutions are less flexible than the United States Constitution, giving state courts less opportunity to avoid a finding of unconstitutionality. In addition to reviewing legislative policies, state courts are a potential check on state administrative agencies, particularly in questioning whether those affected by an agency's decision were given due process.[3] State courts have also used their power of review to limit a wide range of local governmental activity. One study suggests that state courts are likely to be particularly hard on local governmental decisions relating to taxation and local regulations on business.[4] The courts, however, have not been altogether unsympathetic to the value of local control.[5] Over the years, state courts have built up a large body of case law regarding what local governments can and cannot do. As later chapters indicate, they have had an increasingly important impact on local development, planning, housing, and other policies.

Over the last decade, the role of state courts in reviewing the decisions of state and local officials has gained in importance. Interest groups have made increasing use of state courts, and the courts have greatly enlarged their scope of activity.[6] One reason for this is that the United States Supreme Court since the mid-1970s has been more disposed toward keeping issues out of the federal court system so that they can be resolved in state courts under state law. State courts have also become more active because various reform groups

---

BOX 7–1 THE NEW JUDICIAL FEDERALISM

"The new judicial federalism refers to the willingness of state courts to exercise their long dormant authority to base the protection of individual rights on independent interpretations of state constitutional rights rather than U.S. constitutional rights. By pursuing this independent course, state courts can grant rights protections that are broader than those granted by the U.S. Supreme Court. . . .

"The basic dynamic is that, through its interpretations of the U.S. Bill of Rights and the 14th Amendment, the U.S. Supreme Court establishes a floor, namely, a minimum level of rights protections for all persons across the nation. Like the idea of a federal social 'safety net,' no federal or state court may allow rights protection to fall below the federally established floor, but a state court may raise rights protection above that floor within its own state."

Source: John Kincaid, "The New Judicial Federalism," *The Journal of State Government* 61 (September/October 1988): 163–169, at 163.

(for example, those concerned with the environment, consumer protection, and civil rights) have found that litigation, while expensive, is much less costly than intensive lobbying in the legislative and administrative areas and is also often highly successful. These developments have meant that state courts not only have become increasingly important in reviewing the decisions of state and local officials but also have become actively involved in making general policies governing the operation of prisons, schools, and other institutions.

In what observers have labeled an era of "new judicial federalism," state courts in recent years have taken a more aggressive role in protecting individual rights under state constitutions (see box 7–1). This has occurred in cases ranging from gender discrimination to the rights of people accused of crime, and from equality between school districts to free speech in shopping centers. Courts have been most active in the Northeast and West and in places that have a liberal or progressive political tradition.[7]

Often in recent years, state courts have drawn upon state constitutions to provide rights the United States Supreme Court has held are not protected by the United States Constitution. This has occurred, for example, in regard to the use of local property taxes to support education (see chapter 12). It has also occurred on various criminal matters. An illustration came in 1992 when the New York Court of Appeals declared that the open fields doctrine—one allowing police to search unfenced land for a marijuana patch or something else illegal without a warrant—violated the state constitution. Several years earlier, the United States Supreme Court had ruled that nothing in the United

States Constitution prohibited such police practices.[8] Other areas where citizens may receive greater protection of civil liberties in the states under state constitutions are in regard to the right to privacy (which often is explicitly provided in some state constitutions while only implied in the United States Constitution), benefiting the pro-choice side; the right to bear arms; and rights of property owners. In regard to the last of these, state courts have increasingly applied strict limits on the regulations that diminish the value of property.[9]

As state courts have become more active, they have antagonized more groups and have often provoked negative reactions. Sometimes retaliation has come through the election system. Voters in both Massachusetts and California, for example, reinstated the death penalty through constitutional initiatives after their high courts invalidated the practice. In the mid-1980s California voters went further and denied Chief Justice Rose E. Bird her seat on the court because of her opposition to the death penalty. In an effort to curb what some see as excessively liberal state courts, there has been a movement in some states to prohibit these courts from expanding on the interpretations of the United States Supreme Court.

In addition to passing on the validity of state and local policies, state courts also function to some extent as interest groups seeking to secure legislative or executive adoption of desired courses of action.[10] Frequently, judges use court opinions to express their views and preferences on policy alternatives a legislative body might consider. On occasion, court opinions declaring these views are sent directly to legislators and administrators. State court judges may also become involved in policy development by meeting in formal and informal conferences with legislators, governors, and other public officials; by making formal advisory reports to state officials; and by appearing at legislative hearings. The views of judges are often sought out by other state officials on matters concerning court organization and procedure, criminal law, and the regulation of business activity. Judicial recommendations on these matters are often supported by the bar association and appear to be looked on favorably in the legislature. A favorable reception is especially likely on matters relating to court organization and procedure.

ROLE IN REGARD TO NATIONAL POLICY IN THE STATES

Another important aspect of the role of state courts in the political process concerns the application of national policies in the various states. Under Article VI of the United States Constitution, state judges must respect the overriding authority of the Constitution, federal statutes, and treaties. Implementation of this responsibility has largely resulted from the use of the appellate jurisdiction given the Supreme Court by Congress. Congress has granted the right to appeal decisions of state courts when a federal statute has been held unconstitutional or where a state statute has been unsuccessfully challenged as contrary to the federal Constitution. Other cases may be brought up from state courts by a *writ of certiorari*.[11] For practical reasons, the United States Supreme Court has much discretion in determining what cases it will hear.

The United States Supreme Court, through appellate jurisdiction, functions as the final reviewing authority over both federal and state court systems. Its power, however, is subject to several limitations. Congress, if it wished, could eliminate the appellate jurisdiction of the Court or alter it so that the Court could not review certain types of cases. The authority of the High Court, moreover, may be greatly compromised by the activity of the lower courts, both state and federal, that are depended on to implement its decisions. Enough research has been done in this area to demonstrate that the law "depends not only on what the Supreme Court says it is, but also to some extent on what the lower courts say the Supreme Court said."[12]

State courts are likely to have much discretion in determining the meaning of a United States Supreme Court policy. This is partially because the policy directives given them are frequently vague.[13] State courts may not be sure what has to be done, what tests or standards are to be employed in determining the constitutionality of an act or judging attempts at compliance. The meaning of the law in this situation could be expected to vary from jurisdiction to jurisdiction, according to the particular demands of each state court. In the school desegregation cases, for example, the Supreme Court, while demanding an end to "separate but equal" public schools, found it unwise to formulate a single decree outlining a course of action to be followed by all school officials. The lower federal courts and the state courts were given much discretion in the framing of specific decrees and in determining the specific form of compliance.

Diversity is also likely to grow out of the near impossibility of getting all the various judges involved to agree on the merits of a particular policy. It is entirely possible that lower court judges will want no part of the Supreme Court policy or agree only in part, and that their concept of what should be done will be reflected in the specific changes they demand. It is also possible that state and lower federal court decisions will depart from High Court guidelines because the lower court judges give weight to what they feel can be accomplished in the light of particular political situations.

An indication of the different attitudes of state court judges toward federal judicial policy is provided by Kenneth Vines's study of segregation cases.[14] The study concerned race relations decisions of eleven southern supreme courts from May 1954 (the date of the Supreme Court's decision in *Brown* v. *Board of Education*) through December 1963. Some southern state court judges, labeled "Federalists," saw their role to be one of implementing Supreme Court policy to the best of their ability. The "Compromisers" placed greater weight on local needs and problems of race relations and, while often recognizing the authority of the Supreme Court, did so only reluctantly. The third group, "States' Righters," were determined to emphasize the priority of local conditions and the independence of the state judicial process over the duty of implementing Supreme Court policy.

State courts during this period were an important instrument in handling black grievances in the South, though blacks preferred, often with reason, going to the federal courts when possible. Decisions in the state courts were in favor of blacks in about one out of three cases, while southern federal district courts ruled in their favor slightly more than half of the time.

Southern court judges, most of whom were elected and had built political careers in the South, were closer to the sentiments expressed in the actions of the state legislatures than of the federal courts. At the same time, considering the political climate, blacks did far better in state courts than might have been expected. The ability of the state courts to isolate themselves from the political climate, Vines suggested, was related to the fact that the judges served longer terms than the legislators and seldom had to face competition for reelection. They were also isolated somewhat from the effects of public opinion and partisan activities because the style, language, and form of their decisions tended to hide them from public view. The courts were able to make decisions on minor technicalities rather than tackle major issues head-on. State courts, it would appear, may enjoy considerable independence from both the United States Supreme Court and the state political system

The State Courts

Jurisdiction and Powers

State courts are called on to hear two general classes of legal controversies: criminal and civil. In criminal cases, the state is involved in an action against a citizen for a misdemeanor or felony, the latter being more serious. Criminal cases begin with an arrest and proceed through the stages of preliminary hearings, the setting of bail, indictment, arraignment,[15] trial, and sentencing. On the other hand, in a civil case the court acts as a forum for settling disputes between two or more private parties, although in some cases, the government may be the plaintiff or defendant. Typical civil suits involve matters such as violations of contracts, divorces, and automobile accidents.

State courts decide the bulk of civil and criminal cases in this country, for these are usually governed by state law. Federal courts normally refrain from hearing cases where both state and federal laws are involved until the state courts pass on the questions involving state matters.

Faced with the problem of enforcing a decision or implementing a policy, courts can employ various forms of legal and equitable remedies. A legal remedy is given only after the damage is done, usually as a fine or imprisonment. An equitable remedy usually takes the form of an injunction to prevent something from happening (such as a public employee strike) or to make something happen. Most courts have jurisdiction in suits involving both law and equity, though some states have separate chancery or equity courts.

Another common judicial tool is the declaratory judgment, found in the majority of the states. Through this device a court simply enters a judgment defining the rights of the parties. "The fundamental theory of the declaratory judgment," one authority has concluded, "is that in a civilized society people will obey court decisions without the threat of force or punishment."[16]

STRUCTURE

At the top of the state court system—illustrated in figure 7–1—is a court of last resort, usually known as the supreme court, of from three to nine justices. The major work of the highest state court involves hearing appeals from the lower state courts. In addition to this appellate jurisdiction, this court may have original jurisdiction in such matters as the granting of certain writs, cases in which the state is a party, and disputes between counties within the state. In contrast to the United States Supreme Court, which theoretically hears only actual cases and controversies, the highest state courts in some states give advisory opinions to the legislature, governor, or other state officials. Elsewhere, this function is performed exclusively by the attorney general.

Appellate courts of from three to nine justices exist in over thirty states. State legislatures created them in order to reduce the caseloads of the highest state courts. These courts may have original jurisdiction in some cases, but their chief function is to review the decisions of the trial courts to determine whether or not the law has been correctly applied to the facts gathered there. Generally, the appellate courts do not review questions of fact or hold new trials.

General trial courts (called district, circuit, or superior courts) have original jurisdiction in most cases involving state law. These are courts of record; that is, they keep a full transcript of their proceedings. In some states, a single court with several geographical divisions handles cases involving criminal law, civil law, equity suits, and probate matters. In other states, separate courts have been established for each of these purposes. Most litigation terminates at this level, though appeal to the appellate court and sometimes directly to the state's highest court is possible.

At the bottom of the state court system are a number of minor courts or courts of limited jurisdiction. The specific types of minor courts and the responsibilities given to them vary greatly. It is at this level that most citizens have their first and often their only encounter with the courts.

One of the most common minor courts is the justice court, a long-standing institution adapted from English practice in colonial times, presided over by

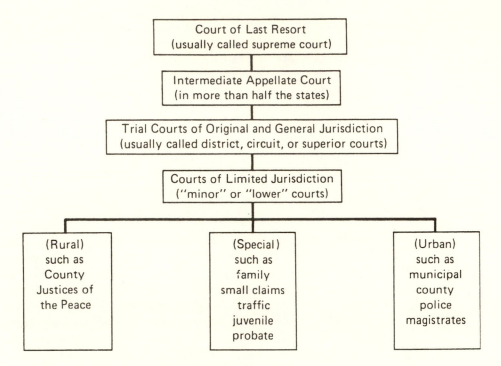

FIGURE 7–1 State Court Organization

Source: Advisory Commission on Intergovernmental Relations, *State-Local Relations in the Criminal Justice System* (Washington, D.C.: Government Printing Office, 1971), p. 88.

a justice of the peace (JP). The JP, usually elected from a township or other subdivision of a county, handles petty civil litigation involving small amounts of money and performs civil functions such as marriage ceremonies. The JP also may issue warrants for arrests and searches, conduct preliminary hearings in felony cases to determine if there is enough evidence to warrant holding an accused person over for trial in a higher court, and settle minor criminal matters such as vagrancy or traffic law violations. Justice courts are not courts of record, and appeals from these courts usually require a trial *de novo* (a completely new trial).

The justice courts have long been one of the main targets of court reformers. Principal complaints have been directed at the JPs' lack of legal training and the practice of paying them on a fee basis. The fee system has undoubtedly encouraged some JPs to drum up business by advertising or entering into agreements with local police—such as ones creating speed traps designed primarily to fleece out-of-town drivers. The legal profession has been foremost among those calling for reform in the justice court system, especially in the drive to act on the JPs' lack of legal education. Several states have now abolished the justice courts and have replaced them with district, county, or municipal courts. JPs are most commonly found in rural and suburban areas.

Large cities may have municipal, magistrate, police, traffic, city, night, or small claims courts. These courts, like the justice courts, are technically part of the state court system but operate quite independently with their own rules of procedure. Municipal court judges are usually paid out of local funds and are either elected locally or appointed by the mayor. Unlike the JPs, the judges of the municipal courts have almost always had legal training. The municipal court is a court of original jurisdiction for many civil and criminal matters involving local ordinances and is usually a court of record. Its jurisdiction is generally somewhat broader than that of the justice courts, in that it can hear cases involving greater amounts of money and more severe criminal penalties. Some cities have integrated all special courts into a single municipal court system with a number of divisions. In other cities, separate domestic relations (family) and juvenile (children's) courts have been established. There may be much overlap in the jurisdictions of the specialized municipal courts and the general trial courts. In some situations, a police officer has the choice of taking someone he or she has arrested before a municipal, county, or state trial court judge.

ADMINISTRATIVE PROBLEMS

State court systems, like the state executive branch, are characterized by fragmented administrative authority. Reformers have long cited the need for an integrated or unified court system and improved judicial administration. In an integrated arrangement, the various courts would be brought into a single system headed by the highest state court or its chief justice. The chief justice would have authority to assign or reassign any judge or magistrate to any court where he or she would be needed. The chief justice or the high court would also prescribe rules of practice and procedure for all courts.

Court systems in less than half of the states can be said to be fully or substantially integrated. To aid in the day-to-day administration of the courts, most states have created an office of court administrator to assist the chief justice in his or her administrative duties. Similar offices have been established to assist trial court judges. The administrator assumes nonjudicial functions such as budgeting, purchasing, and the collection and compilation of data. Nearly all states also have a judicial council, usually headed by the chief justice of the highest state court, designed to study and improve the operation of the court system. Since 1971, a National Center for State Courts has been in existence to perform a similar function.

The heavy caseloads of state and local courts are a long-standing problem. State and local courts handle some three million cases a year, compared to only about 140,000 by the federal courts. The problem of overcrowded dockets has brought both delay and hasty or assembly-line justice. These problems have been most pronounced in the lower courts serving major urban areas. Most of these courts are bogged down with litigation involving traffic violations, automobile accidents, illegal drinking, petty thefts, and bill collecting.

Delay in coming to court is not always bad. Judges, for example, delay sensational cases to wait for a better atmosphere in which to select an impartial jury. Trial delay may also result from the hope that the problem, such as a divorce suit, will be resolved without court action. Delay at other times has less positive consequences, as when the accused is kept in prolonged detention, witnesses die or disappear, and impatient plaintiffs accept too little in civil suits settled out of court.

The problem of overcrowding has generated pressure to increase the number of judges and to make significant changes in the traditional system of justice. For one thing, there has been a tendency to save time by reducing the use of juries, especially in civil cases. Even in criminal cases, states are now free to reduce the size of juries from the traditional twelve to as few as six, and several have done so. Overcrowding has also stimulated the use of pretrial conferences in civil cases and pretrial plea bargains in criminal cases.

A third consequence of the increased burden has been a challenge to the traditional right of each judge to administer his or her own court. In addition to the movement toward an integrated state system, there has been a movement toward appointing an administrative judge with power to control the master calendar and assign cases to each associate of a multimember court system. This method could be used to ensure that each judge did his or her share of the work. The adoption of the system has encountered the resistance of older judges who have been on the bench the longest and are set in their ways.[17]

Another method of attacking the problem of overcrowding is to reduce the number of cases coming into the judicial system in the first place. This can be accomplished by shifting more of the case material to administrative bodies or to arbitration. In the arbitration process each party selects one arbitrator and together they select a third. The arbitrators then decide the issue and their judgment is upheld by the court.

Examples of law reforms that promise to do much to relieve the backlog of the courts are no-fault insurance and the liberalization of divorce laws. The traditional automobile insurance system is based on the concepts of liability and negligence. One party must be shown to be at fault. Under the no-fault system now used in various forms in about half the states, victims are usually reimbursed by their own insurance companies without any court proceedings unless the amount of damage exceeds a certain level. No-fault has been opposed by trial lawyers who make a good part of their living through auto accident cases. Divorce laws have been liberalized in several states in recent years. For example, California legislation allows the dissolution of a marriage on the ground of "irreconcilable difference." One spouse need only go to the county clerk's office to obtain a form for a small fee that informs the other spouse of the divorce proceeding. If there is no contest over property or children, a final decree can be issued in six months.

THE JUDGES: SELECTION AND REMOVAL

Most of the some seventeen thousand state court judges in this country are white and male. Most also are products of an in-state law school. Judges in the states, in contrast to judges in most European nations, while generally trained in the law, are not trained to be judges.[18] Instead, they are recruited from other professions. In most states voters elect the judges. Other judges reach their positions through appointment by the governor, the legislature, or by a system combining appointment and election.[19]

ELECTION OF JUDGES

State judicial elections are held on either a partisan or nonpartisan basis. In a partisan election, the candidate runs in his or her party's primary and the party nominees face each other in a general election. In a nonpartisan election, the candidates are placed on the ballot with no reference to party. In some mixed systems, as noted below, judges are also voted on in *retention elections*, that is, ones in which voters are asked whether they want to retain a sitting judge in office for another term. In these elections judges run without partisan identification and without an opponent.

Partisan elections usually bring a better voter turnout than nonpartisan elections, as many additional voters are motivated by the party cue given them. Party voting on judges, as indicated below, may be rational in that party labels help voters correctly predict how judges are likely to decide particular issues. From the candidates' point of view, it may be easier to mount a partisan campaign because this gives them some organizational and financial support they would otherwise have to secure through their own efforts. Partisan elections also tend to give an advantage to locally born candidates whose local contacts help them get on the ballot. Nonpartisan elections, in comparison, give newcomers more of a chance to get on the ballot. Partisan elections are often criticized on the grounds that party affiliation should have nothing to do with how judges make decisions and thus should not even be considered by the electorate. Judges, from this perspective, should also dismiss party ties and be free of political connections in order to make unbiased decisions.

The election of judges, whether on a partisan or nonpartisan basis, raises several difficult problems. Some of these, as with other elections, have to do with the fairness of the districting or at-large systems employed. Federal courts and attorneys may find that the way state legislatures have drawn district lines for judicial elections has a discriminatory impact on racial minorities and thus violates the 1965 Voting Rights Act. Campaign finance is also a problem in judicial as well as other elections. Though judicial races traditionally have been low-budget affairs, such campaigns may be expensive and appear to be becoming more so. Candidates for the supreme court in large states may spend a million dollars or more on their campaigns. Funds generally come from attorneys and law firms, whose clients may later appear before the judge receiving a contribution. Also contributing directly are business and labor organizations or PACs, which often have a stake in court decisions. Only a few states attempt to limit contributions to judicial campaigns or deal effectively with the potential conflict-of-interest problem.[20]

Other difficulties concerning judicial elections center on voting behavior and differing views about the role of the courts. In theory, elections bring greater popular control over the courts. Assuming for the moment that this is a desirable objective, history indicates that voters have not demonstrated much interest in exercising controls. Turnout in judicial elections is usually far lower than in gubernatorial elections. Voters seldom are aware of the qualifications or even the identity of those who seek judicial office or of the records of those seeking reelection.[21] At times they are overwhelmed simply by the large number of judicial candidates on the ballot. Many voters just skip over the judicial contests. Those who do vote tend to favor the incumbent. This is especially true in those cases where the only question is whether or not to retain a judge in office.[22] It is less true when an incumbent has an opponent. In states where the party affiliation of judges is known, this generally becomes the determining factor in the election.

To some extent the voters' behavior may be related to a belief in the myth of the law—that judges engage in work that is (and should be) beyond the comprehension of the average voter. People tend to have reverence for the courts, even when rulings are against their interests. They may feel unqualified to question or evaluate a judicial decision.[23] If the "myth of the law" inhibits the electorate from active or meaningful involvement in the selection of judges, so, too, do the facts that in many cases judges run unopposed and that the election often amounts to nothing more than a confirmation of a previous appointment made by a governor or other official in filling a vacancy. In some states as many as 70 percent of the "elected" judges in office were initially placed there by appointment. Judges themselves may feel that they cannot be true to the law and campaign like other politicians on the basis of specific promises of favors because justice must be impartial and above politics, not subject to mob passions or popular fashions.

THE APPOINTIVE SYSTEM

It is commonly assumed that the appointive system is the best means of meeting the requirement of judicial objectivity and expertise. To be sure, if these were really the only qualifications considered, it might be argued that the governor and the bar association may well be in a better position to search out and find the most qualified candidates. However, those who appoint judges are more apt to consider the candidates' political loyalty and philosophical dispositions than objective qualifications.

There is no evidence, moreover, that appointed justices are more qualified in legal training than are elected judges. Indeed, one study suggests that gubernatorial appointments place less emphasis on formal education than does the election method.[24] The appointive system does tend to give more opportunity to those who have held past legislative offices (because governors and others who appoint are familiar with legislators) and to those who have had previous judicial experience. The latter is especially true in regard to state supreme court appointments. The elective and combined methods are more favorable to candidates with previous law enforcement experiences, such as district attorneys.[25]

MIXED METHODS OF SELECTION

To secure both responsive and expert judges, several states have combined the appointive and elective methods and have added nonpartisan commissions to screen candidates. Under the California Plan adopted in 1934, the governor nominates a candidate for a state supreme court or district court of appeals vacancy (the only two levels covered by the plan) for the consideration of a Commission on Qualifications composed of the chief justice of the supreme court, presiding judge of the district court of appeals, and attorney general. If the commission approves of the choice, the appointee serves one year and then is up for election for a twelve-year term. The appointee runs for election on his or her own record without any opposing candidate.

Missouri adopted a similar plan in 1940. Various nonpartisan commissions are set up in the state to suggest candidates for judicial office. One commission, composed of the chief justice of the supreme court as presiding officer, three lawyers named by the organized bar, and three laypeople appointed by the governor, nominates candidates for the supreme court and circuit court of appeals. A similar commission performs the same function for other judicial districts affected by the plan. When a vacancy occurs on any bench affected by the plan, the appropriate judiciary commission nominates three persons, and the governor (or mayor or county executive) selects the judge from this panel of names. The appointed judge serves a probationary period of at least one year and runs on his or her record at the next election. The electorate is faced with the task of deciding whether the judge should be retained—they do not choose among candidates. Predictably, turnout is lower than in elections where they have that choice. Also predictably, voters in Missouri and elsewhere with similar systems have turned out very few judges. It is difficult to "beat someone with no one." Some observers have also been critical of the appointment part of the process, contending that the chief executive has usually been able to find a way of suggesting the names to the commission that they eventually submit to him or her.[26]

METHODS OF REMOVAL

The traditional method of dealing with unfit judges in most states is through impeachment proceedings whereby a judge is indicted by one house of a legislature and tried by the other. A judge who is impeached and convicted is removed from the bench and barred from holding any other public office. Thus, impeachment is suitable only for the most serious types of judicial misconduct. Otherwise it is such a harsh, cumbersome, and expensive procedure that it is usually impractical.

Two other procedures for removing unfit judges are the address to the executive, which is a concurrent resolution by both houses of the legislature requiring the governor to remove a judge, and the recall, which requires a popular referendum on whether or not a judge should be removed before expiration of his or her term. These methods are available in a relatively few states. They have been used infrequently and are of even less practical significance than impeachment.[27]

All states now have special boards, tribunals, or commissions consisting of judges, lawyers, and citizens for disciplining and removing judges. California's Commission of Judicial Performance was the first such commission. Established in 1960 by voter-approved constitutional amendment, the commission functions to receive and investigate complaints concerning judicial fitness or conduct. If it believes action is warranted, it may take steps accordingly, possibly leading to retirement or removal of the judge in question. The California Commission has nine members: two judges of courts of appeal, two judges of superior courts, and one judge of a municipal court, all appointed by the California supreme court; two attorneys chosen by the state bar; and two citizens appointed by the governor and approved by the senate. Upon a complaint to an executive secretary, the commission investigates allegations. If it finds them frivolous, it does no more than inform the complainant accordingly. If, however, it encounters a problem of judicial incapacity or misbehavior, it seeks a voluntary solution through a confidential proceeding. When the circumstances warrant retirement or removal and the judge refuses to retire or resign voluntarily, the commission arranges for a hearing. The commission's recommendation for dismissal must be upheld by the state supreme court.

SECURING JUSTICE

CIVIL AND CRIMINAL CASES

As mentioned earlier in this chapter, courts are called on to hear two basic types of controversies—civil and criminal. In civil cases, such as divorce actions or those involving automobile accidents, the court functions largely as a forum for settling disputes between private parties. Civil cases usually begin with a plaintiff's securing a summons from a court clerk that directs the defendant to appear in court to answer charges. Following this, the two parties generally exchange charges and countercharges. The dispute may be settled out of court or through a pretrial conference between the two parties. Those not settled go before a judge and sometimes a jury in a formal court trial. Unlike criminal cases, where guilt must be shown "beyond a reasonable doubt," only "preponderant evidence" is needed in a civil case to determine which party is at fault.

PRETRIAL RELEASE

Criminal cases are normally initiated by the arrest of a suspect by a police officer or sheriff. After the suspect is arrested, taken to jail, and questioned, he or she is brought before a magistrate or a justice of the peace for a preliminary hearing to determine whether or not he or she should be held for trial in a higher court. One of the most important decisions made at this time is whether or not a defendant should be released before trial. In a large number of cases, defendants are released on their own recognizance (promise to appear for trial). This is most likely to occur when the crime involved is relatively minor and when the defendant, according to information the judge is able to gather, appears to be trustworthy and have roots in the community.

Judges may also require bail as a condition of pretrial release. If the judge decides to set bail, the suspect will be required to post a sum of money that will be forfeited for failure to appear for trial. The judge may have considerable discretion as to the amount of bail required or may be guided by rates set in judicial schedules.

Because many defendants are not affluent, they pay a fee (from 5 to 10 percent of the bail required) to a bail bondsman, who then posts a bond guaranteeing the bail and the defendant's presence at the trial. The bondsman may in effect decide who will be released awaiting trial, and in most jurisdictions the bondsman can arrest and return the defendant if he or she tries to run away. In practice, the bail system hurts the poor and helps repeated offenders who have demonstrated to the bondsmen that they will not jump bail. First-time offenders who have not demonstrated that they are a good risk have a difficult time getting aid from the bondsman. Those who are released on bail are free to return to their work and families and, if so inclined, to intimidate potential witnesses against them. Those who are unable to raise bail, on the other hand, are punished without the benefit of a trial by being sent to jail for weeks, even months, awaiting their day in court. Research has found that a person who is free on bail and able to work with his or her attorney may have a substantial advantage over a person who could not secure bail. Those in jail tend to plead guilty more often and in many cases will receive a tougher sentence than those who made bail.[28]

LEGAL AID

Under prevailing laws, individuals who cannot afford to hire their own private attorney are entitled to free legal assistance even for the most minor offenses if the possibility of a jail sentence is involved. The only exception occurs when the accused waives the privilege to legal assistance on a "knowing and intelligent" basis.

In some jurisdictions, the poor may turn to legal aid societies—organizations of lawyers outside of the court system. Most legal aid societies, however, do not accept criminal cases. The two most common sources of legal aid in criminal cases are the systems of assigned counsel and public defenders.

Under the assigned counsel system, an indigent defendant is provided with an attorney in private practice who is appointed by the trial judge. Some states require all lawyers to engage in assigned counsel at one time or another. A majority of states pay a small fee to those who serve. This system has been criticized because lawyers are often young and inexperienced and because the poor are given less priority than the firm's regular clients. A variation on the assigned counsel system is Judicare, which allows an indigent defendant to choose his or her own lawyer, who is then paid at specified rates from public funds. This system is intended to give the defendant some choice and to contribute to the fostering of a more normal lawyer-client relationship.

The public defender system emerged at the beginning of the twentieth century as an improvement over the assigned counsel system. Some states use it exclusively; others use it only in metropolitan areas, retaining the assigned counsel system in other areas. The defender system may be organized on a city, county, judicial district, or statewide basis. The public defender serves on a continuing basis instead of being assigned a specific case and is compensated by salary rather than by individual fee. While the assigned counsel may be a young and inexperienced lawyer, the public defender is by law in most areas required to have at least a certain minimum of experience.

One of the biggest drawbacks of the legal aid system is that, despite the Supreme Court decisions that legal aid be made available immediately after arrest, it is commonly not assigned until the preliminary proceedings before the lower court judge. By that time, the defendant may have made a statement to the police or prosecutor that has effectively destroyed his or her chances for an acquittal or reduced charge.[29]

Prosecutors and Plea Bargaining

What ultimately happens to defendants also depends very much on the activities of public prosecutors who act on behalf of the state in conducting proceedings against persons suspected of crime. The prosecutor is known by a variety of titles, district, county, or state attorney being the most common. Most prosecutors are locally elected by party and are largely independent of the state attorney general, who participates only in appellate cases or when legislation specifically charges him or her with prosecution responsibilities.

The prosecutor has complete discretion in deciding whether or not to prosecute and what the charges will be against an individual.[30] The prosecutor does not bring cases against all arrested suspects and often moves to dismiss a charge he or she has made in the light of new developments. Should a prosecutor seek to bring charges against an individual, he or she may turn to a grand jury for an indictment. A grand jury, composed of from twelve to twenty-three members, is convened by the prosecutor in the jurisdiction to hear evidence against a suspect. The jury does not hear evidence from the defendant or the defendant's attorney. If a majority of the members feels there is sufficient reason to believe the accused should be held for trial, the jury presents a "true bill." If not, it makes a finding of "no true bill." Several jurisdictions have replaced the grand jury system with an information system in which the prosecutor simply submits the charges—in the form of an affidavit of evidence accompanied by sworn statements—to a court of original jurisdiction.

Most criminal cases are ultimately disposed of by guilty pleas. Many of these are the result of *plea bargaining* between the prosecutor and the defense attorney or between the prosecutor and the defendant without legal assistance. The use of plea bargaining varies from locality to locality; for example, it is used more often in Pittsburgh than in Minneapolis,[31] and more often in Chicago than in Baltimore.[32] The basic objective of plea bargaining is to obtain a plea of guilty in exchange for a reduced charge or a favorable sentence recommendation from the prosecutor to the judge. A prosecutor may agree to accept a lesser charge because he or she has a weak case on a more serious charge, because he or she wants to enhance his or her political career by building up a record of convictions, or because he or she may feel that justice would be better served if the court were to go easy on a certain individual such as a young, first-time offender. An offer of a reduced charge or a light sentence may also be made to induce a suspect to testify against another suspect. Of course, the accused is often attracted by the possibility of a lighter sentence. There is a danger, however, that the accused, while innocent of any crime, may plead guilty out of fear that the prosecutor may throw the book at him or her if the case should go to trial.

THE TRIAL

Prosecutors, defense attorneys, and judges—often working as a team in getting through the caseload as quickly as possible with a minimum of expense—rely heavily on plea bargaining as a means to this end. Lower criminal courts, especially in large cities, are characterized by a steady stream of guilty pleas that are disposed of in minutes. The judicial role is often bureaucratic and impersonal as sentences are routinely meted out. Given the high number of guilty pleas, the most common role of the defense attorney is not to prove the client innocent but to convince prosecutors and judges that the client should not be given a harsh penalty.[33]

The federal Constitution, state constitutions, court decisions, and state statutes give those accused of crime certain "fair trial" protections. Legal experts commonly include on the list of such protections the rights of the defendant to be formally notified of the charges against him or her, to confront prosecution witnesses, to have the case heard by an impartial judge and jury, to have legal counsel, and to remain silent (see chapter 15). In addition, the state cannot use certain types of evidence such as hearsay against the defendant. The state must establish guilt beyond a reasonable doubt, and the accused is innocent unless the prosecutor can prove otherwise. In practice, these protections may not be always applied.

When conflict exists in the courtroom, the method employed to arrive at the truth is known as the adversary system. Conflict may arise between a lawyer representing the state and one representing the defendant in a criminal case or between two lawyers representing different parties in a civil case. The judge in theory plays a neutral role and attempts to ensure that the rules of procedure are followed. The "truth" must emerge from fallible witnesses, conflicting testimony, and lawyers fighting to promote their clients' interest rather than to produce all evidence. Jerome Frank has called the system a "regulated brawl" in which the facts are really guesses of what the judge and jury think has happened.[34] In actuality, what emerges from the process is greatly dependent not only on the skills of the opposing attorneys but also on the predispositions of juries and judges.

The trial or petit jury that serves during a trial is usually drawn by lot by a court administrator from a large jury panel. The panel itself is commonly drawn at random from voter or taxpayer lists, though certain people, for example, doctors or nurses who may be needed elsewhere, are exempt from the list. Prospective jurors are also examined by the opposing attorneys and a certain number of jurors can be dismissed without the court's approval, simply on the demand (peremptory challenge) of the attorneys.[35] Once that number has been reached, further removals require the consent of the court. An attorney naturally looks for a jury that will be sympathetic to his or her client's (in the case of the prosecutor, the public's) best interest.

In recent years there has been a move toward more representative juries because of the use of broader source lists, a reduction in exemptions from service, and greater limits on peremptory challenges. Some observers have contended that the emphasis on more representative juries has produced jurors who see their role as being one of representing a constituent group, rather than a member of a deliberative body seeking consensus on the innocence or guilt or an individual. Along with this development, there has been increased concern with *jury nullification*—allowing juries to decide the law as well as the facts of a case. In a criminal case, for example, an individual accused of a crime might be acquitted if the jury disagrees with the law concerning the crime.[36]

TRIAL OUTCOMES

Research on jury behavior suggests that juries commonly do go beyond the facts of a case, some legislating on their own. In civil cases, for example, juries may award generous judgments against large corporations or insurance companies out of the belief that the person who has a claim against them needs the money or that, regardless of merit of the claim, the company can afford the loss. To some extent jurors in the 1995 O.J. Simpson case may have been influenced by how they perceived the record of the Los Angles Police Department in regard to race relations (see box 7–2). In some cases, the outcome depends on how the facts are interpreted. Jurors, as the first trial of police officers involved in the Rodney King beating illustrated, may regard what some see as a clear case of police brutality to be a matter of police officers simply doing their job. Defense attorneys in this 1992 trial were highly successful in showing jurors how to interpret what they saw on the video of King's arrest (see chapters 8 and 15).

Other research suggests that during the jury deliberations some people are more influential than others. Men are more likely to participate in discussions than women, and participation is likely to increase with education and social status. Generally, juries are harsher on defendants of lower socioeconomic status and appear to be favorably impressed by witnesses or defendants who seem most self-confident.[37] Some research also suggests that men and women differ somewhat in how they view accounts of criminal cases. Women tend to give greater weight to mitigating circumstances, that is, the reasons why someone might have committed a crime, before coming to a conclusion. Men focus more directly on the bottom-line question of innocence or guilt.

BOX 7–2   TRIAL OUTCOMES: THE SIMPSON CASE

Trial outcomes, as in the case of O.J. Simpson in 1995, are often controversial, leading some to criticize the quality of the jury system. Opinion surveys indicated that blacks and whites differed sharply on the jury's "not guilty" verdict—blacks overwhelmingly approved, a majority of whites opposed. A majority in both groups, however, agreed that Simpson would have been found guilty if the jury had been all white rather than predominantly black. A majority of both groups also agreed that Simpson would have been convicted if he had not been rich.

Source: Washington Post survey, October 1995.

JUDICIAL DECISION MAKING

The nature of judicial decision making varies to some extent according to the level of court, that is, between trial and appellate courts. A single trial court judge may struggle through a large workload in a routine bureaucratic manner. But in the more isolated multimembered appellate courts, judges appear to approach their task of reviewing lower court cases in a more legalistic manner. To some extent judges in higher state courts pick up cues on how to decide particular cases from decisions made by state courts in other states. Especially important in this regard are the prestigious and more progressive courts located in the largest states.[38]

Behind-the-scene interaction among judges on an appellate court may be characterized by persuasion, bargaining, and compromise.[39] Often the goal is to arrive at a unanimous decision that, it is assumed, will aid in securing compliance with the decision. A court opinion not supported by all the judges lacks the psychological force of a unanimous opinion and suggests the possibility that the court might reverse itself. At times, individual judges will dissent from a majority opinion, though this is rarer in state courts than in the United States Supreme Court. Over a period of time, relatively stable factions also may develop, for example, along liberal and conservative lines.

All judges have benefited from the widely shared belief that the role of a judge is primarily a neutral one of finding the law and applying it to the facts of a case. Even though judges may indeed strive toward neutrality, research indicates that it may be useful to know, for example, something about how the judge was selected and his or her party affiliation in predicting how a case will be decided. Research suggests that there is some difference on policy matters between elected and appointed judges. For example, elected judges may be more liberal than appointed judges in cases involving consumers but less liberal in cases involving the constitutional rights of criminal suspects.[40] These tendencies may reflect the mood of the electorate that put the officials in office in the first place. Research suggests, however, that judges who are scheduled to face the electorate try to avoid electoral opposition by, for example, avoiding unpopular decisions.[41]

Some research studies have found that judges affiliated with the Democratic Party may be more sympathetic than Republican judges to the consumer, the working person, and the defendant in criminal cases, but less sympathetic to businesses such as utilities seeking to avoid regulation.[42] Additional research on trial court judges suggests that the sex of the judge may also be important in certain cases. Women judges, for example, appear to be considerably harsher on female defendants than are male judges.[43] Race may also be an important factor in understanding judicial behavior. Some research indicates, for example, that on the decision to incarcerate, black trial court judges are more evenhanded in their treatment of black and white defendants than are white judges. The latter are likely to be somewhat more lenient to white defendants than they are to black defendants.[44]

A central norm of judicial behavior is impartiality, and it may be assumed that most judges strive toward this objective. At the same time, judges are human and are influenced in their thinking by external influences and their own predispositions.

ENDNOTES

1. See, for example: Fred V. Cahill, *Judicial Legislation* (New York: Ronald Press, 1952); John P. Frank, *Marble Palace* (New York: Alfred A. Knopf, 1958); Alpheus T. Mason, *The Supreme Court: Vehicle of Revealed Truth or Power Group?* (Boston: Boston University Press, 1953); Jack W. Peltason, *Federal Courts in the Political Process* (Garden City, N.Y.: Doubleday, 1955); and Victor G. Rosenblum, *Law as a Political Instrument* (Garden City, N.Y.: Doubleday, 1955).

2. On occasion, the *amicus curiae* brief has been "an agent of the court acting as champion of the court's point of view. . . . In the main, however, the *amicus curiae* has been a means of fostering partisan third-party involvement through the encouragement of group representation by a self-conscious bench. The judges have sought to gain information from political groups as well as to give them a feeling of participating in the process of decision. . . ." Samuel Krislov, "The *Amicus Curiae* Brief: From Friendship to Advocacy," *Yale Law Journal* 72 (March 1963): 694, 720–721.

3. See: Stephen I. Frank, "State Supreme Courts and Administrative Agencies," *State Government* (Spring 1978): 119–123.

4. See: Kenneth M. Dolbeare, *Trial Courts in Urban Politics* (New York: John Wiley and Sons, 1967).

5. See: Richard Briffault, "State-Local Relations and Constitutional Law," *Intergovernmental Perspective* (Summer–Fall 1987): 10–14.

6. Lee Epstein, "Exploring the Participation of Organized Interests in State Court Litigation," *Political Research Quarterly* 47 (June 1994): 335–351.

7. See: John Kincaid, "The New Judicial Federalism," *The Journal of State Government* 61 (September/October 1988): 163–169.

8. See, generally: Stanley H. Friedelbaum, ed., *Human Rights in the States: New Directions in Constitutional Policymaking* (Westport, Conn.: Greenwood Press, 1988); Susan P. Fino, *The Role of State Supreme Courts in the New Judicial Federalism* (Westport, Conn.: Greenwood Press, 1987); Stanley Mosk, "The Emerging Agenda in State Constitutional Rights Law," *The Annals* 496 (March 1988): 54–64; and "Supreme but Not Final," *Newsweek* (12 October 1992): 78–79.

9. See: Thomas Weidlich, "Pro-choice Forces Score Wins in State Courts, Activists Rely on State Constitutions to Secure Medicaid Abortion Money," *The National Law Journal* 17 (7 August 1995): A11; and Timothy Bishop and Jeffrey Sarles, "State Charters Often Have Broad Takings Clauses; Businesses Suffering a Partial Taking of Their Property Usually Find Little Relief in Federal Court," *The National Law Journal* 17 (17 April 1995): C14.

10. See, generally: Henry Robert Glick, "Policy-Making and State Supreme Courts: The Judiciary as an Interest Group," *Law and Society Review* 5 (November 1970): 271–288.

11. *Certiorari* is an order by a higher court to a lower court to send up a record of a case for review.

12. Loren Beth, *Politics, the Constitution and the Supreme Court* (Evanston, Ill., and Elmsford, N.Y.: Row, Petersen, 1962), p. 53.

13. See: Peltason, *Federal Courts*, p. 14. See also: Walter F. Murphy, "Lower Court Checks on Supreme Court Power," *American Political Science Review* 53 (December 1959): 1017–1031.

14. Kenneth N. Vines, "Southern Supreme Courts and Race Relations," *Western Political Science Quarterly* 18 (March 1965): 5–18.

15. Arraignment is the stage in a criminal proceeding when the defendant is called before a judge to have the bill of indictment read to him or her and to determine how he or she will plead.

16. David P. Currie, "The Three-Judge Court in Constitutional Litigation," *University of Chicago Law Review* 32 (Autumn 1964): 1, 16.

17. See: Beverly Blair Cook, "Role Lag in Urban Trial Courts," *Western Political Science Quarterly* 25 (June 1972): 234–248.

18. Some countries, for example, require a minimum amount of courtroom experience of all judicial candidates and a written examination on important branches of substantive and procedural law.

19. Much of the pioneer work in this area is found in Herbert Jacob, "The Effect of Institutional Differences in the Recruitment Process: The Case of State Judges," *Journal of Public Law* 13 (1964): 104–119. See also: Stuart S. Nagel, *Comparing Elected and Appointed Judicial Systems* (Beverly Hills, Calif.: Sage Publications, 1973); Glen R. Winters, *Judicial Selection and Tenure* (Chicago: American Judicature Society, 1973); Richard A. Watson and Ronald G. Downing, *The Politics of the Bench and the Bar: Judicial Selection under the Missouri Nonpartisan Court Plan* (New York: John Wiley and Sons, 1969); and Philip L. Dubois, *From Ballot to*

Bench: Judicial Elections and the Quest for Accountability (Austin: University of Texas Press, 1980).

20. See: Any Young, "In the States," *Common Cause Magazine* (July/August 1990): 41; Sheila Kaplan, "Justice for Sale," *Common Cause Magazine* (May/June 1987): 29–32; and discussion in Harry P. Stumpf and John H. Culver, *The Politics of State Courts* (New York: Longman, 1992): 43–45.

21. See, for example: Charles A. Johnson, Roger C. Shaefer, and R. Neal McKnight, "The Salience of Judicial Candidates and Elections," *Social Science Quarterly* 59 (September 1978): 371–378; and Kenneth N. Vines and Herbert Jacob, "State Courts," in Jacob and Vines, eds., *Politics in American States* (Boston: Little, Brown, 1971), pp. 272–311.

22. See, for example: William K. Hall and Larry T. Aspin, "What Twenty Years of Judicial Retention Elections Have Told Us," *Judicature* 70 (1987): 340–347.

23. Jacob, "The Effect of Institutional Differences."

24. *Ibid.*

25. *Ibid.*

26. *Ibid.*

27. Richard Richardson, *The Politics of Lower Courts in the United States* (Boston: Little, Brown, 1970), p. 51.

28. See, generally: Herbert Jacob, *Justice in America*, 2nd ed. (Boston: Little, Brown, 1972), pp. 60–67.

29. See, generally: Lee Silverstein, *Defense of the Poor in Criminal Cases in American State Courts* (Chicago: American Bar Association, 1963); "Law and Grievances of the Poor," in *Law and Order Reconsidered* (New York: Bantam Books, 1970), ch. 3; and Jacob, *Justice in America*, pp. 60–67.

30. A useful overview of the public prosecutor's role is found in: Jack M. Kress, "Progress and Prosecution," *The Annals* 423 (January 1976): 99–116.

31. Martin A. Levin, *Urban Politics and the Criminal Courts* (Chicago: University of Chicago Press, 1977).

32. James Eisenstein and Herbert Jacob, *Felony Justice: An Organizational Analysis of Criminal Courts* (Boston: Little, Brown, 1977).

33. See: Maureen Miloski, "Courtroom Encounters: An Observation Study of a Lower Criminal Court," *Law and Society Review* 5 (May 1971): 473–538.

34. Jerome Frank, *Courts on Trial* (New York: Atheneum, 1963).

35. An exception to the ability of attorneys to make peremptory or automatic challenges is situations in which they are using race as a basis for excluding jurors from trials. Supreme Court rulings have barred both prosecutors and defense attorneys from preemptions based on race. On the problem this poses for the justice system, see ch. 15.

36. Jeffrey Abramson, *We the Jury: The Jury System and the Ideal of Democracy* (New York: Basic Books, 1994).

37. See: Jacob, *Justice in America*, ch. 7.

38. Gregory A. Caldeira, "The Transmission of Legal Precedent: A Study of State Supreme Courts," *American Political Science Review* 79 (1985): 178–194.

39. See, generally: Henry Robert Glick, *Supreme Courts in State Politics* (New York: Basic Books, 1971).

40. See: Nagel, *Comparing Judicial Systems;* and Melinda Gann Hall, "Constituent Influence in State Supreme Courts: Conceptual Notes and a Case Study,"*The Journal of Politics* 49 (November 1987): 1118–1124.

41. Melinda Gann Hall, "Electoral Politics and Strategic Voting in State Supreme Courts," *The Journal of Politics* 53 (May 1992): 427–446.

42. See: Stuart S. Nagel, "Political Party Affiliation and Judges' Decisions," *American Political Science Review* 50 (December 1961): 843–850; Sidney Ulmer, "The Political Party Variable in the Michigan Supreme Court," *Journal of Public Law* 11 (1962): 352–362; and Dubois, *From Ballot to Bench.*

43. John Gruhl, Cassia Spohn, and Susan Welch, "Women as Policymakers: The Case of Trial Judges," *American Journal of Political Science* 25 (1981): 308–322.

44. Susan Welch, Michael Combs, and John Gruhl, "Do Black Judges Make a Difference?" *American Journal of Political Science* (February 1988): 126–136.

PART THREE

⭐ ⭐ ⭐

LOCAL-LEVEL POLITICS

8

☆ ☆ ☆

THE SETTING FOR LOCAL POLITICS

Previous chapters have suggested much about the general setting in which local politics takes place. This chapter focuses more closely on the movement and distribution of people in various types of communities; differences among cities, suburbs, and small towns; the pattern of local government; and the relations among local government units.

METROPOLIS, CITY, SUBURB, AND TOWN

Around 80 percent of the some 260 million people in this country live in metropolitan areas as defined by the federal government for statistical purposes. Within what the federal government calls Metropolitan Statistical Areas (MSAs) one finds at least one hundred thousand people and, typically, a large central city surrounded by several suburbs. Currently there are some 350 metropolitan areas.[1]

About half of the nation's population lives in metropolitan areas with populations of a million or more. On the other end of the scale, about a quarter of the population lives in the open countryside or in small towns under twenty-five hundred in population that are located in rural (nonmetropolitan) areas. About one out of every thirteen of the people in rural areas lives on a farm.[2]

MIGRATION PATTERNS AND PROBLEMS

One of the dominant factors affecting the character of local politics is the movement of people. Many of the problems of large central cities within metropolitan areas, particularly the older ones in the East and Midwest, have resulted from the exodus of industry and the more affluent citizens to suburban areas. This movement has been accompanied until recent years by a steady influx of a largely unskilled and poor population from rural areas. Industry has left the cities to get away from crime and transportation problems and to take advantage of lower taxes and cheaper land in suburban areas. An exodus of people out of central cities has followed the exodus of jobs. People have also left to get away from traffic congestion, crime, taxes, and, sometimes, integrated neighborhoods. On the positive side, they have sought out cleaner air, improved schools, and better housing.

Many people are now living in *exurbia,* or rural towns and counties within commuting distance of large cities.[3] With the movement of people away from the urban core to suburbs and beyond, several relatively self-contained and self-sufficient settlements have emerged. Metropolitan areas, as a consequence, are far less likely than in the past to be characterized by an economically, socially, and politically dominant central city. Compared to the traditional pattern of a large central city being at the hub of activity, as people commute into it from their homes in the suburbs, the contemporary pattern, particularly in the East and Midwest, is one of a smaller central city, relatively isolated from the suburbs, and increased interaction among the suburbs (see figure 8–1).

Since the 1970s, Americans have viewed small towns and rural areas as the ideal places to live.[4] The decline in appeal of city life has been particularly noticeable among people living in the East, people in their thirties and forties (many of whom are raising families), and blue-collar workers. Population studies show that these people have been more likely than others to move not only out of cities but also out of metropolitan areas. Professionals such as lawyers and doctors, however, have generally preferred to remain in areas with the greatest concentrations of people.

One dominant aspect of migration patterns has been that people who share similar characteristics tend to cluster together. Many large cities are collections of villages composed of distinct ethnic groupings. Often, neighborhoods and even whole suburbs are populated by people with similar lifestyles, income levels, and social ranking. The growth of retirement communities over the past several years has contributed to the separation of people according to age. Most people also live in racially segregated neighborhoods. For nonwhites, however, separation may be less a matter of choice than of their inability to leave predominantly minority neighborhoods.

The problem of *spatial assimilation,* that is, of moving into an integrated

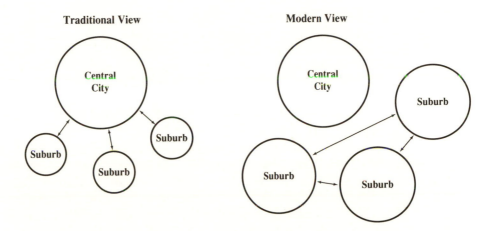

FIGURE 8–1 Central City-Suburban Relations

neighborhood, has been particularly severe for blacks. Although there has been increased movement in recent years, blacks have faced far more difficulties than other minorities in prospering in the cities and moving out to the suburbs or into white middle-class neighborhoods within cities.[5] Nearly 60 percent of the black population resides in central cities, while only 25 percent of the white population lives in these places.

Housing discrimination frustrates the exodus of blacks from ghetto areas. Although federal, state, and local laws prohibit racial discrimination in the sale and rental of housing, these "fair housing" protections have lacked enforcement. Real estate agents commonly discriminate against blacks (and Hispanics) by misinforming them about the availability of housing, making unfavorable rental terms and conditions, and refusing to offer assistance with financing. Realtors commonly engage in *racial steering*, that is, refusing to show minorities certain homes or showing them homes only in established minority residential areas.[6]

Movement out of ghetto areas has also commonly been frustrated by zoning laws that fail to provide for low-cost housing or confine it to existing ghetto areas. Zoning laws requiring large, expensive lots (*fiscal zoning*) have a similar effect. Local laws placing limits on population growth and/or the construction of new homes further limit entry by blacks into middle-class suburban areas. These restrictions, defended on economic grounds, have the effect of limiting population mobility. United States Supreme Court decisions indicate that cities may have considerable authority to limit and control population growth. According to these decisions, for example, cities may limit the number of new housing units that can be built and may refuse to rezone land so that racially integrated, low-cost housing can be built (see chapter 14).

Some observers liken today's black ghetto to an emerging colony. As such, it is a prisoner of the cities, characterized by absentee ownership of most local businesses, low per-capita incomes, a small middle class, low rates of potential economic development, and a large uneducated and unskilled workforce. Blacks, from this perspective, do not control the economic resources of the ghetto but, rather, are systematically exploited by white merchants, landlords, and businesspeople, some of whom live miles from the ghetto and are largely out of touch with its problems.[7]

Frustration in predominantly black communities led to the 1965 Watts riots in Los Angeles and serious outbreaks of violence in Newark, Detroit, and scores of other United States cities in 1967 and 1968. National Guard units and police forces quelled the rioting and restored order. Governments established several commissions to study and report on these disturbances. One of these, the National Advisory Commission on Civil Disorders (also known as the Kerner Commission), concluded that the nation was "moving toward two societies, one black, one white—separate and unequal."[8] The commission rejected the assertions that the riots were the product of organized conspiracies and identified several grievances related to the riots. Heading this list were police practices including physical and verbal abuse, unemployment and underemployment, and inadequate housing.

Even though the 1960s riots generated much concern and reform activity, conditions in ghetto areas have not improved and, indeed, may have deteriorated since the 1960s.[9] Unemployment, for example, continues to affect particularly the residents of central cities, especially black teenagers. Not surprisingly, rioting once again occurred in Los Angeles in the spring of 1992 following the acquittal of four white police officers who had been caught on videotape beating a black motorist, Rodney King. The rioting was largely spontaneous, though street gangs participated in much of the arson and violent crime that took place. Three days of rioting resulted in the death of 53 people and damages of more than a billion dollars. Los Angeles police were widely criticized for not being prepared to handle the violence. Several critics saw the need for closer police-community relations to avoid future violence (see chapter 15).

Although the Los Angeles riots came as no surprise to many observers, a more common pattern in ghetto areas since the 1960s has been what some call *quiet riots*. These have their base in total despair brought on by unemployment, crime, poverty, and housing and school segregation. Some people caught in these conditions have turned inward, seeking relief in drugs. To some extent, drug taking, crime, and other pathological behaviors are the functional equivalent of rioting. Analyses have argued that governments at all levels need to refocus attention on the basic economic problems (unemployment and underemployment) of the urban underclass.[10]

Since the 1960s, black mayors have been elected in a host of large cities:

Atlanta, Chicago, Cleveland, Detroit, Gary, New Orleans, Newark, Los Angeles, St. Louis, and Washington, D.C. Blacks have not been a majority of the population in all these cities (for example, in Los Angeles blacks are but a quarter of the population) and in all these cities black candidates have received some support from white voters. However, unlike other minority groups before them who have been able to capture city hall, blacks have not generally won a great prize. Rather, they have secured political power just at a time when large cities seem ungovernable and local autonomy and success in solving problems seem unlikely.

CENTRAL CITIES

Some observers see the result of population and migration trends to be central cities surrounded by a "noose" of white suburbs, guarded by police to protect against marauding invaders from the cities. The cities, like underdeveloped nations, will have to be sustained by outside assistance. Some observers have wondered if big cities are worth preserving. Eugene Raskin, for example, has noted that cities developed in response to needs for defense, commerce, and excitement, but they no longer serve these purposes. It is no longer feasible to think of large cities defending anyone from outside aggression: indeed, cities are prime targets for nuclear attacks. Industry has found it more profitable to move to the suburbs, and commerce in the central cities is faltering. Crime, blackouts, and traffic jams are the wrong kind of excitement.[11]

Other observers, such as Edward Banfield, are less alarmed about the condition and future of large cities. To Banfield, "the plain fact is that the overwhelming majority of city dwellers live more comfortably and conveniently than ever before."[12] The key problem of large cities lies in the enclaves of various peoples with few skills, limited educations, and low incomes. These people, according to Banfield, are cut off from the rest of the city, feel little attachment to society at large, and lack the ability to imagine a future or sacrifice for future rewards.

By several measurements, governmental and people problems are most pronounced in the oldest and largest central cities in the East and Midwest. Large cities in the East and Midwest have been losing population in recent years, while those in the South and West have generally gained in population. Fueling the growth has been migration from other sections of the country and the liberal use of annexation procedures whereby cities have extended their boundaries and have brought in more people. The losses of jobs and high-income taxpayers have financially crippled many eastern and midwestern central cities. To make matters worse, the increasing numbers of poor and unskilled people have generated heavy expenditures for city health, welfare, and housing programs. Also troublesome to central cities are the commuter-related problems of traffic congestion, parking, air pollution, and street maintenance. Many older cities face unusually large expenditures to repair or replace deteriorating water mains, sewer lines, streets, bridges, and other physical facilities.

Some of the financial problems of the nation's largest cities were dramatically revealed in 1975, when it became apparent that the city of New York would fall some $1.5 billion short of meeting its payroll and debt obligations. Analysts attributed part of this problem to factors peculiar to the city itself. For example, New York had been undertaking expensive welfare responsibilities and had been providing services such as free higher education not commonly provided by other city governments. Like other cities, however, New York had also encountered financial problems caused by a deteriorating tax base, increased demands of municipal unions, and population shifts out of the city. In New York's case, the federal government came to the city's rescue through loans and loan guarantee measures. Recovery also required large cuts in the city's workforce, heavy tax increases, curtailing of government services, and postponement of public improvement projects. Out of the stress, the office of mayor was strengthened as a way of creating greater coordination and efficiency.[13]

Similar problems, plus severe political altercations between the mayor and the business community, help account for the failure of Cleveland to meet its obligations to six local banks and make payments to its firefighter and police pension funds in the late 1970s. Cleveland was the first major city since the Depression years of the 1930s to default on its debts. The amount of the debt, however, was considerably less than that of New York City ($20 million compared to $1.5 billion) and was faced by the city without state or federal assistance.

The financial woes of cities continued into the 1990s. One medium-sized city of some 140,000 people, Bridgeport, Connecticut, declared itself bankrupt. Like other cities, it had an eroding tax base and an increasing welfare population. Bridgeport, again like other cities, had experienced a structural change in its economy—the loss of jobs once supplied by manufacturing—forcing its citizens, particularly the blue-collar poor, to look for new ways to make a living.

Some observers have taken the view that the decline of central cities in older sections of the country is a natural reaction of people and industry to the problems they have encountered and is a phenomenon that should be allowed to run its course. Others have contended that the federal government is at least partially responsible for the plight of the central cities and that it has a major responsibility to help reverse the effects of its past mistakes. Among the federal governmental policies contributing to the decline of the central cities have been mortgage programs that have subsidized new housing in suburban areas, transportation improvements that have made it possible for people to separate where they work (central cities) from where they make their homes (suburbs), and water and sewer projects that have encouraged growth in suburban areas.

Attempts to combat the problems of distressed large cities have produced a number of government programs, many of which are discussed in other sections of this book. Generally, the focus of federal policy has evolved from primary concern in the 1950s with the physical deterioration of central cities to concern in the 1960s with the problems of the urban poor and nonwhites, to concern in the late 1970s with the fiscal problems of large city governments. These problems resulted in an escalation of federal aid programs to cities in the 1960s and 1970s. These programs were cut back in the early 1980s (chapter 2). With the rise of the suburbs, the political significance of large cities in national politics has been on the decline. Presidential elections are won or lost in the suburbs rather than big cities. Budgetary concerns in Washington have also reduced serious attention in Washington to many manifestations of the large-city crisis.[14]

In recent years, some state governments have become more involved in providing aid and development programs targeted for distressed areas in large cities. These actions have enabled several cities to undertake large-scale renewal projects. Particularly active have been cities like Baltimore, Boston, Chicago, New York, Philadelphia, and Washington, D.C. In many places there has been a *gentrification* process bringing middle-class citizens back to the cities. Gentrification, however, increases rent and property values and thus makes conditions more difficult for the poor. Most large cities continue to confront severe fiscal problems. Moreover, population trends indicate that the future may well belong to the suburbs rather than to the central cities.

SUBURBIA

For statistical purposes, analysts use the term suburbia to refer to all areas within an MSA except central cities. Suburbs, thus defined, have more white-collar workers, more college graduates, and more middle-class families than do central cities. On the whole, the suburban areas have had proportionately more children, fewer working mothers, and more single-family dwellings than central cities. Analysts take these measures as indices of a family-centered culture.

There are, of course, all types of suburbs. In regard to legal status, some suburbs are incorporated, often defensively to ward off annexation by a central city, while others are unincorporated and avoid financial strain by allowing the county to minister to the needs of their residents. Suburbs may also be distinguished by social classes. Wealthy people created the first suburbs. They moved just outside the city limits to find high-status, quasi-rural living in luxury estates. Middle-class and working-class suburbs came later.

Many suburbs are so small that they are without a tax base large enough to provide more than minimal services for a bedroom community composed of residents who spend most of their daylight hours in the central city. Other suburbs, particularly older ones close to the central city, have grown so large and heterogeneous their problems and politics resemble those of large central cities. In some parts of the country, suburbs are so spread out and scattered among a wide number of subdivisions there is no center of activity or sense of belonging to a larger suburban community at all. Some suburbs are predominantly black while many others are predominantly white. Politically, suburbia as a whole is safe neither for Republicans nor for Democrats.

Historically, we do find one important difference between city and suburb: While the older central cities have generally grown as settlements without walls, open to everyone, suburbs have a long tradition of exclusivity. As suggested earlier, zoning practices and policies limiting growth may have the effect of keeping the poor and nonwhite out of wealthy and white suburbs, and, conversely, of keeping many of the poor and nonwhite in the central cities or in the minority-dominated suburbs open to them. In a white suburban community politics is likely to revolve around the protection of property values and fighting off unwanted invasions of people or activities that would lower those values.

SMALL (NONMETROPOLITAN) TOWNS

In recent years, scholars have found that some of the historic differences in the attitudes and behavior of urban and rural people have lessened.[15] This has resulted in part from the fact that rural America has found it difficult to remain isolated from the spread of urban culture and lifestyles. Another factor that may minimize the difference between rural and urban dwellers is that many urban residents have rural backgrounds and appear to have retained values and attitudes acquired in a rural society. In predicting attitudes, the community of origin may be more useful than the community of current residence.

Many of the differences between urban and rural people may have lessened. Urban and rural (or metropolitan and nonmetropolitan) populations, however, do continue to differ along religious, ethnic, and racial lines. Metropolitan areas, particularly large cities, have a disproportionate number of Catholics, Jews, and ethnic minorities from eastern and southern Europe. As noted earlier, a large percentage of the black population also lives in metropolitan areas. Nonmetropolitan areas, in contrast, remain largely white, Anglo-Saxon, and Protestant (often fundamentalist) in composition.

Governments in small towns are often viewed as being the closest to the people. Many small-town governments are, indeed, open and responsive to their citizens. On the other hand, compared to larger jurisdictions, political activity in a small town is more likely to be dominated by small cliques, often the most prominent families. Small towns are likely to be populated by people who are conservative in their political, economic, and social views. They are likely to support one party in state and national elections and are seldom the scene of closely contested, issue-oriented local elections. Although the smallness of the jurisdiction gives people a better opportunity to participate, the level of participation in elections or at council meetings may, in fact, be limited to relatively few. As with larger units of government, it might be said that citizens are only occasionally concerned with town council decisions and that much of their involvement with the council is related to issues directly affecting them, rather than the community in general.

Studies on small-town politics in rather stable communities suggest a pattern of laid-back, informal government. Politics is apt to be a major topic of conversation within the village, but the discussion tends to be focused on personalities rather than on issues. The town or village government, moreover, is unlikely to initiate new undertakings or policies and is willing to abdicate much of its authority to state and county agencies. When decisions are made by the local government, they are likely to reflect the *principle of unanimity*. By this rule, dissent and disagreement are ironed out before or during official meetings, so a consensus is reached and decisions are made unanimously.[16]

Small towns face a variety of problems. The nature of these depends, in part, on whether they are declining or growing in population. Many of those on the decline have been dependent on labor-intensive extractive industries such as farming, forestry, or mining. Some of the most noticeable problems have been in farming communities. During the past quarter-century over thirty million people have left the farms for larger urban areas. Much of this exodus has been caused by technological advances that have increased farm productivity and reduced the need for labor. Survival of small, isolated rural towns facing a decline in employment and population is generally seen to depend on considerable outside help, for example, from the state government, in promoting a diverse economy and overall economic growth.

Some small towns experiencing rapid growth have been attractive because they offer a pleasant climate or lifestyle for those in retirement. Many more people have looked on the small town as a place of employment. Much of the employment appeal has been to blue-collar workers.[17] In relatively remote parts of the country there have been "boom towns" populated by an immigration of construction and mining workers. More growth has occurred on the fringes of metropolitan areas where agricultural economies have been replaced by those built on manufacturing and trade. The addition of jobs has not only attracted new migrants to small towns but also reduced the exodus of young people raised in these areas. Growth, of course, has also brought problems of supporting new or expanded services and of mediating conflicts between "newcomers" and "old-timers."

As small communities have grown, there has been an increase in the number of administrative professionals hired by their governments. Trained managers (county, city, and town), police chiefs, planners, and civil engineers are now commonly found serving communities faced with complex problems caused by rapid growth. Growing towns have hired professional managers and planners to help take advantage of federal aid programs and meet state land-use regulations. They have added civil engineers to help design new water systems made necessary by federal and state water standards.

The increased importance of professional administrators in growing areas has been accompanied by a change in administrative style and considerable conflict in various parts of the country. The traditional values of a small town create an administrative style that is informal, simple, and heavily influenced by friendship and primary group relations, but the administrative style of the professional administrator calls for neutrality and rationality in carrying out governmental functions. Long-time residents of a small town, accustomed to a more personal government where legal and procedural requirements are neglected, may become uncomfortable in an environment in which regulations are consistently applied on an impersonal basis.[18]

Survey data suggest that those who live in small towns are happier with the quality of life than are those who live in heavily populated areas. Nevertheless, small towns do have serious problems. The percentage of the nonmetropolitan population living below the poverty line (see chapter 12) is greater than in metropolitan areas (about 20 percent compared to 11 percent). The quality and availability of health care and housing in nonmetropolitan areas also lag behind those of urban areas. What people apparently value about small towns is what they *do not* have much of, for example, crime, high taxes, noise, and pollution, in comparison to large urban areas.[19] Rapid growth of small towns, of course, is likely to lead to an increase in many of these and other problems that people presumably move to small towns to escape.

THE PATTERN OF LOCAL GOVERNMENT

Local government in the United States consists of over 85,000 separate units. This figure includes some 3,000 counties, 19,000 municipalities, 17,000 town or township governments, 14,000 school districts, and 32,000 special districts. Over the years, the most dramatic drop has been in the number of school districts and the most dramatic increase has been in the number of special districts (see table 8–1).

State courts have traditionally viewed local governments as "the legal creatures" of their states. Applying *Dillon's Rule* (after John F. Dillon, a nineteenth-century Iowa jurist and authority on municipal law), they have concluded that local governments have only the powers expressly granted

TABLE 8–1   Types and Numbers of Local Government

Type	1992	1982	1972	1962
County	3,043	3,041	3,044	3,043
Municipal	19,279	19,076	18,517	18,000
Town or township	16,656	16,734	16,991	17,142
School district	14,422	14,851	15,781	34,678
Special district	31,555	28,078	23,885	18,323
Total	84,955	81,780	78,218	91,186

Source: United States Bureau of the Census, *1992 Census of Governments: Government Organization* (Washington, D.C.: Government Printing Office, March 1994 and previous years).

them by the state and that these powers must be construed narrowly. This rule has been challenged from time to time by those who have championed the *Cooley Rule*. Derived from an 1871 decision by Michigan Judge Thomas Cooley, this rule asserts that the right to local self-government is inherent. Nevertheless, the bulk of judicial decisions has clearly been on the side of Judge Dillon rather than Judge Cooley.

Cities, villages, and in some states boroughs and towns are known in law as municipal corporations or governments.[20] The state creates them, defines their authority, determines the possible form of government they may adopt, and may even abolish local governments. State authorities may also, in effect, suspend local autonomy and democracy and take direct control over the activities of local governments (see box 8–1). State interventions of this nature have been most noticeable in recent years with respect to financially distressed municipalities and to "academically bankrupt" school districts (see chapter 12) Yet, such interventions are rare. Whatever desire state officials have to intervene in local affairs is countered by a variety of political and cultural constraints and by managerial problems that work against the exercise of state authority. There is, consequently, often a considerable gap between the potential authority of the states over local governments and how states use their authority.[21]

In practice, the amount of independent authority exercised by local governments varies not only from state to state (see chapter 2) but also by type of local government and by particular functions.[22] Municipalities usually enjoy greater self-government than do counties and other units of local government. Generally, local units enjoy more discretion as to how they would like to be structured or organized than they do as to what functions they may perform or as to how they may raise and spend revenues. Different factors seem to be linked to the amount of discretion given for these different areas of authority. Research suggests, for example, that rapid population growth may prompt a

BOX 8–1 TAKEOVER IN CHELSEA

The ultimate state intervention in recent years came in Chelsea, Massachusetts, a city of some twenty-eight thousand people on the northern edge of Boston. The city experienced a severe financial decline in the mid-1980s. The state initially responded with loans and grants and fiscal oversight. In 1991 it finally put the town in receivership to save it from financial collapse. The state eliminated the post of mayor, reduced the status of other locally elected officials to an advisory one, and gave the receiver broad authority to run the city for up to five years. The receiver proceeded to balance the city's budget by cutting the payroll, renegotiating union contracts, increasing user fees, privatizing some services, and other means. The receivership also produced a new local government structure, in effect since 1994, which was designed to improve the ability of local officials to govern efficiently.

legislature to give local governments more authority on structure, but that changes on what functions a city or county can perform are linked to slower-changing cultural factors.[23] Changes in the policies of the federal government may also trigger changes in the way states regard local units. Recent declines in federal aid to cities, for example, have prompted state governments to give cities more discretion in regard to raising revenues.

MUNICIPALITIES

Cities and other municipalities were at one time under the almost total domination of state legislatures. Up to the early decades of the twentieth century, cities were generally created and governed by special acts of the state legislature. Local communities wishing to achieve the status of municipal corporations would petition the legislature for a charter conferring governmental powers on them. The charters were commonly so narrow that the municipalities had to return to the legislature to secure authority to do such things as have a street paved, install a fire hydrant, or increase the salaries of their officials. At other times, legislation affecting only a particular municipality would be passed without regard to or in spite of local sentiments.

Municipal reformers in the early decades of the twentieth century argued that the powers and status of individual municipal governments should not vary according to the whims of state legislatures and that legislators were ill equipped to make local decisions. This criticism led to state constitutional prohibitions on special legislation and to the adoption of home rule laws or constitutional provisions.

Laws in most states now require that state legislatures deal with municipalities through general rather than special legislation. Depending on factors such as population or the value of property within its jurisdiction, a municipality may be classified, for example, as a first-class or second-class city or as a town rather than a city. These classifications, as discussed later, condition the form of government and powers of the municipality. Once a municipality is classified, it is subject to all state laws affecting that classification. Thus, state legislatures commonly pass laws for all first-class cities or towns as a group rather than for specific municipalities. This practice is intended to comply with prohibitions on special legislation. In reality, however, general laws sometimes amount to special laws when only one municipality falls into a certain classification. For example, in legislating for first-class cities the New York State legislature is really legislating only for New York City.

Currently, municipal governments may be created or incorporated by three basic methods: (1) general laws applying to municipalities with certain classifications, (2) optional charter laws, and (3) home rule procedures. These methods, unlike the older system of creation through a special legislation, require that the question of incorporation be submitted to a popular vote. A municipality incorporated under a general law adopts governmental features established by state law for all municipalities falling into the same classification. Under an optional charter plan available in some states, incorporating municipalities are given a choice of specific governmental plans. For example, a city can choose a mayor-council form or a council-manager form of city government. (These forms are discussed in chapter 10.)

Home rule provisions found in state statutes or constitutions are the most flexible in that they allow qualifying municipalities (for example, those over a certain population size) the right to frame, adopt, or amend their own charters. In order to obtain home rule, a local charter commission is elected to draft a charter for submission to the voters. While home rule procedures have given municipalities (and some counties) greater control over their governmental organization, they have not given local governments a green light to undertake what activities they desire. State courts, on the contrary, have often tended to give a narrow interpretation to home rule powers. On the other hand, local governments lacking home rule are in a worse position in that they must obtain specific legislative authority for just about everything they wish to do. One result of this is that state lawmakers in states where home rule is weak spend considerable time on relatively minor bills affecting local governments.

More than half of the municipalities in the country serve populations of fewer than a thousand people. On the other end of the scale are, ranked in order of population as of 1994, New York City, Los Angeles, Chicago, Houston, Philadelphia, San Diego, Phoenix, Dallas, San Antonio, and Detroit, which serve more than a million people. The functions of the various municipalities (and other units) vary from state to state and within a state, largely on the basis of their populations. Some municipalities, like New York City, for example, have responsibility for welfare programs, although this is normally a state and county function. Some municipalities may also have responsibility for education, though states usually give this function to independent local school districts.

COUNTIES

County governments—in contrast to municipalities—have traditionally functioned as administrative units for state programs in such areas as welfare services, highway construction, education, and the administration of justice.[24] Three out of four counties serve fewer than fifty thousand persons. The range in population size served is from Loving County, Texas, with 107 inhabitants to Los Angeles County, California, with more than 8 million people.

Historically, county governments have operated under the commission form, borrowed by colonial governments from the English shire. This form vests authority in a board of supervisors or commissioners who are usually elected from districts. Authority is further dispersed among several popularly elected officials, including a sheriff, treasurer, prosecuting attorney, tax assessor, and a superintendent of schools. On the plus side, the large number of elected officials increases government responsiveness to the people and brings about checks and balances in the system. On the negative side, the structure makes it difficult for any one person to exert leadership or control over county government. This system also encourages "buck passing," that is, allowing one supervisor or agency head to blame another for what the government does or fails to do. Another problem is that the frequent lack of unity among county officials puts the county in a weak bargaining position vis-à-vis other governments.[25] The commission form of county government is particularly popular in smaller rural counties. In these places county governments continue to function largely as administrative arms of the state government.

Metropolitan pressures, however, have encouraged several states to give counties (or at least certain categories of counties) home rule charters that allow them to provide many of the services once performed only by municipalities. Because they bridge jurisdictional boundaries of municipalities, counties are often viewed as the logical unit of government to provide services on a metropolitan or regional basis. In some cases counties have assumed functions such as health care that could no longer be provided by individual municipalities in an efficient manner. In other cases, counties provide various services to municipalities under contract (see following discussion of Los Angeles County). The new role of counties as providers of metropolitan services has been most prominent in southern states where there has been a tradition of state centralization and where counties have not had to share functions with towns and township governments. County administrators in this and perhaps other parts of the country appear eager to assume responsibility for provision for the full range of services normally provided by cities.[26]

Structural changes have also been made in metropolitan areas in recent years to improve the administration of county governments. While a majority of all counties have the traditional commission form, it has been increasingly popular in urban areas to opt for a council-administrator form or a council-elected executive form. Under a council-administrator plan, the county council appoints a professional administrator (known as a county manager, chief administrative officer, or executive secretary) who has broad authority over personnel, budgeting, and the administration of county departments and agencies. The council-elected executive form provides for separate legislative and executive branches. The elected executive, often known as the county mayor, has administrative powers similar to those of the county manager. In addition, some have the power to vote at council meetings, and many may veto county ordinances. Compared to the council-administrator plan, the county executive plan provides in the office of mayor a strong, easily recognizable political leader. Although the council-manager and council-elected executive forms differ in regard to how policy is made and implemented, the choice between the forms does not appear to make much of a difference in what counties do, that is, in policies adopted or expenditure patterns.[27]

Along with the increased activity and reorganization, county governments in urban areas have become increasingly assertive in their dealings with the state and other local units. While continuing to serve as arms of the state, they have become more assertive in demanding an end to particular state controls, for example, restricting their fiscal authority, and have frequently struggled with municipalities for a prominent role in providing local services.[28]

TOWNS AND TOWNSHIPS

In the New England states, one finds a strong tradition of local government autonomy and the oldest form of municipal government in the nation—the local town meeting. The town meeting, established in colonial times, has constituted an exercise in direct democracy. Originally, all eligible voters assembled at an annual meeting to discuss community issues and make laws. Under traditional arrangements, the voters would elect from three to seven selectmen and a number of other officials to manage the town's affairs between town meetings. Today, because of growing population and the complexity of urban problems, many New England towns have deviated from direct democracy by adopting a system to elect representatives from precincts to attend meetings. The role of participation in town meetings varies greatly, from less than 10 percent of the registered voters to more than 40 percent. Apparently, many who do attend are reluctant to speak because they fear that they may seem foolish or uninformed.[29] Many towns have chosen to professionalize their governments by placing responsibility for management in the hands of a town manager who reports to the board of selectmen.

Town and township governments were created in several eastern and midwestern states to perform functions similar to those performed by New England towns. They, too, are exercises in direct democracy and vest managerial functions in an elected board. Over the years, however, most rural townships have found it increasingly difficult to attract citizens to their annual meetings and have lost authority in areas like highways and law enforcement to counties and cities. On the other end of the scale, township governments act like full-scale municipal corporations providing all local schools and even county-like services.[30]

SPECIAL DISTRICTS

Special districts are quasi-municipal corporations created under state law. Most provide a single function such as fire protection, soil conservation, sewer, water, housing, or mosquito control. They are governed by a small board, usually appointed by state or local officials. Districts usually have their own taxing and borrowing authority.

Special districts have been used to meet problems that transcend local (sometimes state and national) boundaries. They have been popular because they facilitate the provision of services without disrupting the structure of general units of local government. They also provide greater fiscal flexibility by allowing local units to bypass taxation and debt limits placed on them by state law. At the same time, the growth in the number of special districts has further fragmented governmental authority, especially in metropolitan areas, and has added to the complexity of local government. Special districts often operate in isolation from other units of local government and fail to coordinate their programs and plans with them. Because their governing bodies are usually not elected and they seldom attract much public attention, special districts also fail to meet the criteria of public accountability.[31]

The best-known special districts, although in a classification of their own under the census, are school districts. These are usually governed by an elected board of education. The board, in turn, hires a professional administrator to supervise the activity of the system. The number of school districts has been dramatically reduced from 109,000 in 1942 to around 14,000 today. The consolidation of school districts into larger units has been undertaken to enlarge their property tax base and to make them more administratively efficient. We look at school districts in greater detail in chapter 12.

GOVERNMENT IN METROPOLITAN AREAS

THE METROPOLITAN PROBLEM

The "metropolitan problem" that has attracted the attention of scholars and government officials has several aspects. In part, it relates to the growth of

---

BOX 8–2   PROGRAMMED TO FAIL

David Rusk, a former mayor of Albuquerque, New Mexico, has argued that 40 percent of the country's 522 central cities are programmed to fail. They are what Rusk calls "inelastic" cities that are unable to grow, expand their tax base, or create economic opportunities for their inhabitants. These cities also lack the ability to form partnerships and alliances with neighboring communities, which would expand economic opportunities. Rusk sees a solution in state action encouraging regional or metropolitan governments.

See: David Rusk, "Bend or Die: Inflexible State Laws and Policies Are Dooming Some of the Country's Central Cities," *State Government News* (February 1994): 6–10; and, more generally: David Rusk, *Cities without Suburbs* (Washington, D.C.: Woodrow Wilson Center Press, 1993, 1995).

---

suburbs and the subsequent difficulties of central cities, especially in the older sections of the country. In many places we find a mismatch between fiscal needs and resources. The needs are in the central cities but the resources are in the suburbs. Residents of central cities have to tax themselves at a higher rate than suburban residents simply to generate the same revenues and at a substantially higher rate to generate sufficient revenues to address their special needs. Yet, if they try to raise revenues to the necessary level, they are likely to encourage more people to leave for the suburbs.[32]

A central metropolitan problem from this perspective centers on the question: Can the suburban trend be controlled? As indicated earlier, several programs have been undertaken to keep affluent people in cities or to encourage them to return to cities. Solutions to the mismatch problem also have been sought in local government tax-sharing programs and reforms in federal and state aid programs that would more directly target large cities with financial problems (see chapter 11). Some observers have called for new regional or metropolitan governments that could end fiscal imbalances and promote or create equity in services (see box 8–2).

Another aspect of the metropolitan problem simply is that of providing governmental services on an areawide basis. The need for an areawide approach to many problems can be easily demonstrated. A city's mosquito control program, for example, can hardly be effective if the mosquito population merely moves across boundary lines. Other governmental problems, such as water pollution and transportation systems, also cut across local boundaries.

Many jurisdictions have attempted to meet these types of problems through the use of special districts that literally draw a line around the various problem areas. But, as noted above, the use of special districts has meant the creation of relatively invisible governments not directly accountable to the public and, in the metropolitan area as a whole, increased fragmentation of governmental authority. Over the years, other solutions to metropolitan governing and service problems have centered on annexation, consolidation, and bringing about more cooperation among existing units of local government.[33]

ANNEXATION

Throughout much of the nation's history, cities have been able to keep their boundaries concurrent with population growth through the annexation of territory. Through annexation proceedings, a city extends its boundaries into unincorporated areas. Annexation enables cities to secure a new tax base and prevent dwellers on their fringes from benefiting from city services without paying for them. The new areas of the city have often received better services after annexation. Annexation has also prevented the development or creation of local governments that would be potential rivals.

There are, however, legal and political barriers to the use of annexation. Much annexation took place when state law encouraged such activity and when there was plenty of unincorporated territory to annex. Until the beginning of the twentieth century, cities generally had the right to annex by unilateral action. As cities expanded their boundaries, they began to frighten people in unincorporated suburbs and rural areas. An alliance of suburban and rural interests in state legislatures reacted by making annexation more difficult. Most important among the annexation laws were those granting outlying property owners the sole right of initiating annexation proceedings and those providing that cities could annex only after voters in the area to be annexed voted their approval in a referendum election. In addition to these laws, state legislatures made it easier for outlying areas to incorporate and thus avoid annexation.

Recent history has shown that people in unincorporated areas may resist annexation because they fear the loss of area identity, higher taxes, the extension of the city's subdivision and zoning regulations into the area, and political domination by a larger and socioeconomically different city population. Annexation is most difficult where voters perceive lifestyle differences between themselves and those living in the annexing city. There also may be problems from the annexing city's point of view. The city may, for example, find that the outlying area anxious for annexation contains too many low-income residents. Because of this, the city might have to spend far more to extend services than it could gain in taxes.

The most dramatic growth through annexation in recent years has taken place in southern and western states. In many parts of the country, however, restrictive laws and the emergence of incorporated suburban areas have made annexation no longer feasible. In this situation decision makers confront the problem of how to meet effectively problems that spill over local boundaries. Some observers call for greater consolidation of governments. Others place emphasis on voluntary cooperation among existing units of local government.

GOVERNMENTAL CONSOLIDATION

Over the years many academics and practitioners have argued that new metropolitan or regional levels of government should be created either to replace local units or to assume functions that are areawide in nature. Proposals for the consolidation of governments in metropolitan areas have been advanced as necessary to provide services in a rational manner and to end duplication of services and inequities in taxation. Consolidation, some argue, is necessary to create local governments capable of solving their own problems without the support of the national and state governments.[34]

Some proposals have called for the consolidation of governments in a given metropolitan area into a single (one-level) government with general authority over the jurisdiction. Other proposals have been for a two-level metropolitan federation that would provide the advantages of both centralization and decentralization. Such systems are used in London and Toronto and represent an attempt to apply a federal plan of government to a metropolitan area, whereby a central government performs areawide functions and local governments handle local problems. Areawide problems would generally include water supply, sewage disposal, and police protection, and local problems would include refuse collection and maintenance of local streets. There is, of course, apt to be wide disagreement over what is an areawide function and what is a local one.

Thus far, relatively few consolidations have occurred within metropolitan areas.[35] The most successful area of consolidation has been between city and county governments.[36] Much of this, however, has involved only the integration of certain functions to end the duplication of services, increase efficiency, and save the city taxpayers from paying for county services they do not receive. Functional consolidation has been frequently advocated and has taken place with city-county police, health, and welfare departments.

In 1957, a system of government was adopted in Dade County, Florida, that, while something short of a complete consolidation, became the closest thing we have in this country to a metropolitan federation. Dade County, called "Metro," is a union of twenty-six municipalities, each of which continues as a governmental entity. The county government operates under a special home rule charter and has the power to provide regional services (such as water, planning, and mass transit) and to set minimum standards of performance for any service or function performed by cities within its boundaries.

The county may take over functions performed by municipalities that fail to meet its standards. Metro's governing body consists of a thirteen-member board of county commissioners, which appoints a county manager and attorney.

Following the Dade County experiment, more complete consolidations toward a one-level rather than a two-level (federated) government took place in various parts of the country. Three of the most significant of these involved Nashville and Davidson County (Tennessee), Jacksonville and Duval County (Florida), and Indianapolis and Marion County (Indiana). The adoption of a charter for a single consolidated government in Nashville grew out of studies begun in the early 1950s. Voters both in Nashville and the outside areas finally approved the consolidation in 1962. Nashville's Metro resulted in the elimination of the old city and county structures and their replacement by a county mayor and a large metropolitan council of forty members. Under the new government, two service districts were created: a general service district covering the entire area was given responsibility for functions like police, hospitals, and schools; and an urban services district was formed to provide and finance such functions as street lighting and cleaning, refuse collection, and additional police and fire protection.

Consolidation in Jacksonville was greatly facilitated by an exposure of governmental corruption in both the city and the county that led to the indictment of several public officials. On the heels of this scandal, citizen and business groups secured legislative approval to establish a fifty-member study commission to bring about a restructuring of the governments. Four small municipalities within the county took advantage of the opportunity of a separate vote and decided to stay out of the consolidation. The consolidation resulted in the election of a strong mayor and a nineteen-member city-county council.

Unlike that in the Nashville and Jacksonville situations, leadership for consolidation in the Indianapolis area came from within city hall. Consolidation was made easier by the fact that the mayor of Indianapolis, the governor, and a majority of the state legislature were Republicans. Consolidation became almost a party issue since it was supported by Republicans as a means of securing their hold on city hall through the addition of voters in the suburbs and opposed by Democrats for the same reason. The Indianapolis-Marion County merger was also unique in that it was effected by the state legislature without a local referendum. The consolidation did not affect school systems, police departments, the township volunteer fire departments, or three small cities within this county. Under the new system, called "Unigov," county voters elect a mayor and a city council of twenty-nine members.

In the more common situation where voters have been involved, consolidation attempts are apt to be opposed by incumbent officeholders, both elected and appointed, who see the prospect of losing their jobs. Opposition is also likely to come from those who champion home rule and identity of their local units or fear an increase in taxation. Smaller units of government, if given the opportunity, may well refuse to become part of the consolidation.

Blacks in large cities also may see a loss of political power through consolidation with suburban and county units. Indeed, black voting power has been diluted by recent consolidations. In Nashville, the black percentage of the population went from 40 to 25 percent following consolidation. Similarly, in Jacksonville the percentage of blacks went from 43 to 23 percent and in Indianapolis from 25 to 15 percent. This potential loss of minority group voting power, however, may be minimized or overcome by district arrangements that give special representation to minorities in metropolitan councils.

Consolidation proposals are often defeated at the polls. Data suggest that as many as three out of every four city-county consolidation proposals on the ballot since 1945 have been rejected by the voters.[37] Past experience suggests that it is helpful to enlist the active support of leading citizens and to hold numerous public hearings. Perhaps more important, successful efforts toward consolidation may also depend on the existence of a critical situation in the provision of public services or the uncovering of a scandal that will generate public support for reform.[38]

PATTERNS OF COOPERATION

In recent years, emphasis has been placed on meeting metropolitan problems through voluntary cooperation among existing units of local government rather than through the restructuring of local governments. The cooperative approach has been popular with local public officials because it maintains local home rule, fends off restructuring through consolidation, and, at the same time, contributes to increased efficiency and lower costs. Individual municipalities have taken the lead in initiating various types of cooperative undertakings. Cooperation has been further encouraged by the improvement in the administration and services of county governments, by state legislation permitting cooperative arrangements, and by planning requirements attached to federal aid programs.

Two commonly used means of cooperation are contracts and agreements between cities or between cities and counties and voluntary councils of government. Three types of cooperative arrangements frequently used are: (1) those in which one governmental unit contracts with another to perform specific services, such as fire protection; (2) those in which two or more governmental units jointly purchase equipment or operate some facility under contractual arrangements; and (3) those in which two or more governmental units agree to assist one another when the need arises (for example, a mutual aid pact regarding each other's police force during an emergency).

Los Angeles County provides the most prominent example of a local government engaged in the service contract business. Through a general service contract, the county provides a wide range of services to municipalities within its boundaries. Rather than provide its residents with their own police or health services, a municipality can purchase them from the county. Municipal governments under this type of arrangement resemble consumer agencies attempting to get the best buy or package of programs from the county during annual negotiations as they weigh the county's bid against the cost of providing the services themselves. At the same time, becoming incorporated within the county is still worthwhile because the municipalities may have control over local planning and zoning, receive earmarked state aid, and be protected against annexation.

Contracts and agreements, while easy to bring about compared to consolidation, offer at best only a piecemeal solution to areawide cooperation. Very often what results is a patchwork of legal relations without any overall design and system. Contracts and agreements also often exclude those local governments in the area that do not have either the financial resources to contract and pay for services or any services to offer in return.

Another form of intergovernmental cooperation is the voluntary council of government. COGs are associations of local governmental officials within a given area formed to foster cooperation in solving common problems. The council device facilitates cooperation while retaining home rule. Generally, all cities and counties within a metropolitan area are eligible for council membership. Some councils have also extended eligibility to school districts, special authorities, and even Indian tribes. Each member unit selects its representatives to the council. These are generally the chief elected officials of the local governments involved. The power of the COGs is purely advisory. They are supported for the most part by members' contributions, although they also receive planning grants from the national government.

In practice, councils of government take several forms. Some are merely defensive coalitions formed to prevent drastic governmental restructuring or are good-fellowship gatherings that fail to do much in the way of developing a positive plan of action for the metropolitan area. Others function in large part as regional planning commissions or as conduits for federal funds, for example, in regard to transportation. Overall, COGs are limited by the simple fact that they are voluntary and can only be as effective as individual members want them to be.

As the associations gain the confidence of their members and develop staff facilities, however, they may go through an evolutionary process toward becoming regional policymaking and action councils. Going beyond the conventional COG, for example, is Portland, Oregon's, Metropolitan Service District (Metro). This is a metropolitan-wide, multipurpose government run by officials directly elected by voters. Metro has a twelve-member governing board whose members are elected for four-year terms on a nonpartisan basis from single-member districts within the metropolitan area. The government has the authority to perform a wide variety of services and, with voter approval, to draw on its own revenue sources. Metro extends into three counties and is active in area land-use planning, environmental protection, and operating such enterprises as zoo and convention facilities.[39]

COGs, it should be noted, are but one type of several metropolitan or regional bodies. In addition to COGs there are multicounty planning bodies and hundreds of separate areawide organizations or authorities concerned with specific functions like law enforcement, economic development, poverty, homelessness, education, transportation, and air pollution. Regional agencies concerned with only a single function have some disadvantages. They are not directly accountable to the people in the regions they serve and often fail to coordinate their efforts with local governments or with each other. Directly elected multipurpose "umbrella" regional bodies such as the one in Portland appear to be more desirable.

INTERLOCAL RELATIONS, HOME RULE, AND THE FUTURE OF THE METROPOLIS

Relations among governmental units in metropolitan areas may be looked upon as resembling those among nations of the world.[40] Each unit of government is primarily out to protect or maintain its own interest. Each looks to maintain its legal autonomy and territorial integrity and to compete effectively with other units for scarce resources such as profitable business enterprises and high-income residents.

In dealing with other units of government, officials represent their people as ambassadors represent their countries. Within metropolitan areas there are counterparts to "major" and "minor" powers. A central city, for example, may be a major power because it has control over the area's water supply. There are also long-standing feuds and rivalries between central cities and suburbs and among suburbs, just as there are among nations. Competition among local units may produce conflict, bordering on war, but enlightened self-interest also brings diplomatic relations, treaties, agreements, and other cooperative endeavors to avoid conflict or solve common problems.

The international relations analogy is helpful in pointing out the difficulties in restructuring local governments or effecting cooperation among them. Councils of government may be as inherently weak or potentially strong as the United Nations. Cooperative relations between units of local government, as between nations, tend to be structured on a project-by-project or piecemeal basis.

Recent years, however, have brought an increased emphasis on cooperative endeavors and improved regional problem solving. Interlocal contracting has been driven principally by cost considerations, as a way of making up for declining revenues.[41] Improved regional problem solving has been accelerated by public awareness that transportation and other problems transcend local boundaries.[42]

Much of the cooperative activity one finds around the country is voluntary. To a considerable extent, however, what passes for "voluntary" cooperation among local officials reflects the fear that if local units do not cooperate, the state will mandate solutions to areawide problems. There is already a considerable amount of "top down" regionalism emanating from the states rather than "bottom up" regionalism emanating from the voluntary efforts of local units.[43] A growing number of states, for example, require local governments to work together in preparing metropolitan or regional plans addressed to the interrelated goals of controlling growth, combating environmental problems such as air and water pollution, and providing an adequate infrastructure (chapter 14).

Legally, of course, local governments are unlike sovereign nations. Conditions may be imposed on them from above. State governments may insist on the consolidation of local governments, thus confining home rule to those units able to exercise it. State action of this nature may impair not only the autonomy of local government but also the increasing political power of the blacks remaining in the cities. Those subscribing to the "public choice" school of thought have also criticized the development of metropolitan governments. From this perspective, emphasis should be placed on maintaining a large number of diverse local governments in order to give people and businesses a greater opportunity to choose the type of local government and services they desire.[44]

Whether councils of government and/or other regional bodies will develop into full-fledged metropolitan governments is difficult to predict. More certain is the emptiness of home rule if the city cannot be governed by any means. Population and economic trends have not only created pressure for greater intergovernmental cooperation in metropolitan areas, if not a federated metropolitan government of some type or another, but have also increased the role of the state and national governments in what once were only local problems.

ENDNOTES

1. The total includes what the United States Office of Management and Budget calls Consolidated Metropolitan Statistical Areas, containing a million or more people, which are subdivided into Primary Metropolitan Statistical Areas.

2. U.S. Department of Commerce, Bureau of the Census, *Rural and Rural Farm Population* (Washington, D.C.: Government Printing Office, June 1988).

3. See, for example: Nicole Achs, "Exurbia," *American City and County* (June 1991): 65–72.

4. See: Gordon F. DeJong and Ralph R. Sell, "Population Redistribution, Migration, and Residential Preferences," *The Annals* 429 (January 1977): 130–144; and Kenneth M. Johnson and Calvin L. Beale, "The Rural Rebound Revisited," *American Demographics* (July 1995): 46–55.

5. See: Douglas S. Massey and Nancy A. Denton, "Suburbanization and Segregation in U.S. Metropolitan Areas," *American Journal of Sociology* 94 (November 1988): 592–626.

6. See: John Yinger, *Housing Discrimination Study* (Washington, D.C.: U.S. Department of Housing and Urban Development, October 1991). A review of the findings is found in: "New Evidence of Urban Housing Discrimination," *The Urban Institute Policy and Research Report* (Winter/Spring 1992): 4–6.

7. See: William K. Tabb, *The Political Economy of the Black Ghetto* (New York: W.W. Norton, 1970).

8. See: *Report of the National Advisory Commission on Civil Disorders* (Washington, D.C.: Government Printing Office, 1 March 1968).

9. See: *The State of the Cities*, Report of the Commission in the '70s (New York: Praeger Publishers in cooperation with the National Urban Coalition, 1972); and "Watts: Ten Years On," *Newsweek* (18 August 1975): 24–26. See also: Joe Aberbach and Jack Walker, *Race in the City* (Boston: Little, Brown, 1973); and Joe Feagin and Harlan Hahn, *The Politics of Violence in American Cities* (New York: Macmillan, 1973).

10. See, for example: William J. Wilson, *The Truly Disadvantaged: The Inner City, the Underclass, and Public Policy* (Chicago: University of Chicago Press, 1987).

11. "Are Our Cities Dying?" *New York Times* (2 May 1971): sec. 8, p. 1. For an update of this discussion, see: "Are Cities Obsolete?" *Newsweek* (9 September 1991): 42–44.

12. Edward C. Banfield, *The Unheavenly City* (Boston: Little, Brown, 1970), p. 1. The same basic themes are elaborated on in Banfield, *The Unheavenly City Revisited* (Boston: Little, Brown, 1974).

13. See: Robert Bailey, *The Crisis Regime* (Albany, N.Y.: SUNY Press, 1984). See also: Charles Brecher and Raymond D. Horton, "Retrenchment and Recovery: American Cities and the New York Experience," *Public Administration Review* (March/April 1985): 267–274.

14. See: Alan Ehrenhalt, "As Interest in Its Agenda Wanes, a Shrinking Urban Bloc in Congress Plays Defense," *Governing* (July 1989): 21–25.

15. See: Norval D. Glenn and Lester Hill Jr., "Rural-Urban Differences in Attitudes and Behavior," *The Annals* 429 (January 1977): 36–50.

16. Arthur J. Vidich and Joseph Bensman, *Small Town in Mass Society* (Garden City, N.Y.: Doubleday, 1958), pp. 112–139.

17. Lawrence O. Houston Jr., "The New Non-Metropolitan Growth: Where Do Blue Collar Residents Fit In?" *Small Town* (March/April 1981): 8–14.

18. Alvin D. Sokolow, "Small Town Government: The Conflict of Administrative Styles," *National Civic Review* (October 1982): 445–452.

19. See: Don A. Dillman and Kenneth R. Tremblay Jr., "The Quality of Life in Rural America," *The Annals* 429 (January 1977): 115–129.

20. A "borough" in states such as Pennsylvania, Connecticut, and New Jersey refers to villages or towns smaller than a city. The term is also used to refer to units

comparable to counties in Alaska and to the five major subdivisions of New York City: Manhattan, Brooklyn, Queens, the Bronx, and Richmond.

21. See, for example: David R. Berman, "Takeovers of Local Governments: An Overview and Evaluation of State Policies," *Publius: The Journal of Federalism* 25 (Summer 1995): 55–70; and Vincent L. Marando and Mavis Mann Reeves, "State Responsiveness and Local Government Reorganization," *Social Science Quarterly* 61 (December 1988): 994–1004.

22. See: Joseph F. Zimmerman, *State-Local Relations: A Partnership Approach*, 2nd ed. (New York: Praeger, 1995).

23. See: David R. Berman and Lawrence L. Martin, "State-Local Relations: An Examination of Local Discretion," *Public Administration Review* (March/April 1988): 637–641.

24. All states but Alaska, Connecticut, Louisiana, and Rhode Island have county governments. Boroughs in Alaska and parishes in Louisiana, however, are organized and function in the same manner as county governments. In Rhode Island, the county is simply a judicial district. Some limited portions of other states also lack a distinct county government. The United States Census Bureau regards consolidated municipal and county governments as municipal governments. For an update on county developments, see: David R. Berman, ed., *County Governments in an Era of Change* (Westport, Conn.: Greenwood Press, 1993).

25. Henry J. Pratt, "Counties' Role Grows in Urban Affairs," *National Civic Review* (September 1972): 398.

26. Vincent L. Marando and Robert D. Thomas, *The Forgotten Governments: County Commissioners as Policy Makers* (Gainesville: University Press of Florida, 1977).

27. Edward B. Lewis and George A. Taylor, "Policy Making/Implementing Activities of Elected County Executives and Appointed County Administrators: Does Form of Government Make a Difference?" *International Journal of Public Administration* 17 (1994): 935–953.

28. William R. Dodge, "The Emergence of Intercommunity Partnerships in the 1980s," *PM* (July 1988): 1–7.

29. Some of these observations are contained in: Frank M. Bryan, "Policy Making in the Open Forum: Town Meetings in the Rural Tecno Policy," paper delivered at the Annual Meeting of the Southern Political Science Association, Atlanta, Georgia, 4 November 1976. See also: Frank M. Bryan, "Town Meeting Government Still Supported in Vermont," *National Civic Review* (July 1972): 348–351; Rosaline Levenson, "Representative Town Meeting Survives in Connecticut," *National Civic Review* (November 1969): 484; Gordon E. Baker, "The Impulse for Direct Democracy," *National Civic Review* (January 1977): 19–23, 35; and Jane J. Mansbridge, "Town Meeting Democracy," in Peter Collier, ed., *Dilemmas of Democracy* (New York: Harcourt Brace Jovanovich, 1976), pp. 148–167.

30. On the various roles played by towns and townships, see: G. Ross Stephens, "The Least Glorious, Most Local, Most Trivial, Homely, Provincial, and Most Ignored Form of Local Government," *Urban Affairs Quarterly* 24 (June 1989): 501–512.

31. See, for example: Scott A. Bollens, "Examining the Link between State Policy and the Creation of Local Special Districts," *State and Local Government Review* (Fall 1986): 117–124.

32. See, generally: Lawrence J. R. Herson and John M. Bolland, *The Urban Web* (Chicago: Nelson-Hall, 1990).

33. For an overview of approaches to this problem, see: David B. Walker, "Snow White and the 17 Dwarfs: From Metro Cooperation to Governance," *National Civic Review* (January/February 1987): 14–28.

34. Committee for Economic Development, *Modernizing Local Government* (New York: Committee for Economic Development, July 1987).

35. As in the case of annexation, state laws prior to the early 1900s permitted boundary changes through an overall majority vote in the areas involved—a procedure whereby a large city could overwhelm the vote in a small city. City consolidations involving a complete merger took place in the nineteenth century by legislative edict in Boston (1822), Philadelphia (1854), New York (1898), and New Orleans (1813). Currently, thirty-seven states authorize city-city consolidations. Consolidations under these laws have usually involved smaller jurisdictions with declining populations. Voters usually reject city-city consolidations. See: Gary Halter, "City-City Consolidations in the United States," *National Civic Review* (Summer 1993): 282–289.

36. Examples are the City and County of Denver, the City and County of Hawaii, and the City and County of Honolulu. In Alaska one finds similar arrangements in the combined city-boroughs in Anchorage, Juneau, and Sitka.

37. See: Vincent L. Marando, "The Politics of City-County Consolidation," *National Civic Review* (February 1975): 71–81.

38. See: Advisory Commission on Intergovernmental Relations, *Factors Affecting Voter Reactions to Governmental Reorganization in Metropolitan Areas* (Washington, D.C.: Government Printing Office, May 1962).

39. Eileen Shanahan, "Going It Jointly: Regional Solutions for Local Problems," *Governing* (August 1991): 70–75.

40. See: Matthew Holden, "The Governance of the Metropolis as a Problem in Diplomacy," *Journal of Politics* 26 (August 1964): 627–647.

41. See: David R. Morgan and Michael W. Hirlinger, "Intergovernmental Service Contracts: A Multivariate Explanation," *Urban Affairs Quarterly* 27 (September 1991): 128–144.

42. Joy McIlwain, "Regional Approaches Gaining Ground," *American City and County* (August 1989): 38–40.

43. Shanahan, "Going It Jointly."

44. See: Vincent Ostrom, Charles M. Tiebout, and Robert Warren, "The Organization of Government in Metropolitan Areas: A Theoretical Inquiry," *American Political Science Review* 60 (December 1961): 831–842. Among the recent studies on the value of competition are: Mark Schneider, "Intermunicipal Competition, Budget-Maximizing Bureaucrats, and Levels of Suburban Competition," *American Journal of Political Science* 33 (August 1989): 612–628; and Advisory Commission on Intergovernmental Relations, *The Organization of Local Public Economies* (Washington, D.C.: Government Printing Office, December 1987).

9

☆ ☆ ☆

PARTICIPATION AND POWER IN LOCAL POLITICS

Scholars have offered a variety of answers to the question of who governs in local communities. A traditional approach has been to focus on the forms of local government and the relative powers of mayors, city council members, and administrators. This approach does not, however, illuminate the actual relations among the official decision makers or between the decision makers and the public. Nor do the forms indicate much about the differences in political participation and influence in a community or variations in community policymaking.

This chapter examines the historic struggle between bosses and reformers in local politics, the nature of municipal election systems, and the role of political parties and interest groups in local politics. The chapter concludes with some findings and theories on community power.

BOSSES AND REFORMERS

THE GROWTH OF POLITICAL MACHINES

In the closing days of the nineteenth century, many agreed with British historian James Bryce's observation that "the government of cities is the one conspicuous failure of the United States."[1] Many observers attributed the

---

Box 9–1   HONEST GRAFT AND DISHONEST GRAFT

"Everybody is talkin' these days about Tammany men growin' rich on graft, but nobody thinks of drawin' the distinction between honest graft and dishonest graft. . . . I've not gone in for dishonest graft—blackmailin' gamblers, saloonkeepers, disorderly people, etc.—and neither has any of the men who have made big fortunes in politics.

"There's an honest graft, and I'm an example of how it works. I might sum up the whole thing by sayin': 'I seen my opportunities and I took 'em.'

"Just let me explain by examples. My party's in power in the city, and it's goin' to undertake a lot of public improvements. Well, I'm tipped off, say, that they're going to lay out a new park at a certain place.

"I see my opportunity and I take it. I go to that place and I buy up all the land I can in the neighborhood. Then the board of this or that makes its plan public, and there is a rush to get my land, which nobody cared particular for before.

"Ain't it perfectly honest to charge a good price and make a profit on my investment and foresight? Of course, it is. Well, that's honest graft."

Source: Remarks given at turn of the century by ward boss George Washington Plunkitt. William L. Riordon, recorder, *Plunkitt of Tammany Hall* (New York: E.P. Dutton, 1993), p. 3.

---

failure of municipal government to the political machines headed by bosses that flourished in many cities.

The basis of the political bosses' power in many places was the control of immigrant votes. Newcomers to cities often arrived without jobs, money, or command of the English language. Political machines assumed the role of protector of the poor. They provided shelter, food, recreation, and jobs in return for political support. Nearly every neighborhood had a political club-house that served as a link between citizens and city hall.

The machines performed necessary welfare services. These, however, were financed by bribes, kickbacks on contracts, and assessments on pay and were motivated less by philanthropy than by a desire to achieve political power. City hall was regarded as a prize, and to the victor belonged the spoils of power. As one of the most famous (or infamous) local bosses, George Washington Plunkitt of New York City, put it: "I seen my opportunities and I took 'em."[2] Plunkitt and other bosses would, for example, receive inside information from their friends in government that a certain piece of land was to be purchased for a public project, go out and buy the land, and sell it to the city for an inflated price (see box 9–1).

Local bosses like Plunkitt not only controlled city elections but also were often able to influence the course of county, state, and national elections which, in the era of the political machine, were commonly held at the same time as local elections. Party leaders hand picked men to be ward leaders. In return for turning out the vote for the party ticket, ward leaders were allowed to keep their city positions or receive a better-paying public job. Because rewards were based on the number of votes for the machine's candidates, votes were sometimes manufactured from dogs, children, the deceased, and fictitious people. A favorite rallying cry for the party faithful was: "Vote early and vote often!" In order to win elections, the bosses also became masters of campaign strategy, offering balanced tickets representing different ethnic groups, and compiled impressive records as builders of hospitals, parks, civic centers, and other public facilities.

This situation would not have been possible without collusion between the machine and local businesspeople. Collusion and corruption were particularly prevalent in the granting of charters for the establishment of transit facilities, in procurement of city equipment and supplies, and in contracting for municipal public works. As journalist Lincoln Steffens pointed out, anything could be accomplished by a determined individual or businessperson with enough money to bribe a city official.[3]

The emergence of the political machine was also related to the inability of the traditional weak-mayor system, characterized by the multiple election of executives and large, unwieldy city councils to respond to the needs of rapidly growing cities. The long list of elected officials made it difficult for the voters to cast their ballots intelligently or to hold officials accountable. Each elected official had his or her own base of political power and was independent of any formal hierarchy. The machine, through its dominance over elective positions, filled the power vacuum and provided the coordination needed to run the government.

THE MUNICIPAL REFORM MOVEMENT

In response to widespread corruption around the turn of the century, a municipal reform movement sprang up—a movement that resulted in a host of innovations, now common features of city governments. By 1896, citizens had established some 245 national, state, and local organizations to protest and pressure for the elimination of various abuses in municipal government and administration.[4] At the heart of this movement, born out of the Progressive spirit, were white Anglo-Saxon Protestant middle-class businesspeople and civic leaders. The reformers tended to be old-stock Americans who were moved, in part, by fear and resentment of recent immigrants.

The movement was far from unified or consistent in its objectives. By the first decade of the twentieth century, for example, six separate groups were organized to inspect housing conditions in Boston.[5] Reformers called for the short ballot, which would simplify the duties of the voters, and for forms of direct democracy (the initiative, referendum, and recall) that would make the responsibilities of the voters heavier; for the commission form of government with elected department heads and for strong-mayor plans with appointed department heads; and for both centralized administrative leadership and a strong civil service.

The reformers agreed, however, on the necessity of reducing the power and influence of the political machines and on the need to improve the caliber and operation of city government. The reform movement was to contribute to the decline of the machine by: (1) using the ballot to elect reform candidates to enforce laws against graft and corruption, election frauds, and the misappropriation of public funds; (2) adopting civil service regulations to cut off the supply of patronage; (3) replacing party nominating conventions with direct primaries to reduce the influence of the boss within the party and make it easier to nominate reform candidates; (4) promoting the adoption of the initiative, referendum, and recall to ensure greater popular control over the operation of city government; and (5) instituting nonpartisan elections to be held at different times from state and national elections. The last of these represented an effort to insulate city politics from state and national politics and further reduce the power of the boss.

Several of the reforms were designed to improve the operation of city government by taking the "politics" out of it and making it both more democratic and efficient. In an attempt to improve on the traditional weak-mayor system, reformers focused on the commission, strong-mayor, and council-manager alternatives. The latter became the favorite of those who contended that politics should and must be separated from city administration and that government should operate on the same principles as business corporations. Small city councils elected at-large rather than from wards within the city and nonpartisan elections became part of the council-manager package.

A basic assumption of the reformers was that there was no need for politics and conflict in running city government. There was no Democratic or Republican way to collect trash or do other municipal functions. Local governments, according to the reformers, must be insulated from partisan politics as found on the state and national levels and be free to operate on a sound businesslike basis under the leadership of those concerned with the common good of the community rather than their party's interest or personal self-interest. To further this insulation, reformers also often championed the goal of more local home rule.

EFFECTS OF THE REFORM MOVEMENT

The success of municipal reformers varied considerably from city to city. They were, for example, very successful in Cleveland, modestly successful in

New York, and much less than successful in Chicago.[6] From a broad perspective, however, the municipal reform movement left a deep and lasting imprint on the structure and politics of municipal governments. Over the years, thousands of cities have adopted all or most of the reform package. That is, they have chosen a city manager, a small city council, a merit system for hiring personnel, devices of direct democracy such as the referendum and initiative, and elections that are nonpartisan, at-large, and at different times from state and national elections. These "reformed" cities tend to have relatively wealthy, well-educated, and predominantly white Anglo-Saxon Protestant populations.[7] Research suggests that people with these characteristics are most likely to be receptive to reform institutions, practices, and ideology.[8] The reform influence has also been more evident in medium-sized (250,000 to 499,000) but growing cities and in the South and West. Larger and more heterogeneous cities, particularly in the Northeast, are more likely to be mayor-council types characterized by large councils elected from wards on a partisan ticket.[9]

In addition to its effects on local structure, the reform movement gave birth to several organizations that continue to influence the course and direction of city government. Local civic associations in many jurisdictions continue to not only expound the tenets of the reform movement, acting as watchdogs against boss rule, but also often play the role of political parties themselves by recruiting local candidates, nominating them, and campaigning for their election. On the national level, the principal representative of the reform movement is the National Civic League (formerly the National Municipal League), founded in 1894 as an outgrowth of a conference called by local reform organizations. The league has long adhered to the goals of home rule, the council-manager form, the merit system, the short ballot, and nonpartisanship.

The reform movement also contributed mightily to the creation of organizations of public employees designed to upgrade their professionalism by disseminating information through conferences and publications. Examples of such organizations are the International City/County Management Association, the International Association of Chiefs of Police, and the National Association of Assessing Officers. Most of these national organizations have state and local chapters.

On the positive side, the municipal reform movement undoubtedly increased the professionalism of various aspects of municipal administration. On the other hand, some have seriously questioned if whether by helping to destroy the personal government provided by the political machines and fostering professionalism and efficiency, the reformers made local government less sensitive to the demands of the electorate and, indeed, to elected officials. To some observers, the result has been the creation of "new machines" in the form of large and powerful city bureaucracies with their own special systems of rewards and clientele relationships.[10]

The municipal reformers erred, critics charge, in ignoring that city governments not only provide services like police, fire, and water but also serve a political function of managing conflict within the community. By suppressing the political function and moving many decisions out of the recognized political process into a more complex and technical administrative process, the reform movement has made it more difficult for both citizens and their elected officials to influence public policy.

CONTEMPORARY REFORM

In contemporary municipal reform, there has been a tendency to look back with some nostalgia on the era of the political machine, which at least cut through red tape and provided a more personal government. A new breed of reformers looks more for greater decentralization of control over municipal services, improved communications between citizens and city hall, and increased chances for citizens (especially the poor and nonwhite) to provide political input.

Since the late 1960s, demands for greater participation have been accompanied by demands for greater governmental decentralization and more neighborhood government in large cities.[11] Demands for greater neighborhood control have been particularly intense in ghetto areas where there has been discontent over the distribution, delivery, and level of many local services. Decentralization has also served in part as a counterthrust to proposals for even more centralization at the metropolitan or regional levels. Metropolitan government, as noted earlier, is feared on the grounds that it would make government even more remote and inaccessible and would dilute the political strength of racial and ethnic minorities in the central cities.

In response to demands for more decentralization, some cities have set up "little city halls" and municipally operated multiservice centers that have made the provision of city services somewhat more personalized, increased communication with the public, and helped coordinate programs affecting neighborhoods. Multiservice centers provide a common branch office for many municipal and private agencies, such as those involved in employment, community action, and legal aid. Little city halls are normally concerned with the coordination and administration of municipal services within the neighborhood. Other means to facilitate communication between neighborhoods and city hall have included: (1) city council and "meet your mayor" programs and other official meetings on a regular basis in neighborhood areas, (2) citizen complaint machinery, and (3) resident advisory committees. Reforms of this nature have been most common in large mayor-council cities.

Few cities have considered recommendations that neighborhood subunits of government headed by locally elected councils be established to carry out neighborhood functions or control services like education and police. There are, however, more than one thousand neighborhood or community development corporations that are chartered by the states and usually supported by federal funds. These nonprofit corporations perform certain functions, for example, housing construction for low-income groups and neighborhood rehabilitation projects or services such as day-care centers and recreational, health, and legal programs. Some neighborhood groups provide such services without public funds.

Major issues in local politics center on the demands of citizens, particularly minorities, to participate more effectively in the development and administration of programs affecting them. The problem of accommodating demands for greater participation applies to nearly the whole gamut of urban services. Cities have sought greater citizen input through the creation of advisory boards and more open hearings—though these are often deficient because citizens lack information or are consulted only after officials have virtually finalized their plans.

Another type of activity in the 1980s, running counter to the tenets of the municipal reform movement, was the drive to replace at-large elections for city council positions with elections from districts (see detailed discussion in chapter 10). Advocates of this change argued that at-large elections helped insulate city governments from the needs and demands of minority neighborhoods. Courts encouraged abandonment of at-large systems and, in many places, minorities have secured greater representation on city councils through the use of the district or ward system. The more recent widespread movement to place term limits on council members, however, has the effect of reducing the power of the crop of district-based councilmen and women who have recently come to power. Indeed, some observers contended that the term limitation movement at the local level reflects, at least in part, the desire to minimize the political effects of using districts.[12]

VOTING AND ELECTIONS

Basic characteristics of municipal politics are low voter turnout and an election system that, due to the municipal reform movement, features election runoffs, non-partisan elections, and the use of instruments of direct democracy. We look at these, the nature of local campaigning and more theoretical questions involving elections, representation, and influence in the following pages.

VOTING TURNOUT

Voting in municipal elections follows the same general pattern as voting in state and national elections in regard to such factors as age and education. The fact that voter turnout is relatively low in municipal elections, however, means that the composition of the municipal electorate is much less representative of the populace than that of the presidential and other elections where turnout is higher.[13] The more affluent, usually Republicans, are likely to have a greater influence on local elections than on elections at other levels.

In addition to factors associated with individuals (such as income, education, and occupation), participation in local politics is related to differences in governmental structure and in community characteristics. Participation (voter turnout) is lower in reformed than in unreformed cities, that is, lower in cities with nonpartisan elections, elections at-large, and other reform characteristics. Regardless of governmental structure, voting turnout is greater in cities with definite class or ethnic cleavages, in older stable cities than in young growing ones, and in cities in the East than in other regions of the country.[14]

Research further indicates that even though participation is relatively low in small, isolated villages and towns, it is much greater in these places than the socioeconomic characteristics of their population would suggest. Small towns and villages are heavily populated by people with relatively low incomes and levels of education. The nature of the community, especially its small size and isolation, however, appears to encourage participation. Similarly, even though many suburbs are populated by people who might normally be highly active, certain characteristics of the community may discourage turnout. In many suburbs participation is depressed because of a lack of media attention to local politics. Often, what is happening in the community is overshadowed by media coverage of what is happening in a nearby city. Participation also may be depressed in highly homogeneous suburbs. In these places individuals may feel little need to vote because they share basic values and are likely to be happy with the results of an election even if they do not vote. Because of such factors, participation in small suburbs located near large cities is generally even lower than in small towns and villages outside of metropolitan areas.[15]

RUNOFF ELECTIONS

The influence of the municipal reform movement of the early twentieth century on municipal governments is particularly evident when one looks at the election system. One common feature of the local system traceable to the reformers is the use of election runoffs. Municipal reforms insisted on the election of consensus candidates to office. To strengthen the prospect of widespread support for the eventual winners, they stipulated a plan under which a winning candidate for office had to receive a majority of the votes cast rather than simply a plurality of the votes cast. Under their plan, which has been implemented in many cities, two elections are usually held for council seats and other offices. Candidates who receive a majority of the votes cast in the first election are declared elected. Often, however, no candidate gets a majority of the votes and a second or runoff election between the two highest vote-getters is necessary to fill at least some of the positions. Studies suggest that those who receive the most votes in the first election usually win the runoff. Though research is limited, the runoff system does not appear to discriminate against candidates who are minorities or females.[16]

NONPARTISAN ELECTIONS

The unique feature of municipal politics is the widespread use of nonpartisan elections. The device is used in over 60 percent of the nation's principal cities and almost always, but not exclusively, with the council-manager plan.

Technically, "nonpartisan elections" refer to those in which there is no party designation of any kind on the ballot and candidates are nominated by a simple petition process. Some people also use the term to refer to elections in which candidates are identified by local slates or organizations other than those of the Democratic or Republican parties. Political scientist Charles Adrian has suggested there are at least four types of nonpartisan elections in use in the country: (1) those in which the only candidates who normally have any chance of winning are those supported by a major political party, although the party name does not appear on the ballot (Chicago); (2) those in which slates of candidates are supported by various groups, including political parties (Cincinnati and Wichita); (3) those in which slates are supported by various groups but political parties have little or no part in campaigns (Kansas City, Fort Worth, and several cities in Michigan and California); and (4) those in which neither political parties nor slates of candidates are important and each person must develop his or her own campaign organization (particularly common in small cities).[17]

In the more truly nonpartisan cities, the local branches of the national political parties have only a minimal influence on the election process. Party organizations in these circumstances focus primarily on county, state, and national elections. In the absence of party organizations, incumbent city council members, especially in small cities, may assume responsibility for recruiting candidates for vacancies on the council. The ability of a candidate to go on and win a council seat in a nonpartisan small city may depend most heavily on the support of local newspapers, merchants, and service clubs (such as the Lions and Rotary clubs).[18] In larger nonpartisan cities, informal groups of influential businesspeople and professionals regularly recruit, nominate, and campaign for slates of city candidates. Also found in large, nonpartisan cities are more formal local political parties, such as the City Charter Committee in Cincinnati, which perform similar functions.

Municipal reformers at the turn of the century looked at nonpartisan elections as a way to reduce the influence of the local machines in municipal politics and to insulate municipal government from unnecessary and irrelevant conflict. Nonpartisan elections were expected to encourage voters to choose the "best person" and make their decisions on the basis of local issues rather than on the basis of national and state issues or partisan affiliations. Voters were also expected to regard local elections as different from the typical election, that is, as a community rather than partisan activity. Reformers also hoped that nonpartisanship would produce higher-caliber candidates—those interested in the common good of the city, not partisan or personal rewards.

The goals of the reformers have not been fully realized. Studies suggest that what are officially "nonpartisan" contests can easily turn into partisan ones in the minds of the voters.[19] In some places, as suggested above, the parties are actively, if not officially, involved. In others, voters have little difficulty securing partisan information about the candidates. Presumably, some do so and cast their vote largely on this basis.

Even assuming that voters in nonpartisan elections actually ignore partisan cues, it is difficult to tell how much they focus on important local issues. When deprived of the aid of a party label, voters are more apt to depend on the local press for voting guidance. These cues may have little to do with important local issues. In nonpartisan as well as partisan elections, campaigns are often conducted on the basis of personalities more than issues. Even when there is extensive coverage, moreover, evidence suggests that many citizens do not take advantage of the opportunity to inform themselves. Many simply do not vote. Others vote for a familiar name, for a name with a particular ethnic identification, or simply for the first name on the ballot.[20]

It is difficult to conclude that nonpartisan elections produce the "best person." Data suggest, however, that nonpartisan elections produce higher-status council members than do partisan elections. This tendency is reinforced when nonpartisan elections are held on an at-large basis rather than from wards or districts. Minorities are particularly hurt in terms of representation by the at-large method.[21] Thus, compared to the partisan-ward system, nonpartisan elections held at-large appear to produce less representative city councils.[22] One of the saving graces of the nonpartisan system in terms of representation is that it makes it possible for a member of a minority party to get elected. For example, voters in a largely Republican city may vote for a Democrat because they are unaware of his or her party identification or consider it to be irrelevant because of the nonpartisan character of the office.

DIRECT DEMOCRACY

As a result of the reform movement, the initiative, referendum, and, to a lesser extent, the recall are commonly used on the local level. In municipal politics, the initiative may be used to enact an ordinance or amend the city charter. The referendum, as on the state level, may be compulsory, optional, or of a protest nature. The compulsory referendum is especially significant in local politics because of the need to secure voter approval for major bond issues to finance schools, recreational facilities, and other major public projects. The recall is available to localities in thirty-seven states. It may be used against city council persons, sheriffs, school board members, and a variety of other local officials. Overall, the device has been employed only sporadically, usually in relatively small rural communities, for example, to remove a mayor who fired a popular police chief. Explaining a rash of local recall campaigns in Nebraska during the late 1980s, one state official concluded: "Sometimes it's taxes, sometimes it's firing the football coach, sometimes it's because they didn't say 'hi' at the post office."[23] In Nebraska, as elsewhere, the law does not set any criteria for a recall. While the device may be misused, it continues to be valued as a "gun behind the door" that can be used to give incumbents who fall out of touch with public sentiment a vote of no confidence.[24]

Studies on voter behavior on ballot issues show there is often stronger support for bond issues among those with higher income and occupational status than among those at the other end of the scale in these respects. Several years ago political scientists James Q. Wilson and Edward C. Banfield used such evidence to support their thesis that upper-income people are apt to be more "public-regarding" in their voting than are lower-income people.[25] They said that the public-regarding middle- and upper-income people tend to see the interest of the larger community and will vote against their own self-interest by supporting programs of little value to themselves but for which they must help pay. "Private-regarding" low-income people, on the other hand, appear more concerned with family needs and personal loyalties than with the interests of the larger community.

These differences in outlook were at one time associated by Banfield and Wilson with the municipal reform movement. The white Anglo-Saxon Protestant middle-class reformers were seen as public-regarding and the immigrant population and their descendants were seen as private-regarding. These first conclusions, however, were later altered somewhat by the authors. "Public-regarding" became the "unitary ethos" of the upper class or upper-middle class and "private-regarding" became the "individualist ethos" disassociated from any "conjecture about its historical origins" with immigrants.[26]

CAMPAIGNING AND CAMPAIGN COSTS

Campaigns for local office commonly involve attempting to gain the endorsement of various elites such as newspaper editors and organizations such as the business-minded chamber of commerce.[27] The direct or grassroots approach aimed at voters has traditionally involved heavy reliance on personal appearances and the help of volunteer workers to distribute literature. In many large and medium-sized cities, however, serious candidates for the

---

BOX 9–2 WHY DO PEOPLE CONTRIBUTE?

A media consultant who has worked for several big-city mayors once remarked: "People aren't contributing money because they think someone will make a good spokesman for the city. They want him because they want to be able to go downtown and get some help if they need it. They want to know someone will answer the phone if they need a zoning variance, or that they'll be able to get their brother-in-law a job in the summer picking up paper. It's gut-level politics. Everybody is looking for a way to get the administration's ear."

Source: "Mayoral Candidates Enter the Big Time Using Costly TV Ads and Consultants," *National Journal* (6 April 1985): 737–742, quote at 738.

---

office of mayor now rely on more sophisticated campaign techniques such as radio and television advertisements, professional polling, phone-bank operations, and direct mailings targeted to specific groups. The new style is particularly evident in fast-growing cities in the South and West where it has been next to impossible to reach the vast number of new voters through personal contact and where newcomers are unlikely to be aware of the status of individual candidates in the community. Reliance on more impersonal devices and building name recognition is also greater in large cities where partisan ties have been weakened because of nonpartisan elections. Former Cleveland mayor Dennis J. Kucinich has remarked that the difference between the old style of personal or grassroots campaigning and the new style is like "the difference between participatory democracy and selling cornflakes."[28]

One net effect of changing campaign techniques has been an escalation of campaign costs. Running for mayor in a large city may cost anywhere from $500,000 to $1 million. Historically, candidates for local office have relied on individuals and firms doing business with the city and, in particular, on real estate interests. The latter have generally been anxious to support candidates who are most willing to use the powers of local government to promote economic development. Whereas a good many people may donate money to candidates out of friendship or a sense of duty, others may have more limited self-interest goals in mind (see box 9–2).

Although the growing reliance on large "fat cat" contributions has raised serious questions of political favoritism, thus far only a few cities have imposed regulations on campaign finances that, for example, limit how much individuals and corporations can contribute. Some cities, following the lead of Seattle, not only limit contributions but also help finance campaigns out of public funds.

ELECTIONS AND INFLUENCE

Political scientists have long assumed that elections help determine the question of who gets what from government. In regard to local elections, much of our attention has been on how the shifting ethnic or racial base of a city's population affects elections and public policy.

Generally, as the ethnic or racial base of a city's population changes, so too does its electoral politics. Over time, one ethnic or racial group may replace another as the dominant force in local politics. At one time, for example, the Irish replaced the earlier established Yankees as the dominant force in the politics of many cities. In more recent years, blacks and Hispanics have become major forces in the politics of larger cities, challenging or replacing Anglos.

The ability of blacks, Hispanics, or any other social group to influence elections depends, in part, on its numbers—the larger its share of a city's population, the more its potential electoral strength. To have actual influence, a group also has to be mobilized into electoral activity so that its members vote and vote for those who favor the group's interests. Electoral victories, moreover, will not produce much of anything unless the group's representatives are *politically incorporated* into the power structure, that is, brought into the coalitions that dominate city policymaking.[29]

The extent to which blacks and Hispanics have actually been able to use local election systems in recent years to bring about change has been a topic of some debate. Some studies have placed emphasis on the difficulty of mobilizing minorities, in part because of the internal differences within both the black and Hispanic communities, and of their resulting inability to influence policy.[30] Many of the more recent studies, however, suggest that blacks and Hispanics, at least under some circumstances, may be highly mobilized as voters, are able to put minority people into municipal office, and that some of these officials, in turn, are able to bring about changes in policy such as in municipal hiring practices that benefit minorities.[31] The election system, in effect, does work in bringing about change. There are, however, as we note below, overall limits to community power systems in policymaking.

GROUP ACTIVITY

POLITICAL PARTIES

As the municipal reformers anticipated, the urban political party has been considerably weakened by nonpartisan elections, civil service, and other related changes growing out of the reform movement. Also contributing to the decline of the traditional machines have been the economic advancement and social assimilation of European immigrants and their descendants and the governmental assumption of welfare functions once performed by machines.

Strong political organizations continue to exist, but very few operate in the classical style or dominate city politics in the fashion they once did.[32] Most function as loose coalitions of groups or factions, none of which is able to dominate. Urban political parties may be divided among the followings of individual leaders, interest groups, small machinelike organizations operating on the ward level, and political clubs. To some extent, ideological motivations have replaced material motivations for participating in local political organizations. That is, participants have shown a greater concern with issues and policies than with getting a job or an economic advantage.[33]

Urban political parties not only are fragmented but also have to share what influence they have with a multitude of institutions and groups active in city politics. Perhaps the most notable of these represent the many-faceted business community, local newspapers, and neighborhoods.

BUSINESS INTERESTS

Commonly identified as influential economic notables in city politics are bankers, builders, public utility officials, and the owners of large department stores. The influence and importance of the business community is also felt through general organizations such as the chamber of commerce, service organizations like the Lions and Rotarians, and specialized groups such as the "Downtown Merchants Association." Collectively, these business-minded forces function somewhat as the "growth machine" dedicated to expanding the city's economic base.[34]

Individual businesspeople have much to gain or lose by local governmental decisions. Bankers, builders, real estate developers, and others have a logical interest in maintaining property values and are concerned with local planning, building permits, subdivision regulations, and zoning. For bar and club owners the concerns are with local tax policies and regulations affecting the hours they may stay open.

The involvement of businesspeople in local politics often takes the form of direct participation as elected officeholders or as appointees to various boards or commissions, for example, those dealing with planning or zoning. Businesspeople obviously are often in a position to better their own interests by serving the city. While many are "community minded," conflicts of interest have long been a potential, if not actual, problem on the local level.

Businesses are not always united in their demands on local government. Historically, city governments in many places have been caught in the conflict between downtown merchants and their rivals in shopping centers. One may also find differences between businesspeople who own or work for "hometown" firms and those who work in the city as employees of national corporations or chain stores. The latter appear less likely to become involved in local politics out of fear that they may alienate groups or make enemies in city hall. Other reasons for the noninvolvement of managers in local politics are the demands in time and energy of their work and the requirement that they move, often to different parts of the country, to secure promotions.[35]

Groups such as the local chambers of commerce have long been among the strongest advocates of the tenets of the municipal reform movement. Business leaders and groups have also traditionally looked on city government as playing an important role as an instrument of community growth. City officials have generally shared the desire for economic growth—putting the city "on the map" by increasing its population and economic base—and have viewed business cooperation as vital in this endeavor.[36] Economic hard times felt by both city governments and local businesses in the 1990s have, if anything, strengthened the government-business partnership.[37] On the other hand, citizens appear less committed than in the past to the growth philosophy, especially in some suburban areas where many look to government to provide life's amenities and to help keep out undesirable people, housing, and industry. The notion of growth is particularly attractive to bankers and real estate developers but often less so to business owners and people living near the areas to be developed.

THE MEDIA

Local newspapers may be more influential in urban politics than in state and national politics because few other sources of information about local affairs exist and because of the use of nonpartisan elections. In large and small communities, one newspaper or several newspapers under common ownership may have a monopoly on local news. Where nonpartisan elections are employed and political parties are inactive in local politics, voters lose the partisan cue and are more likely to be influenced by what information they receive through the press.

Newspapers are generally in a commanding position to form public attitudes concerning the community's assets and problems. They mold public opinion through the editorial pages and by decisions on what to report and how it is to be reported. In a more direct fashion, newspapers may instruct the voters by endorsing candidates and by making recommendations on charter amendments, bond issues, tax rate proposals, and other measures appearing on the ballot. Overall, daily newspapers are probably more influential among middle-class citizens than among those in the lower economic brackets, who are less likely to read them, and on decisions relating to referenda rather than to candidates, especially where partisan elections are employed.

Another vital role of the newspaper is as a check on city government. Several newspapers have the reputation of being crusaders, conducting investigations, exposing graft and corruption, and undertaking other investigative studies that publicize situations and lead to change. One common theme of newspapers, particularly in reformed cities, is the need to protect against the emergence of strong political organizations or boss rule. Some observers have contended that this position largely reflects the newspaper's own self-interest because, in the absence of strong political organizations, candidates for office and officeholders have to rely on the media to communicate with the public. Strong political organizations, in other words, threaten the dominant position of the press in the local political system.[38]

For a variety of reasons, the press is likely to take it upon itself to inform public officials what "public opinion" demands. Reporters are apt to demand full access to governmental decision makers, condemning closed hearings and other instances of governmental secrecy. Several papers have instituted "hot lines" or "answer lines" whereby citizen complaints or inquiries regarding city services are fielded and investigated by the press.

The popular image of local newspapers as watchdogs over local officials, however, does not apply to all newspapers or to all newspapers all of the time. Critics have contended that large daily newspapers tend to be part of the general probusiness establishment that controls city hall. In a city dominated by a single newspaper, the paper is likely to have much influence over who can be elected to office. Assuming that a paper was responsible for helping an administration get elected in the first place, it can be expected to be more than willing to communicate the accomplishments of the officeholders to the public. At other times, newspapers may support local officials by not reporting certain items or doing so in a manner that minimizes the interest or concern of the reader. Not surprisingly, some researchers have found that the manner in which news is reported tends to support local authority and leading community institutions.[39]

Radio and television stations perform similar functions in municipal politics, although their impact is somewhat limited by legal restrictions on their advocacy role and by financial and time limitations preventing them from giving in-depth local reports. Given the mass audience reached by television, however, station managers are in a far more powerful position than newspaper editors to influence the public's thinking on the area's problems, to expose situations leading to reform, and to enable political leaders to communicate or build an image with the public.

Television stations, radio stations, and large metropolitan daily newspapers are likely to provide the bulk of information on local politics. In most cases, the emphasis is on developments in the large central cities in which the stations and newspapers are located. Reporting of this nature tends to generate a metropolitan consciousness and to provide political leaders in the central city with an opportunity to build a broader political constituency for another elective office. At the same time, the dominance of the metropolitan media may tend to detract attention from the problems and politics of suburban areas within the region. Suburbanites who read "hometown" papers are more likely to participate in local political affairs than are suburbanites who read only metropolitan papers. In many cases, however, suburban papers have only a minimal readership and a sizable number of people are outside the local community's major communication process.[40]

NEIGHBORHOOD GROUPS

Neighborhood groups or associations conduct meetings, elect officers, and perform a variety of functions.[41] They attempt to promote economic development, protect property values, secure more and better governmental services, and instill a sense of identity and pride in their part of the city. They also provide some services on their own, such as crime watch programs with the police. On a political level, they serve as a means through which communities are mobilized into political activity and through which individual leaders can begin their political careers.

Organizations and political activists representing various neighborhoods engage in much of the conflict that characterizes city politics. They are central players in disputes over how police, transportation, sanitation, and other services are distributed among various parts of the city. They also try to avoid unwanted facilities, be they drug rehabilitation centers, hazardous landfills, or major building projects endorsed by the business elite. Neighborhood groups, finally, are also in the business of trying to protect their turf from the invasion of people of different incomes, races, religions, or nationalities. Such conflicts grow out of the movement of minorities into Anglo neighborhoods, the movement of the white middle-class gentry into minority neighborhoods (the gentrification process), and conflicts between minorities, for example, blacks and Hispanics, over control of their turfs.

The various neighborhood groups do not have equal bargaining power. Middle- and upper-middle-class parts of town have the political resources of income and education. These translate into easy accessibility to policymakers with which to protect their neighborhoods. They also have leverage by threatening to vote with their feet, that is, leave the city, if conditions are not to their liking. The poor and nonwhite have sought influence for their neighborhood concerns through mobilization and mass protest action along the lines advocated by Saul Alinksy, a prominent organizer in Chicago in the 1960s. Contemporary neighborhood leaders in inner cities, however, appear to be less inclined toward rent strikes, store boycotts, and other forms of mass protest than toward seeking out collaborative arrangements with businesses and government to improve their part of the city.

OTHER PARTICIPANTS AND INTERESTS

In addition to the official decision makers (who are discussed in chapter 10), the following groups are also active in local politics:

1. Candidate appraisal or slating committees, permanent or temporary groups that play the role of political parties in recruiting and supporting slates of candidates in nonpartisan systems.[42]
2. Citizen leagues, such as the Chicago Civic Federation and the League of Women Voters, that prepare voter information sheets and recommend changes in the operation and structure of city governments.
3. Taxpayer groups striving for lower taxes and more efficient (and/or lower) governmental expenditures.
4. Labor unions, though more involved with national and state policies, are concerned with matters like local taxes and the organization of municipal employees.
5. Churches, often active in the field of civil rights and in programs involving education and welfare.
6. Ethnic and racial groups, often organized on a neighborhood level and involved in electoral activity.

COMMUNITY POWER

THE PEOPLE AND THE ELITE

The question at the beginning of this chapter, "Who governs local communities?" has been answered in a variety of ways.[43] In democratic theory, this question is answered with a reference to the "general public" or "the people." To be sure, most citizens do not appear to be greatly interested in or knowledgeable about the great bulk of decisions made by local governments. Yet official decision makers may be held in check by their perceptions of the way citizens are likely to react to various policy proposals and, beneath this, their needs to meet citizen expectations and maintain citizen support. One may argue that citizens are ultimately in a position to make the most important decisions, such as who holds office and major issues of public policy, if they care to do so.

At the same time, it may also be true that important decisions are not even submitted for citizen consideration, that elections on candidates and issues offer the voter little choice, and that "public opinion," when expressed, is in fact an opinion that has been manipulated by an elite segment of the population. In the end, a relatively small segment of the population may influence the public much more than it is influenced by the public. As for motivation, the members of this elite segment of the population may be interested in serving the general community welfare as they see it or using their power for their own purposes—or they may see no conflict between community interest and their own self-interest.

The existence of a political elite is based in part on the assumption that political resources are unevenly distributed in society. In local politics, elected officials have formal authority to govern and at least the appearance of a popular mandate to do so. Yet, elected officials themselves may be only one part of the elite group or, indeed, may be the pawns of more influential segments of the community. Some observers have found the power structure to go beyond the formal decision makers to include newspapers and the economic notables in the community. Within government, an elite status may also be given professional administrators, whose expertise and control over information for decision making give them vital political resources.

POLITICAL INFLUENCE: CONCENTRATED OR DISPERSED?

One of the most enduring conflicts among scholars has been whether political influence is concentrated in the hands of a small, relatively stable elite that is able to exert control over a wide range of policy matters or is more widely distributed among a number of politically active individuals and groups, none of which has control over a broad range of policy issues. The first type of system is generally identified as *elitist*, and the second type is generally known as *pluralistic*. In the first system, an elite exerts influence by command or by its very presence in the community. In the second system, community policymaking takes on the form of negotiation, bargaining, and compromise among community influentials or separate centers of power.

Some who have taken the pluralist approach have suggested that political systems are generally open enough so that every group or interest within a community has a reasonable chance of influencing public policy. In support of this, the argument is made that the differences in the political resources of various groups are not that great and that what are often viewed as relatively powerless groups actually do have significant political resources. In the case of the poor and nonwhite, for example, a significant political resource may be the ability to threaten disorder. Other observers, while also denying that any one group or set of individuals controls all matters of public policy, see certain elites in control of specific areas of public policy. Thus, in any given community, one may find multiple functional elites or private, semiautonomous subgovernments that control specific policy areas.

Whether a community power structure is found to be elitist or pluralistic appears to depend in part on the size of the community—and on the particular research methods employed in studying community power. Research suggests that the smaller the community, the more likely it is to be watched over by a small group of "first families" or businesspeople that controls the broad spectrum of governmental and community activity. Many large cities have their roots in such an elitist system. One study, for example, suggests that during the second quarter of the nineteenth century, New York, Philadelphia, Brooklyn, and Boston were governed by wealthy lawyers and merchants who used local government to protect and promote their own interests, for example, by making expenditures that would help business but otherwise attempting to keep taxes low and social services at a minimum.[44] Scholars have found some large cities today to be of an elitist nature. Floyd Hunter, for example, found "Regional City" (Atlanta) to be dominated by a small group of economically powerful businessmen. Hunter found power in the city structured in a single pyramid; the elite made important decisions and passed "the word" down to those on the lower levels.[45]

To elite theorists, the chief division between the rulers and the ruled is socioeconomic or class differences. The upper class (whose status is based on family background, wealth, and occupation) dominates those who hold formal authority and through them dominates those in the lower classes. As suggested above, the elite has generally been seen to be most anxious to promote its own interests and has usually been found to be quite successful at doing so. As one study on Oakland, California, concluded: "The city's medium and large businessmen have reaped the major and continuing benefits of local policy, while the nonrich have reaped a harvest of more crowded housing, forced removal, relatively higher taxes, and minimum public services."[46]

Criticisms of studies on elites have often centered on the methodology employed. Many scholars, including Hunter, have used the *reputational approach*, which is based on the response of citizens to the question of who they think "runs" the community or is the most influential (powerful) in it. This approach has generally led to the identification of a business-dominated elite, especially bankers, builders, real estate operators, owners of large department stores, and newspaper editors. Critics of the reputational approach have pointed out that the discovery of an elite is hardly surprising because the questions used (like "Who is the most powerful?") often assume that an elite must exist. Critics also argue that there is really no way of knowing the criteria by which respondents identify someone as "powerful" or "influential" because these terms are imprecise.

Another criticism of the reputational approach is that it identifies only potential influence rather than actual influence. Many scholars have argued that the question of who governs can be determined only by studying actual decisions to see who was involved and who won or lost. However, defenders of the approach point out that a reputational elite need not exercise its power to be influential. Its existence alone may act as a deterrent in policy development. People may well be reluctant to advocate something they feel would be opposed by an elite, and, as a consequence, certain problems may never reach the stage of formal decision making.[47]

Researchers who study actual decisions have generally found pluralistic systems in which power is dispersed rather than consolidated in a single elite. Most studies of decisions or events in large cities suggest that no one group is concerned with or attempts to influence all major questions of public policy.[48] Large-city political systems, in other words, appear to be characterized by a polynucleated or multicentered power structure so that no one person or group has control over all the decisions made. Even such prominent political leaders as the late Mayor Daley of Chicago have had to operate in a highly pluralistic political system and reserve their influence or "working capital" for matters of the most direct importance to them.[49]

Big-city mayors within pluralistic systems function partly as brokers in mediating conflicts among various groups within the community, settling or attempting to settle disputes as they arise. They also function to coordinate programs of action against one or more of the city's ills. The success of a mayor depends to a great extent on his or her ability to gain electoral support; to exercise leadership over the city council and independently elected administrators; to secure the advice and support of highly skilled professional administrators; to mobilize economic elites and other nongovernmental groups like the press and television stations behind his or her programs; and to negotiate successfully with federal, state, and other local officials to overcome the city's problems. In order to maintain power, mayors may have to carefully balance controversial issues with highly visible, noncontroversial issues that the media and public support.[50] In many cases, however, there is a large gap between the big-city mayor's actual influence and the influence needed to deal with the problems he or she faces.[51] In this sense, no one person really governs in a large city.

In considering the scope and effect of community power, attention should also be given to factors largely beyond the direct or immediate control of community leaders or groups. Among the major constraints on local decision makers, regardless of who they may be, are the amount of wealth they can draw on in the community to provide services (see chapter 12) and their relative inability to prevent citizens and businesses from moving to other jurisdictions. What is going to happen in a local community, moreover, is also likely to be shaped in large part by decisions made on the national and state levels and by the decisions of national corporations.

ENDNOTES

1. James Bryce, *The American Commonwealth*, vol. 1 (New York: Macmillan, 1908), p. 637.
2. William L. Riordan, *Plunkitt of Tammany Hall* (New York: E.P. Dutton, 1963), p. 3.
3. See: *The Autobiography of Lincoln Steffens* (New York: Harcourt, Brace and World, 1931).
4. This figure was given at the first National Conference on Good City Government

in 1896. See: W. Brooke Graves, *American Intergovernmental Relations* (New York: Charles Scribner's Sons, 1964), p. 795.

5. See: William Bennett Munro, *The Government of Cities* (New York: Macmillan, 1912), p. 374.

6. See: Kenneth Finegold, *Experts and Politicians: Reform Challenges to Machine Politics in New York, Cleveland and Chicago* (Princeton: Princeton University Press, 1995).

7. See: Robert R. Alford and Harry M. Scoble, "Political and Socioeconomic Characteristics of American Cities," *Municipal Year Book, 1965*, p. 95. See also: Leo F. Schnore and Robert R. Alford, "Forms of Government and Socioeconomic Characteristics of Suburbs," *Administrative Science Quarterly* 8 (June 1963): 1–17.

8. James Q. Wilson and Edward C. Banfield, *City Politics* (Cambridge: Harvard University Press, 1963). For a contrary finding, see: David R. Berman and Bruce D. Merrill, "Citizen Attitudes toward Municipal Reform Institutions: A Testing of Some Assumptions," *Western Political Quarterly* 29 (June 1976): 274–283.

9. See: Raymond E. Wolfinger and John Osgood Field, "Political Ethos and the Structure of City Government," *American Political Science Review* 60 (June 1966): 306–326; and Robert L. Lineberry and Edmund Fowler, "Reformism and Public Policies in American Cities," *American Political Science Review* 61 (September 1967): 701–716.

10. See: Theodore J. Lowi, *The End of Liberalism* (New York: W.W. Norton, 1969), p. 201.

11. See, for example: Advisory Commission on Intergovernmental Relations, *The New Grass Roots Government?* (Washington, D.C.: Government Printing Office, 1972); Alan A. Alshuler, *Community Control: The Black Demand for Participation in Large American Cities* (New York: Pegasus, 1970); Milton Kotler, *Neighborhood Government: The Local Foundations of Political Life* (New York: Bobbs-Merrill, 1969); and Joseph F. Zimmerman, *The Federated City: Community Control in Large Cities* (New York: St. Martin's Press, 1972).

12. See, for example: John Clayton Thomas, "The Term Limitations Movement in U.S. Cities," *National Civic Review* 81 (Spring–Summer 1992): 155–173.

13. Howard D. Hamilton, "The Municipal Voter: Voting and Non-Voting in City Elections," *American Political Science Review* 65 (December 1971): 1135–1140, quote at 1140.

14. See: Robert R. Alford and Eugene C. Lee, "Voter Turnout in American Cities," *American Political Science Review* 56 (September 1968): 796–797. See also: Eugene C. Lee, "City Elections: A Statistical Profile," *Municipal Year Book, 1963*, pp. 74–84.

15. See: Sidney Verba and Norman H. Nie, *Participation in America* (New York: Harper and Row, 1972).

16. Arnold Fleischmann and Lana Stein, "Minority and Female Success in Municipal Runoff Elections," *Social Science Quarterly* 69 (December 1988): 378–385. See related discussion of runoff primaries in ch. 4.

17. Charles R. Adrian, "A Typology for Nonpartisan Elections," *Western Political Quarterly* 12 (June 1959): 449–458.

18. Eugene C. Lee, *The Politics of Nonpartisanship* (Berkeley and Los Angeles: University of California Press, 1960).

19. The same generalizations hold true for other types of nonpartisan elections, for example, judicial ones. See: Peverill Squire and Eric R.A.N. Smith, "The Effect of

Partisan Information on Voters in Nonpartisan Elections," *The Journal of Politics* 50 (1988): 169–179.

20. See: Fred I. Greenstein, "The Changing Pattern of Urban Party Politics," *The Annals* (May 1964): 2–13.

21. T.P. Robinson and T.R. Dye, "Reformism and Black Representation on City Councils," *Social Science Quarterly* 59 (June 1978): 133–141.

22. See, generally: Carol A. Cassel, "Social Background Characteristics of Nonpartisan City Council Members: A Research Note," *Western Political Quarterly* (September 1985): 495–501.

23. "A Contagious Bug in the West," *Newsweek* (4 April 1988): 27.

24. See: Charles M. Price, "Recalls at the Local Level: Dimensions and Implications," *National Civic Review* (April 1983): 199–206; and Charles M. Price, "Electoral Accountability: Local Recalls," *National Civic Review* (March/April 1988): 118–123.

25. Wilson and Banfield, *City Politics.*

26. James Q. Wilson and Edward C. Banfield, "Political Ethos Revisited," *American Political Science Review* 65 (December 1971): 1048–1062. For a challenge to public-regarding theory, see: Harlan Hahn and Sheldon Kamieniecki, *Referendum Voting: Social Status and Policy Preferences* (Westport, Conn.: Greenwood Press, 1987).

27. Susan E. Howell, "Local Election Campaigns: The Effects of Office Level on Campaign Style," *The Journal of Politics* 42 (1980): 1135–1145.

28. "Mayoral Candidates Enter the Big Time Using Costly TV Ads and Consultants," *National Journal* (6 April 1985): 737–742, quote at 739.

29. Rufus P. Browning, Dale Rogers Marshall, and David H. Tabb, *Protest Is Not Enough: The Struggle of Blacks and Hispanics for Equality in Urban Politics* (Berkeley: University of California Press, 1984).

30. See, for example: Bryan O. Jackson, "The Effects of Racial Group Consciousness on Political Mobilization in American Cities," *Western Political Quarterly* 40 (December 1987): 631–646.

31. See, for example: Kenneth R. Mladenka, "Blacks and Hispanics in Urban Politics," *American Political Science Review* 83 (March 1989): 165–191; and Rodney E. Hero, "Hispanics in Urban Government and Politics: Some Findings, Comparisons and Implications," *Western Political Quarterly* (June 1990): 403–414.

32. On the Daley machine of Chicago, see: Mike Royko, *Boss: Richard J. Daley of Chicago* (New York: E.P. Dutton, 1971); and Milton Rakove, *Don't Make No Waves—Don't Back No Losers: An Insider's Analysis of the Daley Machine* (Bloomington: Indiana University Press, 1975). A different view of machine politics (i.e., the theme that it is now "withering away") can be found in: Raymond E. Wolfinger, *The Politics of Progress* (Englewood Cliffs, N.J.: Prentice Hall, 1974). For party activity in five urban areas, see: William Crotty, ed., *Political Parties in Local Areas* (Knoxville: University of Tennessee Press, 1987). See also: John P. Frendreis, James L. Gibson, and Laura L. Vertz, "The Electoral Relevance of Local Party Organizations," *American Political Science Review* 84 (March 1990): 225–235.

33. James Q. Wilson, "Politics and Reform in American Cities," in Robert L. Morlan, ed., *Capital, Courthouse and City Hall,* 4th ed. (Boston: Houghton Mifflin, 1972), pp. 284–292.

34. Harvey Molotch, "The City as a Growth Machine: Toward a Political Economy of Place," *American Journal of Sociology* 82 (1976): 309–332. On the varying role of financial interests in big-city politics, see: Robert F. Pecorella, *Community Power in a Postreform City* (Armonk, N.Y.: M.E. Sharpe, 1994).

35. See: Diane Roth Bard Margolis, *The Managers: Corporate Life in America* (New York: William Morrow, 1979).

36. See, for example: Clarence N. Stone, *Regime Politics: Governing Atlanta, 1946–1988* (Lawrence: University Press of Kansas, 1989).

37. Alan Ehrenhalt, "For Chambers of Commerce and Cities, the Days of Conflict May Be Over," *Governing* (November 1989): 40–48.

38. See: David L. Rosenbloom, "The Press and the Local Candidate," *The Annals* 427 (September 1976): 12–22.

39. See: David L. Paletz, Peggy Reichert, and Barbara McIntyre, "How the Media Support Local Governmental Authority," *Public Opinion Quarterly* 35 (Spring 1971): 80–92.

40. M. Margaret Conway, "Voter Information Sources in a Nonpartisan Local Election," *Western Political Quarterly* 21 (March 1968): 69–77.

41. Many of the following remarks also apply to residential community or homeowners' associations. See: Robert Jay Dilger, "Residential Community Associations: Issues, Impacts, and Relevance for Local Government," *State and Local Governmental Review* (Winter 1991): 17–23.

42. See: Luis Ricardo Fraga, "Domination through Democratic Means: Nonpartisan Slating Groups in City Electoral Politics," *Urban Affairs Quarterly* 23 (June 1988): 538–555; and Chandler Davidson and Luis Ricardo Fraga, "Slating Groups as Parties in a 'Nonpartisan' Setting," *Western Political Quarterly* 41 (June 1988): 373–390.

43. Among the many useful readings in the vast literature on the subject of community power are: Michael Aiken and Paul E. Mott, eds., *The Structure of Community Power* (New York: Random House, 1970); Peter Bachrach and Morton Baratz, *Power and Poverty* (New York: Oxford University Press, 1970); Terry N. Clark, ed., *Community Structure and Decision Making* (San Francisco: Chandler, 1968); William Hawley and Frederick M. Wirt, eds., *The Search for Community Power* (Englewood Cliffs, N.J.: Prentice Hall, 1968); William A. Gamson, *Power and Discontent* (Homewood, Ill.: Dorsey Press, 1968); Nelson W. Polsby, *Community Power and Political Theory* (New Haven: Yale University Press, 1963); and Robert A. Dahl, *Who Governs?* (New Haven: Yale University Press, 1961).

44. Edward Pessen, "Who Governed the Nation's Cities in the 'Era of the Common Man'?" *Political Science Quarterly* 87 (December 1972): 591–614.

45. Floyd Hunter, *Community Power Structure: A Study of Decision Makers* (Chapel Hill: University of North Carolina Press, 1953). See also: Floyd Hunter, *Community Power Succession: Atlanta's Policy-Makers Revisited* (Chapel Hill: University of North Carolina Press, 1980). For an update and other view of Atlanta, see: Stone, *Regime Politics*.

46. Edward C. Hayes, *Power Structure and Urban Policy: Who Rules in Oakland?* (New York: McGraw-Hill, 1972), p. 199.

47. See: Bachrach and Baratz, *Power and Poverty*. See also: Matthew A. Crenson, *The Un-Politics of Air Pollution* (Baltimore: Johns Hopkins University Press, 1971).

48. See, for example: Dahl, *Who Governs?*

49. See: Edward C. Banfield, *Political Influence* (New York: The Free Press, 1961), ch. 8.

50. Barbara Ferman, *Governing the Ungovernable City: Political Skill, Leadership, and the Modern Mayor* (Philadelphia: Temple University Press, 1985).

51. See: Jeffrey L. Pressman, "Preconditions of Mayoral Leadership," *American Political Science Review* 66 (June 1972): 511–524; Robert H. Salisbury, "Urban Politics: The New Convergence of Power," *The Journal of Politics* 26 (November 1964): 775–797; and John P. Kotter and Paul R. Lawrence, *Mayors in Action: Five Approaches to Urban Governance* (New York: John Wiley and Sons, 1974).

10

★ ★ ★

LOCAL GOVERNMENT: THE OFFICIAL POLICYMAKERS

The discussion in chapter 9 focused largely on citizen activity and the influence of unofficial policymakers such as private groups and influential individuals and businesses (including the media) in local politics. This chapter centers on the working environment and activities of the official policymakers and policymaking institutions. We look at the structural environment in which municipal officials function and at the role and activities of city councils, mayors, city managers, and local administrators.

THE STRUCTURAL ENVIRONMENT

Figure 10–1 shows four basic forms of municipal government. These forms, it should be noted, are models only and few governments actually measure up in all respects. A majority of municipalities (54 percent) have some variation of the mayor-council form. Two general categories of the mayor-council form are the strong-mayor and weak-mayor varieties. Close to 40 percent of all municipalities have the council-manager plan and only about 3 percent are using the commission option. The remaining municipalities use the town and other plans discussed in chapter 8.

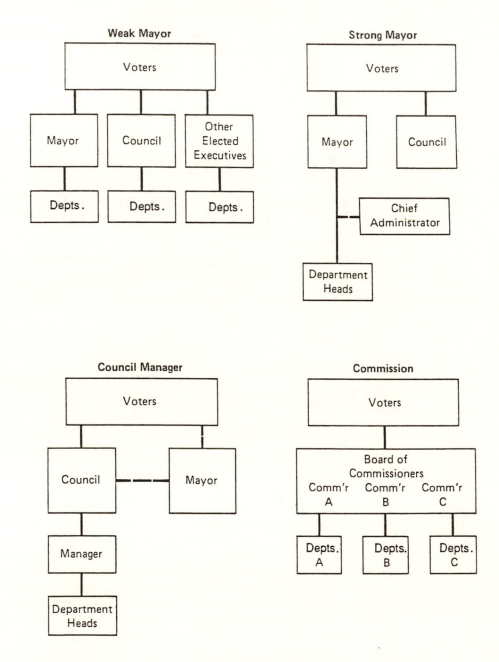

FIGURE 10–1 Forms of Municipal Government

The weak mayor–council type is the oldest form of municipal government. Under this form, the mayor is weak in the same sense that most governors are weak, because he or she shares executive authority with several administrators directly elected by the voters. The weak mayor has only a limited ability to appoint and remove other administrators or to prepare a budget. The mayor is sometimes elected out of the council. Often he or she lacks the veto power. Cities using this form usually also have relatively large city councils whose members are elected from wards (districts within the city). A major defect of the system is that no one individual can assume responsibility for overall policy implementation. In large cities like Chicago, a political organization has filled the power vacuum. The system works best in relatively small, homogeneous communities where the demands for executive leadership are minimal. Indeed, in small municipalities, the job of mayor may be adequately fulfilled on a part-time basis.

Under the strong-mayor form, the mayor and the council are the only officials directly elected by the voters. This arrangement simplifies the demands made on the electorate and gives the mayor a unique status as the only elected executive. In addition, the mayor has considerable authority to appoint and remove departmental personnel, to prepare a budget for submission to the council, and to veto acts of the council (subject to an override). Through these powers and the ability to recommend programs, the mayor can exercise policy leadership. The strong-mayor plan is found in most large cities and many small ones. Large cities where the mayor may not have time for extensive administrative duties have adopted a mayor-administrator plan under which a professional administrator (known as the controller or chief administrative officer) is appointed by the mayor to supervise department heads, prepare the budget, and control personnel matters.

The council-manager form places administrative authority in the hands of a manager who is appointed by the council and serves at its pleasure (though occasionally under the terms of a written contract). The average tenure has turned out to be about five years. Under this plan, the mayor is a member of the council who became mayor by a vote of the council, through a process in which the position is rotated among council members, or because he or she received the highest number of votes among council candidates in the most recent election. In a departure from the original plan, several cities with this form allow voters to choose among candidates running for the office of mayor. This variation is most often found in the larger cities. The council-manager plan, as originally developed, calls for a city council that is relatively small—five to nine members—elected at-large and on nonpartisan basis. Judicial and community pressures in some places have prompted some cities with the plan to abandon the at-large system for one where districts are used.

The council-manager form appears to operate best in relatively homogeneous communities where there is a high degree of consensus on the role and functions of government. It has been adopted mostly in suburbs of under a quarter of a million people (especially middle-class suburbs), although it is also found in some large cities, such as Dallas, Cincinnati, and Kansas City. The objectives of the system are to structure city government on the same principles as an efficient business corporation and to separate politics and policymaking from administration.

Under the commission form used in some three hundred cities, the same governmental body exercises both executive and legislative powers. The plan divides the powers of government among a small number, usually five, of directly elected commissioners. Each commissioner sits on the city council and is in charge of one city department, such as public safety. The mayor may be chosen directly by the voters or selected by the commission out of its own membership. In any case, the mayor has little authority. This plan makes coordinating governmental activity difficult and invites government by log-rolling (the trading of support and favors) among commissioners. In recent years, the commission form has been abandoned by a number of cities (for example, Kansas City, Kansas; Salt Lake City, Utah; and Shreveport, Louisiana) and is currently used in less than 3 percent of all cities in the United States.

Research suggests that two out of every three municipalities have changed their governmental form at least once since their incorporation.[1] The demand for reorganization has often reflected general unhappiness with the delivery of essential services, such as that of the police, under the existing structure. The significance of the choice among the various forms, however, has been a matter of debate. Some observers link the mayor-council system, especially the weak version, with traditional "boss rule" politics, confusion, and waste, and have praised the council-manager form for developing effective and efficient government.[2] Others, however, find the council-manager form inadequate in providing political leadership and citizen representation in large cities and unsatisfactory because it gives too much weight to the influence of professional administrators over the demands of citizens or elected officials. Some research suggests that, whatever stylistic differences exist among types of government, changing from one form to another is not likely to affect such performance indicators as taxing and spending levels.[3]

The City Council

Role and Structural Variations

During the colonial period, the governmental powers of cities were usually vested in a council elected by the small segment of the population eligible to vote. Mayors were chosen by the council or by the colonial governors and did not do much more than preside over meetings of the council. Council members initiated legislation and council committees supervised the performance of administrative tasks. Council members were often justices of the peace and constituted a court when sitting as a body. The council continued to thrive under the weak-mayor system but was limited by the growing complexity of urban problems and the emergence of the strong-mayor and council-manager systems.

Characteristics of current councils vary with their form of government and with the size of the communities they serve. Small (five to nine members) action-oriented councils are common in council-manager forms. Councils in large cities, where the mayor-council system is usually employed, tend to be larger (the largest being fifty in Chicago and thirty-six in New York) and play a more representational and deliberative role, much like that of state legislatures or Congress. In some cities, especially those with a council-manager and commission form, the mayor is also a member of the city council, although he or she may not be allowed to vote on all issues coming before the body.[4]

Municipal voters select council members through partisan or nonpartisan elections (see chapter 9). Many cities elect their council members at-large. Others use districts or wards or some combination of the at-large and district system (electing some members at-large and others from districts).

The choice of wards or at-large elections may affect both the representative nature of the council and the council members' views of their roles. Ward elections encourage the representation of neighborhood interests and give each voter within the city "his or her own" council member to whom he or she can bring grievances and whom he or she can hold accountable. The council members accordingly may see themselves as "errand boys" for the people in their districts and put first priority on what is best for their constituents when making decisions. Elections at-large may be detrimental to the representation of minority interests since the majority race or party can sweep every election and position on the ballot. Indeed, in some cities the adoption of the at-large device appears to have its roots in a desire to diminish the influence of newly arrived ethnic groups and blacks in the local political system.[5]

Elections at-large are defended, particularly in council-manager cities, on the grounds they bring council members with broader, citywide viewpoints and help detract from neighborhood politics. Ward elections are unpopular in this kind of city because of their historical association with boss rule, a central characteristic of which was the "ward heeler" who serviced his neighborhood in return for political support.

Research on the significance of the choice of election systems suggests that, as expected, council people elected at-large are more likely than those elected from districts to make the whole city rather than neighborhoods their chief focus. Also as expected, those elected from districts or wards are more constituency oriented. Yet, the differences in orientation are not great. Moreover, researchers have found it difficult to identify significant differences in policy that are due to the choice between at-large or district systems or between partisan and nonpartisan elections.[6]

It is clear, however, that no local election system is immune from challenge in court as to its validity. Since the United States Supreme Court's 1986 decision in *Thornburg* v. *Gingles,* groups throughout the country have challenged the use of the at-large system for local elections on the grounds that it dilutes the voting power of minorities and thus violates the national Voting Rights Act.[7] Cities that use wards or districts, on the other hand, must grapple with problems of districting.[8]

The Council Members

Formal qualifications for serving on a city council are usually quite easy to meet. Candidates need only be citizens of the United States, qualified voters, and residents of the city for at least one year preceding their election or appointment.[9] In most communities, there is no limit on the number of consecutive terms that a council person may serve. The general movement to limit terms of elected officials, however, has also been felt on the local level. About a third of cities with over a quarter of a million population now have term limits on council members and other officials. Term limits are also found in many smaller cities and towns. Many of the term restrictions on council members were adopted in the last few years by popular vote with little debate over their merits, as opponents, including public officials, were reluctant to speak out against the popular proposals.[10]

Survey data reveal that the majority of council members are white males.[11] Although there has been an increase in the number of Hispanic and black council members in recent years, these minorities still are often underrepresented on city councils. Women members are found on about one-third of all city councils and hold around 18 percent of these positions. Blacks hold an estimated 5 percent of the council positions. For Hispanics, the estimate is about 2 percent. By all available evidence, the turnover rate for city council members is somewhat comparable to that for state legislators (more than half of the members are likely to be serving their first term) and is considerably higher than that for members of Congress.

City council members are generally part-time political amateurs who do not seek careers in politics. Service on city councils has traditionally been regarded as a temporary civic duty, like heading the community chest. One consequence of the part-time status of council members is that they have been largely dependent on the city administrators for information and policy development.[12] The fact that council members often plan to serve only a single term means that short of recall, they are immune from ultimate accountability to the voters. Some studies suggest, however, that even though electoral accountability is lacking, only rarely is there conflict between the views of council members and the views of their constituents. This attitudinal congruence (basic agreement) is especially likely in small, homogeneous communities where citizens and council members share common backgrounds and values.[13]

Although most council members are best characterized as part-time amateurs, one commonly finds council members who take the job seriously, for example, being unusually willing to question city policies and practices.[14] The small, but perhaps growing, number of council members who are politically ambitious for higher office differs from the others in that they tend to seek out information beyond what they receive from city administrators, to think in terms of a larger voting constituency than the one from which they were elected, and to consider problems from a broader (regional, state, or national) point of view.[15] Finally, one should not take the part-time status of council members to mean that the members do not have strong personal interests in governmental decisions. For example, those who are also real estate developers might try to protect or advance their interests in zoning decisions (though they may see no conflict between what is good for the city and what is good for their business). The rezoning of residential property is also apt to be a prime cause of division on the council, with each member's position reflecting how the rezoning would affect his or her property or neighborhood.[16]

Survey research suggests some broad differences in how council people see their representative role. As table 10–1 indicates, council members from small and medium-sized cities see their primary duty to be one of representing the interests of the city as a whole. Council people from large cities, on the other hand, see the representation of their neighborhoods to be of prime importance. This finding, as indicated earlier, may reflect the greater use of wards or districts in large cities. Council members in large cities were also particularly likely to give special representation to racial minorities. Half of the council people in cities of all sizes felt it was very important to give representation to business groups and the elderly.

City councils have become more diverse in their memberships and, apparently, more sensitive to a greater number of groups. Yet, council members also appear to have become more frustrated. As table 10–2 shows, council people from cities of all sizes have become increasingly frustrated by council-member conflict, interest group pressure, long hours, time away from families, campaign costs, low salaries, and a variety of other problems affecting their service.

COUNCILS AT WORK

Regular city council sessions, usually presided over by the mayor, are held at intervals set by state law or by the council's own rules. In large cities, councils may meet more than once a week; in small cities, regular sessions may take place only once a month. In addition to regular sessions, the council may meet in adjourned or study sessions between regular sessions, in special

TABLE 10–1   Attitudes of Council Members Toward Representing Groups in the City

| | Percent who view their representation of group to be very important | | | | | | |
| | Total | Small | | Medium | | Large | |
	%	Rank	%	Rank	%	Rank	%
City as a whole	79	1	85	1	81	2	73
Neighborhoods	74	2	65	2	73	1	82
Business	52	3	55	4	51	4	49
Elderly	51	4	50	3	52	3	51
Racial minorities	38	7	27	5	35	4	49
Environmentalists	35	5	33	6	36	8	34
Women	31	7	27	7	28	6	39
Municipal employees	30	6	31	8	26	9	34
Ethnic groups	26	12	16	9	24	7	37
Good government organizations, e.g., LWV	23	9	25	12	18	10	27
Realtors/developers	22	11	18	11	21	12	26
Labor unions	21	13	12	10	22	10	28
Anti-pornography/vice	18	10	19	13	17	13	19
Political parties	15	13	12	14	16	14	16
Pro-choice	11	16	7	15	11	15	14
Right to life	7	15	8	16	6	16	8

Source: James H. Svara, "Council Profile: More Diversity, Demands, Frustration," Nation's Cities Weekly (18 November 1991): 4. Reprinted with permission.

sessions often called on an emergency basis, and in conference sessions. This last is an executive or closed session, called before the regular session, at which members discuss items that are to come up at the regular session. Often the sessions may result in a consensus and make a "united front" of the council possible during the regular session. Because of the importance of conference sessions, however, several states have required that they, like other sessions of the council, be open to the public. In contrast to the legislative practices on the state and national levels, city councils often make decisions immediately following a public hearing. Council members are briefed on policy matters by administrators and have read the reports of the zoning and other commissions before the regular session begins. The public hearing before the council, however, may be highly charged and result in the presentation of information that the council hears for the first time (see box 10–1). The hearing may also

TABLE 10–2   Sources of Frustration to Council Members, 1979 and 1989

	Percent who feel condition is a serious problem							
	Total		Small		Medium		Large	
	1979	1989	1979	1989	1979	1989	1979	1989
Council member conflict	33	55	36	52	33	55	23	57
Interest group pressure	33	46	35	47	31	47	28	45
Long hours	26	43	22	35	33	43	31	50
Time away from family	24	46	23	35	23	46	26	56
Inadequate staff assistance	24	36	22	21	25	39	29	48
Too much reading	19	40	17	40	19	35	27	44
Problems with media coverage	19	36	18	36	19	34	20	38
Too many meetings	18	35	16	37	20	31	20	39
Losses in private income	14	34	12	31	17	34	15	38
Campaign costs	13	49	12	37	13	50	21	59
Open meeting laws	12	20	13	24	12	18	9	18
Late night constituent calls	12	17	12	13	12	19	12	20
Too much written paperwork	9	19	8	11	9	15	9	32
Inadequate office space	7	23	6	14	8	24	10	31
Public disclosure requirement	7	9	5	8	10	9	5	9
Low council member salaries	n.a.	43	n.a.	34	n.a.	43	n.a.	52

Source: James H. Svara, "Council Profile: More Diversity, Demands, Frustration," *Nation's Cities Weekly* (18 November 1991): 4. Reprinted with permission.

demonstrate political pressure that sways the council members' votes, regardless of the study reports and recommendations made by city staff and commissions.[17]

City council functions vary to a considerable extent with the size of the population they serve. Council members in large cities spend more time on zoning, planning, and the consideration of executive proposals from the mayor or manager than do council members in small cities and towns. Small-city council people, on the other hand, spend more time reviewing administration of city functions, answering constituent requests, and keeping track of personnel matters (hirings and firings) than do their counterparts in large cities. Council members in both sized cities consider zoning and land-use

---

BOX 10–1 LIFE ON THE CITY COUNCIL

"The new councilman or board member soon learns that few if any visitors will attend who do not have an ax to grind. In the few moments before a meeting is formally opened, members survey the audience, recognizing certain groups and the cause they represent, jestingly speculating with one another about those they do not recognize. 'What do they want?' is the standard question. . . .

"Citizens participate from the audience in debate, though, of course, only when recognized to do so, and both the council and members of the audience frequently address one another by first names. Unhappily, from the board member's perspective, while groups of citizens will from time to time appear to support a favorite project, few persons attend with sufficient continuity to gain a broad understanding, and when really tough decisions have to be made, those who are sympathetic to the position of the board are prone to shy away from combat and leave the board to face its critics completely devoid of the inestimable help of visible public backing."

Source: Robert L. Morlan, "Life on the City Council: Realities of Legislative Politics," in Robert L. Morlan and Leroy C. Hardy, *Politics in California* (Belmont, Calif.: Dickenson Publishing, 1968), pp. 103–104.

---

decisions to be their most difficult. In terms of citizen complaints, local officials appear most often to hear grievances over dog and other pet control problems (by far the most common type of complaint), traffic, and rezoning matters.[18] Survey research indicates that council members feel they are very good in responding to constituent needs and demands. Yet, they see themselves doing less well in setting goals and priorities and performing other governmental functions. City councils, in the opinion of the people who serve on them, are, in general, stronger as representative bodies than they are as governing bodies.[19]

EXECUTIVE LEADERSHIP

THE OFFICE OF MAYOR

The central executive officials in municipal politics are the mayor and, in council-manager cities, the city manager. On paper it is only in the strong-mayor form that one finds a chief executive whose official powers and duties resemble those of the president of the United States. Under this system in its pure form, the mayor has the authority to appoint and remove many officials, prepare and execute an executive budget, veto legislation, and prepare a legislative program. The mayor is also the only executive official directly

---

BOX 10–2 PATRONAGE IN THE CITIES

In some large, unreformed cities, the mayor can fill several public jobs on a patronage basis: in Chicago, for example, some twenty-five thousand patronage jobs exist, even though the validity of the patronage system has recently been subject to adverse court rulings. More likely is the situation described by Detroit Mayor Coleman Young: "The general belief in Detroit is that there are a thousand jobs out there on the Christmas tree, and people with limited abilities are promoting themselves as prospective commissioners of major departments. In fact, I have about one hundred appointments open to me, and most of them require special-background qualifications."

Source: Quoted by Roger M. Williams, "America's Black Mayors: Are They Saving the Cities?" *Saturday Review/World* (4 May 1974): 11.

---

elected by the voters, and department heads look to his or her leadership rather than to that of the city council.

The formal position of the mayor in the council-manager or commission form does not give the holder of that office much influence. Rather than an independent political actor, the mayor in theory, as noted earlier, is not much more than another member of the council. Rather than a leading policymaker, the mayor is expected to do little more than preside at council meetings and represent the city on ceremonial occasions. In actual fact, as noted below, even in the commission or council-manager system, there is room for the exercise of strong mayoral leadership.

Mayors in large mayor-council cities may have several immediate staff advisers concerned with the development and implementation of policy and/or with the establishing of working relations with the bureaucracy, the media, community groups, the city council, and officials representing other governments. The growth of staff has been particularly pronounced since the 1960s, when large cities were suddenly faced with a number of crisis situations and the necessities of increasing their abilities to deal with federal agencies and citizen demands.[20] At the same time, however, the number of staff or other jobs that big city mayors can fill on the basis of patronage is usually far less than the demand for such positions (see box 10–2).

In most council-manager cities and in small cities with a mayor-council form of government, the immediate staff resources of the mayor are minimal. The mayor's job in these types of municipalities is considered to be part-time and is rewarded with only a nominal salary. One study based on an analysis of suburban mayors in the Detroit area found that mayors in these communities served relatively short terms (an average of 3.8 years) and seldom were able to use their positions as stepping-stones to higher office.[21]

Variations in governmental forms, city size, and staff appear to be important in shaping the mayor's role and influence in local politics. Other factors, however, are also involved. The fact that a mayor is usually directly elected is conducive to his or her being politically active on behalf of a constituency. Because voters do not appear to know a great deal about the responsibilities of various positions in government,[22] they may hold mayors responsible for functions over which they actually have no formal authority. Thus, regardless of the form of government involved, the expectations of the electorate are important. Furthermore, what a mayor can actually accomplish depends to a large extent on his or her power base (popular appeal, ties to influential community leaders), and his or her own personal objectives and skills.

THE MAYORS

Surveys have shown that mayors, like city council members, are usually white, male, and better educated than the general population. The "average" mayor is in his late forties (slightly older than the average city council member) and is either a businessman or a member of some profession. Many mayors first served on the city council.[23]

As for leadership styles, many mayors appear most comfortable in performing ceremonial functions such as giving speeches at public functions. They are likely to take on community problems only when they develop to the point where some governmental action is necessary. Some mayors appear anxious to evade controversy, while others appear to enjoy functioning as brokers in settling disputes. A number of mayors appear to be "idea people" or reformers actively working for new projects and programs and pursuing long-range as well as short-term goals for their cities. Their chief task (as suggested in chapter 9) is to draw on any official and personal resources they have to mobilize the council, the bureaucracy, citizens, and community leaders toward the solution of problems or the attainment of community objectives.[24]

There are, of course, all types of mayors, with different backgrounds and problems. Historically, different classes of the population have served as mayor. In New Haven, for example, Robert Dahl found three different stages in the nature of mayoral leadership. The period from 1784 to 1842 belonged to the "patricians," long-established New Haven families whose influence in local politics stemmed from their status, education, and wealth. The period from 1842 to 1899 was dominated by mayors who represented the "entrepreneurs," the commercial and industrial elite who, while lacking social status, had considerable influence through their wealth. The period since 1909 has been dominated by the "ex-plebes," those with working-class backgrounds whose ascendancy has been based neither on wealth nor status but on their appeal to the ethnic groups that have flocked to the city.[25]

Over the last few decades, the governing of large cities has been in the hands of men as diverse as John Lindsay of New York, a liberal in an era characterized by taxpayer rebellions and a fear of crime;[26] Frank Rizzo of Philadelphia, a hard-liner on the law-and-order issue; and Dennis Kucinich, the youthful and highly controversial mayor of Cleveland and a populist engaged in conflict with "the money boys" (banks and utilities) in his city and with the city council. In the early 1980s, there were about seven hundred female mayors.

In recent decades a new group of black mayors has emerged, including Richard Hatcher of Gary, Thomas Bradley of Los Angeles, Maynard Jackson of Atlanta, and the late Harold Washington of Chicago. Black mayors have had a special set of problems, one of which is they must contend with racial prejudice in seeking election to begin with. Research indicates that the strongest opposition to black candidates has come from poor whites.[27] Once in office, black mayors have frequently found themselves facing the opposition of whites in administrative positions protected by civil service.[28] Black mayors have also inherited some of the most severely deteriorated cities. At the same time, they have had to meet black citizens' increased expectations that they will solve these troubles.

The extent to which black mayors should and can give special consideration to the problems of the black community is a matter of controversy among citizens, black officials, and political theorists. Mayors who are members of a deprived ethnic or racial group might be expected to be disposed toward helping "their people." Favoritism of this nature, however, may be politically unpopular with other groups. Black leader Julian Bond has described the political problem in these terms: "You can't afford to let Group A know you're helping Group B—but you've got to help them."[29] Black mayors also may find it difficult to keep the support of black voters and, at the same time, form an effective pro-growth partnership with local business interests.[30]

In the late 1980s and early 1990s control of city hall in several large cities shifted to leaders bent on reducing taxes and spending by shedding services and downsizing the bureaucracy. Contrary to historical patterns, the current crop of big-city mayors includes Republicans, such as Richard Riordan in Los Angeles and Rudolph Giuliani in New York, as well as Democrats.[31]

CITY MANAGERS

In council-manager cities, the manager assumes many of the mayor's official functions. Survey data reveal that city managers have an average age of about forty-two and are predominantly male, white, native born, and Protestant.[32] There has been only a modest increase in recent years in the number of women and nonwhites in the profession. In 1971, 99 percent of the managers were male. By 1980, this percentage fell to only 97 percent. The percentage gain for nonwhites has been less than 2 percent over the same period. Overall, there has been a shift away from the once dominant engineering background for city managers toward one in which they have an undergraduate degree in liberal arts (most often political science) and graduate training in public administration. As one study has concluded: "The profession has continued to move away from its early preference for a narrow, technocratic education toward an education with substantially more breadth. This trend has occurred as it has become necessary for those who manage cities to "make more sense out of things in general."[33]

One study, by Richard Stillman, has analyzed the personal and career characteristics of city managers and grouped them into three types: careerists, administrative generalists, and local appointees.[34] Careerists tend to view city management as a lifetime occupation. They have often been trained in public administration and have worked their way up in city administration from positions such as administrative assistant. They consider themselves to be specialists in city administration and are active in national activities of professional groups such as the International City/County Management Association. Careerists tend to be highly mobile, moving to more challenging jobs in other cities, and to identify more closely with their profession than with the locality where they happen to work. Administrative generalists comprise perhaps the largest category of city managers. These managers did not begin their careers with the intention of becoming city administrators but moved into their positions from similar positions in private enterprise. They are, in short, professional managers but not professional city managers.

The local appointee, more common in small communities, is a "local" without a great deal of professional training for the position and with no real interest in pursuing a career in city administration. He or she has taken the job simply because it was available and no one else wanted it.

City managers, according to the formal working of the council-manager plan, must assume sole responsibility for the implementation of policies made by the city council. They must not become involved in politics but instead must play the role of an assistant in helping the council come to policy decisions. Under the formal model, the manager is a professional the council turns to for administrative ability and policy advice. The council is the sole policymaker. The job of the manager is to defend the policy of the council in the community.

In practice, the division of responsibilities between the council and manager is not as sharp as the model would have it. City councils and managers are likely to share responsibilities in the various phases of the governmental process. In what might be considered a typical or average council-manager city, the city council plays a large role in defining the broad mission of the city

DIMENSIONS OF
GOVERNMENTAL PROCESS

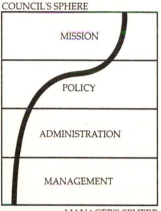

ILLUSTRATIVE TASKS FOR COUNCIL	COUNCIL'S SPHERE	ILLUSTRATIVE TASKS FOR ADMINISTRATORS
Determine "purpose," scope of services, tax level, constitutional issues.	MISSION	Advise (what city "can" do may influence what it "should" do); analyze conditions and trends.
Pass ordinances, approve new projects and programs, ratify budget.	POLICY	Make recommendations on all decisions, formulate budget, determine service distribution formulae.
Make implementing decisions, e.g. site selection handle complaints, oversee administration.	ADMINISTRATION	Establish practices and procedures and make decisions for implementing policy.
Suggest management changes to manager, review organizational performance in manager's appraisal.	MANAGEMENT	Control the human, material and informational resources of organization to support policy and administrative functions.

MANAGER'S SPHERE

The curved line suggests the division between the Council's and the Manager's spheres of activity, with the Council to the *left* and the manager to the *right* of the line.

The division presented is intended to roughly approximate a "proper" degree of separation and sharing. Shifts to either the left or right would indicate improper incursions.

FIGURE 10–2 **Mission-Management Separation with Shared Responsibility for Policy and Administration**

Source: James H. Svara, "Dichotomy and Duality: Reconceptualizing the Relationship between Policy and Administration in Council-Manager Cities," *Public Administration Review* (January/February 1985): 228. Reprinted with permission from *Public Administration Review*, copyright © by the American Society for Public Administration, 1120 G Street NW, Washington, D.C. All rights reserved.

(for example, its basic service and tax level), works with the manager in making specific policy decisions regarding projects and budgetary matters, but is less involved than the manager in administrative or managerial activities (see figure 10–2).

The actual functions of the manager vary in cities of different sizes and political environments. They also depend on the training and attitudes of the managers. The position of city manager may be part-time or combined with another municipal job in some smaller communities. In small towns, the manager may have only a secretary; in larger ones, he or she may have numerous technically trained people on the immediate staff. The larger the city, the less likely managers are to be involved with the daily routines of departments. Conferences with department heads and the council, planning and preparing reports, and intergovernmental work with state and federal agencies are major concerns of managers in large cities. Direct citizen contact and supervision of municipal activities take up much of the manager's time in small cities.

The manager in any city can hardly avoid involvement in policy matters. Usually the manager prepares the agenda for the council and often attends council meetings armed with facts and information on possible courses of action. Council members, seldom in a position to question the information or the suggested alternative policy directions, often find themselves following the manager's recommendations.

MANAGERS AND MAYORS

Just as the actual function of the manager differs from the model, so does that of the mayor, especially in large cities. The traditional literature on the council-manager form gives the mayor only a limited role of presiding over council meetings and performing ceremonial functions. About half of the cities with the council-manager form, however, have considerably increased the position's political base by having the mayor directly elected by the voters.

A study by Robert Boynton and Deil S. Wright of forty-five large (over 100,000) cities with a council-manager plan found that the mayor has often been given more powers than the model of the plan calls for and, in practice, is deeply involved in both political leadership and administration.[35] Several large cities studied give the mayor considerable formal power to appoint administrative committees and citizen advisory boards. In actual practice, the mayors also play a great role in appointing department heads and in setting up the agenda of the council. Even though only 13 percent of the mayors had the formal power of making recommendations to the council, 82 percent actually made such recommendations.

These mayors, the study demonstrated, were not simply slightly more powerful than council members. They functioned as major political leaders in their cities and were far more involved than the average council member in working with the city manager, overseeing administration, and contacting city officials.

The involvement of the mayor in administration conflicts with the model and, not uncommonly, with the expectations of the city manager. Managers have been known to complain about politicians who interfere in administration and whittle away the manager's authority. The basic relationship between the mayor and manager, however, more often involves teamwork (see box 10–3). In the cooperative endeavor, the mayor dominates the political role, though he or she is often involved in administration, and the manager dominates in administrative matters, though he or she also becomes involved in the mayor's political program. Overall, managers play the dominant role in smaller cities, while mayors play the dominant role in larger cities.[36] In either case, the team relationship, as Boynton and Wright note, "is frankly political" and "the tenure of the manager is clearly linked to that of the mayor and/or the stability of community political leadership."[37]

BOX 10–3   THE POLICY ROLE OF THE MANAGER

Recognition of the changing role of the manager and the "team" relationship with the mayor is indicated in the following comment from Thomas W. Fletcher, a professional city manager:

"What is the manager of today? Is he an administrator? professional? technician? or a politician? In all probability the modern city manager has elements of all of these. Certainly the old image of the manager as the professional administrator, dealing with the techniques of engineering and finance, is gone. The human problems that now have the highest priority have removed the manager from the cloisters of his office in city hall and [have] required him to become a modern political animal. . . .

"We must now recognize that the directly elected mayor must assume a much stronger role in our city governments. The leadership of our community must be placed in the hands of our elected political leaders; and the manager must subject himself willingly and enthusiastically to encouraging that shift in responsibility."

Source: Thomas W. Fletcher, "What Is the Future for Our Cities and the City Manager?" *Public Administration Review* 31 (January/February 1971): 14–20, quote at 18.

In the end, a mayor under the council-manager form may actually function little differently from a mayor under the strong-mayor plan. Mayors of large cities, regardless of formal structures and powers, tend to become political leaders.[38] The team approach of the mayor and the manager may find its counterpart in the team approach of the mayor and a chief administrative officer under the mayor-administrator plan. Thus, big cities may receive somewhat the same type of executive team leadership under both structural arrangements.

ADMINISTRATORS AND LOCAL GOVERNMENTAL SERVICES

ADMINISTRATORS AND LOCAL POLITICS

Much of what was said in chapter 7 concerning governmental employment and the role played by administrators in state politics also applies at the local level. Since the time of the municipal reform movement, there has been a trend toward the selection of administrators on the basis of merit and competitive examination. In some cities such as Chicago, however, political patronage is still a prime route for local governmental employment. Reform governments have been in the forefront of those requiring merit and attempting to protect a "neutrally competent" administrative workforce from political pressures and involvement.[39]

Thanks in large part to federal laws, there has been a marked increase in the number of minority group members employed by local governments. This has been especially true in large, northern central cities where the nonwhite percentage of the population has steadily risen. Nonwhites in many localities, however, are generally employed in relatively low-paying laborer and general service jobs. Only a small percentage of nonwhite local employees are police officers or firefighters, though considerable progress was made during the 1980s and early 1990s because of affirmative action litigation (see chapter 15). Of the relatively few nonwhites who hold professional or managerial positions, many are in departments that have social functions, such as housing services and public welfare. Since the 1960s, some nonwhites have been employed as staff members of civil rights commissions and human relations councils and as minority group advisers to high-ranking administrators. These positions have functioned to some extent as a means of giving minorities an input into the development and implementation of local policy and a means of "flack-catching" from the minority community.[40]

Administrators are also involved in local politics in their capacities as developers and implementers of governmental policy. At the top of the administrative hierarchy are commissioners, department heads, bureau chiefs, and their assistants, who provide information to elected policymakers for policy development and who may also have considerable discretion on the level and distribution of services to the public. In performing these functions, high-level administrators in most large cities have the assistance of engineers, planners, lawyers, and financial experts. Experts in areas like planning, budgeting, and local law commonly serve in staff agencies that advise the chief executive and administrators in line agencies, that is, those agencies concerned with the provision of services such as public works or law enforcement. Police officers, social workers, housing inspectors, and other local administrators who are often in direct contact with citizens in delivering services have been called *street-level bureaucrats*.[41]

One task commonly facing high-level administrators is gaining internal control over subordinates within their departments. This may be difficult because subordinates may be protected by political patronage or civil service and/or enjoy a measure of independence by virtue of their expert knowledge. The actual activities of street-level bureaucrats who deliver services on a day-by-day basis in the community may be particularly difficult for high-level administrators to control.[42] For their part, administrators appear to duly acknowledge the right of mayors and council persons to set broad policy. Administrators, however, tend to resent the involvement of their political superiors in the implementation process, because this usually takes the form of what is viewed by administrators to be unfounded complaints or annoying, if not unreasonable, requests for special favors for constituents.[43]

Like their counterparts on the state level, high-level local administrators also commonly assume the task of protecting and/or enlarging the jurisdiction, legal authority, and finances of their organizations. Toward this end, they may set out to create a favorable climate of citizen opinion, cultivate politically influential constituencies, wage war on what are seen to be encroachments by other governmental agencies, and attempt to stand in good favor with the mayor, manager, and council.

In attempting to cultivate a favorable public image, many agencies have public relations programs of one type or another that may involve newsletters, press conferences, or speakers at various meetings. Many organizations are able to show visible proof of accomplishment by providing or improving on various public facilities such as roads, parks, and playgrounds. Other agencies find that the discovery of an actual or potential crisis situation—for example, a dramatic rise in the crime rate or in the amount of toxic substances in the air—functions to secure public and official support for increases in their appropriations and authority.[44]

THE PROVISION OF SERVICES

In providing various services, local governments have the choice of doing so indirectly by contracting out or directly performing the activity. Much of the service contracting local governments do is with other governments. As indicated in chapter 8, a municipality may, for example, enter into an agreement with another municipality or a county for police services. Other contracts are entered into with profit or nonprofit private organizations.

There is a long history of contracting with the private businesses for services like trash collection, ambulance dispatch, and street paving. In recent years, the amount of this type of contracting has increased. Jurisdictions, particularly those under financial pressure, have contracted out services in order to reduce costs. Economic pressures have often overcome the desire of city officials to have direct control over services and the opposition of municipal workers and their unions who, as one might expect, fear job losses.[45]

Contracting with private enterprise has commonly been advanced in the belief that private firms can do the job for less money than public agencies. Cost savings, however, do not always result. When they do, it is largely through personnel efficiencies, that is, having fewer workers or paying lower wages because union and civil service restrictions are bypassed. Critics of contracting out argue that private firms are often unreliable (that is, they may go out of business and leave citizens without essential services) and could actually lead to higher costs, poorer service, or both.[46] In order to encourage city departments to be competitive with private contractors, some cities, such as Phoenix, allow city departments to compete with private bidders for services like refuse collection and street cleaning.

When directly distributing benefits among people or among neighborhoods, local administrators appear to rely on a number of criteria.[47] Among these are the willingness of those who receive the services to pay for them, need, equality, and political acceptability. Many urban services, such as mass transit or refuse collection, are provided to those who are willing or able to pay in whole or part for the benefit of the services. The criterion of need may be determined through objective tests. For example, city officials may take a traffic count at an intersection to determine whether or not there is enough traffic to justify a stop sign. Administrators with limited resources (for example, staff and money) may find that all such needs cannot be immediately taken care of and will give priority to the worst problems. Thus, street repairs are made to avoid accidents or traffic jams on the most heavily traveled routes, and additional police personnel are sent into the most crime-ridden sections of the city. In regard to street improvements, priority may be given to arterial or feeder streets over neighborhood streets because state aid is earmarked for the former and because professional street engineers appear to see their major role to be one of providing fast, efficient, and safe traffic circulation on major routes.[48]

Contrary to the principle that services should be distributed on the basis of need is the principle that all people or areas of a city should be treated equally. Administrators are made aware that each council member expects his or her part of the city to have the same quality of police and fire protection and other city services as any other part of the city.

On a more purely political level, the distribution of services may be determined by the desire to appease or enlist the support of certain groups. At the request of prominent merchants, for example, police may be required to patrol shopping areas even though their services are needed more or could be more effectively used elsewhere. At other times, services may be given only somewhat reluctantly to those who have taken the time and the effort to complain loud and long enough to be heard.

SERVICES AND THE CITIZEN-CONSUMER

Decisions regarding the distribution and level of services are inherently controversial, although administrators often attempt to make them on the basis of objective criteria. Controversy often has also resulted from the manner in which administrators provide services. In recent years, much attention has focused on the behavior of local officials, such as police officers, who are in direct contact with citizens while enforcing laws and providing services. Another area of concern has been the often complex and confusing formal procedures imposed on those who wish to receive licenses, permits, and other governmental benefits.

BOX 10–4 APPEALING TO SUPERIORS

"An evil that commonly grows up in any government office which handles a large volume of small cases involving individuals who are typically unrepresented by counsel is the systematic effort of officers to discourage aggrieved parties from taking their case to superior officers. Even when the agency's published rules provide for review, parties are often given the impression that the initial decision is final. Even when the practice borders on falsification, superiors sometimes purposefully manage not to know about it: appeals to them add to their work load...."

Source: Kenneth Culp Davis, *Discretionary Justice: A Preliminary Inquiry* (Baton Rouge: Louisiana State University Press, 1969), pp. 143–144.

The delivery of police and other local services is discussed in some detail in Part Four of this book. Suffice it to say at this point that citizens, particularly but not exclusively the less educated and affluent, may perceive themselves to be confronted by a massive, complicated, and impersonal bureaucracy. What are seen as highly rational and efficient procedures by administrators may appear as meaningless, frustrating, and dehumanizing "red tape" to citizens. Citizens of all ages, races, and areas of a city may be confronted with low-level administrators who declare, "Sorry, I don't make the rules, I just apply them." Low-level administrators, in business as well as government, function to buffer the higher-level administrators who make the rules from the people affected by these rules. Even though individuals may be given the right to appeal the decision of an administrator to a superior official, the exercise of this right is often discouraged (see box 10–4).

Citizens unhappy with the distribution, level, quality, and delivery of local governmental services do have other means of registering their complaints. Assuming that a complaining party is able to afford the time and expense of litigation, he or she may be able to secure relief through judicial action. Citizens may also express their grievances through action line services set up by news media or ombudsman-type devices offered by local governments. These services channel complaints to the appropriate agency. To try to contact local elected officials directly, however, has been the common route.

Some research suggests that those who are generally most active in politics—most likely to vote, take part in party and group activities, and be on a first name basis with governmental officials—and who have a strong sense of political efficacy are also those who are most likely to complain about governmental services.[49]

In several of the concluding policy chapters we refocus on relations between citizens and the street-level bureaucrats—be they teachers, social workers, or police officers—and the difficulties of trying to involve citizens, especially the poor and nonwhite, in the development and implementation of policies affecting them.

ENDNOTES

1. Heywood T. Sanders, *Governmental Structure in American Cities* (Washington, D.C.: International City Management Association, 1980).
2. See: *Forms of Municipal Government* (New York: National Municipal League, 1973), p. 2.
3. David R. Morgan and John P. Pelissero, "Urban Policy: Does Political Structure Matter?" *American Political Science Review* 74 (December 1980): 999–1006.
4. Robert A. Barrett and B. Douglas Harman, *External Relationships of City Councils* (Washington, D.C.: International City Management Association, March 1972).
5. See: Chandler Davidson and George Korbel, "At-large Elections and Minority-group Representation: A Re-examination of Historical and Contemporary Evidence," *Journal of Politics* 43 (June 1981): 982–1005. See also: Richard L. Engstrom and Michael D. McDonald, "The Election of Blacks to City Councils," *American Political Science Review* 75 (June 1981): 344–354. For an account of how a switch to district elections benefited Hispanics, see: Jerry L. Polinard, Robert D. Wrinkle, and Tomas Longoria Jr., "The Impact of District Elections on the Mexican American Community: The Electoral Perspective," *Social Science Quarterly* 72 (September 1991): 608–614.
6. See, for example: Susan Welch and Timothy Bledsoe, *Urban Reform and Its Consequences: A Study in Representation* (Chicago: University of Chicago Press, 1988).
7. 106 S. Ct. 2752 (1986). Some, but not all, social science research suggests that at-large elections adversely affect the representation of minority ethnic and racial groups. See literature review and findings by Ted P. Robinson, Robert E. England, and Kenneth J. Meier, "Black Resources and Black School Board Representation: Does Political Structure Matter?" *Social Science Quarterly* 16 (December 1985): 976–982. For the theme that the ill effects of nonpartisan and at-large systems have been exaggerated, see: Susan A. MacManus and Charles S. Bullock III, "Minorities and Women Do Win At Large!" *National Civic Review* (May/June 1988): 231–244.
8. The "one-person, one-vote" rule was first extended to local governments in the case of *Avery* v. *Midland County* (Texas) in 1968 (390 U.S. 474). In a 1970 case, *Hadley* v. *Junior College District of Metropolitan Kansas City* (397 U.S. 50), the United States Supreme Court decided that the rule applied to any legislative body that has taxing power or any of the normal functions of a legislature. In one significant case, however, the Court has ruled that it would not insist on strict adherence to the population standard if this would inhibit attempts to consolidate governmental units in a metropolitan area. In this case a single unit had been formed through the merger of six towns and the county of Virginia Beach. Each of the seven units was used as a single-member legislative district for the election of council members,

though the districts were unequal in population. Had the Court invalidated the plan, it would have made future consolidations more difficult because local governments have usually been unwilling to participate in structural changes of this nature without being assured of an equal voice in the new government.

9. George S. Blair, *American Legislatures* (New York: Harper and Row, 1967), p. 59.

10. Mary A. Schellinger, "Today's Local Policymakers: A Council Profile," *Baseline Data Report* vol. 20, no. 4 (Washington, D.C.: International City Management Association, July/August 1988). See also: John Clayton Thomas, "The Term Limitations Movement in U.S. Cities," *National Civic Review* 81 (Spring–Summer 1992): 155–173.

11. See: Susan A. MacManus and Charles S. Bullock III, "Women and Racial/Ethnic Minorities in Mayoral and Council Positions," *The Municipal Year Book: 1993* (Washington, D.C.: International City/County Management Association, 1993), pp. 70–84. See also: Alan Klevit, "City Councils and Their Functions in Local Government," *Municipal Year Book: 1972*, pp. 15–54. See also: Michael S. Deeb, "Municipal Council Members: Changing Roles and Functions," *National Civic Review* (September 1979): 411–416; and United States Department of Commerce, Bureau of the Census, "Popularly Elected Officials in 1987," in *1987 Census of Governments: Preliminary Report* (Washington, D.C.: Government Printing Office, December 1988).

12. See: Cortus T. Koehler, "Policy Development and Legislative Oversight in Council Manager Cities: An Information and Communication Analysis," *Public Administration Review* 33 (September/October 1973): 433–441.

13. See: David R. Morgan, "Political Linkage and Public Policy: Attitudinal Congruence between Citizens and Officials,"*Western Political Quarterly* 26 (June 1973): 209–223.

14. See: Deeb, "Municipal Council Members."

15. See: Kenneth Prewitt and William Nowlin, "Political Ambitions and the Behavior of Incumbent Politicians,"*Western Political Quarterly* 22 (June 1969): 298–308.

16. See: Robert J. Huckshorn and Charles E. Young, "Study of Voting Splits on City Councils in Los Angeles County,"*Western Political Quarterly* 13 (June 1960): 479–497.

17. For a former mayor's views on public hearings, see: Robert J. Horgan, "City Council Decisions: Can We Make Them Better?" *Nation's Cities* (September 1972): 57–61. See also: Robert L. Morlan, "Life on the City Council: Realities of Legislative Politics," in Morlan and Leroy C. Hardy, *Politics in California* (Belmont, Calif.: Dickenson Publishing, 1968), pp. 103–104.

18. Klevit, "City Councils."

19. James H. Svara, "Council Profile: More Diversity, Demands, Frustration," *Nation's Cities Weekly* (18 November 1991): 4.

20. Arnold M. Howitt, "The Expanding Role of Mayoral Staff,"*Policy Studies Journal* 3 (September 1975): 363–370.

21. See: "Suburban Mayors' Jobs Studied in Detroit Area," *National Civic Review* (April 1977): 193–194.

22. See, for example: David R. Berman and Bruce D. Merrill, "Citizen Attitudes toward Municipal Reform Institutions: A Testing of Some Assumptions," *Western Political Quarterly* 29 (June 1976): 274–283.

23. See: Raymond L. Bancroft, "America's Mayors and Councilmen: Their Problems and Frustrations," *Nation's Cities* (April 1974): 14–24.

24. More extensive typologies of mayors may be found in: John P. Kotter and Paul R. Lawrence, *Mayors in Action: Five Approaches to Urban Governance* (New York: John Wiley and Sons, 1974); and Douglas M. Fox, *The Politics of City and State Bureaucracy* (Pacific Palisades, Calif.: Goodyear, 1974).

25. Robert A. Dahl, *Who Governs?* (New Haven: Yale University Press, 1961).

26. See: James Q. Wilson, "The Mayors vs. the Cities," *The Public Interest* (Summer 1969): 25–27.

27. Richard Murray and Arnold Vedlitz, "Racial Voting Patterns in the South: An Analysis of Major Elections from 1960 to 1977 in Five Cities," *The Annals* 493 (September 1978): 29–39. See also: Charles S. Bullock III and Bruce A. Campbell, "Racist or Racial Voting in the 1981 Atlanta Municipal Elections," *Urban Affairs Quarterly* 20 (December 1984): 149–164.

28. William E. Nelson Jr., "Black Mayors as Urban Managers," *The Annals* 439 (September 1978): 53–67.

29. Quoted by Roger M. Williams, "America's Black Mayors: Are They Saving the Cities?" *Saturday Review/World* (4 May 1974): 11.

30. See, for example: Clarence N. Stone, *Regime Politics: Governing Atlanta: 1946–1988* (Lawrence: University Press of Kansas, 1989).

31. See: Rob Gurwitt, "Indianapolis and the Republican Future," *Governing* (February 1994): 24–28.

32. Data on city managers reported here are found in Richard J. Stillman II, *The Modern City Manager: A 1971 Profile* (Washington, D.C.: International City Managers Association, 1971). See also: Richard J. Stillman II, *The Rise of the City Manager: A Public Professional in Local Government* (Albuquerque: University of New Mexico Press, 1974). On the policy role of managers, see: Timothy A. Almy, "City Managers, Public Avoidance, and Revenue Sharing," *Public Administration Review* 37 (January/February 1977): 19–27; and Ronald O. Loveridge, *City Managers in Legislative Politics* (Indianapolis: Bobbs-Merrill, 1971). Recent data on managers are summarized in Richard J. Stillman II, "Local Public Management in Transition," *Public Management* (May 1982): 2–9.

33. Stillman, "Local Public Management," p. 3.

34. Stillman, *The Rise of the City Manager*.

35. Robert Paul Boynton and Deil S. Wright, "Mayor-Manager Relations in Large Council-Manager Cities: A Reinterpretation," *Public Administration Review* 31 (January/February 1971): 28–35.

36. David R. Morgan and Sheilah S. Watson, "Policy Leadership in Council-Manager Cities: Comparing Mayor and Manager," *Public Administration Review* 52 (October 1992): 438–446.

37. Boynton and Wright, "Mayor-Manager Relations," p. 33.

38. For a case study of change in a council-manager city, see: Glen Sparrow, "The Emerging Chief Executive: The San Diego Experience," *National Civic Review* (December 1985): 538–547.

39. On the differences between reform and nonreform cities in regard to administration, see: Glenn Abney and Thomas P. Lauth, *The Politics of State and Local Administration* (Albany, N.Y.: SUNY Press, 1986).

40. Adam W. Herbert, "The Minority Administrator: Problems, Prospects, and Challenges," *Public Administration Review* (November/December 1974): 556–563.

41. See: Michael Lipsky, "Toward a Theory of Street-Level Bureaucracy," in Willis D. Hawley et al., *Theoretical Perspectives on Urban Politics* (Englewood Cliffs, N.J.: Prentice Hall, 1976), pp. 196–213.

42. See the discussion on the police in chapter 15.

43. See: Judith E. Gruber, *Controlling Bureaucracies: Dilemmas in Democratic Governance* (Berkeley: University of California Press, 1987).

44. See: Wallace S. Sayre and Herbert Kaufman, *Governing New York City: Politics in the Metropolis* (New York: Russell Sage Foundation, 1960), pp. 249–264.

45. See: James M. Ferris, "The Decision to Contract Out: An Empirical Analysis," *Urban Affairs Quarterly* 22 (December 1986): 289–311; David R. Morgan and Michael W. Hirlinger, "The Decision to Contract Out City Services: A Further Explanation," *Western Political Quarterly* 41 (June 1988): 363–372; Evelina R. Moulder, "Privatization: Involving Citizens and Local Government Employees," *Baseline Data Report* no. 26 (Washington, D.C.: International City/County Management Association, 1994); and James D. Ward, "Privatization and Political Culture: Perspectives from Small Cities and Towns," *Public Administration Quarterly* 15 (Winter 1992): 496–522.

46. C.J. Hein, "Contracting Municipal Services: Does It Really Cost Less?" *National Civic Review* (June 1983): 321–326.

47. This section relies in part on: Frank S. Levy, Arnold J. Meltsner, and Aaron Wildavsky, *Urban Outcomes: Schools, Streets, Libraries* (Berkeley: University of California Press, 1974). See also: Bryan D. Jones and Clifford Kaufman, "The Distribution of Urban Public Services: A Preliminary Model," *Administration and Society* 6 (November 1974): 337–359.

48. See: Levy, Meltsner, and Wildavsky, *Urban Outcomes*.

49. Phillip B. Coulter, *Political Voice: Citizen Demand for Urban Public Services* (Tuscaloosa: University of Alabama Press, Institute for Social Research, 1988). See also: Michael W. Hirlinger, "Citizen-Initiated Contacting of Local Government Officials: A Multivariate Explanation," *The Journal of Politics* 54 (May 1992): 553–564.

Part Four

★ ★ ★

Problems and Policies

11

★ ★ ★

THE POLITICS OF FINANCE

In this and the following four chapters, we examine what state and local governments have done or have failed to do in regard to various demands, problems, or situations. We also examine national government policies because they frequently affect the problems and activities of state and local governments. This chapter looks at state and local finances. It opens with an overview of expenditure and revenue patterns and goes on to examine the nature and effect of specific state and local taxes, state and local borrowing, and some broad factors that affect taxing and spending decisions.

EXPENDITURES AND REVENUES

TRENDS

The general level of state and local spending has varied considerably over the past several decades. From the 1940s to the late 1970s, state and local governments experienced a rapid growth in the amount of money they spent. In the late 1970s this began to decline. Changes in federal policy helped force state and local governments to be more dependent on their own revenues and less dependent on federal aid. Another factor slowing state and local spending was the taxpayers' rebellion, which started in California in 1978 with the adoption of Proposition Thirteen limiting local property taxation. The rebellion, along with taxing and spending restrictions, spread to other states.[1]

Further compounding the fiscal problems of state and local officials were increases in costly federal mandates and economic downturns in the early 1980s and again in the early 1990s.

State and local financial conditions have improved in recent years. This has been due in part to an improved national economy and in part to actions taken by officials to improve their fiscal positions. An improved economy has improved state and local revenue flows. It has also somewhat reduced the mandate problem. As their financial burdens have lessened, the federal government has had less reason to mandate costs on state governments and state governments have had less reason to shift costs to localities. Helping to balance their own budgets, state and local governments have raised taxes and fees, cut programs, and saved funds by contracting out for services and, especially on the local level, by entering into agreements with other governments to undertake projects and provide services jointly. The financial pinch in recent years encouraged state and local governments to come up with creative and cost-effective programs, and many were able to do so.

Although the economies of states and localities have recovered somewhat, state and local officials still must live with relatively less federal aid and a host of new restrictions on their abilities to tax and spend. Budgetary pressures, moreover, remain strong in many places because of infrastructure and capital spending needs. Because of structural changes in their economies, some large cities also continue to have a particularly strong need for continued intergovernmental aid from their states or the federal government. More broadly, the fiscal problems of all local governments are vitally affected by decisions made at other levels, particularly the state.

State and local governments, though beset with revenue problems, in the aggregate are spending more dollars than ever before—some $1,145 billion in the early 1990s. These units of government have spent more than 60 percent of all public monies used for domestic programs, though some of the money they have spent comes from the federal government. By far the largest area of state-local expenditure has been education, which now constitutes about 33 percent of the total amount spent by state and local governments. Elementary and secondary education take up about 24 percent of the total, and around 9 percent goes to higher education. Public welfare accounts for about 13 percent of the spending. Other significant expenditures are for health and hospitals, around 9 percent, and highways, some 7 percent.

Education expenditures, though relatively high, have steadily declined as a percentage of the budget since the late 1960s, when they were almost 40 percent of total expenditures, to the current 35 percent. Transportation spending, most of which goes for highways, was in the 18 percent range in 1961, rapidly declined over the next decade, and has leveled off to between 8 and 9 percent since then. Growth has been most pronounced in the area of health, particularly because of the increase in the Medicaid program. Medicaid alone claims around 7 percent of all expenditures. Public safety expenditures, a category that includes costs for police and corrections, have also increased dramatically in recent years (see chapter 15).

On the income side, state and local governments receive about 16 percent of their revenues from the federal government. The rest of their funds—84 percent—come from their own resources. Among these, the most productive sources are sales taxes, property taxes, income taxes, and various types of charges. Compared to the 1960s, state and local governments are far less reliant on the property tax—down from about 40 percent total state-local own-source revenues to around 22 percent. There has been a conscious effort to reduce reliance on this source because of taxpayers' resistance. There has also been somewhat less reliance on the sales tax. State and local governments, on the other hand, have become more reliant on the income tax and various types of charges.

Looking at state government finances separately from local government finances, one finds that, over the years, education, public welfare, highways, and hospitals have been the largest areas of expenditure. The first of these categories has been by far the greatest. Elementary and secondary education take about 22 percent out of the average state budget, and higher education takes another 12 percent. Rapid increases have been most noted in recent years for corrections and Medicaid. Though declining, federal aid is the single most important source of revenue, followed by the individual income tax and the general sales tax.

Education is also by far the largest local government expenditure. Independent school districts not affiliated with a city or county government spend most of this money. Health and hospitals and public welfare have become the largest categories of expenditure for county governments. For municipalities, police and fire expenditures rank as the leading area of spending. As cities increase in size, a greater percentage of their budgets goes to welfare, health and hospitals, housing, and other essential social services, and proportionately less is spent on highways, police and fire protection, and sewage and sanitation services.

Local governments raise nearly 60 percent of their own revenues—for municipalities the percentage is over 70—with the property tax being the largest source of their own-source income, some 47 percent of the total. Next in line as a source of revenue are user fees and charges, at around 23 percent.

Intergovernmental revenues from the federal and state governments are also of considerable importance to local governments. For cities, the amount of intergovernmental aid as a percentage of all revenues is generally greatest in the largest cities. Around 33 percent of all the revenues of cities of a million or more comes from the federal or state governments. The figure is about the same for county governments.

Local governments receive about four times as much from state governments as they do from the federal government. State aid to local governments consists of grants and shared taxes.[2] Revenues from these sources account for about 30 percent of all city and county revenues. Most state aid (some 60 percent) goes to support education. Following education in funding are public welfare (15 percent of the total), general local government support (around 8 percent), and highways (4 percent). Relatively little state aid—only about one out of every eight dollars—goes to cities to support traditional municipal programs such as police and fire protection.[3]

Generally, state governments in the poorer parts of the country have assumed the lion's share of the state-local financial burden because they are in a more favorable position to tap what resources are available.[4] State aid programs appear to have had a modest equalization effect, that is, they have somewhat reduced the revenue gap between poorer and wealthier localities.[5] Only a handful of states, however, have made a conscious effort to target funds on the basis of local needs.[6] Differences among the states in the nature and level of local assistance programs are related to a wide variety of factors. The level of benefits, for example, appears to increase with increases in per capita income and the percentage of Democrats in the state legislature. The importance of particular factors, however, varies with different types of assistance programs.[7]

Over much of the history of the home rule movement, cities have called for an extension of their authority to draw on tax sources other than property. Contemporary reformers have placed equal emphasis on having state governments assume the costs of more programs now borne by local governments and increasing the local share of state-collected revenues. State assumption of expenditures in areas like education could reduce problems, for example, disparities in spending, now resulting from reliance on the local property tax, and would free that tax for other local functions.

While much of the innovative thinking on revenues has involved state-local relations, one should also note unusual relationships among local units. A unique approach to the problem of local finance is a tax-base sharing practice used in the Minneapolis-Saint Paul area. Some three hundred taxing jurisdictions located in seven counties pool 40 percent of the revenue derived from increases in nonresidential property taxes. This money is allocated to communities in the area on the basis of their populations and relative needs. Research suggests that this system severely reduces the differential in the tax base between the richest and poorest cities, from twenty-two to one to four to one, and eases what would be destructive competition among localities for economic growth. At the same time, however, local officials in Minnesota or elsewhere cannot depend on the system to bring a great deal of revenue to central cities, the places where local governments have been most vulnerable to fiscal stress. Nor do they serve as an effective alternative to other types of reforms, such as greater state assumption of the costs of various local functions.[8]

MEASURES OF LEVEL, EFFORT, AND FAIRNESS

State and local spending can be evaluated in several ways. For example, one can look at expenditures on a per capita basis, as a percentage of personal income, or as a percentage of total expenditures. The first of these provides a measure of the level of expenditure that is useful in comparing one government with another or the performance of a particular unit of government over time. Looking at expenditures as a percentage of personal income in a given state or locality takes the analysis a bit further by providing an indication of the effort made by governments to tap available income and of the burden they impose on their taxpayers. When attention is shifted to expenditures for particular functions as a percentage of total expenditures, one gets an indication of what functions are given priority.[9]

Historically in some places there have been relatively high levels of state and local spending per capita but, because of high levels of personal income, relatively low percentages of personal income being drawn upon for revenues. In 1990, Connecticut, New Jersey, and Massachusetts fell into this category (see table 11–1). Utah, on the other hand, was an example of a state where the level of state and local spending was relatively low (thirty-eighth in the nation), but because of low levels of personal income, the effort or burden on taxpayers was relatively high (sixteenth in the nation). Wyoming was an example of a state with relatively high levels of spending and taxing, while Missouri ranked low in both regards.

Generally, in recent years, the level of expenditure on a per capita basis has been lowest in the Southeast and highest in the Mideast or Middle Atlantic states. Burdens, on the other hand, have been heaviest in the Rocky Mountain region and lowest in the New England area. In terms of priorities, one finds relatively little variation among the states in the proportion of budgets given to schools, but considerable variation in the proportion of budgets given to programs such as welfare (11.5 percent in the Rocky Mountain region to 19.2 percent in New England). Variations in priorities, of course, are greater when one looks at individual states (see table 11–2).

In evaluating state and local tax policies, one must begin with the recognition that they serve a number of purposes. Some are intended to encourage certain types of behavior or activity. During the height of the energy crisis, for example, states offered tax reduction incentives to encourage the use of solar energy. Several types of taxes are levied less for revenue than for regulation. An example is the license tax requirement for the owners of pool halls and bars.

The most common purpose of taxation, obviously, is to raise revenue. But who should pay? The answer to this question depends to a great extent on whether a regressive or a progressive tax is employed. A *regressive tax* takes a greater percentage of the income of those with lower incomes than of those with higher incomes. A tax based on the ability to pay, taking proportionately

TABLE 11–1   State Rankings for State-Local Expenditure Items per Capita and as a Percentage of State Personal Income, FY 1992

Rank	General Expenditure			
	State	Per Capita	State	Percent of Personal Income
1	AK	$10,047	AK	45.6%
2	NY	5,670	WY	28.4
3	WY	5,294	NM	24.5
4	HI	5,230	HI	23.6
5	NJ	4,687	NY	23.5
6	CT	4,594	LA	23.1
7	MN	4,506	ND	22.9
8	RI	4,408	MN	22.0
9	CA	4,289	MT	21.9
10	DE	4,238	VT	21.7
11	WA	4,210	RI	21.7
12	MA	4,145	OR	21.3
13	VT	4,089	WI	21.0
14	WI	3,997	ME	20.7
15	NV	3,973	WV	20.6
16	OR	3,966	UT	20.6
17	ND	3,910	DE	20.5
18	PA	3,793	MS	20.4
19	NM	3,785	AZ	20.2
20	MI	3,778	CA	20.1
21	ME	3,765	SC	20.0
22	CO	3,707	WA	19.8
23	LA	3,688	IA	19.7
24	NH	3,664	MI	19.3
25	MD	3,650	KY	19.3
26	IA	3,606	OK	19.1
27	MT	3,561	AL	18.8

Source: Advisory Commission on Intergovernmental Relations, *Significant Features of Fiscal Federalism*, vol. 2 (Washington, D.C.: Government Printing Office, 1995), p. 191.

more from the rich than the poor, qualifies as a *progressive tax*. A tax that takes the same percentage of income from all taxpayers is proportional or flat. Over most of this century, progressive taxes have generally been viewed as the most desirable, though this goal has been difficult to achieve in practice because of the many tax advantages given relatively wealthy people. In recent years,

| Rank | State | General Expenditure | | |
		Per Capita	State	Percent of Personal Income
28	AZ	3,509	SD	18.6
29	FL	3,495	ID	18.4
30	IL	3,472	PA	18.4
31	NE	3,456	NV	18.3
32	KS	3,402	NE	18.2
33	OH	3,401	NJ	18.0
34	VA	3,302	CO	17.9
35	GA	3,300	OH	17.9
36	SC	3,235	GA	17.8
37	WV	3,218	FL	17.7
38	UT	3,207	AR	17.6
39	IN	3,193	KS	17.5
40	SD	3,192	MA	17.5
41	KY	3,184	NC	17.4
42	TX	3,146	IN	17.4
43	OK	3,144	TX	17.1
44	NC	3,111	TN	17.0
45	AL	3,109	CT	16.9
46	ID	3,064	NH	16.7
47	TN	3,006	IL	15.9
48	MO	2,885	VA	15.8
49	MS	2,868	MD	15.7
50	AR	2,757	MO	15.2
	US	3,826	US	19.0
	DC	7,561	DC	27.1

however, the progressive tax has fallen somewhat from grace and the notion that taxes should be flat, that is, based on the same percentage for all taxpayers, has become more popular.

Other than the ability-to-pay criterion, taxes may be justified on the basis that the taxpayer receives some type of benefit from the tax money collected. An example of a benefit tax is the gasoline tax. This tax is primarily paid by motorists and is normally earmarked for highway expenses. Another example is the local special assessment (in effect a service charge) collected from owners

TABLE 11–2   State and Local Expenditures, Percentage Distribution, FY 1992

Region and State	Total	Elementary and Secondary Education	Public Welfare	Health and Hospitals	Higher Education	Highways
United States	$975,817.0	23.5%	15.8%	8.3%	8.6%	6.8%
New England	55,392.9	22.1	19.2	7.1	5.9	6.4
Connecticut	15,064.4	24.5	16.5	7.5	5.1	7.2
Maine	4,653.5	25.5	21.6	4.5	7.7	8.4
Massachusetts	24,843.0	19.6	20.4	8.6	5.2	5.3
New Hampshire	4,085.2	24.2	24.0	3.8	6.7	6.9
Rhode Island	4,412.0	19.7	17.0	5.7	6.5	5.1
Vermont	2,334.8	27.4	15.9	2.9	11.5	10.3
Mideast	210,119.4	23.1	19.0	4.4	6.4	5.6
Delaware	2,928.7	21.3	10.0	5.4	13.3	9.3
District of Columbia	4,423.3	14.1	19.7	12.1	2.7	2.8
Maryland	17,945.4	24.0	15.1	5.0	9.5	6.2
New Jersey	36,649.1	26.9	16.0	4.7	5.9	6.9
New York	102,675.2	21.6	20.3	3.2	4.9	5.0
Pennsylvania	45,497.7	24.0	20.3	5.8	8.8	5.9
Great Lakes	151,476.3	25.1	16.4	8.3	10.0	7.2
Illinois	40,323.4	23.1	15.4	6.5	8.3	8.8
Indiana	18,068.4	26.9	15.0	10.8	12.1	6.6
Michigan	35,644.8	26.8	15.8	10.1	11.0	5.3
Ohio	37,482.7	24.4	18.6	8.5	9.5	7.3
Wisconsin	19,957.0	25.5	16.6	6.3	10.7	7.6
Plains	64,047.0	25.2	15.5	8.8	10.4	9.8
Iowa	10,107.7	25.5	13.8	10.8	12.4	12.3
Kansas	8,556.8	25.3	10.6	8.6	14.3	11.0
Minnesota	20,133.3	23.6	18.0	9.3	8.3	8.4
Missouri	14,976.3	27.1	17.2	8.2	8.6	8.5
Nebraska	5,533.6	26.8	13.5	8.8	12.5	10.2
North Dakota	2,479.1	21.4	14.7	3.4	14.9	11.3
South Dakota	2,260.2	25.8	13.3	5.1	8.1	13.6

Source: Advisory Commission on Intergovernmental Relations, *Significant Features of Fiscal Federalism,* vol. 2 (Washington, D.C.: Government Printing Office, 1995), pp. 122–123.

of property who benefit by a public improvement such as street paving, sidewalks, or sewer lines. Cities also commonly impose user charges, making those who use public transportation, refuse collection, and other services pay for them.

A third type of tax may be described as "a tax on sin." State and local governments have, for example, found it relatively easy to justify sales taxes on alcoholic beverages and tobacco with the theory that they are luxuries or on the grounds that people should not be buying these items in the first place

Region and State	Total	Elementary and Secondary Education	Public Welfare	Health and Hospitals	Higher Education	Highways
Southeast	199,132.2	23.3	14.4	11.7	9.1	7.6
Alabama	12,865.8	18.8	14.7	18.2	11.2	7.2
Arkansas	6,599.9	25.6	17.9	8.3	11.6	9.6
Florida	47,117.5	23.5	11.4	9.7	6.5	7.2
Georgia	22,352.5	24.3	15.1	16.0	7.0	6.2
Kentucky	11,954.4	20.6	20.1	6.8	10.0	8.9
Louisiana	15,780.0	22.1	16.1	12.1	7.9	7.7
Mississippi	7,501.0	22.3	15.6	15.1	11.4	9.6
North Carolina	21,266.6	25.4	14.1	12.1	12.0	7.4
South Carolina	11,654.9	24.7	13.9	15.6	10.8	5.4
Tennessee	15,104.3	19.5	17.4	12.2	10.0	8.7
Virginia	21,113.5	25.8	11.0	8.8	9.9	8.3
West Virginia	5,821.8	26.9	18.8	7.0	9.5	9.4
Southwest	85,140.9	26.6	13.5	8.9	10.6	7.8
Arizona	13,448.3	23.8	14.0	5.5	11.0	7.9
New Mexico	5,988.4	21.8	12.4	9.3	12.5	12.2
Oklahoma	10,076.5	24.8	14.8	11.2	10.8	9.3
Texas	55,627.7	28.1	13.2	9.3	10.3	7.1
Rocky Mountain	27,305.9	25.1	11.5	7.2	11.7	9.1
Colorado	12,843.5	24.3	11.8	6.6	11.3	8.1
Idaho	3,266.0	25.3	11.7	8.7	11.1	10.4
Montana	2,927.4	26.3	12.2	5.8	8.4	12.1
Utah	5,807.4	26.0	11.7	6.9	15.2	7.1
Wyoming	2,461.6	25.1	7.9	11.1	9.9	14.1
Far West	183,202.6	20.8	14.1	9.3	8.4	5.4
Alaska	5,907.9	17.0	7.2	3.7	5.0	10.4
California	132,500.8	20.2	15.2	9.9	8.4	4.7
Hawaii	6,046.3	13.5	9.9	6.7	8.5	7.2
Nevada	5,308.5	22.4	9.1	7.5	7.1	8.2
Oregon	11,786.4	24.3	11.5	7.6	10.0	6.7
Washington	21,652.7	24.8	12.8	9.1	9.3	6.4

(though, given the revenue they produce, tax collectors might well be heart-broken if people stopped "sinning").

In practical terms, state and local policymakers evaluate taxes and other revenue sources not only by their equity, but by whether the burden they impose can be shifted in whole or in part to nonresidents. One way of doing this is through the adoption of a general sales tax. Shifting some of the tax burden to residents of other states can also be accomplished through severance taxes on natural resources. Thus, in the late 1970s, as western states increased the severance tax on oil, gas, and coal mined within their boundaries, eastern states dependent on these energy sources complained that the taxes were being unfairly passed along to their citizens in the form of higher prices. In an indirect manner, states can also shift much of their burden to nonresidents by securing favorable federal taxation and spending policies that, for example, take funds from taxpayers in wealthier states to support expenditures for people in poorer states.

Historically, state and local tax systems have tended to be regressive in nature.[10] The systems have been in great flux, however, and, by some measures are now moderately progressive. Certainly, their impact varies around the country. Table 11–3 depicts the burdens imposed by state and local sales, income, auto, and real estate taxes on families with different levels of income in the largest cities in each state and in the District of Columbia (only selected cities are shown). Averaging out the tax burdens of all cities, one finds that a hypothetical family of four making $25,000 a year pays 7.9 percent of its income for state and local taxes. Going up the income scale, we find a rate of 8.6 percent at the $50,000 level, 9.7 percent at the $75,000 level, and 9.9 percent at the $100,000 level. The system, by these measures (which exclude regressive user fees), is mildly progressive. Looking at individual cities, we find considerable variety. Taxes, for example, seem high and virtually flat in Newark, New Jersey, low and modestly progressive in Albuquerque, New Mexico, and both low and somewhat regressive in Memphis, Tennessee. Perhaps worst of all, they are both relatively high and regressive in Philadelphia. In many cities, there is not a consistent pattern.

In terms of public attitudes, since the early 1990s, public opinion polls have shown the local property tax and the federal income tax in a virtual tie for the distinction of being considered the worst tax in the country. Americans have viewed these taxes as far less fair than the Social Security tax, the state income tax, or state sales tax.[11] As table 11–4 indicates, among those giving the federal income tax the most negative rating are people most actively involved in the workforce (aged 25–44), college graduates, and those in the professional/manager/owner category. The local property tax, on the other hand, is particularly disliked by retired people, people in rural areas, and people with relatively large incomes. The federal income tax is particularly unpopular in the South, while the local property tax is particularly unpopular in the Northeast and North.

REVENUE SOURCES

In addition to federal aid, discussed in chapter 2, state and local governments receive the bulk of their revenues from three major types of taxes: sales, income, and property, and a host of special types of taxes, charges, and fees.

TABLE 11-3   Estimated State and Local Taxes Paid by a Family of Four in
Selected Large Cities: 1992

[Preliminary. Data based on average family of four (two wage earners and two school age
children) owning their own house and living in a city where taxes apply. Comprises state
and local sales, income, auto, and real estate taxes.]

City	Total Taxes Paid, by Gross Family Income Level (dollars)				Total Taxes Paid as Percent of Income			
	25,000	50,000	75,000	100,000	25,000	50,000	75,000	100,000
Albuquerque, NM	1,478	3,434	5,943	8,461	5.9	6.9	7.9	8.5
Atlanta, GA	2,838	5,593	9,107	12,019	11.4	11.2	12.1	12.0
Baltimore, MD	4,068	8,246	12,791	16,659	16.3	16.5	17.1	16.7
Bridgeport, CT	4,519	9,416	16,270	21,185	18.1	18.8	21.7	21.2
Burlington, VT	1,909	4,132	7,197	10,134	7.6	8.3	9.6	10.1
Charleston, WV	1,691	3,542	6,373	8,836	6.8	7.1	8.5	8.8
Charlotte, NC	2,085	4,412	7,253	9,734	8.3	8.8	9.7	9.7
Chicago, IL	2,954	5,938	9,326	12,084	11.8	11.9	12.4	12.1
Columbus, OH	2,151	4,713	7,712	10,650	8.6	9.4	10.3	10.7
Columbia, SC	1,971	4,799	8,151	10,905	7.9	9.6	10.9	10.9
Des Moines, IA	1,844	4,120	6,770	9,109	7.4	8.2	9.0	9.1
Detroit, MI	4,723	9,680	14,773	19,290	18.9	19.4	19.7	19.3
Honolulu, HI	1,853	4,306	7,272	9,921	7.4	8.6	9.7	9.9
Indianapolis, IN	2,017	3,703	6,268	8,061	8.1	7.4	8.4	8.1
Jackson, MS	1,451	3,421	6,080	8,237	5.8	6.8	8.1	8.2
Kansas City, MO	1,965	4,358	7,024	9,224	7.9	8.7	9.4	9.2
Louisville, KY	2,439	5,100	8,099	10,777	9.8	10.2	10.8	10.8
Memphis, TN	1,718	2,896	4,506	5,702	6.9	5.8	6.0	5.7
Milwaukee, WI	3,274	7,288	11,425	15,071	13.1	14.6	15.2	15.1
Newark, NJ	5,853	11,445	17,696	23,420	23.4	22.9	23.6	23.4
New York City, NY	2,603	6,579	11,199	15,247	10.4	13.2	14.9	15.2
Omaha, NE	2,159	4,529	7,872	10,668	8.6	9.1	10.5	10.7
Philadelphia, PA	3,956	7,610	11,361	14,755	15.8	15.2	15.1	14.8
Portland, ME	2,132	5,144	9,361	12,759	8.5	10.3	12.5	12.8
Portland, OR	2,428	5,369	8,263	11,542	9.7	10.7	11.5	11.5
Providence, RI	4,271	8,393	13,542	17,945	17.1	16.8	18.1	17.9
Salt Lake City, UT	2,038	4,682	7,564	10,020	8.2	9.4	10.1	10.0
Sioux Falls, SD	1,837	3,180	5,312	6,701	7.3	6.4	7.1	6.7
Virginia Beach, VA	2,089	4,423	7,521	9,930	8.4	8.8	10.0	9.9
Washington, DC	2,278	5,041	8,416	11,556	9.1	10.1	11.2	11.6
Median[1]	1,970	4,306	7,253	9,921	7.9	8.6	9.7	9.9

[1]Median of all 51 cities.

Source: Government of District of Columbia, Department of Finance and Revenue, *Tax Rates and Tax Burdens in the
District of Columbia: A Nationwide Comparison* (annual).

TABLE 11-4   Which Do You Think Is the *Worst* Tax—That Is, the *Least* Fair:
Federal Income Tax, Social Security Tax, State Income Tax, State
Sales Tax, Local Property Tax? (percent)

	Federal Income Tax	Social Security Tax	State Income Tax	State Sales Tax	Local Property Tax	Don't Know / No Answer
Total public	27.2	12.4	7.4	13.6	28.4	11.0
Male	28.9	12.0	7.9	11.9	28.5	10.8
Female	25.6	12.8	6.9	15.2	28.3	11.2
Total head of household	28.3	12.6	6.7	13.3	29.0	10.1
Male head	29.5	11.1	7.1	12.2	30.5	9.5
Female head	27.2	13.9	6.3	14.2	27.7	10.7
Under 35 years of age	29.9	14.2	9.3	13.2	21.8	11.5
18–24	21.1	14.4	10.2	16.9	20.9	16.5
25–34	34.6	14.1	8.8	11.3	22.2	8.9
35–44	33.8	13.8	6.9	11.5	26.8	7.2
45–65	24.1	10.6	7.2	15.1	33.9	9.1
Over 65	17.1	10.7	5.0	13.6	35.9	17.7
High school incomplete	21.5	8.2	7.2	15.8	30.9	16.4
High school graduate	26.1	14.7	6.9	11.2	30.3	10.8
College incomplete	24.4	14.1	8.3	17.2	27.4	8.6
College graduate	37.3	9.6	7.8	13.0	24.0	8.3
Household income						
Under $15K	22.8	11.1	7.3	15.9	28.3	14.6
$15–24.9K	28.4	12.6	6.1	11.5	29.8	11.7
$25K+	27.6	12.4	8.5	14.0	29.6	8.0
$25–29.9K	18.4	17.6	6.5	15.0	31.5	11.0
$30–39.9K	29.9	12.7	12.3	17.3	22.3	5.6
$40K+	28.9	10.6	6.7	11.7	33.6	8.5
Own	26.1	12.8	5.5	12.8	33.3	9.5
Rent	29.7	11.1	11.6	15.4	17.6	14.6
White	26.0	12.8	7.6	13.0	29.0	11.5
Black	32.1	11.5	5.8	17.7	26.8	6.0

Source: U.S. Advisory Commission on Intergovernmental Relations, *Changing Public Attitudes on Governments and Taxes* (Washington, D.C.: Goverment Printing Office, 1994), p. 11.

SALES AND INCOME TAXES

The general, or broad-based, sales tax has been a major source of tax
revenue for state governments.[12] It is levied in all but three states. Local
governments in twenty-eight states have the option of levying a sales tax. They

	Federal Income Tax	Social Security Tax	State Income Tax	State Sales Tax	Local Property Tax	Don't Know/ No Answer
Employed	30.8	13.3	8.4	13.1	25.5	9.0
Employed female	29.4	14.6	6.7	15.8	24.7	8.8
Nonemployed	21.0	11.5	6.1	14.0	33.5	13.9
Nonemployed female	20.6	11.4	7.4	14.2	33.0	13.4
Professional/manager/ owner	34.4	12.0	7.6	12.1	23.8	10.1
White collar/sales/clerical	24.8	19.6	5.1	19.6	22.5	8.3
Blue collar	26.8	10.9	8.8	12.7	30.3	10.4
Retired	21.4	10.1	4.3	14.3	37.9	11.8
Married	28.9	12.9	7.7	12.1	29.3	9.2
Not married	24.9	11.8	7.0	15.7	27.1	13.5
Household size						
1–2 people	27.6	12.8	7.2	13.0	28.1	11.2
3–4 people	24.3	11.2	8.5	15.5	31.4	9.1
5+ people	29.1	11.2	5.7	21.0	15.4	17.6
Children in household under 18	26.7	13.4	7.5	15.8	27.9	8.7
No children	27.6	11.9	7.7	11.9	28.9	12.0
Northeast	21.9	9.5	10.7	16.0	33.1	8.8
North	25.7	13.9	4.9	15.2	33.0	7.3
South	31.7	10.3	6.7	13.3	27.0	11.2
West	25.9	17.9	8.3	9.8	20.8	17.2
Nonmetro	27.7	13.2	6.4	12.5	34.7	5.4
Metro: 50,000 and over						
Fringe	27.9	10.0	8.5	13.1	28.9	11.6
Central city	26.0	13.7	7.5	15.2	21.2	16.4

may, in some places, collect their own sales taxes, but in most states, state revenue departments collect the tax and pass it along to the local jurisdictions. This route is easier on retailers (who would otherwise collect the tax for two jurisdictions) and is a more efficient method of collection. At the same time, cities may feel more comfortable assuming authority over the collection of their sales tax revenues.

The sales tax has several advantages. It is a lucrative and fairly predictable source of revenue. It has also been publicly accepted (as much as a tax will be), in large part because it is paid, often unconsciously, in small doses when purchases are made. Sales taxes are effective ways for cities to shift revenue burdens to tourists or commuters. However, sales taxes are regressive because the poor spend a higher percentage of their income on goods on which a sales tax is levied than do the rich. To get around this problem, at least partly, several jurisdictions exempt food and utility outlays from the sales tax. Medicine is also exempted in nearly all states. Too many exemptions, however, threaten the value of the tax as a collector of revenue. Over the last few years, efforts have been made to extend the sales tax to various services as well as goods. These moves have encountered fierce resistance. Florida, in 1987, adopted such a measure. Protest led by advertisers and other businesses affected by the measure, however, prompted the legislature into three stormy special sessions and, finally, to repeal the five-month-old law.

Several states also levy an income tax on individuals, corporations, or both. Though state income taxes are normally not as progressive as the federal income tax, increases in income do tend to put people in higher income brackets established by the states so that they pay more in state income tax. Since the early 1970s, incomes have generally increased, thus forcing people into higher income brackets. And because of inflation in the prices of goods and services, citizens have generally gained little, if anything, in real purchasing power. To reduce the effect of inflation on the citizenry, some states now index the personal income tax so that exemptions and deductions are increased annually by the rate of the rise in the general price level.

A municipal income tax is allowed in eight states, mostly in the East. In some cases it provides cities with between one-third and one-half of their revenues. Local income taxes are usually regressive because no exemptions or deductions are allowed and the tax rate is levied at a flat percentage (usually about 1 percent) on all individuals. The municipal income tax has also encountered problems because it may be levied on residents and nonresidents alike, since it may be imposed on the place of residence or on the place of employment. States differ in how they handle the problem. Pennsylvania gives priority to the municipality of residence, except in Philadelphia, where the place of employment is the basis of the tax. In Ohio, the place of employment is the basis.

THE PROPERTY TAX

Until the 1930s, the property tax was the primary source of revenue for state and local governments. Today, most states rely less on the property tax and more on sales and income taxes. Property taxes, however, constitute more than two-thirds of all locally collected revenue and are the mainstays of the tax system for all units of local government. For this reason, the property tax merits extended discussion.

The property tax applies to real property (land and buildings) and personal property, which, in legal terms, may be either tangible (things of intrinsic value such as jewelry, clothing, or automobiles) or intangible (evidence of wealth such as stocks or bonds). In determining the real property tax (of central concern here), all land is assessed, theoretically at its "full cash value," by a locally elected county assessor. Although state constitutions may require that all land be taxed at a uniform rate, state legislatures have been allowed to assess properties at different percentages of their full cash value. Residential and farm land, for example, may be assessed at 18 percent of their value while large utilities may be assessed at 40 percent of their full cash value. Thus far, this discrimination among properties has escaped judicial challenges. Courts have also upheld California's "welcome stranger" system, required by Proposition Thirteen, that makes assessments and, thus, property tax bills much higher for those who purchased their homes after 1978. Property acquired before the proposition took effect is frozen at low levels, that is, at values defined in the 1975–1976 assessment. Property acquired since 1978 is valued essentially at its purchase price.

Once the total assessed value of the property in a given jurisdiction is determined, the legislative body (council, county board, or school board) determines how much money is needed from the property tax and sets a tax rate to secure that amount. For example, if the assessed value of the property within a city is $20 million and the city determines that it will need $600,000 from the property tax, it would set the rate at 3 percent. An individual owning a house valued at $60,000 and assessed at 15 percent, or $9,000, would pay a property tax of $270. State law commonly limits the tax rate—but not the number of times the same property can be taxed. Thus, a homeowner may pay the maximum rate to the county, the city, a school district, and any number of special districts in which his or her property may be located.

Several factors affect the fairness of the property tax and its ability to keep up with economic growth. One inherent problem is the difficulty in determining property values. Assessed values vary widely not only among taxing jurisdictions but also within each taxing jurisdiction. Among the methods used by assessors to determine property value are estimating the replacement cost of the property (building), determining the selling price on the open market if the seller had ample time to find the right buyer, and comparing prices paid for similar properties. Some assessors attach a dollar amount to every square foot in a house or building, no matter how it is constructed or where it is located.

Standards to determine value, in short, are less than scientific. To compound the problem, county assessors are often poorly trained for their jobs. Salaries for assessors are considered to be far below those needed to attract trained and competent people. Few states have laws stipulating qualifications for assessors or their performance. Often local assessors have been lenient in placing values to facilitate their reelection or have been guilty of accommodating influential persons and businesses.

A second problem has been that much property is not placed on the tax rolls. The usefulness of the property tax in many jurisdictions suffers from exemptions made at the state level that reduce its base. Veterans, widows, and the elderly have been granted exemptions or partial exemptions from the property tax in many states, regardless of their actual wealth. Church property is often exempt from taxation, including that property used for nonreligious purposes. Governments, educational institutions, charitable organizations, and hospitals also own tax-exempt property. Often, additional exemptions or reductions of property taxes are offered to lure businesses. Some counties and cities find that 60 percent or more of the property base has been exempted from taxation.

A third problem of the property tax is that it is regressive. One reason for this is the fact that assessors tend to value high-priced houses at lower figures relative to the market value than cheaper ones because of the political influence of wealthy people. Second, richer families spend a smaller percentage of their incomes for housing than do poorer families. According to data prepared by the Advisory Commission on Intergovernmental Relations, the average urban household pays about 4 percent of its income for local property taxes, but many low-income families pay as much as 50 percent of their incomes for local property taxes. The tax is particularly hard on those who own houses but have relatively small incomes. To offset the regressive effect of the tax, some states have laws that set a limit on the amount of taxation.

The property tax also discourages property improvements. Those who improve their property are "rewarded" with higher taxes. One effect of this has been to encourage the deterioration of slum housing in inner-city neighborhoods. The system also benefits speculators who hold unimproved land at low levels of taxation, while waiting to sell for profit. Some jurisdictions have bypassed this problem by taxing land at its highest and best use. Unimproved farmland, for example, may be taxed as if it were a residential subdivision. This system brings in more revenue but, on the downside, it may conflict with the goal of preserving open space.

Two other effects of the property tax system should also be mentioned. First, the property value in a given jurisdiction usually conditions how much a governmental body can borrow through general obligation bonds (those redeemed or paid back through general taxation). Property value, however, may be a poor indicator of the jurisdiction's ability to pay off debts, because it does not reflect wealth in the form of wages, and the property may be undervalued. Another effect of the property tax, discussed more fully in the following chapter, is the extreme disparities it creates on financing education.

The property tax, as indicated earlier, has long been politically unpopular and has become increasingly so in recent years. Indeed, much of the search for state and local revenue in recent years has represented an effort to decrease reliance on the property tax. At the same time, however, despite all its difficulties, the property tax is still important to local governments because it is a lucrative source of revenue. It is also highly flexible in that the rate of property values can be adjusted to bring in more revenue.

OTHER SOURCES

In addition to the big-three tax sources (sales, income, property), state and local governments collect revenue through special taxes, fees, and charges. Some states, such as Louisiana, Montana, Oklahoma, Texas, and Wyoming, use severance taxes on the removal of natural resources for significant amounts of revenue. As indicated previously, during the 1970s severance taxes on resources became particularly important in many western states because of soaring energy prices. The United States Supreme Court has upheld the right of states to impose a severance tax on resources mined in their jurisdictions as long as the tax does not discriminate against out-of-state consumers.[13] The Court has also upheld the somewhat controversial unitary tax method employed by fourteen states.[14] Through this approach, a state can tax what it calculates to be its fraction of a corporation's total, often worldwide, profits. Where such a tax is not used, corporations are taxed only on the basis of their assets and activities within state boundaries.

Over the past two decades, user fees have become a popular means of financing a variety of services. Fees are commonly used to finance water, sewage, and transportation services. The notion that the direct user of a service should pay for it is popular throughout the country. Because of this, user fees are a relatively acceptable way of raising revenues. They are also attractive to local officials because they can commonly levy fees without a grant of permission from state legislatures. Localities have also had much discretion imposing impact fees on developers to offset the costs of building or expanding facilities such as roads, sewers, and parks and to serve the growth engendered by projects.

Additional revenues are available in some jurisdictions from state or locally owned enterprises and through legalized gambling. Seventeen states earn a considerable amount of revenue through state-operated liquor stores. On the local level, one may find municipal power systems that bring large amounts of revenue into city treasuries and/or sell power to consumers at relatively low rates.

A growing number of states in recent years have turned to legalized gambling to secure more revenues. Many allow betting on horse or dog races and sports gambling. A few allow casino gambling in at least some of their cities. In 1992, the Louisiana legislature allowed New Orleans to go into the casino business as a means of raising revenue and promoting economic development. South Dakota also is among the states allowing casino gambling. Nevada, which legalized casinos in 1931, derives nearly half of its general fund revenues from taxes and license fees on the gambling industry. New Jersey's first casino opened in Atlantic City in 1978 and produced more than $1 million a month in gambling taxes during its first year in operation. Still, gaming in New Jersey has had mixed results. Adverse consequences have been seen in increase of street crime, escalating prices of real estate (especially hard on the rents and property taxes of the elderly), and increased costs for public services such as transportation. Generally, the experiment has not brought about the expected revitalization of Atlantic City.[15]

Better than two-thirds of the states conduct lotteries although, thus far, these attractions have contributed to only a small portion (around 3 percent) of the revenues of the states that use them. States showing the earliest interest in lotteries were those with the highest tax burdens. They were seeking alternative, less painful, ways to generate more revenues. They also tended to be states with a good potential market for a lottery, that is, they were relatively affluent, densely populated, and could attract tourists or players from neighboring states that did not have lotteries.[16] Lotteries, on the other hand, have been difficult to establish in states with relatively large percentages of Protestant fundamentalists in the population.[17] People with this religious background take a dim view of gambling and, apparently, have been effective in some states in turning back efforts to establish lotteries.

Lotteries are publicly popular, and, quite understandably, politicians have found them preferable to levying new taxes or increasing existing ones. Many people, however, continue to question if states should be in the business of operating a gambling enterprise or encouraging people to gamble. Evidence suggests that lotteries have attracted heavy and frequent bettors—about 10 percent of those who play account for half of the total amount bet—some of whom, like alcoholics, have trouble quitting. Prominent among the heavy bettors are minorities (blacks and Hispanics), Catholics, and middle-aged citizens.[18] In some places the states and casinos have used gambling revenues to set up programs to cure compulsive gamblers.

Critics have also found lotteries to be relatively expensive ways of collecting revenue (over half of the gross income may go for prize money and administrative expenses) and as being regressive in impact. On the latter point, however, most data suggest that lotteries are not a "tax" on the poor.[19] Though poor minorities often are frequent bettors, lottery tickets are generally purchased by middle- and upper-income persons. Data are also lacking to support the common charge that lotteries have encouraged more illegal gambling. In some areas, lotteries may have cut into illegal street games.[20] Illegal numbers rackets appear to have been able to survive elsewhere because they actually offer better odds than the legal lotteries, are willing to offer credit, and don't withhold taxes.[21]

BORROWING

BORROWING DECISIONS

State and local governments must often borrow money. They most often incur debt to finance major projects such as the construction or improvement of schools or sewage treatment plants and for the purchase of land or expensive machinery. Federal aid has given state and local governments an alternative to borrowing for some of these expenditures and has been an important factor in determining whether or not to borrow.

In situations when federal aid or, in the case of local governments, state aid is not available or desired, the choice narrows down between borrowing or waiting and paying for needed projects when the money becomes available. Although pay-as-you-go financing is generally advisable for individuals, state and local governments have found it difficult to meet large expenditures in this manner. Waiting is likely to be more expensive. By the time a government saves up enough for a major purchase, the original cost (of a piece of land, for example) is likely to have multiplied several times over.

BONDS

States and localities borrow money by issuing bonds for sale. The two most common types of state and local bonds are the general obligation bond and the revenue bond. *General obligation bonds* are backed by the full faith and credit of the issuing government. This means that they are supported by the jurisdiction's general taxing and revenue powers. General obligation bonds are the least expensive form of borrowing because investors regard them as safe (there have been very few defaults) and are willing to accept a relatively low rate of interest. *Revenue bonds* are supported only from the revenues derived from the project for which money is borrowed (for example, tolls from a turnpike). These usually cost the government more in interest because investors see them as more of a risk than general obligation bonds.

One of the more controversial areas of municipal bonding has been the use of tax-exempt industrial development bonds. These are used to provide relatively cheap financing for private businesses. The bonds are issued by a municipality to raise funds for a private developer or some commercial venture such as a fast-food chain. Since the developer, in effect, borrows at the municipal rate, the cost of borrowing is considerably lower than he or she would have paid. Cities have defended the use of such bonds as a means of attracting new industries and development. Critics have argued that the sale of these tax-free bonds not only costs governments in terms of lost revenue but also has given an unfair subsidy to large private enterprises that do not need such incentives to expand. Problems of this nature prompted Congress in the Tax Reform Act of 1986 to limit the ability of states to use their tax-exempt bonds for "private purposes."

FACTORS AFFECTING ABILITY TO BORROW

Three general factors condition the ability of state and local governments to borrow funds: legal restrictions, the tax-exempt feature of municipal bonds, and bond ratings.

State constitutions and laws place two general types of restrictions on borrowing: maximum limits on the amount of debt and requirements that public referenda be held to permit the issuance of bonds. Debt limits most often apply to borrowing through general obligation bonds. Limits are often expressed as a percentage (from 15 to 25 percent) of the value of the property within the jurisdiction, but may also be stated in specific dollar amounts. One effect of these restrictions has been to encourage state and local governments to turn to revenue bonds, which cost much more than general obligation bonds. They have also resulted in the invention of special districts, authorities, and various other kinds of complicated financial arrangements to bypass the limits.

The requirement for a referendum brings about another set of decision-making problems. Public officials have to calculate public sentiments and determine how to promote the issue, educate the voters, and gain the support of various neighborhoods and the media.[22] During the height of the taxpayers' rebellion in the 1970s, approval rates were between 60 and 70 percent; since then, they have been closer to 80 percent. If success looks unlikely, officials in about half the states can avoid going to the voters and avoid debt limitations by issuing certificates of participation (COPs). Under these arrangements the government leases what it wants, for example, new equipment or a new building, from a third party, such as a private company, that owns the assets. COPs, however, are usually more expensive to issue than bonds because of the involvement of third parties.

State and local governments have been aided in selling their bonds to investors by federal law that exempts income earned from "municipals" (a term used to designate both state and local bonds) from the federal income tax. This policy (from time to time seriously questioned in Congress) has enabled state and local governments to borrow money at a lower rate of interest than private corporations can. Although low interest rates do not appeal to the average investor, they do appeal to large institutions and to those in the higher income brackets who stand to gain greater benefits from tax-free income. Municipals have been particularly attractive to commercial banks and to insurance companies.

The attraction of municipals to investors and the rate of interest states and cities must pay investors depend in large part on the way firms such as Moody's Investors Service and Standard & Poor's rate the bonds. Whether a municipal bond is given a prime Triple-A rating or a low C rating depends on the bond rating firm's determination of a jurisdiction's ability to pay its debts (for example, its current and potential fiscal condition). The higher the rating, the less interest state and local borrowers have to pay. Municipals have generally been a safe investment. There have, however, been notable defaults. One of the most dramatic of these was the failure, in 1983, of the Washington Public Power Supply System, known not too affectionately by its critics as "Whoops," to make good on funds borrowed to finance the construction of nuclear reactors in the state of Washington.

TAXING AND SPENDING DECISIONS

Decisions on how to raise and spend revenue are at the heart of the governmental process. State government officials most directly involved in financial decision making are legislative leaders (especially those sitting on appropriations, taxation, and budget committees), governors and their staffs, and the heads of various departments. Legislative leaders appear to have a greater direct influence over taxing and spending decisions in smaller states. In the larger states, influence shifts to governors who, with the help of large, professional staffs, are considered better able than legislative committees to grapple with a large bureaucracy and complicated financial problems.[23] Similarly, financial decision making in large cities appears to reside in the hands of the executive, the mayor or manager, while council involvement is more effective in smaller communities.[24]

Financial decisions take place within a broader environment that imposes certain constraints on state and local decision makers. As indicated in several places in this book, the spending and revenue problems of one level of government are often influenced by shifts in policy by another level of government. For example, states and local governments, in recent years, have had to live not only with changes in federal policy regarding aid but with changes in the federal tax system that make it more difficult for state and local governments to borrow funds (see above) or impose various types of taxes.[25]

At any given time, state and local financial decision makers also have to live within the constraints imposed by legal, economic, and political conditions and the budgetary system itself. These constraints are examined below.

LEGAL CONDITIONS

Several legal limitations, in addition to those noted above on borrowing, condition the ability of state and local governments to raise and spend money. Under the United States Constitution, state and local governments are prohibited from: (1) levying taxes on the property, functions, activities, or instrumentalities of the national government; (2) taking tax action that interferes with interstate commerce; and (3) levying taxes on imports or exports. The first of these has perhaps had the most important effect in that it removes a great deal of property from the property tax rolls.

State constitutions and statutes, though somewhat liberalized in recent years, place more crippling burdens on state and local finance. They contain prohibitions on levying certain types of taxes (for example, a graduated income tax) and on raising tax rates beyond certain levels. Recently, voters have adopted measures allowing state or local government to raise taxes or expenditures only if two-thirds or more of its members agree to do so. Another popular reform idea makes tax increases and spending increases above a certain level dependent on voter approval.

In the 1970s, many states placed limits on the ability of local officials to raise revenues (especially through property taxes) and placed limitations on overall local spending. Although these tax and expenditure limitations appear to have had little effect on total spending, they have helped change the composition of local revenues. Specifically, they have encouraged local governments to become less reliant on the property tax in meeting their expenditures (though property taxes have increased), more reliant on state aid, and more reliant on locally collected fees and sales taxes. The result, some have argued, has been to encourage both greater centralization at the state level and greater reliance on more regressive revenue sources.[26]

Other limits on discretion come in the form of earmarked funds, balanced budget requirements, and collective bargaining arrangements. States commonly earmark or dedicate revenues by law for particular purposes or programs. As noted earlier, states often earmark revenues derived from state gasoline taxes for highway programs only. States have also determined that certain percentages of the general sales tax or the receipts from the sale of lottery tickets should be automatically allocated for particular purposes, such as school aid. Supporters of new revenue measures or increased taxes often use earmarking to improve the chances that voters or legislators will approve the changes. A state lottery, for example, may be more acceptable to the voters if it is known in advance that the revenues will be put to some good purpose, such as education.

Earmarking funds limits the discretion of governors and legislators. The lack of flexibility may be particularly harmful in regard to the use of the highway fund. By putting gasoline taxes in the highway fund, one can guarantee a certain level of support for road building and maintenance. At the same time, the practice ties up a great deal of revenue and limits the ability of lawmakers to respond to other pressing problems. Thus, even though lawmakers might feel that revenue in the highway fund would be more effectively used for other purposes, the law prevents them from making such a diversion. Earmarking appears to be a particularly strong characteristic of western states, perhaps suggesting an unusual level of governmental distrust in that part of the country.[27]

Most states also have legal (constitutional or statutory) requirements that their budgets be balanced. This limitation is largely symbolic—there is no punishment for failing to balance the budget and states occasionally find that they have to run deficits. In most states, the limitation only applies to operating budgets and thus excludes long-term debts for capital projects like new buildings. Also excluded are various off-budget agencies with their own funds. Budget balancing is often accompanied by sleight-of-hand techniques—sometimes revenues are counted that have not yet been received or bills are not paid until the next budgeting year, and shortfalls are made up by short-term borrowing, tapping into off-budget funds such as retirement accounts, or selling assets that are later leased back by the state. The concept of a balanced budget, however, is important in a political sense, and public officials may be subject to attack for spending more than they take in from revenues.

Another set of important legal restraints in state and local finance has been the agreements reached as a result of collective bargaining with public employee groups. Given the fact that from 70 to 80 percent of most state and local budgets are devoted to salaries and fringe benefits, collective bargaining negotiations may have a tremendous effect on expenditure patterns and revenue needs.

ECONOMIC CONDITIONS

At any given time, one of the broadest constraints on state and local decision makers is the amount of wealth within their jurisdictions that can (at least on a political level) be drawn on for taxation. The amount of wealth, in turn, depends in large part on the area's economic development and its success in encouraging high-income people and prosperous businesses or industry to settle or remain in the area. Places with low economic bases obviously can afford only low levels of service.

For some states and localities, the more fundamental problem is not so much a lack of economic growth as a lack of economic diversification. Without diversification, the local economy is likely to be unstable and the area may be subject to feast-or-famine conditions. An example is the state of Alaska which, with an essentially "one crop" (oil) economy, has found its revenues highly dependent on the price of energy. After a fall in world energy prices in 1986, state revenues declined by around 40 percent. With this came a dramatic cutback in state programs. A similar fate befell Texas, where oil is also a major part of the economy, and several midwestern farm states when agricultural prices declined in the 1980s.

Local officials in communities of all sizes have seen growth as a way of raising additional revenues without increasing taxes. With economic expansion, it is assumed that they can increase their revenues from existing sources and provide improved services. In practice, of course, the expected benefits of growth may not materialize. A city, for example, may find that a new plant does indeed create jobs, increase personal income, and raise retail sales, but that, because of restrictions on the local tax structure, the local government gains virtually nothing from the increased income or sales activity. It is thus left with more demands for services and relatively few funds to provide them. Growth, in short, does not pay for itself unless the tax structure is able to tap the new wealth.[28]

In pursuing growth, state and local governments have, historically, placed considerable emphasis on creating a climate favorable for business investment. For incentives, businesses have commonly been offered reduced taxes, free land, and cheap credit to invest or locate in a particular state or locality. These inducements have been made to encourage business relocations from one state to another or from one community to another in the same state. Increasingly, state and local officials have set out to woo foreign investors with such offers. A growing body of research demonstrates, however, that such enticements generally have little effect on business development. Companies considering relocation are more likely to be influenced by economic factors such as the productivity of the labor force and proximity to markets and by factors involving the quality of life for employees. To some extent, states and localities, caught up in a competitive situation or development "arms race," have given benefits they need not have given. It has also become apparent that states and localities seriously interested in economic development would be far better off nurturing indigenous businesses and industries than resting their hopes on relocation policies. Indeed, in recent years state development agencies have adopted a wide range of policy tools to spur homegrown entrepreneurship, improve the quality of the workforce, and otherwise strengthen the competitiveness of local businesses and the communities of which they are a part.

There is a great deal of diversity of wealth among the states. In general, per capita income is higher in the more populous and urbanized states. However, exceptions exist in states such as Delaware, Nevada, and Alaska. Each of these states has unique economic assets: Delaware is the home of several large corporations because of its favorable laws; Nevada has a large gambling industry (taxes and license fees on gambling bring in close to half of the state's general fund revenue); and Alaska has large oil reserves. In the early 1980s, revenue from the oil industry permitted Alaska to launch a "share-the-wealth" program that abolished the state's income tax for most of its citizens and distributed cash dividends from an oil-reserve trust fund to Alaskans.

As one would expect, the combined expenditures of state and local governments are generally higher in the relatively rich states than in the poor ones. State and local taxes also draw more revenue on a per capita basis in the wealthier states. In short, governments in wealthier states spend more and take in more in taxes. But governments in wealthier states do not necessarily make the greatest tax efforts—that is, collect the highest percentage of wealth within their states. When we relate state and local taxes to personal income, we discover that tax efforts have been relatively high in lower-income states like Vermont and Arizona. On the other hand, tax efforts have been relatively low in wealthy states like Ohio and Texas.

POLITICAL CONDITIONS

Some theorists look upon governments as predators living on a steady diet of taxation.[29] From this perspective, the appetite is driven by the desire of administrators to expand their programs, the constant demands of interest groups for more benefits, the willingness of politicians to expand benefits so as to secure reelection, or a combination of these and other factors.[30] The victim taxpayers caught up in this quest, according to public choice or rational actor theory, have the alternatives of exiting the jurisdiction or trying to change the policy. Some people and businesses may react by "voting with their feet," that is, by moving to a municipality, county, or state with a lower tax rate.[31] Others may decide to stay where they are at least for the time being and, through protesting, try to bring tax rates down and throw those responsible for the situation out of power. Central to the assumptions behind either the exit or protest strategy is that people are aware of the taxes they pay and will rebel once the level of taxation reaches a certain point.

In practice, however, it is possible, and indeed likely, that many people may not respond at all to changing levels of taxation. Some may do nothing because they do not keep track of taxation levels and are not aware of the situation—a condition, some assert, encouraged by government officials who do all they can to hide the taxes. Some of those who realize their taxes are rising may stay where they are and fail to protest the situation because they are not mobile (do not have the ability to leave or anywhere to go) and do not think that protest would do much good.

Some researchers have concluded that while, indeed, there have been organized tax protests, for example, the Proposition Thirteen movement in

California and similar movements in other states during the 1970s and 1980s, voters who supported these efforts were not distinguished by their knowledge of taxation (they knew very little about actual taxation levels). Instead, they were responding to symbolic messages (for example, antigovernment themes) of political leaders.[32] Other research, however, suggests that voters are indeed sensitive to levels of taxation and, as might be predicted, their hostility is likely to increase as the level increases, and that they are likely to take out their hostility on those in power.[33]

While academic researchers debate the relationship between tax levels and voter behavior, those in office, especially in recent years, appear to accept the proposition that there are political limits to taxation and that excessive taxation can cause businesses and people to leave the jurisdiction or (even worse) engage in protest directed at those officials responsible. Fear of protest and people "voting with their feet" may, in fact, deter state and local officials from even considering tax increases.

Such considerations, along with the competition for economic development, function to keep state and local taxes at low levels. In their desire to lure and retain businesses and affluent citizens, states and local officials are extremely sensitive to how their tax rates compare with those of other jurisdictions. They look at unusually high rates as putting them at a competitive disadvantage. A similar phenomenon occurs within metropolitan areas as local policymakers show their desire to "stay in line" by avoiding intercommunity tax rate differentials that would inhibit their economic development.[34]

When it comes to taxation, politicians do appear, when possible, to seek out less visible taxes or fees and to raise taxes when political conditions are most favorable, that is, when voters are least likely to retaliate. Research suggests that the decisions by state officials to increase taxes depends in large part on political opportunity. Officials, for example, are more likely to adopt new taxes immediately after a general election than just before one, when they can point to a clear fiscal crisis facing the state, and after a neighboring state has already adopted a particular tax. Such conditions help shield lawmakers from adverse political fallout and increase the likelihood of tax adoption.[35]

Along with the politics of taxation, one finds a politics of spending. While taxation is often a salient issue, it is also true that revenues must be found to support at least a minimum level of services, and state and local officials may face severe political repercussions for not taxing and spending. A good many governors and mayors have found themselves faced with a no-win situation: "they cannot operate their governmental programs without increased revenues, and they cannot increase their revenues and be reelected to office."[36]

Adverse reactions appear particularly intense when service levels must be reduced. The relevant question then becomes: "Who gets hurt?" Does a city, for example, lay off police officers, firefighters, dog catchers, or refuse collectors? Any reduction in service personnel is likely to be met by union resistance and the ire of at least some segments of the community. If seniority is employed in reducing the workforce, the last hired—those who are usually minorities and women—will be the first to go, and discontent is likely to be voiced by these elements of the population.

Going from policy area to policy area, one finds the most purely political factors most involved in explaining variations in welfare spending.[37] Spending for welfare, like other programs, varies with the level of income in a state, being highest where income is highest. Beyond this, however, it is also influenced by which party controls the government (being higher in states controlled by Democrats) and in states where participation rates are the highest. The party differences make sense in that low-income people are much more a part of the Democratic Party than they are of the Republican Party. In political terms, higher rates of participation mean that more low-income people are voting and, thus, having more of an impact on public policy.[38]

Pressures for at least certain forms of spending, finally, are also connected to the politics of intergovernmental relations, that is, the effort to stay in line with competing jurisdictions. Within metropolitan areas, for example, increased spending on police by one jurisdiction is likely to be matched by increased spending by others. Increased expenditures for welfare, on the other hand, are not competitive; as one jurisdiction increases its expenditures, others decrease theirs.[39]

THE BUDGETING SYSTEM

The budgeting system constitutes another influence on the character of state and local finances.[40] This system performs the functions of coupling anticipated revenues with spending needs and of allocating funds among different programs.

Legislators consider budgets each year in some states and biennially in others. The actual significance of these different systems is unclear. Those who favor a two-year cycle often do so on the grounds that it offers a greater opportunity for planning and more in-depth program analysis. Those in favor of annual budgeting argue that it provides greater immediate control over spending. On the political level, annual budgeting has been seen by legislators as most conducive to maximizing their ability to control the budget. Biennial budgeting, on the other hand, has been equated with an increased role for the governor and his or her staff at the expense of the legislature.[41]

For many jurisdictions, the primary purpose of preparing a budget is to control expenditures. Allowable expenditures for a governmental agency are commonly listed as items like rent, wages, and supplies. In most states and large cities, greater focus is placed on the programs to be carried out than on the items of expenditure, and at least some effort is made to determine if limited resources are better allocated to one program than another.

Many states and localities have sophisticated budgeting systems characterized by heavy reliance on computers and administrators skilled in economic analysis. Ideally, budgeting is a rational procedure in which revenue projections and spending proposals are brought together, evaluated, and acted upon. Even the most sophisticated systems, however, fail to perform these functions perfectly. Inflation, unanticipated economic slumps, and cutbacks in federal aid, for example, can raise havoc with revenue projections. As one state economist has noted: "Even using state-of-the-art techniques, revenue forecasting is going to be wrong. The important question is how wrong and why? Policymakers need to realize that forecasting is not an exact science."[42]

In about half of the states, revenue forecasting is largely the responsibility of a budget or revenue agency in the executive branch. Legislative staffs, however, frequently make independent estimates. Many states use a consensus revenue estimating method, which draws upon the combined judgment of people in the legislative and executive branches and representatives from business and the academic community. There is no reason to believe, however, that the consensus method is likely to be more accurate than other approaches.[43] More often than not, revenues are underestimated, not overestimated. Revenue shortfalls, however, do occur. This and unanticipated expenditures sometimes create the need for midyear cutbacks in ongoing programs. As a hedge against miscalculations, some jurisdictions maintain "rainy day" funds or budget stabilization accounts.

The long-term trend on both the state and local levels has been toward an executive budgeting system under which responsibility for preparing a single budget document and submitting it to the legislature is vested in the chief executive. Executive budgeting has made great headway in the states and in local governments with the increased adoption of the strong-mayor and council-manager forms.

Under an executive budgeting system, department heads are given forms and official or unofficial guidelines for listing proposed expenditures for the next fiscal year or next two years in a biennial system. The departments submit their proposals to a budget officer (finance director) reporting to the chief executive. The budget officer reviews the requests in the light of the chief executive's policies and in the light of expected revenues. Members of the governor's staff also compare the departments' requests with their current and previous expenditures.

Once the budget is approved by the chief executive, it is sent to the legislature for approval or rejection. Often, the legislature is given the departments' original requests along with the governor's recommendations. Several states now have a full-time budget agency serving as a joint legislative budget committee that analyzes the governor's budget and develops a modified version of it for the consideration of the entire legislature. Once the budget is approved, it is sent to the chief executive for approval or rejection.

The process is generally similar, though less formal, in local governments. Few local councils have a separate staff to assist them in interpreting the budget; they must depend on the assistance of the mayor's or manager's office and normally consult in their recommendations. Many local jurisdictions do not use the executive budgeting system. In some, departmental requests are submitted to a council committee that in turn makes recommendations to the entire council. In others, the initial requests are reviewed by a board of administrators or a group composed of administrators and council members.

During the budgeting process on both levels, most attention is focused on noncommitted revenues (that is, those that are not by law earmarked for a specific purpose), which flow into what in most jurisdictions is called the "general fund." Departmental heads can generally be expected to request more than they spent last year—those who wish increases are well advised to spend all they were given last year.

Research on the state level suggests that department heads often "seize the governor's philosophy" as expressed in press statements, campaign slogans, and elsewhere in justifying their requests.[44] In anticipation that the governor or legislature might well reduce their requests, administrators may "pad" their budgets and ask for more than they expect to receive. The budgeting strategy employed by administrative agencies that derive all or most of their revenues from the general fund, however, also depends in part on the level of anticipated revenues. When revenues are seen to be on the increase, agencies are likely to seek gubernatorial and legislative support for new or expanded programs. When general revenues appear to be on the decline, agencies are likely to see their mission to be one of fighting off cuts in their existing programs.

Governors and legislators give special attention to politically important programs, especially new ones, and to those in which they have a personal interest. Most budgets, however, are incrementally built on the basis of the last year's budget and major attention is given only to unusually large requests over last year's expenditures. Seldom, if ever, is the entire budget given close and exhaustive program-by-program scrutiny. This procedure occurs partly because of lack of time and staff assistance. The limited focus, however, is also valuable because it avoids reopening past and often politically explosive controversies. One broad consequence of incrementalism, as political scientist Ira Sharkansky has written, is the fact that while spending on the state level goes up, "high-and-low-spending states retain their relative status over a period of many years."[45] Once a pattern of spending is established, it is dramatically changed only in times of war, depression, the addition of new revenues, or intense political pressure.

From the 1940s through the 1970s, economic times were generally good for states and localities and spending at these levels increased incrementally, providing benefits for a variety of groups. In recent years, intense pressure has been applied against increased taxation and spending. As a consequence, many jurisdictions have been engaged in "cutback management" (that is, the finding of ways to save money and operate more efficiently) and, in some cases, taking away benefits. One reform undertaken by some state and local governments has been the adoption of *zero-base budgeting* systems. In this approach, each governmental program is completely and periodically reviewed as to its costs and benefits during the budgeting process. The approach differs from sunset proceedings in that the major review is done by the executive branch under the supervision of the governor rather than by the legislature. Zero-base budgeting differs from the traditional budgeting review process in that it requires the examination of all requests for expenditures in an agency's budget (starting from point zero instead of the base) rather than simply on an agency's request to spend more than last year.

Studies on the actual use of zero-base budgeting indicate that it does improve the quality of information going into budgeting decisions. Zero-base budgeting, however, does not appear to be more effective than traditional budgeting methods in reducing state expenditures. In other words, how much a state or locality spends may be more directly related to broad financial conditions and political attitudes than to a choice of budgeting techniques.[46]

Endnotes

1. David B. Magelby, "The Movement to Limit Government Spending, in American States and Localities, 1970–1979," *National Civic Review* (May 1981): 271–276, 282. On the taxpayers' revolt, see also: Robert Kuttner, *Revolt of the Haves: Tax Rebellions and Hard Times* (New York: Simon and Schuster, 1980); David Lowery and Lee Sigelman, "Understanding the Tax Revolt: Eight Explanations," *American Political Science Review* 75 (December 1981): 963–974; D. Sears and J. Citrin, *Tax Revolt* (Cambridge: Harvard University Press, 1982); and M. Neiman and G. Riposa, "Tax Rebels and Tax Rebellion," *Western Political Quarterly* 39 (1986): 435–445.

2. State grants are similar to those made by the national government. They are usually designated for specific programs such as streets, airports, and public health and contain several restrictions. On shared taxes, the states act essentially as tax collectors and return a portion or all of the yield to local governments either according to an allocation formula or on the basis of origin of collection. Much of this shared revenue is earmarked by the states for specific purposes, for example, a city's share of a gas tax must be spent on highway or street improvements. Sales and income taxes are also among the state taxes that are often shared.

3. Randy Arndt, "NLC Study Shows States Lag on City Aid," *Nation's Cities Weekly* (12 September 1988): 1, 9.

4. See: Ira Sharkansky, *The Politics of Taxing and Spending* (Indianapolis/New York: Bobbs-Merrill, 1969), pp. 215–216.

5. See: Thomas R. Dye and Thomas L. Hurley, "The Responsiveness of Federal and State Governments to Urban Problems," *The Journal of Politics* 40 (February 1978):

196–207; and John P. Pelissero, "State Aid and City Needs: An Examination of Residual State Aid to Large Cities," *The Journal of Politics* 46 (August 1984): 916–935. For a more pessimistic view, see: Robert M. Stein and Keith E. Hamm, "A Comparative Analysis of the Targeting Capacity of State and Federal Intergovernmental Aid Allocations: 1977, 1982," *Social Science Quarterly* 68 (September 1987): 447–477.

6. David R. Morgan and Mei-Chiang Shih, "Targeting State and Federal Aid to City Needs," *State and Local Government Review* (Spring 1991): 60–67.

7. Keith J. Mueller, "Explaining Variation in State Assistance Programs to Local Communities: What to Expect and Why," *State and Local Review* (Fall 1987): 101–107. Compare this with: David R. Morgan and Robert E. England, "State Aid to Cities: A Causal Inquiry," *Publius: The Journal of Federalism* 14 (Spring 1984): 67–82.

8. See: D.A. Gilbert, "Property Tax Base Sharing: An Answer to Central City Fiscal Problems?" *Social Science Quarterly* 59 (March 1979): 681–689; Roy W. Bahl and Walter Vogt, *Fiscal Centralization and Tax Burdens: State and Regional Financing of City Services* (Cambridge: Ballinger, 1975); and Eileen Shanahan, "Going It Jointly: Regional Solutions for Local Problems," *Governing* (August 1991): 70–75.

9. See, generally: J. Edwin Benton, "Dimensions of Public Spending," *Policy Studies Journal* 12 (December 1983): 233–246.

10. See: Donald Phares, *Who Pays State and Local Taxes?* (Cambridge: Oelgeschlager, Gunn and Hain, 1980).

11. U.S. Advisory Commission on Intergovernmental Relations, *Changing Public Attitudes on Governments and Taxes* (Washington, D.C.: Government Printing Office, annual).

12. See, generally: John F. Due and John L. Mikesell, *Sales Taxation: State and Local Structure and Administration* (Washington, D.C.: The Urban Institute Press, 1994).

13. *Commonwealth Edison Co., et al.* v. *Montana, et al.* (1981).

14. *Container* v. *Franchise Tax Board*, 463 U.S. 159 (1983).

15. See: Ronald G. Ochrym, "Gambling in Atlantic City: The 'Grand Vision' Blurs," *National Civic Review* (December 1983): 591–596; and George Sternlieb and James W. Hughes, *The Atlantic City Gamble* (Cambridge: Harvard University Press, 1983).

16. John E. Filer, Donald L. Mozak, and Barry Uze, "Why Some States Adopt Lotteries and Others Don't," *Public Finance Quarterly* 16 (July 1988): 259–283. See also: Frances Stokes Berry and William D. Berry, "State Lottery Adoptions as Policy Innovations: An Event History Analysis," *American Political Science Review* 84 (June 1990): 395–415.

17. Cathy M. Johnson and Kenneth J. Meier, "The Wages of Sin: Taxing America's Legal Vices," *Western Political Quarterly* 43 (September 1990): 577–595.

18. See, generally: Charles T. Clotfelter and Philip J. Cook, *Selling Hope: State Lotteries in America* (Cambridge: Harvard University Press, 1989).

19. See, for example: John L. Mikesell, "A Note on the Changing Incidence of State Lottery Finance," *Social Science Quarterly* 70 (June 1989): 513–521.

20. "States Win in Lotteries,"*National Civic Review* (September 1983): 446–450.

21. "The Lottery Craze," *Newsweek* (2 September 1985): 16–20.

22. See, for example: Penelope Lemov, "How to Win (or Lose) a Bond Referendum," *Governing* (February 1990): 34–40.

23. See, generally: Sydney Duncombe and Richard Kinney, "The Politics of State Appropriation Increases," *State Government* (September/October 1986): 113–123.

24. See, for example: Alvin D. Sokolow and Beth Walter Honadle, "How Rural Local Governments Budget: The Alternatives to Executive Preparation," *Public Administration Review* 44 (September/October 1984): 373–383.

25. In the late 1980s several states had to reshape their tax systems because of the Tax Reform Act of 1986, which ended the practice of allowing taxpayers to deduct state and local sales taxes from their federal income tax payments. This change, at least theoretically, made sales taxes less acceptable to taxpayers, particularly in comparison to state and local income taxes, which continued to be deductible on federal returns. Consequently, states and localities were encouraged to abandon the sales tax in favor of other sources of revenue.

26. Advisory Commission on Intergovernmental Relations, *Tax and Expenditure Limits on Local Governments* (Washington, D.C.: Government Printing Office, March 1995). See also: Phillip G. Joyce and Daniel R. Mullins, "The Changing Fiscal Structure of the State and Local Public Sector: The Impact of Tax and Expenditure Limitations," *Public Administration Review* 51 (May/June 1991): 240–253.

27. David R. Berman, "Financing State and Local Government," in Clive S. Thomas, ed., *Politics and Public Policy in the Contemporary American West* (Albuquerque: University of New Mexico Press, 1991), pp. 305–326.

28. See: Barry M. Rubin and C. Kurt Zorn, "Sensible State and Local Economic Development," *Public Administration Review* (March/April 1985): 333–339.

29. See, for example: Margaret Levi, *Of Rule and Revenue* (Berkeley: University of California Press, 1968).

30. See review by D. Lowery and W. Berry, "The Growth of Government in the United States," *American Journal of Political Science* 27 (1983): 665–694.

31. C. Tiebout, "A Pure Theory of Municipal Expenditure," *Journal of Political Economy* 64 (1956): 416–424.

32. See review by Shaun Bowler and Todd Donovan, "Popular Responsiveness to Taxation," *Political Research Quarterly* 48 (March 1995): 79–99.

33. *Ibid.*

34. See: Advisory Commission on Intergovernmental Relations, *Urban America and the Federal System* (Washington, D.C.: Government Printing Office, 1969).

35. Frances Stokes Berry and William D. Berry, "Tax Innovation in the States: Capitalizing on Political Opportunity," *American Journal of Political Science* 36 (August 1992): 715–742.

36. Frederick C. Mosher and Orville F. Poland, *The Costs of American Governments* (New York: Dodd, Mead, 1964), p. 1.

37. For an overview, see: Sung-Don Hwang and Virginia Gray, "External Limits and Internal Determinants of State Public Policy," *Western Political Quarterly* 44 (June 1991): 277–298.

38. See: Kim Quaile Hill and Jan E. Leighley, "Lower-Class Mobilization and Policy Linkage in the U.S. States," *American Journal of Political Science* 39 (February 1995): 75; and Robert D. Brown, "Party Cleavages and Welfare Effort in the American States," *American Political Science Review* 89 (March 1995).

39. Kee Ok Park, "Expenditure Patterns and Interactions Among Local Governments in Metropolitan Areas," *Urban Affairs Quarterly* 29 (June 1994): 535.

40. This section relies in part on: Ira Sharkansky, *Public Administration: Policy Making in Government Agencies* (Chicago: Markham Publishing, 1970), pp. 230–231. See also: Aaron Wildavsky, *The Politics of Budgetary Process*, rev. 4th ed. (Boston: Little, Brown, 1984); Thomas Anton, *The Politics of State Expenditure in Illinois* (Urbana: University of Illinois Press, 1966); John P. Crecine, *Governmental Problem Solving: A Computer Simulation of Municipal Budgeting* (Skokie, Ill.: Rand-McNally, 1969); Edward J. Clynch and Thomas P. Lauth, eds., *Governors, Legislatures, and Budgets: Diversity across the American States* (Westport, Conn.: Greenwood Press, 1991); and Irene S. Rubin, *The Politics of Public Budgeting: Getting and Spending, Borrowing and Balancing* (Chatham, N.J.: Chatham House, 1990).

41. See: The Council of State Governments, *Annual or Biennial Budgets?* (Lexington, Ky., 1972). A more recent review of state practices is found in: United States General Accounting Office, *Budget Issues: Current Status and Recent Trends of State Biennial and Annual Budgeting* (Washington, D.C.: General Accounting Office, July 1987). This and other reports are reviewed by Richard G. Higgins Jr., "Biennial Budgeting for the Federal Government?" *Public Administration Review* (September/October 1988): 938–940; and Ronald K. Snell, "Annual vs. Biennial Budgeting: No Clear Winner," *Spectrum* (Winter 1995): 23–27.

42. Quoted by J. Dan Olberding, "State Crystal Balls," *State Government News* (May 1992): 8, 9, 35, quote at 35.

43. Eileen Shanahan, "Cracks in the Crystal Ball," *Governing* (December 1991): 29–32.

44. See: Gary C. Hamilton and Nicole Woolsey, *Governor Reagan, Governor Brown, A Sociology of Executive Power* (New York: Columbia University Press, 1984).

45. Sharkansky, *Politics of Taxing and Spending*, p. 113.

46. See: Allen Schick, *Zero Base '80* (Washington, D.C.: National Governors Association, 1980).

12

★ ★ ★

THE POLITICS OF EDUCATION AND WELFARE

The mayor of Williamsport, Pennsylvania, once identified the major problems facing city governments as "money, finances, and revenue."[1] Historically, the heaviest demands on the budgets of many state and local governments have been in the areas of education and welfare. Each of these policy areas, moreover, has been characterized by racial tensions and by severe conflicts over the proper role of government. This chapter examines the functions and governance of public education, school integration and finance, the nature of poverty, and the welfare system.

THE POLITICS OF EDUCATION

SCHOOL FUNCTIONS, PROBLEMS, AND CONTROVERSIES

What are the functions of public elementary and secondary schools in American society? Undoubtedly, one has been to act as a custodian or "aging vat" for children. This function, maintained by compulsory school attendance laws, frees parents for activities other than raising children and hopefully keeps children off the streets and out of trouble. Required school attendance and prohibitions on child labor also operate to help prevent overburdening the job market. In a rural farm-based economy, children were economic assets, providing needed and inexpensive labor. In today's urban society, one might well wonder, "What would all those kids do if they were not in school?"

Americans have also depended on public schools to introduce students to the values of society, helping to make them good citizens and to give them skills necessary for future success. For the poor, schools ideally function to provide a gateway for equality in society. The educational level of young people is also of concern to employers, who need an educated workforce to compete in a globalized economy. To many people, investment in education is an essential part of economic development policy.[2]

Contemporary critics of public elementary and secondary education contend that most of the above functions are being performed poorly, if at all. Some argue that rather than introducing children to the values of society (that is, to their parents' values), schools subject children to a hostile "youth culture," which, if anything, is antiestablishment in nature. Schools, some contend, fail in their basic educational function of "teaching Johnny and Jane to read" or providing them with skills to make a productive living or contribute to the economy. For many a student, as Charles E. Silberman has written, schools constitute an "oppressive, grim, and joyless" environment in which the prime emphasis is placed on control rather than education.[3]

Many of the most pronounced problems in contemporary education exist in the inner-city schools of the nation's largest cities. Inner-city schools, largely attended by nonwhites, are characterized by overcrowding, obsolete buildings and equipment, violence, high dropout rates, and academic failures. Some observers, however, feel that academic failures are related more to the environment from which inner-city students come than to anything the schools may or may not do.[4] Schools by themselves, in other words, cannot provide equality of opportunity. Still others contend that the schools themselves are at fault. One complaint has been that ghetto teachers usually have middle-class values and backgrounds and have not been trained to teach in inner-city schools.

The early 1980s brought considerable attention to the failures of public education. The federal National Commission on Excellence in Education set the pace in 1983 by concluding that public education had become engulfed in "a tide of mediocrity." Faced with such criticism, state governments began experimenting with measures to improve the quality of education, such as higher standards for teacher certification and basing pay for teachers entirely on merit. Reform also took the form of minimum-competence tests for students and more emphasis in curriculum on science and mathematics.

In many states, however, the promise of reform failed to materialize because of budgetary cutbacks or because reforms were not pursued to the extent that it made a difference to educationally disadvantaged youths. Often, too, reforms became a matter of bitter controversy. For example, some viewed minimum-competence tests for students as culturally biased against members of minority groups. Teacher organizations sometimes became suspicious of merit reforms, pointing out that "merit" is not easy to measure and, as a consequence, such systems could subject teachers to considerable abuse by school administrators. Teacher organizations also were less than happy about programs allowing people to obtain teaching credentials through nontraditional forms of certification, for example, by simply having a bachelor's degree and undertaking some preservice training, rather than going through years of formal college training in education.[5]

One major thrust of current educational reform has been toward giving parents greater choice regarding where and how they want their children educated. Toward this goal, some reformers have advocated school voucher programs and charter schools (see box 12-1).

Currently, private schools enroll about one out of ten children. Most private schools are affiliated with some religious group. The education provided by private schools may be superior to that provided by public schools, but this is not always the case. Authorities, such as University of Chicago sociologist James Coleman, have long contended, moreover, that public schools could match the higher standard attained by many private schools if more homework were given and greater discipline were achieved in the classroom.[6]

Much of the current mode of education reform has been directed against public school bureaucracies. Some reformers argue that if private schools do better than public ones, it is largely because they have fewer levels of bureaucracy. Bureaucrats in public schools, they contend, consume too much of the money that could be better used for classroom instruction and, more generally, simply get in the way by imposing meaningless rules and regulations that restrict the autonomy of teachers and prevent them from doing their job. Others counter that the size of the education bureaucracy has, in fact, no relation to student performance. Bureaucrats, moreover, perform necessary functions, and reducing the number of administrators will only lead to the imposing of more administrative duties on teachers, thus impairing their performance.[7]

Whatever the merits of the opponents' arguments, much public school reform has been aimed at reducing the size and influence of the bureaucracy. The goal of getting away from public school bureaucracies altogether has been part of the charter school movement, the decision of some school districts to hire private companies to run the school system, and decentralization proposals to shift more authority from the state to local districts and from local districts to individual schools.

The politics of education involves many additional actual or potential controversies. In several situations, conflict has reflected differences over values and lifestyles. Such concerns have been involved in the opposition of conservative groups to United States Supreme Court decisions banning prayer from public schools and, as in Kanawha County, West Virginia, in the

Box 12–1 Vouchers and Charter Schools

Voucher programs give parents public funds to send their children to schools of their choice, including private ones. The amount of money in most plans is roughly equal to what it costs to send a child to public school. Proponents argue that vouchers are valuable because they give parents a greater choice in choosing education services. They also argue that forcing public schools to compete in an educational free market for pupils and their voucher dollars will ultimately improve the educational offerings of the public schools.

Opponents argue that voucher programs would drain needed funds from public schools, many of which are already financially hard pressed. In the short run, at least, opponents point out, such programs could cause a dramatic increase in governmental expenditures because they would extend to students already in private schools.

Vouchers have encountered the resistance of public school teachers and, because they often involve aid to religious schools, those who claim such programs violate the federal constitution, specific state constitutions, or both. Some researchers have suggested that the end result of forcing public schools to compete with private ones is not likely to improve the overall educational product, but is likely to encourage private schools to satisfy demands for religious services in schools and racial segregation in education (see: Kevin B. Smith and Kenneth J. Meier, "Public Choice in Educational Markets and the Demand for Quality Education," *Political Research Quarterly* 46 [September 1995]: 461–478).

The movement toward vouchers was somewhat stemmed when California voters turned down a proposed program in 1993, though a program was authorized by the Wisconsin legislature in 1995. Charter schools, which have raised similar controversies, however, have caught on in several states. These schools are designed by groups of parents, teachers, school administrators, and others in the private sector under charters with school districts or various state agencies. They receive public funds but operate much like private schools under various funding arrangements and plans for assessing student performance.

1970s, to textbooks that were found to be "anti-religious, communistic, and pornographic."[8] Values of the "New Right" religious fundamentalists have also been reflected in demands that "creation science" (the biblical version of creation) be given equal time in public schools with evolutionary theory. As indicated above, there has also been considerable demand for public aid to private education, which has resulted in lawsuits concerning the legality of such aid.

Other conflicts in the realm of elementary and secondary education have involved questions of who should control education (which level of government, which group of interests), racial integration, and school finance.

FEDERAL, STATE, LOCAL RELATIONS

Most major decisions regarding public education are made at the state and local levels. The federal government has played a relatively minor role in school finance and, for the most part, has attempted to influence educational policy in specific areas by encouraging states and localities to adopt special programs such as those targeted for minority group students. In this tradition, one major federal initiative in recent years was the Goals 2000 Educate America Act, signed into law by President Clinton in 1994, which provides funds to states that wish to develop education reform plans to upgrade curriculum and student performance.

Within the states, ultimate authority over educational policy resides in the state governments. Nearly all states have state boards of education with general authority over the provision of elementary and secondary education. Some of these boards are elected and others are appointed, usually by the governor. Under the state board of education, there is a state department of education, headed by a superintendent of public instruction or a commissioner of education, who may be directly elected by the voters. The state department's responsibilities range from rendering a wide variety of services to school districts to regulating school district activity in areas such as finance and the selection of textbooks. In several states, county governments perform the state service and regulatory activities.

States have traditionally left the provision of elementary and secondary education services to local governments (either general-purpose units or independent school districts). They have, however, long assumed the right to set minimum standards of performance on the type and level of services to be provided by local school districts. Along with this, states have reserved the right to take over the function when local officials prove unable or unwilling to adhere to state standards. Under what are known as *academic bankruptcy laws*, a state department of education may take direct control over a local school district, dismissing elected school board members and local administrators. Takeovers have taken place in several places in recent years. The most publicized takeovers have been large school systems in Jersey City and Paterson, New Jersey. State intervention has brought improved management and improved curricula, but when it comes to educational achievement, particularly in large urban systems, thus far there is little reason to believe that state administrators can do a better job than local administrators.[9]

In recent years, the states have reclaimed some of the authority they have delegated to local school districts. Increased state involvement has resulted in part from the pressures on states to give greater financial aid to elementary and secondary education—a development prompted by efforts to limit dependence on local property taxes and by court directives for greater equity in the funding of education. As the states have provided more aid, they have felt compelled to impose more requirements on local school districts. The effect of this has been an undercutting of the authority of local school officials.

Another broad reason for increased state involvement has been the desire to improve the quality of elementary and secondary education. Toward this end, some state legislatures have exerted greater direct controls over curriculum (for example, requiring that certain courses be taught) and have imposed higher standards on teachers and graduating students. Increased state involvement of this nature has been welcomed by educators who share the desire to improve the quality of education. In several parts of the country, however, the new role for the state has conflicted with deeply rooted traditions of local control of public schools and, as a consequence, has encountered resistance.

One can find several examples of increased centralization at the state level in recent years. In some parts of the country, however, a countermovement has set in to reduce the states' role. As part of the anticentralization and antibureaucracy movement, state legislatures have considered downsizing, even abolishing, state departments of education. States also have given school districts exemptions from various regulations and some have considered creating "home rule" school districts with far greater autonomy. Within school districts there has been a comparable move to shift more responsibility to the individual schools.

School District Governance

On the local level, municipal governments at one time assumed the provision of elementary and secondary education. The political machines that dominated city politics in the early years of the twentieth century, however, looked on public school systems as sources of patronage and plunder. The influence of machine politics was found in a partisan selection of school board members, the appointment of political hacks to school administrative posts, and in kickbacks to politicians who awarded school construction contracts. The municipal reform movement described in chapter 9 led to the adoption of measures to insulate schools from city politics. These included the establishment of independent school districts, the use of nonpartisan school board elections held separately from municipal elections, and the employment of professional school managers. These reforms, as noted later, did not take education out of politics but only brought a different type of politics.

Some school districts continue to be dependent on municipal, county, or township governments for financial support. Better than 90 percent of the sixteen thousand school districts in this country, however, are independent of other local units and thus are free to raise their own revenues and frame their own budgets, subject only to conditions imposed by state law. Some of the districts coincide with the political boundaries of villages, towns, cities, or counties; others extend into two or more of these jurisdictions. Some school districts contain only elementary schools; others contain secondary schools; and still others contain both elementary and secondary schools, often along with junior colleges and a variety of technical and special schools.

School districts are officially governed by school boards. These are usually composed of unpaid private citizens. Most boards have a small, odd-numbered membership of five, seven, or nine members, though those in the largest cities may have as many as fifteen members. More than 90 percent of the school boards are elected. Elections are usually held on a nonpartisan, at-large basis and separately from other elections. Nominations are made by individual declaration, community caucus systems, and even formal primary systems. Teacher organizations, minority group leaders, and small, informal groups of civic leaders may actively recruit and sponsor board candidates. In recent years religious conservatives across the country have been active in school board elections, seeking curriculum changes, opposing sex education programs, calling for prayer in the classroom, and seeking to purge objectionable materials from libraries. Most often, however, school board campaigns are likely to be low in issue content and to attract relatively little public attention.[10]

As on the municipal level, the use of nonpartisan elections and the practice of separate elections for school board members have reduced voter turnout without any verifiable improvement in issue voting. As also found on the municipal level, the at-large system for electing school board members has made it more difficult for racial minorities to secure representation.[11] This may have policy consequences because increased minority representation on school boards appears to bring about an improvement in programs benefiting minority children. This appears to occur through a process in which black school board members are instrumental in hiring high-level black administrators who, in turn, hire black teachers. Black teachers, the end product of this sequence, appear to respond to black students in more effective ways than do white teachers.[12]

Appointive boards are most commonly found in large cities and in communities in the South. Appointments may be made by city councils (especially in smaller jurisdictions), judges, city commissioners, county supervisors, county boards of education, and, more frequently than any of these others, mayors. Citizen committees, representing the major groups or segments of the community, are often used in large cities to recommend board members for appointment. In some states, largely in the South, the appointive system has been challenged in the courts as being discriminatory to blacks.

Whether elected or appointed, school board members are apt to be better educated than most of the community, to be from the middle and upper classes, and to hold business and professional positions. The percentage of school board positions held by women and minorities is small when one considers their percentages in the general population. On the other hand, women hold a larger percentage of school board positions than any of the elected offices in local government. For example, while women hold around 31 percent of the school board seats, they hold but 22 percent of the seats for elected municipal offices. One is unsure what accounts for this. Women may run for school board positions more often than they do for other local offices. One might also speculate that women candidates are generally viewed as having special qualifications in matters regarding children. Blacks and Hispanics also have a higher percentage of school board seats than they do municipal elective offices, though their percentages of school board positions are small, 6 and 3 percent, respectively.[13]

In terms of motivation and behavior, one study has characterized school board members in the following manner:[14]

1. The Client, who functions as the spokesperson for children's interests, for example, that they get a "quality" education through good teaching, curriculum, and guidance and are prepared for college or a vocation.
2. The Guardian, who functions as the protector of the community, especially the taxpayers, and is concerned with budgetary matters and methods of getting the best return on the dollar.
3. The Benefactor, who functions as the champion of school personnel, either teaching or nonteaching, and is concerned with matters like salaries, fringe benefits, and working conditions.
4. The Politico, who ran for the board to become known in the community, with the objective of stepping up to a higher office or improving his or her business possibilities.
5. The Maverick, who has gotten involved because of a pet peeve or goal (for example, returning to the "three Rs" or compulsory swimming).

Board members may play all of these various roles at one time or another, but the first two appear to be most predominant.

The field of education, like other areas of governmental service, has been characterized by a reliance on a large and professionally trained bureaucracy. The relation between school boards, composed of part-time, unpaid laypeople, and the superintendent they hire to supervise administration is somewhat comparable to that between the city council and city manager. The superintendent and professionals on the central administrative staff are in a position to influence board policy by controlling the flow of information to the board, defining policy alternatives, making policy recommendations, and setting the agenda for board meetings.[15]

To some extent, the influence of both the educational bureaucracy and the school board has been countered by the growth of teacher organizations and unions. The largest of these are the National Education Association and the American Federation of Teachers (AFL-CIO), both of which have state and local chapters. Leaders of teacher groups are commonly involved in recruiting and sponsoring school board candidates and often sit in on meetings of school district advisory and policymaking bodies. Bargaining agreements between teachers and school board members are common. Negotiations between the two condition the allocation of school resources and often relate to policy matters such as class size and curriculum.

Citizen participation in school district politics, as measured by voting in school board or bond elections and attendance at board meetings, is normally very limited. As researchers noted some time ago, "relatively few citizens use whatever channels are available to register their educational needs. Popular participation is episodic, providing more a spasm than a steady flow of demands."[16] Turnout for school board elections may have trouble reaching 10 percent of the potential vote. As might be expected, people with children in the school system appear more likely than others to participate in these elections.[17] Public interest, when aroused, is usually concentrated on a specific issue like busing proposals or a particular bond issue rather than on overall school policy. Bond issues appear to be in jeopardy of going down to defeat if turnout is heavy, an indication that voting to many people is a form of protest. Some research suggests that older citizens, whose children, if any, are beyond school age, are particularly likely to be opposed to bond issues.[18]

Parent associations occasionally have had some influence on particular school matters, but their overall function has been, perhaps, more to create the illusion of parent representation in public education because they tend to support the "prevailing educational order."[19] Other groups more actively involved in school politics are those representing reform-oriented citizens concerned with school finances and efficiency or issues of morality; civil rights, poverty, and neighborhood groups concerned with school matters affecting minorities; and business interests who may benefit by educational expenditures (for example, construction firms, suppliers). Many of these groups, as well as associations of teachers, school administrators, and school board members, may also be active in state educational politics.

Since the late 1960s, demands have been heard for greater neighborhood control of schools. Much of the impetus for this has come from ghetto dwellers in reaction to what they see as nonresponsive school systems that have failed miserably to educate their children. School governance, they contend, is beyond the ghetto community's control because of the middle- and upper-class dominance of school boards, the remoteness of professional administrators, and the growing influence of teacher groups. If New York City's experience in the late 1960s can be taken as an example, efforts to decentralize control of education down to the neighborhood level are likely to become extremely controversial. Efforts to gain local control, particularly over the hiring and firing of teachers and curriculum, may be expected to be strongly opposed by teacher unions, school administrators, and central school boards.

In recent years, a broader movement for local control, called *site-based management,* has been advanced on the theory that the quality of education can be improved if more powers are devolved down to the individual school level. Freed from the control of central bureaucrats, local authorities, it is contended, will be better able to shape instruction best suited to the needs of students. Thus far, however, there has been little actual decentralization, even where site-based systems are supposedly installed.[20]

SCHOOL INTEGRATION AND FINANCE

SCHOOL INTEGRATION

Of the several policy problems in the area of public education facing state and local decision makers, two of the most difficult are school integration and finance.

In *Brown* v. *Board of Education* in 1954,[21] a unanimous United States Supreme Court ruled that school systems established separately by law for black and white students violated the equal protection clause of the Fourteenth Amendment. The Court found no rational reason for the continuance of "separate but equal" school facilities. Aside from the legal arguments, the court took note of evidence that segregation had an adverse psychological effect on black students, generating a "feeling of inferiority" in them.

Rather than force immediate compliance with its decision, however, the Court decided to give the states, especially in the South, time to adjust to the new ruling. In 1955, following hearings on the problem of implementation, the Court delegated further authority to implement its decision to the lower federal courts. The lower courts were told to act "with all deliberate speed."[22] During the next ten years, there was considerably more deliberation than speed, particularly in the eleven states of the old Confederacy, where segregated schools existed in every state at the time of the *Brown* decision. In 1956, southern states greeted the decision with a widespread policy of "massive resistance" that included state laws allowing school boards to shuffle schoolchildren among districts to maintain segregation, permitting parents to withdraw their children from public schools, providing state support for segregated private schools, and closing schools federal courts had ordered integrated.

In 1957, the refusal of the state of Arkansas, led by its governor, to follow federal court orders for the gradual desegregation of Little Rock High School was overcome only by President Dwight Eisenhower's decision to call out units of the United States Army to enforce the court's order. Faced with such obstacles, by the fall of 1965 only 2 percent of the black student population in the South was attending integrated schools.

By the early 1960s, it was apparent that the federal courts, having neither the "sword" nor the "purse," were in need of presidential and congressional support in implementing the *Brown* decision. The sword (physical force) was necessary in 1962, as it had been in 1956, to overcome state defiance of federal court orders. In 1962 President Kennedy supported federal court orders to integrate the University of Mississippi and sent three thousand federal soldiers and National Guardsmen to the campus to quell riots over the orders. The power of the purse was later exercised by Congress in Title VI of the Civil Rights Act of 1964, which withheld federal funds from institutions, including schools, that were segregated.

The 1964 Civil Rights Act shifted much of the burden of enforcing compliance from the courts to the Department of Health, Education, and Welfare. Administrative activity, along with continued court action, brought the percentage of black students in integrated schools (where at least half of the students are white) in the South up to 44 percent by the late 1970s. Much of this integration, however, was only on paper. In some cases, the classrooms were divided between white and black students. There was also a mushrooming of private, segregated schools, often staffed by former public school personnel.[23]

During the 1960s and 1970s, battles over the implementation of the *Brown* decision spread to northern cities. Many public school systems were placed under court-ordered decrees to achieve racial integration. Most of the integration came about peacefully, but crises developed in certain northern cities such as Boston in the mid-1970s. In many cases, the underlying problem was one of *de facto segregation*, that is, school segregation resulting from segregated neighborhoods. Conflict often centered on the busing of children to overcome such segregation. Busing clearly upset many Americans. A national survey by the Lou Harris organization in the mid-1970s, for example, found 74 percent of those polled were in opposition to school busing. Opposition to busing was defended on numerous grounds other than racial considerations, such as the belief that children should attend neighborhood schools and that busing is expensive, time-consuming, and inconvenient. More sophisticated research indicates that opposition to busing has reflected racial attitudes formed early in life rather than simply being personally affected by the situation (for example, having a child bused).[24]

The United States Supreme Court has unanimously upheld the constitutionality of busing as a means to desegregate schools.[25] There is some doubt, however, concerning the ability of a federal court to order a metropolitan-wide desegregation plan that would require busing across district lines (for example, between central city and suburban school districts).

Along with the conflict over busing have come disputes over the value and ultimate success of school desegregation. There have been conflicting conclusions over whether or not integrated schools, created by busing or other

TABLE 12–1   Percentage of Black and Hispanic Students
in Predominantly Minority and Intensely
Segregated Schools

Years	Predominant Minority (50% or more)		Intensely Segregated (90–100%)	
	Blacks	Hispanics	Blacks	Hispanics
1968–1969	76.6	54.8	64.3	23.1
1972–1973	63.6	56.6	38.7	23.3
1980–1981	62.9	68.1	33.2	28.8
1986–1987	63.3	71.5	32.5	32.2
1991–1992	66.0	73.4	33.9	34.0

Source: Carl Orfield et al., "The Growth of Segregation in American Schools," United States
Department of Education (Washington, D.C.: Government Printing Office, December 1993), p. 7.

means, aid black students academically.[26] Some research suggests that even
though blacks may indeed learn better in integrated schools, the drive for
desegregation in large northern cities has contributed to the flight of whites
to the suburbs with a consequent resegregation of city schools.[27] From this
perspective, desegregation efforts are self-defeating. Other scholars and the
United States Civil Rights Commission, however, have concluded there is no
evidence that school desegregation, by itself, provokes a white flight to the
suburbs.[28]

In the early 1990s school segregation appeared to be on the increase. A
higher percentage of black and Hispanic children attended predominantly
minority schools in which more than half of the students are minorities in the
early 1990s than was the case in the early 1970s. Hispanic children have been
even more likely than black children to be in predominantly minority schools
and, though slightly, in intensely segregated schools (those with 90–100
percent minority) (see table 12–1). For blacks, segregation decreased in the
early 1970s because of court-ordered busing, held steady in the 1980s, and
began to creep back up in the 1990s perhaps, in part, due to the tendency of
courts to lift desegregation orders.

SCHOOL FINANCE

State and local governments over the past several decades have also been
faced with serious problems of school finance.[29] The cost of public elementary
and secondary education is high—totaling some $230 billion in 1992, close to
a quarter of all state and local spending. There is a large gap among the states
in revenues generated per student, ranging from $8,865 in Alaska to $2,908 in

Utah. The amounts generally have been comparatively low in southern states. Since the 1970s, increases have been most dramatic in Alaska (thanks to its oil resources) and Wyoming. While the amount spent on education tells something about a state's priorities, there is no strong or consistent relationship between the amount spent on education and educational performance or achievement.

Traditionally, local governments have provided the bulk of support for elementary and secondary education out of local property taxes. The share provided by state governments, however, has increased over the last several years, and now, on a national basis, is close to that provided by local governments.[30] Hawaii is the only state that pays the full public cost of local schools out of state funds. State aid elsewhere amounts to between 40 and 50 percent of all money spent on elementary and secondary education.

State aid has increased for two primary reasons: to reduce reliance on the local property tax and to increase equalization of expenditures among school districts. In many parts of the country, an increased use of the property tax to support education has prompted a taxpayers' rebellion, as evidenced in the defeat of school budget proposals and bond issues and, in some places, the closing of public schools.

Since the early 1970s, several state courts have invalidated the use of the local property tax as a method of financing education, on the grounds that its use results in great disparities in the amount of money supporting the education of students. In California, for example, a state court invalidated a property tax system under which the school district of Baldwin Park in Los Angeles spent $577 educating each pupil while a school district in Beverly Hills spent $1,232, or more than twice as much, on each pupil. The United States Supreme Court in 1973 refused to concur with lower court decisions invalidating the use of property taxes to finance education.[31] Several state courts, however, continued to find fault with the funding of local schools, often basing their decisions on state constitutional guarantees of a right to education. These decisions have often been followed by prolonged struggles between courts and legislatures. Equalization proposals often do not play well in the wealthier parts of the states. Several states have been able to adopt plans giving aid to districts that fail to meet certain per pupil expenditures, but these formulas do not fully balance financing resources among rich and poor districts.[32]

Efforts to shift funding to the state have commonly been opposed not only by those who object to equalization plans but by those who contend that more state aid would bring greater state control over a function traditionally performed on the local level. Research suggests that shifting to the state level has been most pronounced in states where property tax pressures have been the greatest and where the degree of "localism" in the culture and history of the states, and, thus, the resistance to state control, is the weakest.[33]

Increases in state aid, while appreciated by local districts, have some drawbacks. In many states the increase has been coupled with limits on the ability of school districts to make greater use of the property tax. A common state regulation to this end is that of requiring school officials to secure voter approval to raise budgets (and thus the property tax rate) above a state-prescribed percentage increase. The shift to the state has also made financial support of education less stable. Education financing is tied to ups and downs in the fiscal health of the state economy, less dependable tax sources, and how effectively education competes with a host of other demands on state funds.

Federal aid to education comes through several programs. Among these are one giving aid to local schools placed under the strain caused by armed service personnel and federal workers in the area and those that provide special programs for minority group students or curriculum development. Federal funds, while important for innovation, have amounted to only some 7 percent of all school district revenues and, like other forms of federal aid, have been on the decline. Federal funds have been used to finance educational innovations, but their flow has been unpredictable. Often, federal aid has been opposed on ideological grounds (the fear of federal control) and the supposition that localities will have to pick up additional bills once the federal funding stops.

POVERTY AND WELFARE

THE MEANING OF POVERTY

The United States Social Security Administration measures poverty in the United States by determining the cost of the minimum human diet (how much it costs an average person to eat) and comparing this to family income.[34] If the household income is less than three times the cost of the diet, that household is officially defined as poor. Measurements are adjusted and updated each year. In 1980, for example, the poverty level for a four-person household in an urban area was set at $8,414. In 1990, it was $13,359, and by 1994 the poverty level for such a family had risen to $15,141.

Using the federal government's official measurements, we find that better than one out of five people in this country was poor in the early 1960s (see figure 12–1). The rate declined sharply after the passage of President Lyndon Johnson's War on Poverty program in 1964, hovering between 11 and 12 percent during the 1970s. Since then, the rate has ranged from 13 to slightly over 15 percent. In 1994, some 38 million people, representing 14.5 percent of the population, qualified as poor by the government's measures.

Who are the poor? When we look at the total number of poor people, the 38 million, we find that the vast majority of them, around 67 percent, are non-Hispanic whites. Over 40 percent of those classified as poor are children under eighteen, and some 10 percent are sixty-five or older. Around two-thirds of the poor are in families in which someone is working.

Percent of poor persons: 1959-1994

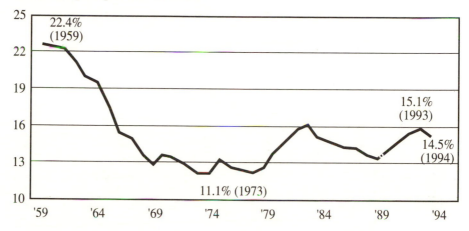

FIGURE 12–1 Poverty Rate Dips, but Remains Higher Than It Was
During the 1970s

Source: U.S. Census Bureau, Department of Commerce, *Income, Poverty, and Valuation of Noncash Benefits: 1994*, Series P60–189 (Washington, DC: Government Printing Office, 1995).

In looking at the poverty rate, or the percentage of a particular population group classified as poor, we find, over the years, that poverty has been far more of a problem for blacks and Hispanics than for non-Hispanic whites, and for children under eighteen than those eighteen or older. In 1990, for example, the poverty rates varied from 11 percent for non-Hispanic whites, to 28 percent for Hispanics, to 32 percent for blacks. For black children, the rate was 44 percent.[35]

Since the late 1960s, we have seen a rapid decrease in the poverty rate for people sixty-five and over. Since the mid-1970s, they have been replaced by children as the age group most likely to be classified as poor. Poverty, once associated with old age, is now associated with children. Another striking development in recent years has been the feminization of poverty. More than a third of all families headed by a female with no husband present are poor. For black and Hispanic families of this nature, the poverty rate is over 48 percent. Generally, poverty rates have been higher outside metropolitan areas than within metropolitan areas (though the highest rates are found in central cities), and in the South more than other regions of the country (see table 12–2).

These statistics, while helping to identify the problem of poverty, do so only

TABLE 12-2　Income and Poverty—Where Your State Stands

Median household income and percent of persons in poverty, by state: 3–year average, 1992–1994

	Median Income	Poverty Rate		Median Income	Poverty Rate
Alabama	$26,727	17.0	Missouri	$29,503	15.8
Alaska	44,518	9.8	Montana	27,599	13.4
Arizona	31,198	15.7	Nebraska	31,779	9.9
Arkansas	24,807	17.6	Nevada	35,436	11.9
California	35,715	17.5	New Hampshire	38,613	8.8
Colorado	35,839	9.9	New Jersey	41,671	10.1
Connecticut	41,589	9.7	New Mexico	27,221	20.0
Delaware	36,849	8.8	New York	32,402	16.4
District of Columbia	30,023	22.6	North Carolina	29,669	14.8
Florida	29,155	16.1	North Dakota	28,531	11.2
Georgia	31,453	15.1	Ohio	32,371	13.2
Hawaii	43,498	9.3	Oklahoma	26,877	18.4
Idaho	30,868	13.4	Oregon	33,056	11.7
Illinois	34,036	13.9	Pennsylvania	31,806	12.5
Indiana	29,408	12.6	Rhode Island	32,814	11.3
Iowa	30,946	10.8	South Carolina	28,566	17.2
Kansas	30,303	13.0	South Dakota	28,639	14.6
Kentucky	25,468	19.5	Tennessee	26,690	17.1
Louisiana	26,511	25.5	Texas	29,915	18.3
Maine	29,914	12.8	Utah	36,199	9.4
Maryland	39,819	10.7	Vermont	34,087	9.4
Massachusetts	38,973	10.2	Virginia	38,454	10.0
Michigan	34,289	14.4	Washington	35,303	11.7
Minnesota	33,638	12.1	West Virginia	22,657	21.0
Mississippi	23,296	23.1	Wisconsin	34,384	10.8
			Wyoming	31,749	11.0

Note: The Current Population Survey is designed to collect reliable data at the national level and secondarily at the regional level. When data are tabulated by state, the estimates are considered less reliable; therefore, particular caution should be used in trying to interpret the relative standing of the states and the District of Columbia.

Source: United States Census Bureau, Department of Commerce, *Income, Poverty, and Valuation of Noncash Benefits: 1994,* Series P60–189 (Washington, D.C.: Government Printing Office, 1995).

in arbitrary and absolute terms. The incomes of the statistically poor and their standards of living may be relatively high when compared with the poor of other countries or relatively low when compared with other people in this country. Poverty, in short, is perhaps more meaningfully seen as a relative concept rather than as an absolute one. The distinction is important in fashioning solutions to the problem of poverty. Absolute poverty could be eliminated by increasing incomes above a certain level. The elimination of relative poverty, on the other hand, requires a redistribution of wealth.

Poverty, whether measured in absolute or relative terms, has long presented difficult problems for government decision makers. What may be called the "hard line" on poverty has been based largely on the belief that many of the poor are morally deficient and have no one to blame but themselves for their plight. According to this philosophy, government should have only a minimal role in aiding the poor and must be careful of generating dependence on its generosity. Those who do receive aid, moreover, should be subject to whatever conditions, including work requirements, that the government chooses to impose. Viewing poverty as a problem of individual character and morality is compatible with the desire to keep costs down. There is no use, the hard-liner argues, to try to help those who cannot or will not help themselves. The hard line has long been prominent in debates over government programs aiding the poor. The "soft line," on the other hand, places emphasis on poverty as a product of environmental or circumstantial forces, rather than personal failings. Cures are to be found in job training, education, and other social programs.

The American people have been suspicious of those receiving welfare, even though the Depression of the 1930s dramatically brought home the point that poverty could result from impersonal economic forces over which the individual had little or no control. Yet, government's main role was seen even in that period to be one of providing temporary relief until the economy could be stimulated and general prosperity would trickle down income to those who had become poor through no fault of their own.

Americans, historically, have stressed the need for each individual to take responsibility for his or her own welfare. In addition, research suggests that the resistance to public welfare reflects an unwillingness to share income with the less fortunate and, among whites, negative attitudes toward blacks. Particularly popular among whites who are hostile to public welfare is the notion that the aid goes disproportionately to blacks because blacks are not committed to the work ethic, that is, do not try hard enough to overcome economic inequality.[36]

Over the years, efforts have been made to combat poverty through programs like job training and through the removal of racial barriers in employment, which would help a segment of society improve its economic position. Another approach to the poverty problem has been to target governmental aid and economic development programs into distressed communities or pockets of poverty such as in the Appalachian area. Of more direct benefit to the poor have been public assistance programs providing cash benefits, and various types of in-kind benefit programs.

PUBLIC ASSISTANCE PROGRAMS

Public assistance programs in the United States have their roots in the Elizabethan poor laws of the seventeenth century and in the special public assistance programs developed by state and local governments from the 1850s to the early 1930s. The early local governments, adapting English poor law concepts and practices for this country, acknowledged their responsibility to provide aid, but only on a minimal basis, and after applicants had met means tests and residency requirements and were able to demonstrate complete destitution. If the city or county could not send an applicant back to another jurisdiction or charge one of the applicant's relatives with support, the pauper was placed in a poorhouse or almshouse.

Later, assistance programs financed and administered by local governments with relative degrees of state supervision were designed to provide pensions to specific groups of individuals, for example, the blind, aged, mentally ill, and needy children. In establishing and administering these special programs, an attempt was made to give preference to the "worthy poor," that is, those who were not morally responsible for their plight or beyond moral regeneration. Mothers who had been deprived of a spouse's support had to be of "good moral character" in the eyes of the administrator. The amount of aid they received varied greatly from jurisdiction to jurisdiction, depending on local practices and property taxes.

By 1934, a majority of the states had public assistance programs, but the benefits generally were not available statewide and were grossly inadequate to meet the demand generated by the 1930s Depression. The federal government, which previously had given aid only to VIMS (veterans, Indians, and merchant seamen), undertook to support the states' assistance programs through the passage of the Social Security Act of 1935.

The Social Security Act, which has been amended several times since 1935, currently provides two basic public assistance programs: Supplemental Security Income (SSI) and Aid to Families with Dependent Children (AFDC).[37] Both of these programs provide cash benefits to lower-income groups. The SSI program provides cash assistance to the needy aged (sixty-five years or older), blind, and disabled. In the mid-1990s, over six million persons received aid under the program. The federal government pays for the basic SSI benefit. Many state governments, however, have supplemented the basic benefit with their own funds.[38]

Of all the public assistance programs, Aid to Families with Dependent

Children has undergone the greatest growth and has generated the most controversy. While other public assistance programs have remained relatively stable, AFDC has grown from covering 372,000 families in 1940 to covering 2 million families in 1970, and, despite tighter eligibility requirements, to nearly 3.8 million in the late 1980s, and to a record 4.7 million during the economic recession of the early 1990s.

The Social Security Act originally extended federal grants to states to aid needy children whose dependency stemmed from the incapacity or death of a parent or from a parent's continued absence from the home. Benefits were denied to families if the husband was in the home and found to be employable. One effect of this was that unemployed husbands would desert their families so that the mother could receive aid. Confronted with this problem, Congress in 1961 extended the program at the state's option to permit families with both parents present but one or both unemployed to qualify for assistance. Only twenty-one states adopted the more liberal program. To keep costs down, other states have insisted on the absence of a father or a "substitute father" (any able-bodied man) as a condition for receiving aid. Some of these states have used legally questionable midnight or early morning raids by welfare officials on the homes of mothers on welfare in an attempt to find a returning husband or a man who could conceivably qualify as a substitute father.

The federal government, state governments, and, in some parts of the country, local governments share the costs of the AFDC program. The federal government picks up at least 50 percent of the expenses in each state. Generally, benefits are higher in the North and East than in the South and West. In 1993 benefits ranged from $120 per month for a family of three in Mississippi to $923 per month in Alaska, with the median state paying $376. Two-thirds of the more than fourteen million people receiving AFDC funds were children. Thirty-four percent of the recipients were Anglo, 39 percent black, and 10 percent Hispanic.

State laws generally require recipients to file monthly reports on their circumstances. State laws also require that recipients, with certain exceptions such as the elderly and incapacitated, register for work. Along with work requirements, several states have coupled participation in the program with a system of penalties and rewards that are designed to change behavior. Among the former have been reforms reducing benefits for recipients who continue having children or for those staying in the program for extended periods. Along the same line are measures to discourage people from migrating into a state to take advantage of higher benefit levels. One way to do this is by restricting migrants to the level of funding they would have received in the state they came from. On the positive side, some states have attempted to use the lure of benefits to encourage recipients to get married or stay in school. As we note below, many of these restrictions reflect myths or at least untested assumptions about the behavior of people on welfare.

In addition to SSI and AFDC, one finds several other programs that provide assistance to low-income persons. Some of these, such as Old Age Survivors and Disability Insurance (OASDI), Medicare, and unemployment compensation, are available to the general public.[39] More specifically targeted for low-income persons are General Assistance Programs (GAPs) and various types of in-kind benefits. GAPS are found in several states. They provide benefits for poor persons who are not eligible for SSI or AFDC. The benefits vary from state to state. They also vary greatly within states where levels are determined by local governments.[40] GAP benefits reach about 1.1 million persons and have been especially important to urban minorities.

In-Kind Benefits

Among the in-kind benefits are the federally funded food stamp program, which furnishes needy households with coupons redeemable for food, housing assistance programs that subsidize rents and mortgage payments, and the Medicaid program, which provides needy people with the means to obtain various types of medical care. These programs, like SSI and AFDC, are means-tested; that is, they are provided only if the applicants can demonstrate their need for the aid.

Medicaid has been by far the largest item of state spending for health purposes. It is also the chief source of health care for low-income citizens. The program is jointly financed by state and federal governments and provides medical assistance for low-income people who are aged, blind, disabled, members of families with dependent children, and, in some thirty states, for those who are otherwise "medically needy." The term medically needy refers to those whose incomes are adequate to purchase food, clothing, and housing but not medical care.

The federal government's share of expenses has ranged between 50 and 83 percent of the medical costs. The share paid by individual states depends on their per capita incomes. They range from 20 percent in the poorer states to a maximum of 50 percent in the high-income states. The federal government requires states to offer certain services, such as inpatient and outpatient hospital care. States may also provide, at their discretion, a variety of other services, such as eyeglasses and dental care.

Expenses under Medicaid grew from about 10 percent of all state expenditures in 1985 to over 15 percent in the early 1990s. Behind this increase was higher unemployment, more poverty, and a general increase in the cost of health care. To control costs, some states have adopted a prospective payment system under which the hospitals or doctors fix a fee for services, regardless of the patient's actual condition or length of stay in the hospital. Others have imposed limits on fees paid to nursing homes and on the expansion of nursing home facilities. Oregon in the early 1990s gained national attention with a plan to limit and ration benefits.

THE POLITICS OF REFORM

ISSUES, CONFLICTS, AND MYTHS

Over the last several decades, many people have looked at the welfare system as being in a state of crisis. The maze of programs, each with its own rules and regulations, is confusing to welfare workers as well as to the poor. As a result, many of the federally financed programs do not reach those truly in need. Only around 40 percent of those persons below the poverty level receive cash assistance through such programs as AFDC and SSI. Some 28 percent of the poor have received no benefits at all, including food stamps.[41] On the other hand, many of those who do receive assistance may be discouraged from working because they can make more money through the various assistance programs or because they will lose benefits when they earn additional income.

The social costs of staying on assistance have sometimes been marital instability and paternalistic, if not demeaning, treatment of the poor. Social workers appear to regard the poor as irresponsible children who need to be taught how to live.[42] Some believe that this approach fosters client dependency and conflicts with the goal of reducing assistance expenditures. Others have argued that assistance programs are used less to help the poor than to avoid social unrest and serve the interests of employers. Welfare, to some extent, services the needs of employers by taking people out of the job market when they are not needed and forcing them to work at low wages when they are needed.[43]

Underlying the conflicts over welfare reform have been disputes, as we have noted, over whether poverty is related to personal factors (intellectual or moral deficiencies) or environmental factors (such as a lack of education) that can be corrected. Related to this dispute is the debate over whether the poor are a permanent group caught up in a culture of poverty in which dependency is handed down from generation to generation or a dynamic group, constantly changing in composition.[44] Some recent research suggests that for most of the poor, poverty is not a constant state of affairs (see box 12–2). Conflict has also been centered on the question of whether aid should come as cash assistance, thus giving the poor a free choice of how to spend their money, or whether that aid should come as in-kind benefits. Those who advocate the latter route contend that low-income persons, if given a choice, may not spend their incomes on the essentials of living, like housing.

Further confounding the debate over welfare reform are several widely believed myths concerning the characteristics of those receiving government assistance, particularly under the AFDC program. Among these are:[45]

1. Welfare families have more children in order to receive more money. Only one-third of families on welfare have four or more children; most have one

---

BOX 12–2   THE DYNAMICS OF POVERTY

Although one finds relatively little change from year to year in the total number of people in poverty and in the percentage of the population considered poor, there is considerable movement in and out of the poverty category. Studies suggest that poverty is but a temporary though often recurring condition for millions of Americans. For example, around 20 percent of those who were poor in 1991 were able to move out of that category by 1992. In 1991–1992, moreover, only about 5 percent of the population was consistently poor for all twenty-four months. Poverty came and went with changes in employment and income. The average poverty spell was about four months. Getting out of poverty at any time during this period, however, was far more difficult for children and the elderly, blacks, Hispanics, and for female-headed households.

Source: Martina Shea, *Dynamics of Economic Well-Being: Poverty, 1991 to 1993* (Washington, D.C.: United States Bureau of the Census, July 1995).

---

or two children. An additional twenty-five or thirty dollars (a standard payment) a month may not be much of an incentive to have more children.

2. Most children on welfare are illegitimate. In fact, a majority of children in families receiving welfare were born in wedlock. Over the past two decades, the number of never-married mothers on AFDC has increased, reaching just over half in the early 1990s. This increase, however, reflects a national trend in the number of never-married mothers.

3. Welfare rolls are full of able-bodied loafers. Most of those on welfare are unemployable because of age or disability. Over 66 percent of the people in AFDC are children and another 10 percent are old. Studies indicate that less than 1 percent of those on welfare are able-bodied males. Much welfare, at least, results from life crises over which recipients have little or no control, for example, accidents, desertion, illness, or involuntary unemployment.

4. Most welfare families are black. Sixty percent of all welfare recipients are white. A higher percentage of blacks than whites, however, are on welfare, and the percentage gap seems to be widening.

5. Welfare mothers stay on the rolls for years and years and refuse to work. Welfare mothers tend to go on and off welfare. Some 70 percent get off welfare within a two-year period, largely because of marriage or employment. About 45 percent come back on welfare after losing a job or getting a divorce or other development. Only some 15 percent stay on welfare more than five years.

6. The disparity in welfare payments encourages the poor to migrate to areas where payments are highest. Available evidence, however, does not altogether support this assumption. Some suggest, for example, that the migration of poor people is patterned after the migration of the population in general. They move to find employment; welfare considerations are secondary at best.[46] In large cities such as New York the vast majority of those receiving welfare appear to be either born in the city or long-time residents there.[47]

THE WAR ON POVERTY

State and local governments, historically, have shown little enthusiasm over framing broad and expensive programs that redistribute income from the relatively wealthy to the less fortunate. Though they have served as laboratories or testing grounds in welfare policy, state and local governments have been far more comfortable distributing benefits among their general populations or promoting the goal of economic development. Much of the responsibility of initiating and financing social welfare reform has been assumed by the federal government.

Along with Social Security, one of the most comprehensive efforts ever undertaken to remedy the problems of the economically disadvantaged in this country was the War on Poverty launched by the administration of Lyndon Johnson in the mid-1960s.[48] Under the Economic Opportunity Act of 1964, a number of programs were initiated with the intent not simply of alleviating poverty, as in the public assistance programs, but of attacking many of the problems, such as poor health care, lack of education, and poor job skills, that were thought to be the cause of poverty. Reformers also sought to involve the poor in putting together programs to help themselves. Such participation, they hoped, would improve poor people's sense of confidence and self-worth and enable them to control their own destinies better.

As it turned out, the poor probably had less impact on community action programs than anticipated. Major priorities were established by the federal government, and many program decisions were made by representatives of social welfare agencies; school, county, and city governments; and private agencies. For those who represented the poor on neighborhood councils, the real choice often came down to one of whether or not to apply for funds for a particular program, and even this decision was hastily made with reliance on the professional staff.[49]

Overall, the War on Poverty appeared to enjoy at least some short-term success. The poverty rate declined after poverty programs were adopted, though it is difficult to determine whether this was because of the programs or other factors (for example, the general economic growth in the period).[50] By the late 1960s and early 1970s, enthusiasm for the antipoverty effort began to decline, in part because of the war in Southeast Asia, which both distracted attention from poverty and drained money away from poverty programs. Following the 1972 presidential election, the Nixon Administration declared the War on Poverty to be a failure. Not long thereafter, the central antipoverty agency was abolished, though many of its programs were transferred to other federal agencies. Lack of finances and conservative opposition were important elements in the abandonment of the War on Poverty. It had also become increasingly unpopular. Some have argued that its unpopularity supports the general proposition that government cannot single out and attempt to help a specific class of people without other people becoming resentful.[51]

CHANGING THE SYSTEM

While the War on Poverty was going full speed ahead in the mid-1960s, AFDC and other programs came under the increasing attack of the poor and their spokespersons. Chief among the state practices condemned by the national and several *ad hoc* local organizations were residency requirements of up to one year to become eligible for welfare (designed to protect taxpayers against drifters), substitute father or "man in the house" rules, underestimation of the amount of an applicant's actual need, and limitations on how much aid could be given, regardless of need.

Part of the pressure for reform in the welfare system emanated from the activities of storefront lawyers working through the Legal Services Program established as part of the War on Poverty. Most of the cases handled under the program involved representing individuals in matters like divorce, garnishment of wages, and evictions. Legal services in several areas (especially California, Texas, Florida, New York, Colorado, and the District of Columbia), however, early took on the cause of law reform as cases involving basic constitutional issues were selected and class action suits involving thousands of poor people were filed and pursued as far as the Supreme Court.

Meanwhile, welfare clients themselves began to form organizations, such as MAW (Mothers for Adequate Welfare in Boston), and began to press their grievances through social action techniques (sit-ins, demonstrations) comparable to those employed in the civil rights movement. In June 1967, many of these local organizations became affiliated with the National Welfare Rights Organization (NWRO). NWRO later served as a means of calling national attention to the rights of the poor and the need for welfare reform.

If the numerous groups involved in the welfare reform movement had a common strategy, it was centered on the belief that if all those eligible for welfare were to demand the benefits to which they were legally entitled, the system would collapse and have to be replaced by a national guaranteed annual income system.[52] Despite the persistent efforts of state governments to keep people out of the AFDC program, the rolls continued to grow at an

ever-accelerating pace throughout the 1960s under the impact of court decisions and political action. The result of the enlargement of the welfare rolls
was a search for alternative methods of providing welfare.

What finally emerged from a welter of ideas was the Nixon Family Assistance Plan, proposed in 1969, which would have established a national minimum level of welfare support. The plan was lost in Congress. Another
proposal lost in Congress in the Carter years was one proposing that the
federal government assume nearly all of the welfare costs borne by states and
local governments. Coming to power in 1980, the Reagan Administration took
the opposite position in calling for a shift in responsibility for welfare from
the national to state and local levels. (See discussion in chapter 2.) State and
local officials showed little enthusiasm for this course of action. The national
government and the states, however, working together, did cut welfare spending, largely by raising eligibility standards.

During the 1980s the federal government gave the states considerable
discretion in devising programs known as *workfare* that encourage able-bodied recipients to participate in job-related activities in exchange for their
benefits. Building on the experience of the states, Congress in 1988 passed the
Family Support Act, which requires that all states have a Job Opportunity and
Basic Skills program (JOBS) for those on welfare.

Thus far, the effects of workfare experiments seem limited. As part of the
hard-line view discussed earlier, it has been assumed that many people go on
welfare simply to avoid work. If this is true, work requirements should help
reduce the number of people receiving various public assistance programs.
Several researchers, however, have contended that workfare programs have
not had much of an effect, if any at all, on the number of people who are on
welfare.[53] Workfare programs do not appear to discourage people from
seeking public assistance. While workfare may help get people off the rolls, it
is difficult to determine if the numbers involved are much different than they
would have been in the absence of such programs.

During the mid-1990s states showed an eagerness to experiment with
welfare reform and were given a green light by the federal government to
do so. States, following the lead of pace setters such as Wisconsin, placed
emphasis on work and responsibility, put time limits on assistance, and
placed caps on overall benefits. More revolutionary proposed changes in
the welfare system, however, were being considered in Washington; they
would put AFDC, Medicaid, and other federal welfare programs into a
large block grant that would be spent in the states largely as each state
government chose. Proponents, principally Republicans in Congress,
argue that states can run Medicaid and other programs more efficiently if
given more discretion. Others are not sure of this result and are fearful
about turning over to the states the responsibility for maintaining a social
safety net for citizens.

ENDNOTES

1. *Nation's Cities* (February 1970): 67.

2. See Sung-Don Hwang and Virginia Gray, "External Limits and Internal Determinants of State Public Policy," *Western Political Quarterly* 44 (June 1991): 277–298.

3. Charles E. Silberman, *Crisis in the Classroom: The Remaking of American Education* (New York: Random House, 1970).

4. See, for example: Mary Joe Bane and Christopher Jencks, "The Schools and Equal Opportunity," *Saturday Review* (16 September 1972): 37–42; and Christopher Jencks, *Inequality* (New York: Basic Books, 1972). See also: Robert J. Staaf and Gordon Tullock, "Education and Equality," *The Annals* 409 (September 1973): 125–134; and Joseph F. Stiglitz, "Education and Inequality," *The Annals* 409 (September 1973): 135–145.

5. Janice Penkalski and Linda Wagar, "School Reform under Scrutiny," *State Government News* (August 1988): 8–11.

6. James S. Coleman et al., *Equality of Educational Opportunity* (Washington, D.C.: Government Printing Office, 1966).

7. Kevin B. Smith and Kenneth J. Meier, "Politics, Bureaucrats, and Schools," *Public Administration Review* 54 (December 1994): 551–558. On the broader issues, see and compare: John E. Chubb and Terry M. Moe, *Politics, Markets, and Schools* (Washington, D.C.: The Brookings Institution, 1990); and Kevin B. Smith and Kenneth J. Meier, *The Case Against School Choice: Politics, Markets, and Fools* (Armonk, N.Y.: M.E. Sharpe, 1995).

8. See: Ann Page and Donald Clelland, "The Kanawha County Textbook Controversy," *Social Forces* 57 (December 1984): 265–281; and Matthew C. Moen, "School Prayer and the Politics of Life-Style Concern," *Social Science Quarterly* 65 (December 1984): 1065–1071.

9. See, generally: David R. Berman, "Takeovers of Local Governments: An Overview and Evaluation of State Policies," *Publius: The Journal of Federalism* 25 (Summer 1995): 55–70.

10. Harmon Zeigler and M. Kent Jennings, *Governing American Schools* (North Scituate, Mass.: Duxbury Press, 1974).

11. Ted P. Robinson, Robert E. England, and Kenneth J. Meier, "Black Resources and Black School Board Representation: Does Political Structure Matter?" *Social Science Quarterly* 66 (December 1985): 976–982.

12. Kenneth J. Meier and Robert E. England, "Black Representation and Educational Policy: Are They Related?" *American Political Science Review* 78 (1984): 392–403. See also: Kenneth J. Meier, Joseph Stewart Jr., and Robert E. England, "The Politics of Bureaucratic Discretion: Educational Access as an Urban Service," *American Journal of Political Science* 35 (February 1991): 155–177; Joseph Stewart Jr., Robert E. England, and Kenneth J. Meier, "Black Representation in Urban School Districts: From School Board to Office to Classroom," *Western Political Quarterly* 42 (June 1989): 287–305.

13. Statistics are from: *1992 Census of Governments, Popularly Elected Officials* (Washington, D.C.: Government Printing Office, June 1995).

14. Joseph M. Cronin, "A Typology of School Board Members," manuscript, Harvard

University, 1966. Cited in Robert Bendiner, *Politics of Schools* (New York: New American Library, 1969), pp. 24–25.

15. See: Frederick M. Wirt and Michael W. Kirst, *The Political Web of American Schools* (Boston: Little, Brown, 1972).

16. *Ibid.*, p. 76.

17. Delbert Taebel, "Politics of School Board Elections," *Urban Education* 12 (July 1977): 153–166.

18. James W. Button, "A Sign of Generational Conflict: The Impact of Florida's Aging Voters on Local School and Tax Referenda," *Social Science Quarterly* 73 (December 1992): 786–797.

19. Mario Fantini, Marilyn Gittle, and Richard Magat, *Community Control and the Urban School* (New York: Praeger Publishers, 1970), p. 74.

20. See: Bruce Bimber, *The Decentralization Mirage: Comparing Decisionmaking Arrangements in Four High Schools* (Santa Monica, Calif.: Rand Corporation, 1994).

21. 347 U.S. 483 (1954).

22. 349 U.S. 294 (1955).

23. See: *Civil Rights Digest* (December 1971): 5–10.

24. See: David O. Sears, Carl P. Hensler, and Leslie K. Speer, "Whites' Opposition to 'Busing': Self-Interest or Symbolic Politics?" *American Political Science Review* 73 (June 1979): 369–384; and John B. McConahay, "Self-Interest versus Racial Attitudes as Correlates of Anti-Busing Attitudes in Louisville: Is It the Buses or the Blacks?" *The Journal of Politics* 44 (1982): 620–720.

25. *Swann v. Charlotte-Mecklenberg Board of Education,* 402 U.S. 1 (1971).

26. On the argument that busing to integrate schools improves the education of blacks, see: United States Commission on Civil Rights, *Racial Isolation in the Public Schools,* 2 vols. (Washington, D.C.: Government Printing Office, 1967). For a contrary argument, see: David J. Armor, "The Evidence on Busing," *The Public Interest* (Summer 1973): 90–126.

27. See: Coleman et al., *Equality of Educational Opportunity;* and Christine H. Rossell, "School Desegregation and White Flight," *Political Science Quarterly* 90 (Winter 1975–1976): 675–695.

28. See, for example: Rossell, "School Desegregation and White Flight"; and United States Commission on Civil Rights, *Fulfilling the Letter and the Spirit of the Law—Desegregation of the Nation's Public Schools* (Washington, D.C.: Government Printing Office, 1976).

29. On school finance, see generally: John E. Coons, William H. Clune, and Stephen D. Sugarman, *Private Wealth and Public Education* (Cambridge: Harvard University Press, 1970); John Pincus, ed., *School Finance in Transition: The Courts and Educational Reform* (Cambridge: Ballinger, 1974); and Robert D. Reishauer and Robert W. Hartman, with the assistance of Daniel J. Sullivan, *Reforming School Finance* (Washington, D.C.: The Brookings Institution, 1973). See also: Rochelle L. Stanfield, "Why Johnny Can't—The Problem of State School Financing," *National Journal* (24 April 1976): 556–562.

30. In 1971–1972 state governments contributed about 38 percent of all revenues for public elementary and secondary schools. By 1986–1987 this had increased to nearly

50 percent. In actual dollars state governments were spending four times as much in 1986–1987 they were in 1971–1972. While total state expenditures have continued to grow, the state percentage has declined to about 46 percent as of the latest count for 1991–1992. See: United States Department of Education, Office of Educational Research and Improvement, *Digest of Educational Statistics 1994* (Washington, D.C.: Government Printing Office, 1994).

31. See: *Serrano* v. *Priest*, 5 Cal. 3d 584 (1971); and *San Antonio Independent School District* v. *Rodriguez*, 411 U.S. 1 (1973).

32. Coons, Clune, and Sugarman, *Private Wealth.*

33. Kenneth K. Wong, "Fiscal Support for Education in the American States: The Parity-to-Dominance View Examined," *American Journal of Education* 97 (August 1989): 329–357.

34. Official poverty statistics consider only the cash income of a family. When benefits such as food stamps, Medicare, and housing subsidies are included as income, the number of people living below the poverty line is considerably reduced.

35. United States Department of Commerce, Bureau of the Census, *Poverty in the United States: 1990* (Washington, D.C.: Government Printing Office, 1991), p. 1.

36. See: Marin Gilens, "Racial Attitudes and Opposition to Welfare," *The Journal of Politics* 57 (November 1995): 994–1014.

37. The original program, and one still used in many states, is Aid to Dependent Children.

38. The SSI program consolidated what had been three separate programs: Old Age Assistance, Aid to the Blind, and Aid to the Permanently and Totally Disabled.

39. Old Age Survivors and Disability Insurance (OASDI) is handled exclusively by the national government through the Social Security Administration. The Medicare program, also handled by the national government, provides medical insurance for people sixty-five years of age or older. Unemployment compensation is a joint national-state program with the states playing the major role. The system is financed by payroll taxes on certain employers, and the amount of benefits depends on state policies.

40. See: Robert B. Albritton and Robert D. Brown, "Intergovernmental Impacts on Policy Variations within States: Effects of Local Discretion on General Assistance Programs," *Policy Studies Review* 5 (February 1986): 529–535.

41. United States Department of Commerce, Bureau of the Census, *Poverty in the United States* (Washington, D.C.: Government Printing Office, 1991), p. 19.

42. See, for example: William B. Eimicke, "Professionalism and Participation: Compatible Means to Improved Social Services," *Public Administration Review* (July/August 1974): 409–414; and Clarence N. Stone, "Paternalism among Social Agency Employees," *The Journal of Politics* 39 (August 1977): 794–804.

43. See: Frances Fox Piven and Richard A. Cloward, *Regulating the Poor: The Functions of Public Welfare* (New York: Pantheon Books, 1971). See also: Mitchell B. Chamlin, "General Assistance among Cities," *Social Science Quarterly* 68 (December 1987): 834–846.

44. On the culture of poverty, see: Oscar Lewis, *Five Families* (New York: Basic Books, 1959) and *The Children of Sanchez* (New York: Random House, 1961); and Charles A. Valentine, *Culture and Poverty* (Chicago: University of Chicago Press, 1968).

45. Based on data from: United States Department of Health, Education and Welfare, *Welfare Myths v. Facts* (Washington, D.C.: Government Printing Office, 1995). See also: Mark Robert Rank, *Living on the Edge: The Realities of Welfare in America* (New York: Columbia University Press, 1994).

46. Sanford F. Schram and Gary Krueger, " 'Welfare Magnets' and Benefit Decline: Symbolic Problems and Substantive Consequences,"*Publius: The Journal of Federalism* 24 (Fall 1994): 61–82.

47. See: George S. Sternlieb and Bernard P. Inkid, *The Ecology of Welfare: Housing and the Welfare Crisis in New York City* (New York: Transaction Books, 1973).

48. Among the many programs established were: Community Action Programs (CAPs), which provided funds to local public and nonprofit Community Action Agencies (usually located outside the administrative structure of municipal governments) to undertake various projects like job training and Head Start (designed to improve the health and physical skills of disadvantaged children); Job Corps, which established residential centers to train youths in various job skills; Volunteers in Service to America (VISTA), a domestic Peace Corps through which volunteers worked in places like Indian reservations, mental hospitals, and urban slum areas; Neighborhood Youth Corps, for full- or part-time work experience; Work Study Programs, providing part-time employment for eligible college students on and off campus; and a Legal Services program. Responsibility for implementing these programs was shared by a number of federal agencies, including the Office of Economic Opportunity (OEO), created under the 1964 legislation. State and local governments, as well as private organizations and individuals, were brought into a number of these programs. Governors initially were given the right to veto projects (for example, CAP and Job Corps) within their states. Legislation in 1965, however, allowed the national OEO director to override these vetoes.

49. See: David M. Austin, "Resident Participation: Political Mobilization or Organizational Co-optation," *Public Administration Review* 32 (September 1972): 409–420.

50. See: John C. Donovan, *The Politics of Poverty* (Indianapolis: Bobbs-Merrill, 1973). For the theme that the War on Poverty was more effective than commonly assumed, see: Sar Levitan and Robert Taggart, *The Promise of Greatness* (Cambridge: Harvard University Press, 1976).

51. See: Mark R. Arnold, "The Good War That Might Have Been," *The New York Times Magazine* (29 September 1974). Reprinted in *Congressional Record* (4 December 1974): S20497–S20500.

52. See, generally: Piven and Cloward, *Regulating the Poor*. See also: Joyce Gelb and Alice Sardell, "Organizing the Poor: A Brief Analysis of the Politics of the Welfare Rights Movement," *Policy Studies Journal* 3 (Summer 1975): 346–354.

53. See: Leonard Goodwin, "Do Work Requirements Accomplish Anything?—The Case against Work Requirements," *Public Welfare* 16 (1978): 39–45; Mildred Rein, "Work in Welfare," *Social Science Review* 57 (1982): 212–232; and Charles Rodgers, "Work Tests for Welfare Recipients," *Journal of Policy Analysis and Management* 1 (1981): 5–17. For a review of this and other literature, and a more positive finding regarding workfare, see: Valerie Englander and Fred Englander, "Workfare in New Jersey: A Five-Year Assessment," *Policy Studies Review* 5 (August 1985): 33–41.

13

☆ ☆ ☆

POLITICS, POLLUTION, AND ENERGY

Many of the most intense and enduring conflicts in state and local politics have had to do with the development and use of natural resources. Political disputes over water, for example, have stemmed from its scarcity and the competing uses of it.[1] Water scarcity, especially in the western United States, has provoked many struggles among states and localities that see their prosperity dependent on expansion of their share of this resource. Rivers and lakes provide drinking water, recreation, electrical power, commercial transportation, irrigation, and a convenient place for industries and municipalities to dispose of waste materials. Different groups such as conservationists, outdoor sports people, farmers, and businesspeople have conflicting views on the ways rivers and lakes should be used. Of course, the absence of restrictions on dumping waste can effectively destroy the use of water for nearly any other purpose.

In recent years, governmental policies on the use of natural resources have been directed toward resolving problems made apparent in the environmental crisis that first gained public attention in the 1960s and in the energy crisis beginning in the mid-1970s. This chapter is concerned with these crises and, more specifically, with problems and policies relating to water, air, and land pollution and to the development, use, and price of energy resources.

THE POLITICS OF POLLUTION

THE COURSE OF REFORM

Until recent years, Americans have not been overly concerned with how they use their natural resources. Farmers, ranchers, and lumber workers depleted the land and, because there was plenty of it, moved on to new acreage with little or no regard for the land they left behind. The tendency of farmers to buy land and sell it when prices went up prompted one historian to note: "What developed in America was an agricultural society whose real attachment was not to the land but to land values."[2]

As with land, Americans have sacrificed the quality of air and water to support industrial and economic development. The environmental movement of the late 1960s and early 1970s, however, challenged these practices and produced several measures designed to protect and enhance the environment and agencies to implement them. Courts also became involved in the reform movement. State courts in much of the country, for example, applied and expanded on the *public trust doctrine,* that is, the common law doctrine that the government holds certain natural resources in trust for the benefit of the people, to support governmental intervention. Courts considered the most professional (those that best meet standards established by the American Bar Association in regard to merit selection, salary, tenure, and other matters) and courts in states with moralistic cultures have been the most likely to expand the public trust doctrine.[3]

The movement made some immediate gains in attacking long-standing problems such as sewage dumping practices that had contaminated bodies of water like Lake Erie. As the problems became more complex, progress on pollution control became more difficult to document. In the 1970s and early 1980s, moreover, the nation experienced economic difficulties, and pollution control was increasingly viewed by many as an impediment to economic recovery and growth. With the election of Ronald Reagan in 1980, environmentalists became convinced they faced an administration hostile to the nation's environmental laws.

This fear led to a recharging of the environmental movement. Environmental groups experienced considerable growth. In a very short time, one of the oldest of these, the Sierra Club, increased its membership from 181,000 to 300,000.[4] The environmental cause was also aided by several new issues such as acid rain (the transport of air pollutants over long distances), groundwater contamination, and a host of questions relating to hazardous materials. Events such as the death of nearly two thousand people in Bhopal, India, as a result of an accidental release of poison gas from a pesticide manufacturing plant, and the nuclear disaster in Chernobyl, USSR, added to the concern over the adequacy of environmental protection in this country.

From the early 1970s to the mid-1990s, the American public's sense of urgency over environmental deterioration and the need for immediate action declined considerably, in part because of the progress made. Since the 1970s, however, Americans have been highly supportive of the governmental activity intended to protect the environment. Survey data suggest, moreover, that when asked to choose between protection of the environment and economic growth, most Americans (better than 60 percent), favor environmental protection.[5]

Environmental protection appears to have general public support and particularly strong support among younger adults. Age differences over environmental protection appear to have less to do with the aging process than with generational differences. Thus, the fact that the young are unusually supportive of environmental measures is not simply because they are young (and presumably will change their minds over time) but because they have had a unique experience that makes them see environmental issues in a different way from older people. Environmental problems have been more central to those who have been socialized (educated) into the political system since the 1960s than to those who have lived longer and were initially socialized under different circumstances.[6]

Historically, the environmental movement has also been particularly attractive to the relatively well educated and relatively wealthy. The poor and nonwhite have been less attracted. The poor have cared less about clean beaches than the basics of life such as food, shelter, and clothing. They have found little to cheer about over changes that others contend could lead to higher prices and unemployment.[7] Similarly, there is some evidence that although environmental issues are of concern to black Americans, there is more of a tendency among blacks to see environmental issues as one set of issues needing attention, and not as important as other economic or social issues.[8]

In recent years, however, groups representing the poor and minorities have become alarmed over *environmental racism*. This refers to the fact that hazardous waste dumps and other environmental dangers, such as municipal incinerators and landfills, are far more likely to be found in the neighborhoods of poor blacks and Hispanics than elsewhere. Minorities suffer disproportionately from toxic contamination and have increasingly taken their complaints to environmental agencies.[9]

FEDERAL ACTIVITY

Up to the 1970s, most of the responsibility for pollution control rested with state and local governments. The efforts of the national government on air and water pollution consisted of helping state and local governments carry out their responsibilities. It provided research, technical aid, and money to state and local governments to improve their pollution control programs.

The environmental movement brought about major changes in the direction of federal policy. The Water Quality Act of 1965 required the states to establish water quality standards and plans for implementing these standards. The act gave the states and other affected jurisdictions the options of either setting up their own quality standards for their streams, rivers, lakes, and coastal waters or having the federal government do it for them. A major breakthrough in the area of air pollution was the Air Quality Act of 1967, which established air quality regions and required governors to set air quality standards and plans to implement the standards in their regions. The Clean Air Act Amendments of 1970 followed up on the 1967 legislation by authorizing the Environmental Protection Agency to establish national ambient air quality standards and requiring the states to carry out approved implementation plans in accordance with these standards.

The National Environmental Policy Act of 1969 committed the national government to the broad goals of improving and protecting the environment. The act created a three-person Council on Environmental Quality, appointed by the president, to prepare studies, advise the president, and work with other agencies on environmental problems. Another section of the act required that all proposed federal actions be accompanied by an environmental impact statement "to ensure that environmental considerations are given careful attention and appropriate weight in decision making." Impact statements continue to be part of the law. They are to be reviewed by other agencies having a claim to jurisdiction or special expertise and must be made available for public review. Impact statements have at times forced agencies to alter or abandon plans for highways, airports, and other projects.[10]

The national government over the years has assumed much of the responsibility for setting environmental protection policies. It has preempted some areas of pollution abatement, such as control of automobile exhaust emissions.[11] In other areas of environmental control, the national government shares authority with state and local governments. Under current court rulings, for example, even though Congress has passed legislation regulating pesticide use, states and localities can impose standards that exceed those adopted by the national government.

Historically, much of the environmental activity of the national government has taken the form of inducing state and local governments to reduce their own pollution and to crack down on the pollution of others. At one time, the federal government used grants to encourage state action. In more recent years, however, it has shifted the responsibility for financing various environmental programs to the states. This shift has placed a considerable burden on state and local governments. They have had to come up with revenues to comply with federal regulations on such matters as the safety of drinking water, wastewater treatment projects, underground storage tanks, and disposal of solid waste.

The major federal antipollution laws are administered by the Environmental Protection Agency (EPA), which was established in 1970. The EPA has multiple tasks in developing programs and standards regarding water and air quality, solid waste disposal, and noise, radiation, and pesticide control. The EPA not only regulates in cooperation with the states and local governments but also may take direct action to enforce antipollution laws. One enforcement tool of the EPA has been the Refuse Act of 1899, which outlaws waste discharges into navigable waters or their tributaries. Among the early actions taken by the EPA was the issuance of violation notices to thirty-two cities that were discharging sewage into Lake Erie.

One of the most well-publicized responsibilities of the EPA in recent years has been the implementation of laws relating to toxic wastes. Since 1980, the agency has administered a Superfund, derived in part from a tax on the producers of chemicals, to clean up hazardous waste dumps. Leading to the creation of the Superfund was a public outcry over chemical waste dumping in the Love Canal community of Niagara Falls, New York, which caused hundreds of people to abandon their homes. The EPA determines the most dangerous hazardous waste sites and can sue those responsible for the condition to reimburse the government for the cleanup. The EPA provides money for the cleanup in those situations where a responsible party cannot be found or is unable to pay for the damages. The agency has put some thirteen hundred of the worst waste sites on its Suprefund national priorities list. Twenty percent of those on the priority list are municipal landfills. State governments have their own Superfund programs, patterned after the federal model, for the contaminated sites not on the EPA's list. Altogether there are some seventy thousand suspected contaminated sites.[12]

When Congress extended the Superfund in 1986, it added a measure known as the community right-to-know-law, which requires local officials to notify people of what types of hazardous materials exist in the areas where they live and that plans be formulated by local officials to deal with emergencies involving hazardous substances such as a chemical spill or an explosion at a local refinery.

The EPA's most direct relationship with state and local officials has been in the implementation of pollution laws. National pollution laws have met with some state resistance in the name of states' rights and have generated lengthy negotiations between national and state officials on pollution standards. At times, state regulators have been far more willing than federal regulators to sacrifice air quality for what they see to be gains in employment and economic development. At other times, differences between the two have had to do with means rather than ends.[13]

In implementing national policy, the EPA has at times taken on the appearance of a paper tiger, unable to mobilize political and economic resources to implement its objectives in the states. For example, the agency frequently has had to back down in implementing the congressional requirement that states meet clean air standards for their regions. Because of state and local opposition, the EPA was forced to modify a proposal in 1973 that severe traffic control plans be adopted in thirteen metropolitan areas. The regulations would have imposed limits on gasoline sales and parking space and banned some vehicle use in downtown areas. After a loud protest from state and local officials, the EPA abandoned the proposals. More recently, similar protests from governors and other state and local officials forced the EPA to back away from proposals requiring stringent vehicle inspection and maintenance programs and the use of reformulated gasoline from ethanol or methanol.[14]

During the 1980s, some of the more serious intergovernmental problems in regard to environmental protection involved sewage treatment goals. Under the Clean Water Act of 1972, Congress mandated that municipalities had five years to meet federal secondary treatment guidelines for sewage, that is, to reach the point where 90 percent of all solid wastes were removed from the effluent. In 1977 Congress extended the deadline to 1983. In 1983 it reextended the deadline to 1988. Deadlines were extended, in part, because it was clear that most cities would have to build new treatment facilities or greatly expand existing facilities. Many municipalities put off building or expanding treatment facilities in the expectation of federal aid. This position seemed quite logical. As one observer noted: "A Mayor would get creamed if he ignored the fact that his city could get x million federal dollars if it just waited a couple years."[15] Court suits, however, resulted in rulings that compliance with the Clean Water Act requirements were unconditional and could not be postponed because of a lack of federal aid for treatment plants or for any other reason. Faced with these rulings, the EPA began to take enforcement action against some seventy municipalities from 1984 to 1988 to force compliance with the law. States and localities in various parts of the country have been compelled by federal law to come up with considerable amounts of revenue from their own sources to meet the federal environmental mandates for sewage treatment.[16]

Although one can point to EPA actions that appear to have been imposed on states and localities, this type of domination has not generally characterized the process. On the whole, the implementation of environmental policies has been a matter of bargaining between federal administrators and state and local officials, with the latter often able to tailor implementation of national programs to fit their own needs and desires. Some leeway in the application of the national laws stems from technical and informational problems in defining exactly the pollution problem in a given area of the country. More generally, the EPA must rely on the cooperation of state and local officials who may be unwilling or unable to cooperate. The EPA is ill equipped (in regard to money and staff) to do the job of pollution control activities for the states, even though in some programs it has the legal authority to do so.[17]

The EPA has had to adjust not only to demands of state and local officials but also to the conflicting demands of environmentalists for more controls and the demands of industry for fewer controls. The EPA's direction is also subject to changes in national administrations. Environmentalists were the dominant influence on the agency during its early years, but by the late 1970s and through the Reagan years in the 1980s, the agency became more attentive to the problems of those subject to pollution control standards.[18] Presidential and congressional action can greatly reduce the level and extent of environmental enforcement activity. On the other hand, such controls may do little to change the commitment of administrators to environmental goals. In the long run, moreover, such controls may mobilize supporters of environmental protection who generate pressure to restore active enforcement.[19]

STATE ACTIVITY

The national government has inspired much of the recent environmental activity on the state level. States, however, have often gone beyond federal standards and, particularly during the 1980s when the EPA was less aggressive, have filled in by developing their own standards on such problems as toxic air pollution and groundwater contamination.

Variations in state activity on environmental protection reflect several factors. Generally, wealthier and more liberal states with more professional legislatures tend to have the toughest environmental regulations. State regulations, moreover, do matter. States with the toughest regulations, for example, have had greater success in reducing the amount of air pollution. The connection between state regulation and water pollution, however, is less clear.[20]

Since the early 1970s, all states have had basic air and water pollution legislation. They have also formed monitoring systems to enforce air pollution regulations and have established systems for the inspection and testing of motor vehicles to ensure that national emission standards are met. State water control programs either impose minimum quality standards for all bodies of water within a state or classify certain waters for different uses and impose particular standards for these uses (for example, those classified for industrial uses may be more polluted than those classified for recreational uses).

Most air and water pollution programs are administered by a single state agency. Some of these agencies follow the model of the EPA while others combine the pollution control responsibilities with the older conservation programs. Several states have their own environmental impact statement requirements. In some states, the requirement applies only to projects proposed by state and/or local governments. Other states, such as California, Massachusetts, and Minnesota, also require statements on private projects having a potentially significant impact on the environment.

The states use several approaches to secure industry compliance with air and water pollution regulations.[21] Through publicity showing the seriousness of the pollution problem and through informal communications with polluters, they seek to secure voluntary compliance. These approaches may be effective if public pressure can be built up to the point where a polluting industry begins to worry about its public image. At the same time, an industry that voluntarily cuts down on pollution runs the risk of losing out in its competition with those that refuse to comply, because its production costs will increase. Industries, thus, often have little economic incentive to comply voluntarily with environmental regulations.

States have strengthened the prospect of compliance through direct regulatory devices (fees and permits) and more positive means such as tax incentives. Some require permits for industrial discharges into the air or water. Fees for permits are presumably set high enough to induce polluters to install pollution abatement equipment. Otherwise permits become little more than licenses to pollute. Tax benefits offered by the states include exemption of pollution control facilities from property taxation or from sales taxes and credits on income taxes for antipollution expenditures.

A movement toward a softer, less combative, approach has been recently evident in regard to state superfund or hazardous waste laws. Rather than rely on coercion, states have initiated voluntary cleanup programs. Under these programs owners of a contaminated site and those interested in redeveloping the property cooperate in making cleanups in exchange for some type of protection against liability.[22]

Several states have also adopted environmental self-audit laws that encourage businesses to monitor their operations more closely for adverse environmental effects by allowing them to keep such audits confidential and exempting the companies from fines and penalties if audits reveal a violation of the law. Supporters argue that companies are likely to do a better job of detecting and correcting environmental problems if shielded from adverse publicity and penalties. Opponents call such legislation "polluter protection acts." Opponents contend that the people in the community have the right to know about pollution problems affecting them and that companies will not correct environmental problems unless forced to do so by law and threats of fines and penalties. At the heart of such disputes are differences over the proper and most effective relationship between regulators and the regulated, cooperative or adversarial.

Critics have faulted the states in general for showing little desire to crack down on industrial polluters. One of the most difficult problems has been the political opposition of large industries that are important to the state's economy and, by virtue of their importance, are politically able to defend their interests. State officials fear that stringent enforcement of antipollution regulations could force companies to close down or move. Indeed, while some state agencies are fighting industrial pollution, others are actively recruiting industry from states with more stringent pollution laws.

Politically, each proposal to protect the environment creates its own particular pattern of opposition. A few years ago, for example, a proposal in the Arizona legislature designed to protect wilderness areas by making it unlawful to drive off established roadways or to travel on abandoned roads or trails was scuttled through the combined efforts of prospectors (some with large companies), hunters, people who like to fish, picnickers, four-wheel-drive enthusiasts, and rockhounds.

Legislation such as that first adopted in Oregon in 1972 that attempts to end the use of throwaway bottles by requiring a deposit can be expected to engender opposition from the container and bottling industry, which sees economic hardships and unemployment; from soft drink and beer manufacturers, who fear a loss of sales; from retailers, who face new costs of handling, refunding, sorting, and storing returnable bottles; from vendors, who must convert their machines to handle returnable bottles; and from recycling industries, which, as one might expect, would rather have bottles and cans returned to them than to retailers. Opponents of bottle bill initiatives have spent considerable funds to oppose such measures. In 1982, for example, Coca-Cola and Pepsi-Cola joined brewers, grocery store chains, and manufacturers of bottles and cans and spent some $5 million to $7 million to defeat such a measure in California.[23]

Even though the opposition to this type of reform has been considerable, ten states have passed laws placing a deposit on beverage cans or bottles, which is refunded when turned in for reuse or recycling. Deposit laws do not appear to be having the anticipated adverse industrial consequences and, moreover, have had a considerable positive impact in reducing litter in parks and along roadways. Some analysts cite the success of such laws as an example of the effectiveness of a *market-based* or *pocketbook* incentive approach to environmental problems.

LOCAL GOVERNMENT ACTIVITY

The extent of local governmental involvement in antipollution efforts has depended largely on permissive state legislation and on the financial and technical assistance of national and state governments. Cities and counties, however, have taken much action on their own. Many large cities, for example, have air and water pollution abatement ordinances and industrial waste ordinances. Some of the effluent standards, such as those in New York City, are more stringent than those of the state or national government. Local ordinances have also banned open burning and the use of phosphate detergents and nonreturnable bottles. Some large cities have air pollution emergency plans to warn citizens of dangerously high levels of pollution so they can take precautionary measures. Several local agencies have also been established to implement environmental programs. Altogether there are several

---

BOX 13–1 THE FLOW CONTROL PROBLEM

Local governments have invested a considerable amount of money in waste management facilities such as landfills, waste incinerators, and recycling and composting facilities. To ensure that these facilities will generate enough revenues to pay for themselves, localities have sometimes passed "flow control" laws requiring that wastes be turned over to designated facilities. Private waste companies, however, have challenged the legality of such laws. The United States Supreme Court sided with the private waste companies in a 1993 ruling (*Carbone Inc.* v. *Town of Clarkstown*) by finding that solid waste flow control was economic protectionism and violated the commerce clause of the United States Constitution.

---

hundred city-county or joint local air pollution agencies. Joint local programs, even multicounty ones, have become increasingly popular.

Much responsibility in the area of waste disposal continues to rest with local governments. Local officials have given considerable attention in recent years to the disposal of solid wastes (for example, metal, paper, wood) collected from homes and businesses as refuse. Historically local officials have disposed of solid wastes by burning, dumping into a body of water, or burying in landfill sites. Burning and dumping have only added to pollution and health problems. Local governments have also found it increasingly difficult to find landfill sites for burying trash. In trying to locate a landfill, local officials often encounter the NIMBY syndrome discussed earlier. Local officials apparently have found that "everybody wants you to pick up their garbage, but no one wants you to put it down."[24] In recent years the landfill situation has worsened because many have been forced to close because they cannot meet stringent and costly state and federal environmental standards.

In some places, localities have adapted to the problem of scarcity in landfill space by burning solid wastes to generate electricity. This helps to both reduce the volume of solid wastes and provide a needed product. Incinerators, however, present difficult problems regarding toxic air pollution and ash residue. Politically, they often provoke considerable controversy over their location. The facilities also may be so expensive to construct and operate that the energy produced may not be cost competitive.

Faced with these difficulties, many communities have given attention to the recovery of solid wastes for reuse (see box 13–1). Indeed, localities in several states have been forced into establishing such programs by state recycling laws. These laws generally require the formulation of local waste management plans, local source separation and recycling programs, and that localities together meet specific statewide reductions in solid waste, for example, from 25 to 50 percent over a period of five to ten years. Some states mandate citizen participation in recycling programs. Many of the states to act early were those faced with severe landfill capacity storages. Older recycling programs in states such as Rhode Island, New Jersey, and Oregon have been effective in recovering from 14 to 24 percent of the waste stream.

Localities have generally discovered that achievement of solid waste reduction goals requires supportive action on the state level. This includes providing technical assistance to localities putting together recycling programs and, perhaps more important, help in developing markets for recycled materials. Several states have been active in helping to market recycled materials, especially paper. Most states, for example, have laws expressing a preference for buying products made with recycled materials. A few states also provide tax credits for the use of recycled paper. To help create a market for recycled paper, some states have required newspapers to increase their use of this material.

Finally, one of the more spectacular local environmental problems in recent years has been that of the purity of local water supply systems. In the early 1900s, many communities put chlorine into their water supply systems as an antibacterial agent to combat typhoid, cholera, dysentery, and similar diseases. The systems appeared to be effective until the 1950s, when the rate of waterborne disease outbreaks began to increase. During the 1960s, there were some 128 reported outbreaks of illness due to drinking water, which killed some 20 people and injured more than 46,000.[25] Observers placed much of the blame on primitive, deteriorating water systems, particularly in small communities where there was the additional problem of inadequately trained personnel. Local officials and citizens, it was suggested, had become complacent about their water systems. Added to this was the steady increase in discharge of industrial waste into drinking supplies. Existing systems had been effective in dealing with bacterial substances, but they were ineffective in protecting against modern forms of pollution.

· By the early 1970s, several studies of the problem had been undertaken. A national survey by the United States Public Health Service in 1969 indicated that 36 percent of the tap water samples they studied did not meet standards (thought to be relatively low) set by the federal government for water served aboard interstate carriers. In 1973, a study of 446 water systems in six states conducted by the General Accounting Office for Congress disclosed that only 60 of these systems produced water that met federal standards. The report did not name the systems, an omission defended on the grounds that water system operators were promised confidentiality in return for their cooperation in the study and that the information could cause a public panic. One observer noted cynically, however, that "publicizing the information would embarrass public officials and cause the loss of valuable tourist trade in some areas."[26] Perhaps for similar reasons, New Orleans officials angrily denounced the findings of an EPA study in 1974 that chemicals in the city's drinking water might be carcinogenic and possibly linked to the fact that the city's cancer death rate is 25 percent above the national average.

The report on New Orleans and other cities spurred Congress into adopting the Safe Drinking Water Act of 1974. This legislation, which had been before Congress since 1970, gives the EPA authority to set minimum standards for all forty thousand water systems in the country. Enforcement is left to state and local governments, although the EPA is authorized to step in and establish the standards if state and local officials fail. In the early 1980s, a report by the General Accounting Office, an investigative arm of Congress, concluded that at least fourteen thousand community water systems had not yet met federal water quality standards and would not be able to do so without a great improvement in their facilities. Small communities had the most pronounced problems; many had suffered an increase in waterborne diseases. Data gathered by the EPA in the mid-1980s, moreover, suggested that from 1 to 2 percent of the water drawn from public and private wells is contaminated with toxic materials. Contaminated groundwater has resulted from the use of pesticides, chemical waste dumps, and the seepage of wastewater and solid waste disposal systems. When the Safe Drinking Water Act was reauthorized in 1986, Congress directed the EPA to control a long list of additional contaminants. State and local officials have since objected to expensive water testing requirements, many of which they feel are not necessary.

PROBLEMS AND PROGRESS

As indicated earlier, public support for environmental protection has generally been strong. Support, however, does vary somewhat from time to time. For example, the inclination of Americans to approve of governmental spending on environmental controls tends to vary somewhat with the condition of the economy, being highest when economic conditions are good and lowest when economic conditions are poor. In periods of economic decline there is a tendency to turn from environmental concerns to matters of more immediate economic well-being such as employment. To some extent, public support for more spending on environmental programs is also influenced by the amount of coverage the media give to environmental problems—the more coverage given, the more support there is for environmental spending.[27]

Even in the best of economic times and during the most intense media campaign one finds certain barriers to environmental reform. One is hard put to find people who are willing to champion water or air pollution or other types of environmental deterioration. Leaders of industries directly affected by proposed regulations, however, are likely to contend that the seriousness of various pollution problems has been overemphasized or exaggerated and that blind panic in cleaning up the environment could have adverse effects on the economy, throwing thousands of people out of work. To some extent, at least, industries have been able to draw on their status and economic importance as an employer in a given community to prevent "dirty air" from becoming or going very far as a political issue. Industry resistance to pollution control has been greatest in the areas of the country where pollution has been greatest and where it has appeared that the cleanup would cost the industry the most.[28]

At any given time, the American people, in general, appear to be committed to environmental controls, but perhaps only up to the point at which they result in higher taxes or prices and seriously interfere with their lifestyles.[29] Another barrier to effective environmental action has been the refusal of many to take the possibility of environmental catastrophe seriously. In part, this may reflect faith in the ability of technology to correct environmental abuses and to find means to support continual economic growth.

On a more technical level, environmentalists have had difficulty in deciding on pollution control standards and in backing up their case with specific proofs that a health issue is involved. More must be learned about the precise relationship between air and water quality and public health problems. Often, health problems that are related to pollution or to the use of pesticides take years to become apparent. In the meantime, court cases may be lost because those who argue that dumping, burning, or other polluting practices be halted have been unable to show a cause-and-effect relationship between the pollutant and a specific health problem.

Despite these obstacles, environmentalists have achieved some major accomplishments in recent years. Since the 1970s, reports of the President's Council on Environmental Quality have noted that considerable progress has been made in regard to cleaner air, although the situation continues to vary among metropolitan areas, and that the line has been held on water pollution (see box 13–2). This has occurred, federal reports indicate, with only a minimal impact on the nation's economic growth, unemployment, and inflation.[30]

THE POLITICS OF ENERGY

OIL, COAL, AND NUCLEAR POWER

Historically, many of the most important decisions on the development, use, and price of energy have been made at the state level. The politics of oil in the states, for example, originally took the form of efforts by those in the industry to seek governmental protection against the effects of competition. During the early 1900s, competition in the oil industry led to the drilling of many wells to obtain the greatest amount of oil in the shortest possible time. Under the *law of capture,* drillers could take all the oil they could get from their wells, even if the effect of their drilling was to drain a pool of oil from beneath someone else's property. The competitive effort to "get there first" led to rapid

---

BOX 13–2 ENVIRONMENTAL PROGRESS AND PROBLEMS

"The environmental protection scheme of the United States is 25 years old, relatively new compared to other systems. In those 25 years, EPA came into existence, the federal and state governments passed environmental legislation, and many local governments created environmental protection programs. We have created an infrastructure of programs, laws, and agencies to protect the air, land, and water resources.

"There have been many significant accomplishments. We no longer have rivers that catch on fire. The skies are cleaner. There still are problems, however. For example, one out of five Americans lives in a city where air quality does not meet federal air quality standards. Twenty-five years after passage of the Clean Water Act, 40 percent of our rivers, lakes, and streams are not suitable for fishing and swimming. Despite the progress in dealing with industrial-type discharge into our waters, solving some problems unmasked more. Fourteen years after Superfund, one out of four Americans lives within four miles of a toxic dump."

Source: Carol M. Browner, EPA administrator, "Protecting the Environment: A New Generation," *Intergovernmental Perspective* (Summer–Fall 1994): 11.

---

depletion of the oil pools, an overproduction of oil with resulting low prices, and much waste and inefficiency.

In the early twentieth century, state governments, prompted by the oil companies, came to the aid of the industry. State agencies were authorized to limit oil production by "conservation" measures that placed quotas on the production of each well in the state on the basis of market conditions. State agencies, such as the Texas Railroad Commission, have restricted production of oil wells in their state to maintain high prices. Before the formation of the Organization of Petroleum Exporting Countries (OPEC), state agencies, with the help of federal import quotas against foreign oil, largely controlled the price of crude oil in this country, keeping it above the world price.

Along with influencing the development and price of domestic oil, state governments have performed numerous regulatory duties concerning coal mining, the use of nuclear power, and the price consumers pay for electricity. Much of the controversy concerning coal has had to do with strip mining. This method has been found to be less costly to producers than deep mining. Although strip mining requires fewer workers than deep mining, it has been favored by unions because it is safer than deep mining and results in higher pay for miners. On the other hand, environmentalists and others have been appalled by the devastation of the land caused by strip mining and have linked the practice to soil erosion, stream pollution, destruction of farmland,

and dangers to wildlife. Effective state regulation has been particularly difficult in areas such as West Virginia and Kentucky, where mining is a major industry and therefore a major source of employment and tax revenue.[31] Although there has been considerable effort to strengthen regulation in recent years (including the adoption of federal legislation), critics contend that these efforts are "too little, too late." One observer, for example, concluded that land "restoration has been largely a fiction or a failure; two of every three acres touched by stripping remain almost totally abandoned."[32]

Conflict within the states over the use of nuclear power has taken place between conservation and environmental action groups on one side and utilities on the other. Since the late 1970s, the "No-Nuke Movement" has taken the form of mass protest and civil disobedience somewhat comparable to the civil rights and antiwar movements of the 1960s. The pronuclear position of the utilities has been supported by large industrial concerns, banks, construction firms, and unions, all of which desire continued economic growth and consider nuclear power to be the chief means of creating the cheap and abundant energy necessary for a continued high standard of living. Many, but not all, scientists and engineers associated with the nuclear energy industry have supported increased use of nuclear power and have claimed that the safety risks of using this source are minimal.

During the 1970s, however, the safety of the some seventy plants in operation was brought into question by a string of accidents, the most dramatic of which produced a leak of radioactive steam from the Three Mile Island power plant near Harrisburg, Pennsylvania, in 1979. A presidential commission looking into this accident concluded that fundamental changes were needed to keep the risks associated with nuclear power within tolerable limits. Particularly noted by the commission were the needs for stronger federal, state, and local safety standards; improvement in the training and supervision of plant operators; and the preparation of plans to deal with emergencies. Governments have made many of these reforms.

Currently, there are 109 commercial nuclear power reactors licensed to operate in thirty-two states. Combined, they produce about 20 percent of the total electric energy generated by utilities. Most of these are found in the eastern part of the country. The number of planned units has been on the decline since the early 1970s. In some cases, states have effectively vetoed licensing for nuclear plants by refusing to cooperate in the development of emergency evacuation plans, which are required under federal law.[33]

Behind much of the concern over nuclear power is the safety issue. Studies suggest that the odds are great against a "class nine accident" or a major calamity such as a nuclear core meltdown, which would spread radioactive gases and kill thousands of people over a period of years. Opponents of nuclear power contend, however, that the benefits derived from this source are not worth the price that might have to be paid in the event of a serious accident. Opponents have also been concerned over the possible long-term effects of exposure to low levels of radiation (many possible consequences of exposure, such as cancer, may not be apparent for a number of years), the hazards of uranium mining, and the transport and disposal of radioactive materials. Questions concerning the disposal of radioactive wastes were not given much attention until recently because it was assumed that a technological "fix" would surface before the problems became serious. As the nation entered the 1980s, the environmental movement and a series of failures in the management of wastes led many to question the assumption that technology could be depended on to find solutions. More and more state and local officials also became skeptical about the ability of the federal government to control radioactive wastes.[34]

Since the late 1970s, problems associated with nuclear waste have prompted state and local governments to take several courses of action. Following the accident at the Three Mile Island power plant, some states placed a ban on the construction of new nuclear plants. In 1983, the United States Supreme Court held that the states may take such action until the federal government develops a safe method for the disposal of high-level radioactive wastes. About the same time, some cities banned transport of nuclear materials within their boundaries.

There is considerable debate concerning the extent to which state and local governments may regulate or prohibit the transportation, storage, and/or disposal of nuclear waste. Jurisdiction over some of these matters appears to have been preempted by the national government, leaving no room for state and local activity. At the same time, however, federal officials have been forced by political and practical realities to accommodate state and local officials on such matters. The Department of Energy during the early 1980s, for example, was following an internal policy allowing states to veto the creation of waste disposal sites within their boundaries.

Many of the continuing political struggles, often occurring on the intergovernmental level, have had to do with the disposal of nuclear wastes. Policymakers, for example, have given considerable attention to highly radioactive nuclear wastes, such as used fuel, that take thousands of years to reach safe levels. Congress, in the Nuclear Waste Policy Act of 1992, required that fuel from nuclear energy plants must be stored in deep geographical cavities or chambers. The Department of Energy has long favored designating Yucca Mountain, Nevada, a volcanic rock area, as a storage area for high-level nuclear wastes. The governor and legislature of Nevada have opposed this recommendation, contending that the site is a dangerous place to dump wastes (see box 13–3).

Disposal of low-level radioactive waste (LLW), a task historically handled by the states, has also caused some intergovernmental problems.[35] These

---

BOX 13–3   BECOMING A NUCLEAR WASTE DUMPING GROUND

"So little effort is required to figure out why Yucca Mountain—only one hundred miles northwest of Las Vegas—has been unfairly singled out as America's nuclear waste dumping ground. Nevada only has two U.S. representatives, and, in the minds of some federal officials, the state is far enough away from Washington, and isolated enough, that political reverberations would be comparatively minor."

Source: Governor Bob Miller, quoted in "Should the States Be Forced to Accept Nuclear Waste?" *State Government News* (January 1990): 16–17, at 17.

---

wastes include items like contaminated tools and equipment, which are much less toxic than high-level wastes. But it could still take several decades for them to deteriorate to safe levels of radioactivity. Concern over the problem of disposal of LLWs in the late 1970s caused the governors of the only states with commercial waste dumps (Washington, Nevada, South Carolina) to consider closing their facilities, at least temporarily, until safety problems could be corrected. Pressure from the three governors, who made it clear their states would no longer be the nation's nuclear waste garbage dumps, and a heavy lobbying effort from the nuclear industry produced federal legislation in 1980 requiring all states either to go it alone in constructing dumps for low-level radioactive waste or form interstate compacts for this purpose. Congress gave the states until 1 January 1993 to come up with a solution. Public opposition to the construction of waste sites—another manifestation of the NIMBY syndrome—made it difficult for some states to comply with the federal mandate. Because of this and a lengthy licensing process, only a few states met the deadline.

UTILITY REGULATION

In addition to decisions regarding the development and use of various energy resources, state governments exercise regulatory authority over privately owned companies providing electricity. State regulation of electric companies developed out of the Progressive movement in the early decades of the twentieth century. Contrary to a view once commonly held by historians, these regulations were not adopted over the strenuous objections of the industry. Indeed, state regulation was supported by leaders in the electric power industry because: (1) it was preferable to the major and, at the time, highly popular alternative of municipal ownership of electric utilities; and (2) it would allow the industry to reduce the risks inherent in a competitive market and thus enable it to borrow capital at lower rates. Progressive reformers felt that because of the corruption found on the local level (see discussion of political machines), regulation would have a much better chance if entrusted to state officials.[36]

Currently, regulation of the rates, services, and business transactions of privately owned power systems is done by public service commissions—which may also be known by other names such as utility or corporation commissions. These agencies, the heads of which (usually called commissioners) are elected in some states and appointed in others, also have jurisdiction over telephone, water, railroad, and other "public utilities" operating within their states.[37] The interstate aspects of these enterprises fall under the jurisdiction of federal agencies.

Until the 1970s, the activities of public utility commissions in setting electric rates were largely routine and of little concern except to the engineers, lawyers, and accountants directly involved. The lack of controversy resulted from the status of electric utilities as growth industries, which supplied more and more electricity at stable or even reduced rates because of economies of scale. As the nation entered the 1970s, however, this best of all possible worlds began to crumble as general inflation and dramatic hikes in fuel prices led the industry to demand greater rate increases. At the same time, utility commissions began to hear demands from consumer groups for lower rates and from environmental groups for more energy conservation. The federal government also took a new interest in state utility proceedings through the passage of the Public Utility Regulatory Policies Act of 1978, which, among other things, encourages state commissions to help conserve energy, make more efficient use of energy resources and facilities, and ensure that rates are equitable.[38]

Public service commissions have traditionally looked at three basic factors in determining the rates that electric power companies may charge their consumers: (1) the rate base, (2) the rate of return, and (3) operating expenses. The most difficult of these to determine is the rate base. The rate base is the monetary value of the physical plant, equipment, and other items on which the utility earns a rate of return. Some utility commissions establish the value of the rate base on the original cost of the property minus depreciation. Others have used the "fair value" or reproduction method, which involves finding the cost of reproducing the property at present prices. States also differ as to which items in addition to plant and equipment are to be included in the rate base. Some, for example, include utility property under construction but not yet placed in service and property held for future use; others do not include these items. Regardless of the method of determining the value of the rate base and the types of items to be included in it, state utility commissions—often poorly staffed and financed—generally have had difficulty in checking the data supplied to them by the utilities regarding the amount of their investment. Critics have long contended that companies often inflate the value of their rate base by making unnecessary investments.

The rate of return is set with the intent of giving investors a "fair return" on their investment and one that will help in attracting the capital (private investment) necessary for financing growth. Rates of return are generally set somewhat low on the theory that a protected monopoly runs less of a risk of loss than does an unregulated competitive industry. Operating expenses include salaries, taxes, fuel costs, and other routine costs of doing business including, in some states, the cost of advertising and donations to charity. Since the energy crisis of the early 1970s, state commissions have generally allowed the utilities automatically to pass on tax and fuel cost increases to the consumer. The amount of money that has to be collected in rates to consumers is determined by multiplying the rate base by the rate of return and then by adding the operating expenditures.

The efforts of regulated utilities to secure rate increases have been made more difficult in recent years because several other parties have become involved in rate-making hearings. More than twenty states now have agencies that regularly represent the interests of utility consumers in rate cases. Private consumer groups and officials from the federal Department of Energy have also intervened in rate hearings. Nevertheless, electricity rates have been increasing faster than the overall cost of living since the mid-1970s. Utilities argue that higher rates are needed because of increased fuel costs; increased taxes; higher costs of borrowing money; and greater expenditures for wages, construction, and the purchase of antipollution equipment. Although often successful in securing rate increases, utilities complain that, because of *regulatory lag* (the time it takes for a commission to act on a rate increase request), rates have not kept up with their costs. The amount of lag ranges from a month to a year.

Pressure from consumer and environmental groups and federal legislation has prompted several states to revise their electricity rate structures to discourage the demand for energy. Many states have had rate structures under which large industrial users of electricity pay lower rates per kilowatt-hour than do residential consumers. The effect of this has been to encourage high levels of electricity use and the building of new power plants. Under a "lifeline rate" structure, now used in about a dozen states, the structure has been turned around both to relieve the burden on residential consumers and to discourage heavy use. Several states have also adopted time-of-day rate systems, which encourage consumers to use energy during "off peak" hours (nighttimes or weekends). Changing consumer habits so consumers use electricity more evenly is intended to reduce the maximum demand on utilities and thus the need for costly new plants.

ENERGY SHORTAGES AND DEVELOPMENT

The reaction of state and local governments to the energy crisis of the late 1970s has taken several forms (see box 13–4). Several new agencies have been created to: (1) gather data on the energy resources and needs of particular states, (2) make recommendations on energy development and conservation, and (3) plan for energy emergencies caused by fuel shortages. Some states have followed the federal lead by creating a department of energy to handle these and related tasks; others have energy offices within commerce or natural resources commissions. On the legislative level, several states have offered tax credits to encourage the development and use of solar and other renewable sources of energy. To further the goal of conservation, several states and localities have encouraged car pooling, thermostat cutbacks (especially in public buildings), the construction of more energy-efficient buildings (a goal pursued through building codes and energy audits designed to improve insulation), greater use of mass transportation, and more energy-efficient land-use practices (for example, those leading to higher density housing).[39]

Much of the energy-related activity on the state and local levels has been prompted by federal policy initiatives. Many of the federal programs are administered by the Department of Energy, created in 1977. Broadly, federal energy policies have centered on (1) encouraging greater energy conservation and (2) increasing the domestic supply of energy. While conservation has been encouraged by a number of measures, federal officials have relied greatly on the workings of the price system to achieve this goal (that is, the assumption that people will use less energy as the price of gasoline or electricity increases). Large price increases for these products, however, have thus far not greatly abetted the cause of conservation. The chief barrier appears to be that the demand for energy is linked to lifestyles people find difficult to change. Regarding development, there has been considerable controversy over which particular energy resource should be encouraged. Coal and nuclear power have been considered the principal immediate alternatives to oil and natural gas, but, as noted above, objections have been made as well to these alternatives. In the early 1980s, the federal government was encouraging utilities to increase their use of coal.

Congressional action since the mid-1970s has provided federal aid to help states develop conservation programs. The national government has also become far more involved in public utility regulation, although, thus far, it has only "requested" that states consider energy conservation in making rate structures. Perhaps more significant to states and localities have been federal policies intended to increase the domestic supply of energy. Among the steps taken by the national government in recent years to develop energy sources have been the decision to proceed with the construction of the Alaska pipeline, acceleration in the leasing of nationally owned oil and gas rights in the outer

---

BOX 13–4 SAVING ENERGY: AN UNINTENDED CONSEQUENCE

Energy-related reform often brings some unintended negative consequences. Several years ago, for example, local officials found that millions of gallons of gasoline could be saved each year by allowing cars to turn right on a red light, thus reducing idling at stoplights. The problem was that turning right also increased dramatically the number of pedestrian injuries, as right-turning cars collided with people trying to cross the street.

---

continental shelf, an increase in the leasing or mining or coal resources in public lands, and promotion of the development of new energy sources, such as solar energy.

The energy growth policies have had or are likely to have numerous economic, social, and political impacts in the various states. The decision on the Alaska pipeline, for example, has led to a boom in the state's population and economy, but it has also meant increased inflation and social problems. Community growth, leading to "boom towns," with increased demands on local services and quality-of-life problems, is also likely in areas where leases are given for offshore drilling and the development of coal resources. The question of where new power facilities (power plants, refineries, and pipelines) are to be located is apt to raise conflict and difficult problems in land-use planning and control.

The energy shortage of the 1970s had its most pronounced effect in the energy-poor northeastern states, which long depended on the importation of petroleum. Because imported oil became more expensive and its supply undependable, these states became more reliant on energy produced in other states, for example, Texas, Louisiana, and states in the Plains and Rocky Mountain areas. This increased dependence, in turn, spawned sectional conflicts over the distribution and price of the energy. Conflicts among energy-rich and energy-poor states were particularly noticeable in Congress in the 1970s during the debates over deregulation of natural gas. Members of Congress from gas-producing states worked for deregulation and thus for higher prices for this product. Those efforts were opposed by representatives from states where natural gas was greatly depended on as a source of energy. As a compromise measure, Congress decided to let the price of natural gas increase by 10 percent a year until 1985, when the controls would be lifted.

Generally, conditions were good for the energy-rich states during the 1970s and early 1980s. In the mid-1980s, however, oil became plentiful because the OPEC nations could not agree on production limits. This produced cheaper energy costs in the United States, but energy-producing states like Texas suffered from a decline in prices for the products.

A broader regional issue that has been raised by the energy crisis is whether or not the environment and quality of life in some areas of the country should be sacrificed to produce energy for other areas. Concerns of this nature have been expressed by governors in coal-rich states like New Mexico, Montana, North Dakota, and Wyoming, who have seen severe costs in becoming the "boiler rooms" of the nation. The same problem has been evident since the mid-1960s in the debate over the construction of coal-burning power plants in the remote areas of the Southwest to produce electricity for the use of heavily populated areas, especially southern California. Opponents of the plants have condemned them for bringing air pollution, threatening an already scarce water supply (much water must be diverted for plant cooling), causing land degradation through strip mining, and destroying sacred ancestral Indian land along with national parks and recreational areas.

ENDNOTES

1. See: Frank E. Moss, *The Water Crisis* (New York: Praeger, 1967); and Norris Hundley Jr., *Water and the West* (Berkeley: University of California Press, 1975).
2. Richard Hofstadter, *The Age of Reform* (New York: Random House/Vintage Books, 1955), p. 41.
3. See: James J. Lawler, "Expansion of the Public Trust Doctrine in Environmental Law: An Examination of Judicial Policy Making by State Courts," *Social Science Quarterly* 70 (March 1989): 134–148.
4. "Environmental Activists Taking a New Tack," *National Journal* (3 August 1985): 1808. For an update on the activities of environmental groups, see: Tom Arrandale, "The Mid-Life Crisis of the Environmental Lobby," *Governing* (April 1992): 32–36.
5. David W. Moore, "Public Sense of Urgency about Environment Wanes," *The Gallup Poll Monthly* (April 1995): 17.
6. See: Paul Mohai and Ben W. Twight, "Age and Environmentalism: An Elaboration of the Buttel Model Using National Survey Evidence," *Social Science Quarterly* 68 (December 1987): 296–315. See also: Frederick H. Buttel and William L. Flinn, "Social Class and Mass Environmental Beliefs: A Reconsideration," *Environment and Behavior* 10 (September 1978): 433–450.
7. See: Peter Schrag, "Who Owns the Environment?" *Saturday Review* (4 July 1970): 6–9, 48.
8. Robert Emmet Jones and Lewis F. Carter, "Concern for the Environment among Black Americans: An Assessment of Common Assumptions," *Social Science Quarterly* 75 (September 1994): 560–579.
9. See, for example: D.R. Wernette and L.A. Nieves, "Breathing Polluted," *EPA Journal* (March/April 1992): 16–17.
10. On background see, generally: Lynton K. Caldwell, *Man and His Environment: Policy and Administration* (New York: Harper & Row, 1975), ch. 4.
11. Somewhat unfairly, the ability of states and localities to reach the clean air goals

required by federal law depends, in no small part, on the existence of strong federal emission standards for new cars.

12. Sean Cavanagh, "Brownfields Dilemma," *State Legislatures* (September 1995): 30–32.

13. See: William T. Gormley Jr., "Intergovernmental Conflict on Environmental Policy: The Attitudinal Connection," *Western Political Quarterly* 40 (June 1987): 285–303.

14. "State Resistance Worries EPA," *State Legislatures* (March 1995): 1.

15. Robert Gurwitt, "The Tap Has Run Dry on EPA Extensions to the Clean Water Act," *Governing* (January 1988): 15–19, quote at 18.

16. *Ibid.*

17. See: Robert D. Thomas, "Intergovernmental Coordination in the Implementation of National Air and Water Pollution Policies," in Charles O. Jones and Robert D. Thomas, eds., *Public Policy-Making in a Federal System* (Beverly Hills, Calif.: Sage Publications, 1976): 129–148. On the nature of the conflict that has and might be expected to occur between federal and state administrators on environmental policy, see: William T. Gormley Jr., "Intergovernmental Conflict on Environmental Policy."

18. Alfred Marcus, "Environmental Protection Agency," in James Q. Wilson, ed., *The Politics of Regulation* (New York: Basic Books, 1980), pp. 267–303.

19. Evan J. Ringquist, "Political Control and Policy Impact in EPA's Office of Water Quality," *American Journal of Political Science* 39 (May 1995): 336–363.

20. Evan J. Ringquist, *Environmental Protection at the State Level* (Armonk, N.Y.: M.E. Sharpe, 1993). See also review by James P. Lester and Emmett N. Lombard, "The Comparative Analysis of State Environmental Policy," *Natural Resources Journal* (Spring 1990): 301–319.

21. See: *Pollution Control: Perspectives on the Government Role* (New York: Tax Foundation, 1971).

22. Cavanagh, "Brownfields Dilemma."

23. David D. Schmidt, "Corporate Funds Fuel Initiative Campaigns," *Public Administration Times* (1 October 1982): 1, 4.

24. Diana Wahl and Raymond L. Bancroft, "Solid Waste Management Today: Bringing about Municipal Change," *Nation's Cities* (August 1975): 24.

25. See, generally: Ron Tunley, "Better Drinking Water Is on the Way," *National Review* (June 1975): 299–306; and Jack Ryan, "Safe Drinking Water," *Family Health* (September 1974): 23ff.

26. Ryan, "Safe Drinking Water."

27. Euel Elliott, James L. Regens, and Barry J. Seldon, "Exploring Variation in Public Support for Environmental Protection," *Social Science Quarterly* 76 (March 1995): 41–52.

28. See: Matthew A. Crenson, *The Un-Politics of Air Pollution* (Baltimore: Johns Hopkins University Press, 1971), pp. 11–18.

29. See: Margaret Sprout and Harold Sprout, *Ecology and Politics in America: Some Issues and Alternatives* (New York: General Learning Press, 1971), p. 9.

30. See: Environmental Protection Agency and Council on Environmental Quality, *Macroeconomic Impact of Federal Pollution Control Programs* (Washington, D.C.: Government Printing Office, 1975); and Paul H. Templet, "The Positive Relationship

between Jobs, Environment, and the Economy: An Empirical Analysis and Review," *Spectrum* (1995): 37–49.

31. See: Walter A. Rosenbaum, *The Politics of Environmental Concern* (New York: Praeger, 1977), ch. 8; and Marc Karnis Landy, *The Politics of Environmental Reform: Controlling Kentucky Strip Mining* (Washington, D.C.: Resources for the Future, 1976).

32. Rosenbaum, *Politics of Environmental Concern,* p. 225.

33. On this and related questions, see: Richard T. Sylves, "Nuclear Power Plants and Emergency Planning: An Intergovernmental Nightmare," *Public Administration Review* (September/October 1984): 393–401.

34. See: Richard C. Kearney and Robert B. Garey, "American Federalism and the Management of Radioactive Wastes," *Public Administration Review* (January/February 1982): 14–24.

35. Richard C. Kearney and John J. Strucker, "Interstate Compacts and the Management of Low Level Radioactive Wastes," *Public Administration Review* (January/February 1985): 210–220.

36. Douglas D. Anderson, *Regulatory Politics and Electric Utilities: A Case Study in Political Economy* (New York: Auburn House, 1981).

37. The term *public utility* is used to refer to a variety of businesses that have been found by the courts or legislatures to be "affected with a public interest," and thus subject to special regulations.

38. See: Claude M. Vaughan Jr. and James K. Sharpe, "The Public Utility Regulatory Policies Act: Implications for Regulatory Commission Reform," *Public Administration Review* (May/June 1981): 387–391.

39. See: *Energy Conservation: Policy Considerations for the States* (Lexington, Ky.: The Council of State Governments, November 1976).

14

☆ ☆ ☆

THE POLITICS OF PLANNING AND DEVELOPMENT

State and local governments make numerous decisions that affect the physical environment in which people live. Some of these decisions relate to the quality of air and water and to the development of energy resources (see chapter 13). Of primary concern in this chapter are problems and policies regarding community development, land-use planning, housing, and transportation systems.

COMMUNITY DEVELOPMENT AND PLANNING

DEVELOPMENT OF CITIES

The physical character of communities has been largely the product of economic forces and the decisions of private industries and individuals.[1] Many eastern cities were built to accommodate industrial needs: rivers were used to dump industrial waste, noisy and soot-belching railroads were sent through areas adjacent to central business districts, and immigrant families were housed in six-story tenements that became slums. At the same time, the successful could move into suburban areas, away from the pollution and blight.

As the nation moved westward, land use was pioneered by speculators who constructed minimally "habitable dwellings" in order to receive 160-acre tracts of land at a bargain price from the national government. The life and death of frontier settlements were later determined by the laying of railroad tracks. Settlements bypassed by the trains usually withered and died. Others went on to attract industry and often experienced unplanned, sprawling growth heavily dependent on automobile transportation.

Especially important in the development of cities in all parts of the country have been the activities of corporation leaders who decide when and where they will locate and expand, and of those in real estate, banking, and construction. Local governmental planning up to the beginning of the twentieth century was largely confined to designing street layouts. Beginning in the 1880s, in reaction to industrialization, emphasis was placed on the aesthetic nature of cities. Planning became a means of making the "city beautiful," though beauty was often sacrificed to efficiency.

In more recent years, greater emphasis has been placed on governmental land-use planning and the imposition of controls over the right of individuals and businesses to use their land as they wish. In addition, the environmental movement has challenged the equation of economic and population growth with progress and a way of life characterized by low-density living and a heavy dependence on the automobile and freeway. Controls and basic changes in governmental policies are felt necessary to preserve open space, scenic areas, and natural resources; to build cities that are not only efficient and rational but also compatible with human needs; and to combat problems like air and water pollution and energy shortages

LOCAL PLANNING ACTIVITY

Much of the current planning activity has been stimulated by federal program requirements. Planning is mandatory, often on a metropolitan-wide basis, for federally aided programs in housing, transportation, and other areas. In recent years the states have also required localities to undertake more planning activities.

One consequence of these developments has been the increased importance of professional planners in community decision making. This importance stems not only from their expertise but also from the reluctance of elected officials to become involved in planning activities. Decisions that must be made concerning developmental priorities can intensify conflict and lead to the defeat of officeholders who become associated with an unpopular decision.

The assumption of responsibilities, however, does not necessarily mean that planners have great influence over the course of community development. "Urban governments," as one observer has noted, "have shown a tremendous capacity to ignore development pressures and the expert's advice."[2] The ability of a planner to secure the political backing of governmental officials appears greater when planning is regarded as a staff function under the mayor or manager rather than as part of the jurisdiction of an independent planning commission. In either organizational arrangement, planners are apt to consider their dominant role to be essentially one of offering technical advice rather than one of "selling" developmental programs.[3] There are, however, conflicts within the urban planning profession, and some planners, at least, function as social and political activists who attempt to influence public policies, particularly in the interest of the poor and nonwhite.[4]

Many cities, especially the larger ones, have developed land-use (master, comprehensive, or general) plans intended to guide the future development and use of land within their jurisdictions. The traditional textbook sequence of steps in land-use planning is to determine community goals, study the patterns of existing land use, investigate all relevant social and economic trends, forecast the future needs for land and facilities, and prepare a plan reflecting these findings.

It is difficult, of course, to design a statement of goals that reflects the opinions of all the various groups within a large and heterogeneous community. Planners, despite improvements in information systems, are hard pressed to secure the necessary data to make projections. Much of what will happen to a city is unpredictable. Much depends on decisions made at other levels of government and by private individuals and corporations. Plans, in short, often imperfectly project trends rather than chart a clear course toward well-defined or radically new objectives.

Land-use plans commonly divide the city into different types of zones, such as residential, commercial, and industrial. These basic zones may be further broken down into categories such as light and heavy industry or high-density (apartments, townhouses) and low-density (single-family dwellings) residential areas. Plans also designate the present and future locations of parks, schools, streets, highways, and other public facilities.

Land-use plans are implemented in various ways. Specific public projects must be legally authorized by the council, not simply adopted as part of a plan, and must be funded, usually through borrowing or intergovernmental aid. To secure land for a public undertaking, local jurisdictions may exercise the power of *eminent domain*. Through this power, they may take private property without the owner's consent, giving the owner "just compensation" as prescribed by law. To implement urban renewal programs, property may even be taken from one private party and sold to another.

The basic methods of implementing decisions regarding the use and condition of private property are official map ordinances, zoning ordinances, and various types of controls over how individuals or businesses can develop their properties (see discussion of subdivision regulations in the following section). An official map ordinance is designed to prevent the building of structures on private property that is intended for future public use. A city, for example, although not yet in a position to purchase a particular piece of property, may plan to run a street through it and thus be anxious to prevent it from being developed with buildings. The adoption of an official map designating the land as a future public acquisition accomplishes this objective.[5]

Zoning ordinances commonly limit private land use to the patterns (residential, commercial, industrial) stipulated in the general land-use plan. The zoning ordinance may also regulate matters such as the height of buildings, the size and location of signs, and minimum lot sizes. Zoning ordinances are primarily enforced through land-use permits issued by building officials who check for compliance with the requirements.

Individuals and businesses may challenge the decisions of a building official before a zoning board of appeals or adjustment, usually appointed by the mayor. The board has the power to grant exceptions or variances to those who would suffer undue hardship from the strict enforcement of zoning regulations. Land uses established before the adoption of a zoning ordinance and conflicting with it are generally allowed to continue under a nonconforming use permit. Normally all land within a given jurisdiction is zoned, and municipalities (in some states) may extend their zoning powers one-half to five miles beyond their boundaries to control fringe area development. While rezoning hearings are sometimes highly controversial, the vast majority of them involve only local officials and those seeking changes. Local elected officials often unanimously ratify staff recommendations on zoning matters.[6]

Zoning ideally serves as an effective means of guiding the development of private land use in accordance with a general land-use plan for the jurisdiction. In practice, it has fallen short of this ideal and served other, and often less laudable, purposes. The original purpose of zoning ordinances was to protect existing residential property from incompatible land uses or nuisances. Residential areas were protected, for example, from businesses like machine shops or slaughterhouses that impaired the enjoyment of the property and its economic value. Zoning was valued largely for negative purposes—to prohibit certain types of land use and to protect against change, rather than guide community development. In several jurisdictions it still performs these purposes. Often zoning is not connected with any attempt at formal developmental planning, or the planning itself is designed to preserve and protect existing land uses. In some places people who own junkyards, disposal plants, and pollution-causing industries may find it difficult to meet zoning standards.

Zoning ordinances also may have the intended or unintended effect of preserving patterns of economic and racial segregation. Mobile homes, if allowed at all, may be confined to industrial areas. Mobile homes are associated with urban blight (in large part because they have been confined to blighted areas) and, often incorrectly, with poor, transient citizens with large families. In the more conservative suburbs, zoning may be used to screen out low-income families and families with a large number of children, who would increase educational costs. These restrictions fall most heavily on nonwhites. Such restrictions are made by increasing housing costs through zoning mostly for large single-family dwellings on exceptionally large lots and by prohibiting low-cost multiple dwellings. As noted below, however, some courts have invalidated such practices and ruled that localities must develop affirmative zoning plans that provide housing for those in the low- and moderate-income groups.

Local governments have long been recognized by the courts to have a broad power to regulate the uses of private property in the interests of public safety, health, or welfare. Yet, there are limits to this power. Local land-use regulators may find that they have exceeded the power delegated to them by the state enabling legislation or have, through their regulation, violated due process rights, the guarantee of equal protection, or the right to travel. Zoning and other land-use regulations can be so oppressive and so burdensome that they amount to illegal taking of private property for public use without just compensation. Indeed, under a recent United States Supreme Court decision, developers injured by such regulations may now receive money damages against a local government for even a temporary confiscation of property.[7] In recent years, federal and state courts have heard several "takings" cases brought by property rights advocate groups challenging zoning and other governmental restrictions on the use of private property.

Courts in some states have also reminded local governments that they cannot engage in *exclusionary zoning,* that is, to exclude the poor and nonwhite. Court cases based on the charge of racial discrimination often fail because plaintiffs have failed to supply proof of the actual intent of localities to discriminate in making zoning decisions. Some courts have held, however, that because local governments derive their zoning power from the states, they must use that power in the interest of the state as whole, not simply for the well-being of local residents. Some courts have held that the interests of the state require that each locality provide its "fair share" of housing for low-income groups.[8]

CONTROLLING GROWTH

Citizens, historically, have looked forward to an expansion of their localities' population and economic base. Those already established in a community tend to link growth to higher land values, more or better jobs, and improved shopping or recreational opportunities. Residents in rural areas often see development of value for encouraging young people to stay in their communities. On the other hand, public officials have not been altogether oblivious to the problems growth brings with it and have seen the need to protect communities in their jurisdictions from a massive influx of new residents. "No growth" or "limited growth" sentiments and "quality-of-life" issues have been reflected in city council races around the country in recent years. Citizens have also been called upon to decide on "slow growth" proposals placed on the ballot by the initiative process. Some communities in California, for example, have adopted initiative measures that prohibit further development in unincorporated areas until problems of traffic congestion are resolved.

Supporters of limiting growth have a variety of reasons for their positions.

Some cite the need to prevent further environmental deterioration. Others want to control growth so as to avoid high taxes that could be necessary to expand services and facilities. Others are simply concerned with preserving the character of their communities and the quality of life. Growth limitation policies, however, are not favored by local building interests. Other groups oppose growth limits because their effect, if not actual intent, may be to exclude low-income people and minority groups from a community.[9]

Local governments have several means by which they may attempt to control population growth. Growth may be encouraged or discouraged, for example, by governmental purchase of land and by decisions regarding the expansion of facilities like roads and sewer lines. Within the general limits of the law, local governments are free to experiment with tools and techniques such as development moratoria, low-density zoning, and various types of regulatory and taxation policies to control growth. Moratoria on development can be achieved in the short run simply by blocking the issuance of building permits for new construction or by refusing to issue permits for water and sewer extension. Through the adoption of an "adequate public facilities" ordinance—a device that first gained national prominence when adopted by the Township of Ramapo, New York, in 1969—a locality may take a more positive step to control the rate of development by limiting the issuance of building permits to areas of the community that are adequately served by public facilities. To limit density, cities might restrict development to single-family homes, require larger lots, or mandate that homes meet minimum square footage requirements. Such land-use decisions, however, as noted previously, might be found to be inequitable to the poor.

Subdivision controls also provide local officials with an opportunity to guide growth and pay for its impact. These controls are aimed at developers of new residential, commercial, or industrial properties. In addition to complying with zoning regulations, developers might be required to put in streets, sidewalks, and sewage systems meeting certain specifications and to set aside land for future public use, for example, for parks and schools. Subdivision regulations are intended to avoid creating city problems in the future, such as street widening, the relocation of utility lines, or slum buildings. In a like manner, local officials often impose taxes and fees on developers to help offset the costs engendered by the approved growth. Underlying the practice is the assumption that "new growth must pay its own way."

Localities sometimes also pursue more redistributive goals (policies and programs helping the poor) through the leverage they have over developers in being able to approve or disapprove their land-use proposals. A municipality may, for example, require developers to set aside part of their unit for low-income housing. The idea that development should, when possible, be directed toward benefiting needy areas within a city appears generally supported by city council members, especially minority council members.[10]

The number of exactions (required improvements, property set-asides, fees, and taxes) on developers has increased greatly in the past two decades. To some extent this reflects a rejection of the older notion that growth was inevitably the key to greater local revenues and prosperity. Many localities found that growth actually meant increased municipal costs for services that were, at best, only partially offset by new revenues. The growth of exactions has also stemmed from the financial difficulties of many localities. Just as the federal and state governments tried to cope with their economic problems by passing expenditures off to local governments, local governments attempted to ease their economic difficulties and ease the burden on current taxpayers by passing off costs to developers. That developers have not protested more may be due to their ability to pass the costs on to residential or commercial buyers.[11]

Research on the actual effects of growth control policies over time indicates that they have relatively little effect on overall population growth—that, as time goes by, the forces pushing for development are much stronger than the forces pushing against development. Growth control policies do appear related to changes in the composition of the population, particularly in the exclusion of blacks. As indicated earlier, however, exclusion of blacks may have more to do with practices in the housing market (chapter 8).[12]

LOCAL CONTROL AND REGIONAL PLANNING

Most states have adopted permissive legislation allowing local governments to regulate land use within their boundaries purely on the basis of local concerns and politics. Zoning is perhaps the most highly valued local governmental power because of the control or protection it gives over neighborhood development.

Local control over land use, however, has its weaknesses. Often, as noted above, the decisions of local officials are criticized for being unfair to property owners or minorities trying to move into an area. Another criticism is that local officials in many jurisdictions are unable or unwilling to do the work involved. The ability to plan land use and to implement plans requires a level of professionalism, organization, and management expertise that is very often lacking in local governmental units, especially smaller ones in nonmetropolitan areas. Another problem also found in some small jurisdictions is an unwillingness among political leaders to change their ways of doing things and to recognize the need for planning and land-use controls. Resistance to capacity building appears to be strongest in communities faced with stagnating populations and economies. Yet, without improved capabilities, such communities seem destined to continue on the decline.

Perhaps the most basic problem of relying on municipal units is that each unit is likely to consider its own needs first and only incidentally the needs of the broader metropolitan area or region. Imposing a moratorium, requiring larger lots, or requiring a fee on developers may help a rapidly developing city, at least in the short run. These same actions, however, are not likely to do anything to help neighboring jurisdictions and, indeed, may prove harmful to them and to the region as a whole. Similarly, while cities might solve certain service problems within their boundaries, those problems that transcend municipal or even county boundaries, such as pollution and traffic congestion, require a regional approach to land-use planning.

Problems caused by unplanned, poorly planned, or uncoordinated land development have created pressure to shift much of the planning and control responsibilities to states and broad-based planning agencies. Comprehensive metropolitan or regional planning and increased state involvement have been encouraged by federal programs. The federal government encourages local comprehensive planning, particularly on a metropolitan-wide basis, through metropolitan planning organizations, a function sometimes performed by voluntary councils of government.

State land-use planning controls have become increasingly popular. Hawaii in 1961 was a pioneer of this trend by establishing a State Land-Use Commission with powers to zone the state into urban, rural, conservation, and agricultural districts. Counties are allowed to adopt more detailed zoning regulations than those required by the state. In the late 1960s, Vermont adopted statewide land-use planning, with a permit system to implement the plan. All developments of consequence must be certified by the Vermont Environmental Board, which issues land-use permits. New York State's Urban Development Corporation, established in 1968, has authority to override local zoning regulations inconsistent with the state's urban development program. In Maryland and other states, an office of local or community affairs must approve major local community development decisions.

A more recent trend has been for state governments to require localities to adopt comprehensive land-use plans that are consistent with state comprehensive plans. Such plans focus on the interrelated goals of controlling growth, combating environmental problems such as air and water pollution, and providing an adequate infrastructure. Several states, including Florida, New Jersey, and Washington, have laws that limit new development to places where an adequate infrastructure is already in place or will be in place concurrent with the development being considered.[13] State planning mandates and requirements appear to have been successful in forcing localities to address particular problems. State mandates, for example, have caused local planners to resist pressure for development of high-hazard areas, such as land on earthquake faults and floodways.[14]

Some observers label the approach taken by the states to land use-planning "top down" regionalism, as opposed to "bottom up" regionalism, and worry about the adverse impact of state planning requirements on local authority.[15] In some places, municipalities and state governments have struggled over their relative roles in regard to growth management, especially when it comes to infrastructure financing.[16] For local officials new growth management responsibilities present difficult problems of resolving conflicts among groups and individuals with divergent interests. State-imposed planning also generates considerable costs for local officials.[17] Another problem with state-imposed comprehensive planning is that it sometimes ignores limitations on the ability of local governments in rural areas to do the job. A state mandate for sophisticated planning may be, in effect, negated in rural areas by the insufficient capacities of the governments involved.[18] Several states now make an effort to assist rural governments to adapt to their new land-use management responsibilities.

SLUMS, HOUSING, AND RENEWAL

NEIGHBORHOOD AND HOUSING QUALITY

The definition of slum conditions, like the definition of poverty, is a matter of individual interpretation. Middle-class reformers have often objected to what they see as slums because of their visual ugliness and because the slums appear to contribute to the social problems of the people living there. Slum conditions have commonly been linked to a deterioration of character (involving vice and criminal behavior) and problems of health caused by unsanitary conditions. A long-standing assumption of reformers has been that better housing and neighborhoods (that is, an improved environment) can make better people. Housing reformers have been motivated not only by humanitarian considerations but also by the fear that slum conditions will lead sooner or later to civil disorder and threats to the general welfare.[19]

Others have objected to what they have defined as slums largely on economic grounds. These individuals feel that the land could be more profitable if it were cleared and used for other purposes or other people. The destruction of what is declared to be a slum or blighted area, however, may destroy a viable pattern of social life and cause much psychological stress to those who have to relocate.

In the search for data on which to evaluate the quality of living conditions, attention has commonly been given to the physical characteristics of housing and general neighborhood conditions.[20] Generally, housing units with severe structural defects or inadequate plumbing facilities are regarded as substandard. The percentage of households living in such substandard units has greatly declined over the past few decades. If one looks simply at age of housing, one generally finds a far higher percentage of older units in the Snow Belt East and Midwest than in the Sun Belt South and West (see table 14–1)

Evaluations of neighborhood quality have been based largely on the

TABLE 14.1   Housing Units and Housing Characteristics, by State: 1990

Division and State	Total Housing Units (1,000)	Percent of Units Built		Percent of Households with—	
		1980 to 1990	1939 or Earlier	No Vehicles Available	2 or More Vehicles
U.S.	102,259	20.7	18.4	11.5	54.7
N.E.:					
ME	587	20.7	34.9	8.7	57.1
NH	504	27.7	27.1	6.3	61.7
VT	271	22.4	36.5	8.0	58.0
MA	2,473	13.8	38.9	14.3	49.3
RI	415	15.1	34.0	10.6	54.5
CT	1,321	15.7	25.5	10.0	58.6
M.A.:					
NY	7,227	9.4	35.7	30.0	37.5
NJ	3,075	14.8	24.6	12.9	52.5
PA	4,938	12.4	35.1	15.2	49.5
E.N.C.:					
OH	4,372	12.2	25.8	10.2	56.8
IN	2,246	14.5	24.2	8.5	59.1
IL	4,506	11.7	27.1	14.0	50.9
MI	3,848	13.6	20.8	10.1	56.8
WI	2,056	14.5	28.5	9.3	57.8
W.N.C.:					
MN	1,848	18.5	24.5	8.6	60.0
IA	1,144	10.0	35.0	7.1	61.7
MO	2,199	18.3	20.4	9.8	57.0
ND	276	16.6	24.7	6.5	63.2
SD	292	14.8	30.4	6.5	64.1
NE	661	12.9	30.7	7.2	62.5
KS	1,044	16.9	24.5	6.4	61.7
S.A.:					
DE	290	24.3	14.3	8.2	59.3
MD	1,892	21.6	15.5	12.3	56.0
DC	278	5.5	37.7	37.4	21.2
VA	2,496	26.3	11.0	9.0	59.8

Source: United States Bureau of the Census, *1990 Census of Population and Housing Data Paper Listing (CPH-L-80).*

Taken from: *Statistical Abstract* (Washington, D.C.: Government Printing Office, 1992), p. xvii.

Division and State	Total Housing Units (1,000)	Percent of Units Built		Percent of Households with—	
		1980 to 1990	1939 or earlier	No Vehicles Available	2 or More Vehicles
S.A.: *(cont.)*					
WV	781	17.7	23.7	13.7	50.4
NC	2,818	28.6	9.9	9.6	59.2
SC	1,424	29.0	8.5	10.9	57.2
GA	2,638	32.1	8.1	10.3	58.8
FL	6,100	35.0	3.7	9.2	49.8
E.S.C.:					
KY	1,507	20.0	15.9	11.5	56.0
TN	2,026	24.2	10.2	9.8	58.2
AL	1,670	23.5	9.3	10.3	58.7
MS	1,010	24.1	8.6	12.1	54.2
W.S.C.:					
AR	1,001	24.2	9.4	9.8	56.2
LA	1,716	22.1	10.6	13.9	49.9
OK	1,406	22.1	12.4	7.5	58.1
TX	7,009	29.7	7.1	8.1	55.9
Mt.:					
MT	361	17.5	21.8	6.7	63.5
ID	413	18.0	15.9	4.6	67.3
WY	203	21.4	15.6	4.7	66.9
CO	1,477	24.7	13.0	6.9	60.9
NM	632	27.5	8.1	6.9	59.0
AZ	1,659	37.8	3.2	7.8	53.3
UT	598	24.4	13.5	5.4	66.1
NV	519	40.1	2.9	7.8	54.8
Pac.:					
WA	2,032	23.1	15.7	7.5	61.4
OR	1,194	16.6	16.8	8.0	59.9
CA	11,183	22.9	10.7	8.9	57.9
AK	233	38.0	3.0	11.9	54.0
HI	390	20.8	6.7	9.9	54.1

BOX 14-1   NEIGHBORHOOD CONDITIONS: CAMDEN

"In Camden, New Jersey, where I was last weekend—where a third of the people live below the poverty line—you see block after block of deteriorating housing, graffiti-covered buildings and vacant lots. There is virtually no jobs base. The central business district is a ghost town; the only new construction there is government buildings. . . . There are no major supermarkets in the neighborhoods, just small mom and pop grocery stores.

"And in the neighborhoods, on the blocks of attached, two-story brick row houses, you see a truly unsettling sight. People have erected heavy wrought-iron fences with locked gates in front of their houses to keep out intruders. They have barricaded themselves in their own homes. They have turned their front porches into fortresses, because in a community like Camden, where the poverty rate is so high, where the chance of finding a decent-paying job is so low, crime is rampant and no one is safe."

Source: Secretary of Housing and Urban Development Henry G. Cisneros, speech at Dartmouth College, Hanover, N.H., 9 August 1995.

---

residents' perceptions. Survey data collected in the mid-1970s reveal that most people rate their neighborhoods as good or excellent. General discontent has been highest among central-city residents. In 1975, for example, 16 percent of those surveyed in central cities wished to move because of neighborhood conditions, whereas only 10 percent of the suburban residents and 7 percent of the residents of nonmetropolitan areas wished to do so.[21] Not surprisingly, survey data also indicate that whites are more satisfied with their neighborhoods than nonwhites are.[22]

To many people, however, especially the poor and nonwhites in the inner city, substandard housing is a minor problem compared with general neighborhood conditions like overcrowding, poverty, frustration, and crime (see box 14–1). The lack of access to the broader community because of deficient transportation systems also may work to make even a relatively good neighborhood a poor place in which to live. Such factors, for example, were behind the riots in Los Angeles several years ago.[23]

Confinement in a slum neighborhood has also meant racially segregated and usually inferior education and frequent exploitation by local merchants. Prices for food and most commodities are generally higher in inner-city slum areas than in more affluent suburban ones. Slum dwellers are also more likely to be the victims of consumer frauds. Another traditional enemy of the poor has been the slum landlord, who is seen as ignoring human problems and neglecting needed repairs to squeeze every cent out of his or her investment.

Many jurisdictions have housing codes intended to ensure that existing housing meets certain minimum safety standards. Codes commonly set forth standards for sanitation, ventilation, structural upkeep, and lighting and may prohibit overcrowding. Housing codes are generally not well enforced, a condition that is particularly evident in the inner cities, where many buildings have been allowed to remain in obviously substandard condition. Problems of enforcement are attributed in part to a lack of inspectors. To make up for the lack of personnel, most code-enforcing agencies act on the basis of complaints and confine their activities to the most flagrant violations. A second problem has been that fines for code violation have been set so low that landlords have found it cheaper to pay the fines than to make the repairs. Finally, and more fundamentally, the high cost of making repairs works against improving the housing situation. High repair costs could well result in higher rents beyond the means of the poor, who would thus be displaced. The high costs encourage the property owner to abandon his or her property, as many have, in lieu of making repairs.

Improvement of housing and neighborhood conditions has also been frustrated by the refusal of mortgage lenders to make real estate or home improvement loans in inner-city areas. This practice, known as *redlining*, has been defended on the grounds that loans to property owners in these areas are too risky. The federal government and some states attempt to discourage redlining by requiring mortgage lenders to disclose where in a city they make their loans.

HOUSING SUPPLY AND THE HOMELESS

Most of the new homes built in this country are intended for those in higher income brackets. The theory is that as the upwardly mobile and affluent move into new homes, their old homes will "trickle down" or become available to those on the economic rung below them. One problem with the trickle-down theory is that very often the poor cannot afford even the vacated housing. Another problem is that even those who do have the means may find their access to the housing shut off by racial discrimination.

In recent years the nation has been faced with problems of inadequate housing supply. Many young families have had difficulties in financing the purchase of a first home. More dramatic have been the homeless (see box 14–2). These are people who are living in the streets or in housing not of their choice, such as temporary shelters. The estimated number of people who are homeless ranges from 350,000 to over 3 million.[24]

Scarcity in low-cost housing is due, in part, to massive federal cutbacks in subsidized housing over the 1980s. Because of cuts in federal funds, the supply of this housing has actually decreased since the 1980s, even though the demand has become greater than ever. It also reflects the gentrification of poor neighborhoods over the same period that brought the conversion of low- or moderate-income rental units to relatively high-priced condominiums or

---

Box 14-2 The Homeless

Chief among the general factors contributing to the homeless problem have been programs that deinstitutionalized the mentally ill (in effect, putting them on the streets), high levels of unemployment and poverty, and the scarcity of low-income housing. Many of the homeless, perhaps a third, are mentally ill. To a considerable extent, as Boston Mayor Raymond Flynn, speaking to the United States Conference of Mayors, noted in 1991, "homeless shelters and city streets have become the de facto mental institutions of the 1980s and 1990s." Some of the homeless are people with an addiction to alcohol or drugs. Interspersed among these are migrant workers, runaway children, and veterans who did not recover from their war experiences. Also among the homeless are people with families who are out of work or unable through their current employment to afford permanent housing.

Quote from: "Streets Becoming Home for Mentally Ill," *The Arizona Republic*, Reuters wire service story (9 November 1991): A12.

---

co-ops. A report of the United States Department of Housing and Urban Development (HUD) attributes much of the scarcity to excessive governmental regulations having to do with growth controls, zoning, restrictions on low-income housing, and other matters. Regulations of this nature, HUD concluded, drive up the costs of housing 20 to 35 percent.[25]

The federal government has acted in recent years to help state and local officials deal with the homeless crisis.[26] State and local officials, however, have assumed the major burden. For city officials, the more practical day-to-day problems of homelessness range from finding temporary shelters to the provision of food and various social services. In recent years, a hardening of attitudes toward the homeless has produced stronger prohibitions against such practices as begging, loitering, and sleeping in public parks.

In the long run, the homeless problem requires, at a minimum, a major increase in the supply of low-income housing. Some states have acted to authorize funds for multifamily low-income housing programs, while others have offered developers various types of incentives to build low-income housing. Overall, the state-local effort has been limited, and state and local officials have called for renewed federal aid in the low-income-housing area.[27]

Public Housing

National governmental policies have long stimulated the development of housing for those in the middle- and upper-income brackets and those who wish to move to suburban areas. Until the mid-1960s, the Federal Housing Administration limited its home insurance program to the suburban areas, feeling that central-city housing was economically risky. Middle- and upper-income homeowners have also benefited from tax advantages given them through federal income tax regulations, most importantly the right to deduct interest payments on mortgages.

The national government has not equally encouraged the provision of housing for low-income groups. Government-subsidized public housing has largely been of a rental nature. These, in theory, provide temporary residences for the "deserving poor" who are expected to improve themselves and to move to private housing "trickling down" to them.

The national government's involvement in public housing began during the Depression of the 1930s in part, at least, as an effort to supply jobs in the construction industry. The modern public housing program stems from the Housing Act of 1937, under which the national government began lending money to local governments (with the permission of their states) to acquire land and to construct and maintain low-cost public housing units.

In 1949 Congress established a goal of constructing some eight hundred thousand units of low-cost public housing by 1955. Congress never reached this goal, partly because of the opposition of those involved in the private housing sector (banking, real estate, and construction). The failure of Congress to appropriate enough funds to make realization of the goal possible was also due to the discovery that instead of benefiting a cross section of American people, the program benefited the urban poor and nonwhite.[28] Nevertheless, during the 1970s, as many as two hundred thousand units of low-cost housing were created each year. With the advent of pressures to reduce federal domestic spending, annual production fell to around twenty-three thousand units per year in the late 1980s.

Local housing authorities (LHAs) set up under state law as special districts independent of city government have control over public housing projects. The jurisdiction of an LHA may cover a city, a county, or a number of cities and counties. Boards generally consist of five unpaid members appointed by the mayor. Salaried directors and other employees oversee the day-to-day operation of the LHAs. The LHAs determine when and where public housing projects are to be built. The approval of city councils, and often of the voters, is, however, needed for specific projects. Once built, the LHAs own and operate the projects, determining such matters as eligibility requirements and rent schedules.

Currently, there are thirty-four hundred housing authorities scattered throughout every state in the union. Close to four million persons live in public housing units. For both political and economic reasons, local authorities have chosen to build most public housing in the inner cities. Many of these projects have taken the form of high-rise buildings and resemble maximum security prisons. Public housing projects are commonly overcrowded, iso-lated from the surrounding community, and plagued by maintenance prob-lems and youthful vandalism. Studies have found that in some projects, 20 to 30 percent of the units are uninhabitable.[29]

Public housing projects have had the effect of furthering the concentration of low-income families in inner-city slum areas. To counter this, efforts have been made in recent years to encourage "scatter site" housing, that is, to place small units of low-income housing in middle-class neighborhoods. As noted above, courts in some states have furthered this effort by requiring that each locality provide its "fair share" of housing for low-income groups. These efforts, however, have often encountered the resistance of people in the targeted neighborhoods—another example of the NIMBY siting problem.

Also on the reform agenda for public housing is the notion that residents be given greater control over their living conditions by assuming responsibil-ity for the management of public housing complexes, rather than rely on outside agencies. To reformers like former Housing and Urban Development Secretary Jack Kemp, resident or tenant management is a step toward the more desirable goal of allowing public housing residents to purchase the dwellings they now rent. This view no longer looks at public housing as temporary or transitional housing, but as providing permanent homes. Moving away from a system described by Kemp as one of "federal plantations" toward private ownership would "empower" the poor in controlling conditions affecting them and, it is hoped, would lead to a better living environment.

URBAN RENEWAL AND COMMUNITY DEVELOPMENT

State and local governments have occasionally used their own funds to eliminate slums, provide better housing, and improve neighborhood condi-tions. Nearly all states, for example, have housing finance agencies (HFAs) that raise funds for rental housing development, home improvement loans, and home mortgage loans for people who would otherwise not be able to purchase a home.[30]

Most urban renewal and community development activity in small as well as large cities, however, has been undertaken with aid provided through national programs. The Housing Act of 1949 provided for a national urban renewal program under which grants and loans were made to local units to acquire, clear, and prepare what were found to be blighted areas for new construction. Congress adopted the Model Cities Act of 1966 in an attempt to mesh all governmental and private resources into a total attack on the prob-lems of slum areas.

In 1974 Congress consolidated the urban renewal, Model Cities, and other programs into a broad Community Development Block Grant (CDBG) pro-gram. The block grant program has distributed about $3 billion a year to local governments (municipalities and large counties), which have had considerable discretion as to how the money is to be spent. Since 1981, state governments have received and distributed grants for smaller cities. Previously, this function was performed by the federal government through the Department of Housing and Urban Development.

The CDBG program has long been the object of critical evaluations. Studies conducted by the Brookings Institution found that the original formula for distributing funds favored small towns and suburbs over large central cities, and favored central cities in the rapidly growing South and West over those in the North and East.[31] Civil rights groups have claimed, moreover, that too much of the money has been used for projects that benefit upper-income groups rather than the intended beneficiaries—low- and moderate-income families.[32] Some scholars have found that the shift in control over the Small Cities Block Grant Program from federal to state officials has, indeed, meant less attention to the needs of the less affluent. Rather, the states have been more likely to fund programs such as infrastructure repair, benefiting all income groups.[33]

In the traditional urban renewal program, important decisions are made by local renewal agencies created by state legislation. The local renewal agency may be organized as a part of city government, combined with the local housing authority, or created as a separate legal entity (special district). The agency designates a certain area of the city as blighted, purchases the land (using the power of eminent domain if necessary), and clears the land for reuse. The cleared land may be used for public housing or sold to private builders for redevelopment. Urban renewal programs have generally been dominated by local businesspeople and local officials, though, by law, there must at least be a hearing in the affected neighborhood. Success in getting renewal programs through appears to depend largely on the ability of the renewal agency to gain the support of community political and economic elites and on the failure of those in the affected neighborhood to unite in opposition.[34]

Urban renewal programs have long been the object of criticism. "Blight" has often been determined less on the inadequacy of existing housing than from a desire to do something "better" with the land.[35] Often this desire has been to "save downtown" by converting land used for housing the poor into valuable commercial property and constructing the type of housing that is suitable only for the more affluent. Private developers have not been required to build low-cost housing but have been free to build housing beyond the means of the families who are displaced. Overall, the emphasis has been on the removal of the slums, but little has been done to provide replacement housing for the poor. Displaced people have had to keep one step ahead of the bulldozer. They usually find about the same quality of housing they had before urban renewal, but pay more for it because of the increased demand. Urban renewal has also been criticized on the grounds that it destroys neigh-

borhoods, which are often viable communities, and that it has had a particularly adverse effect on small-business owners, who lose their clientele because
of relocation.

In recent years, greater emphasis has been placed on the purchase and
rehabilitation of homes in slum areas rather than on clearance and renewal.
This approach preserves neighborhoods and often provides standard housing
more quickly and at less cost than new housing. Several local governments
also have adopted urban homesteading programs offering abandoned buildings at bargain prices to people who are willing to make repairs and live there
for a five-year period.[36] Although most of the homesteaders are people who
were already living in the city and who moved to take advantage of the
program, others are former suburbanites who are part of a back-to-the-city
movement. There is some reason to worry, however, that such programs, like
urban renewal in general, displace the poor because renovation leads to higher
rents or higher property taxes and reduces the supply of low-cost housing.

Another approach to the renewal problem has been the use of enterprise
zones. The basic idea is that by offering private investors tax relief and other
incentives, such as low-interest loans and exemptions from regulations, state
and local governments can encourage them to invest in the redevelopment of
blighted areas. Around forty states have either designed enterprise zones or
allowed local governments to do so. A number of zones have experienced
business expansion and job creation. It is unclear, however, how much of this
would have occurred without the incentives offered.[37] Critics also contend
that the primary impact of tax and other incentives is simply to displace
economic activity, for example, shifting investment from one neighborhood
to another, thus causing as much harm as good.[38] Going beyond enterprise
zones, the Clinton Administration promoted Empowerment Zones and Enterprise Communities as ways to combine the efforts of governments at all
levels and private business and foundations to improve impoverished neighborhoods.

THE AUTOMOBILE AND TRANSPORTATION POLICIES

EFFECTS OF AUTOMOBILE DEPENDENCE

One of the central characteristics of contemporary American life has been
a heavy dependence on the automobile. Around 55 percent of the households
in this country have two or more vehicles, though there is considerable
variation on a state-by-state basis, ranging from 38 percent in New York to
around 67 percent in Idaho and Montana (table 14–1)

Historically, the automobile has facilitated movement from central cities to
low-density, single-family residential developments in the suburbs. It has

made it possible for many people to separate living locations from working locations. Other, more negative effects of the automobile include:[39]

1. *Air pollution.* The auto now produces more air pollution in some areas than all other sources combined. Exhaust from motor vehicles constitutes by weight about 75 percent of all urban smog.
2. *Traffic congestion.* This is especially pronounced during rush hours to and from work. It has produced frustration and a loss in time to the average commuter of from forty to seventy days a year. Because of congestion, traffic in some cities moves at a pace of twelve miles per hour—the same rate it did a hundred years ago when horse-drawn carriages were used. Traffic congestion has also made other forms of transportation less effective. Including the time it takes to get to and from airports, it now takes as long to fly from Boston to New York as it did in the 1930s. Congestion tends to be self-perpetuating. As streets are improved, new shops locate along them, traffic builds up, and the street is congested once again.
3. *Land use.* About one-third of all land in an average American city is occupied by streets and parking facilities. More than 60 percent of the land in central business districts is devoted to the moving and storage of automobiles. This has resulted in a loss of space for parks, residential areas, and other land uses. It has also resulted in the loss of scenic and historic areas.
4. *Governmental costs.* Billions of dollars are spent yearly by governments on all levels in building highways and maintaining streets. At the same time, the property tax base is reduced because the large amount of paved land is taken off the tax rolls. Some argument can be made, however, that in the long run, the effect on tax rolls is favorable because highways usually stimulate the development of any vacant and unimproved land they cross. Congestion is a particularly serious problem for those who must commute long distances daily to where they are employed.
5. *Specific hardships.* One frequent victim of highway building has been the low-income neighborhood. Downtown businesspeople have also suffered from traffic congestion and the lack of parking space, losing business to outlying shopping centers. Dependence on the automobile, finally, has limited the mobility of the aged, young, poor, and handicapped. This affects access not only to stores but also to medical care and employment.
6. *Safety concerns.* Some twenty-five thousand people die each year in motor vehicle accidents. Motor vehicle crashes are the leading cause of death for people under thirty-five. Rural roads are more dangerous than urban roads and smaller cars are more dangerous than larger cars, though there has been a movement toward smaller cars in the interest of fuel efficiency.

THE POLITICS OF HIGHWAYS

While reliance on the automobile has been a mixed blessing, a number of forces continue to support the resulting need for highway and street expenditures. Those with a direct interest involved in such expenditures include automobile manufacturers, the trucking industry, gas and oil companies, auto-related businesses (sales, repairs, parking, gas stations), highway builders, owners of roadside businesses like motels and drive-ins, firms that supply materials for automobiles (rubber, plastic, steel, copper, aluminum), and the millions of employees and stockholders associated with these enterprises.

The antihighway coalition has been a diverse group. Railroads, worried about competition for freight hauls, were among the first to oppose the building of new highways and, largely failing in this, have been able to secure fuel taxes, weight restrictions, and heavier tolls for commercial truckers. City officials have occasionally contested the need for more highways or have disagreed with state officials over their design and location. Cities in some states have what amounts to a veto power over the building of state highways within their boundaries. San Francisco in 1959 vetoed freeways in most parts of the city. More consistent in their opposition to highways have been planners and others in favor of increased reliance on mass transit (see below).

Other elements of the antihighway group consist of those who may lose their homes or small businesses or fear a decline in their property values because of a highway location, parents and school authorities concerned about the safety of children attending schools in the affected area, and environmentalists concerned about air pollution. Tactics of opposition have included the formation of *ad hoc* groups, lobbying, picketing, and taking advantage of federal requirements attached to grants for highway building that call for citizen involvement (for example, attendance at hearings) in highway planning. Several antihighway groups have gone to court, claiming that projects lack adequate environmental impact statements and relocation plans, both of which are required by federal law.

Historically, both the federal and state governments have placed heavy reliance on highway and road building. The federal government has given cash grants to the states for highway building since 1916. In 1956, the federal government began picking up 90 percent of the costs of building interstate highways and 75 percent of the bill for constructing other main roads. Congress, at the same time, established a Highway Trust Fund to finance the system. All federal taxes on motor vehicles, gas, oil, and ancillary equipment have gone into the fund.

State highway agencies, now usually found in a state department of transportation, have had a considerable degree of autonomy from other state political actors and local politicians. Much of the money they spend comes directly from the national government via the Highway Trust Fund. The remainder mostly comes from state revenues that are earmarked or dedicated to highway building. The practice of earmarking state revenues (from motor fuel taxes, automobile registration fees, and road user fees) for highways puts the agencies' state financial support beyond the control of governors and legislators.

Over the years, major transportation decisions have been made in an administrative subsystem involving the state highway agencies and the Bureau of Public Roads (now in the United States Department of Transportation, from which much of the money for highways comes) and local highway officials. Highway planners on all levels share a common desire to expand their programs, and each has had a strong clientele group in the business community. Elected public officials, in the past at least, have given their support to these groups because they have seen highway building as an effective way to make public records.

After completion of the 43,000–mile interstate system in the early 1990s, Congress switched its attention to other transportation problems. It passed the Intermodal Surface Transportation Efficiency Act of 1991, commonly known as ISTEA, that equals funding (80 percent federal and 20 percent state and local) to highways and public transportation spending. The new legislation also encourages more local involvement in transportation planning. The old interstate program was generally a federal-state partnership, with local governments only minimally involved. Under the legislation, major decisions on how to spend federal funds for highways, mass transportation facilities, and other transportation projects are made by Metropolitan Planning Organizations. These local agencies are to coordinate their activities with state highway agencies. Implementation of the legislation requires working out the details of a federal-state-local partnership and arrangements for a coordinated approach to transportation, air quality, and growth management problems.[40] While coordination has been difficult to achieve, the act has had some general success in placing more emphasis on public transportation and in improving the influence of local governments in transportation planning.[41]

THE MASS TRANSIT ALTERNATIVE

One obvious alternative to the automobile and continued highway spending is greater reliance on mass transportation, which includes facilities such as buses, subways, and surface or elevated trains. The golden age of mass transportation in this country began in the 1880s and lasted through the first few decades of the twentieth century. The earliest systems consisted of street railways pulled by horses or mules. By 1900, San Francisco had installed a cable car system, Boston had opened a subway, and Richmond's pioneering experiment with an electric railway had been copied by several other cities. By the 1960s, however, only a handful of large cities (New York, Chicago,

Philadelphia, Boston, Cleveland, and San Francisco) had any significant mass transit systems other than buses. Some twenty-three billion people were carried by public transit in 1945, but only around eight billion were carried by public transit in 1974. Many of the earliest transit companies were privately owned. With a decline in ridership, private transit companies steadily lost money and withdrew from the mass transportation field, leaving it up to local public transit authorities to assume the burden.

Major deterrents to mass transit have been problems of finance, service, and public support. Mass transit has suffered in comparison to automobile-highway transit in securing governmental funds. Only since 1973 has the national government supported mass transit out of some of the revenues in the national Highway Trust Fund. Transit systems have been supported by state funds in only a few states. For the most part, demands for state aid to public transportation have fallen on deaf ears in state legislatures because often the bulk of a state's population (outside large cities) would receive no visible benefits.[42] Federal funding for mass transportation has historically been only a small fraction of what it has funded for highway building, though this, as noted above, has recently changed.

With limited funding, mass transit systems have been characterized by poor connections and transfers, infrequent service, unreliability, crowding, noise, and lack of comfort. Not surprisingly, these systems have not had much appeal to those who have the choice of driving their own automobiles. The most reliable customers have been the poor, aged, young, and disabled—people who cannot rely on private transportation.

Mass transit has been increasingly promoted to minimize several auto-related problems. Mass transit is a more efficient carrier of goods and services. While autos may carry an average of 1.3 persons, buses carry from thirty to fifty people, take up only a little more space, and cut down on pollution. The "new era" in mass transportation is evident in increased public expenditures to improve current systems and for the construction of new systems. In most cities, this has resulted in more buses. San Francisco's Bay Area Rapid Transit System (BART), opened in 1971, was the first all-new rapid transit system since Philadelphia's in 1907. Other cities, such as Washington, D.C., have opened transit systems. Since 1981, San Diego has operated a light rail transit service, which has eased overcrowding on buses and highways. Some cities have limited parking of private autos in downtown areas to foster dependence on buses and other means of mass transit and to generate public support to improve these systems. Cities have also reserved existing freeway lanes for express buses and have given serious consideration to providing free mass transit. Both the federal government and state governments have shown an interest in funding high-speed intercity rail systems along the lines found in France, Germany, and Japan, which travel between urban centers at speeds up to two hundred miles per hour.

Even though a number of factors have converged to produce a new emphasis on mass transportation, the battle to entice people away from their automobiles (which offer such benefits as convenience and privacy) has been a difficult one. There has been an increase in the number of passengers carried by local mass transit companies since 1975. Yet, one study has found that even as gasoline prices soared in the 1970s, the use of public transportation in several metropolitan areas actually declined. Moreover, more than half the commuters in the areas studied drove alone to work.[43]

PAYING THE BILLS

"Congested and often inadequate roads, potholes, and crumbling bridges are daily stories in our cities, suburbs, and rural areas,"[44] the mayor of Buffalo Grove, Illinois, told a congressional committee in 1990. Local officials all over the country in the early 1990s had massive transportation problems. Over 40 percent of paved roads were deficient and in need of surface repairs. About half of all bridges were structurally deficient or functionally obsolete.

Compounding the problem of state and local officials in the 1970s and 1980s was that, while construction costs increased, there was a decline in revenues from gasoline taxes, in part because of the switch to more fuel-efficient cars. States responded to this revenue problem with higher gasoline taxes. To keep up with inflation, some states now set the tax as a percentage of the price, wholesale or retail, of a gallon of gas rather than at a flat rate. Voters, while not generally enthusiastic about new taxes, have been willing to pay more in gasoline taxes if the revenues are dedicated to improving deteriorating highway systems.

Among other changes given serious consideration in the states to cope with the costs of maintenance and construction is the use of toll roads. These place the financial burden on those who use the roads. States and localities have also looked into the feasibility of various forms of *congestion pricing*, which make those who contribute to congestion pay stiffer charges than others. An example of congestion pricing is making those who use mass transit at rush hour pay more than those who travel at other times.

While financing of transportation has increasingly become a state and local responsibility, Congress has not altogether ignored the demand for federal assistance. With passage of the ISTEA legislation discussed earlier, Congress not only gave state and local governments more discretion in spending funds, but increased federal funding for transportation improvements. Under the act, some $151 billion is to be spent over a six-year period, largely for highways, bridges, and mass transportation projects.

ENDNOTES

1. For differing views on the effect of governmental policies on urban development, see: Robert G. Wood, *1400 Governments: The Political Economy of the New York*

Metropolitan Region (Cambridge: Harvard University Press, 1961); Michael N. Danielson and Jameson W. Doig, *New York: The Politics of Urban Regional Development* (Berkeley: University of California Press, 1982); Paul Peterson, *City Limits* (Chicago: University of Chicago Press, 1981); and Clarence N. Stone and Heywood T. Sanders, *The Politics of Urban Development* (Lawrence: University Press of Kansas, 1987). For a brief historical account, see generally: C.W. Griffin Jr., "Frontier Freedoms and Space Age Cities," *Saturday Review* (7 February 1970): 17–19, 58–59.

2. Francine F. Rabinovitz, *City Politics and Planning* (New York: Atherton Press, 1969), pp. 6–7.

3. See *ibid.*, pp. 1–4.

4. See: Anthony J. Catanese, *Planners and Local Politics: Impossible Dreams* (Beverly Hills, Calif.: Sage Publications, 1974).

5. Donald H. Webster, *Urban Planning and Municipal Public Policy* (New York: Harper & Row, 1958), pp. 284–289.

6. See: Arnold Fleishmann, "Politics, Administration, and Local Land-Use Regulation: Analyzing Zoning as a Policy Process," *Public Administration Review* (July/August 1989): 337–344.

7. *First Evangelical Lutheran Church of Glendale* v. *County of Los Angeles*, 96 1 Ed 2d 250, 107 S. Ct. 2378 (1987).

8. See: Richard Briffault, "State-Local Relations and Constitutional Law," *Intergovernmental Perspective* (Summer/Fall 1978): 10–14.

9. See: Michael N. Danielson, "The Politics of Exclusionary Zoning in Suburbia," *Political Science Quarterly* 91 (Spring 1976): 1–18.

10. James C. Clingermayer and Richard C. Feiock, "Council Views Toward Targeting of Development Policy Benefits," *The Journal of Politics* 57 (May 1995): 508–520.

11. Alan A. Altshuler and Jose A. Gomez-Ibanez with Arnold M. Howitt, *Regulation for Revenue: The Political Economy of Land Use Exactions* (Washington, D.C., and Cambridge, Mass.: The Brookings Institution and Lincoln Institute of Land Policy, 1993).

12. Todd Donovan and Max Neiman, "Local Growth Control Policy and Changes in Community Characteristics," *Social Science Quarterly* 76 (December 1995): 780–793. See also: John R. Logan and Min Zhou, "Do Suburban Growth Controls Control Growth?" *American Sociological Review* 52 (1989): 802–825.

13. Studies on state programs include: Scott A. Bollens, "State Growth Management: Intergovernmental Frameworks and Policy Objectives," *Journal of the American Planning Association* (Autumn 1992): 454–466; Forster Ndubisi and Mary Dyer, "The Role of Regional Entities in Formulating and Implementing Statewide Growth Policies," *State and Local Government Review* (Fall 1992): 117–127; Dennis E. Gale, "Eight State-Sponsored Growth Management Programs: A Comparative Analysis," *Journal of the American Planning Association* (Autumn 1992): 425–439; Raymond J. Burby and Linda C. Dalton, "Plans Can Matter: The Role of Land Use Plans and State Planning Mandates in Limiting the Development of Hazardous Areas," *Public Administration Review* (May/June 1994): 229–238; and K.T. Liou and Todd J. Dicker, "The Effect of the Growth Management Act on Local Comprehensive Planning

Expenditures: The Southern Florida Experience," *Public Administration Review* (May/June 1994): 239–244.

14. Burby and Dalton, "Plans Can Matter."

15. See, for example: Eileen Shanahan, "Going It Jointly: Regional Solutions for Local Problems," *Governing* (August 1991): 70–75.

16. Robyne S. Turner, "Intergovernmental Growth Management: A Partnership Framework for State-Local Relations," *Publius: The Journal of Federalism* (Summer 1990): 79–95.

17. Liou and Dicker, "The Effect of the Growth Management Act on Local Comprehensive Planning Expenditures."

18. This apparently has been the experience in Florida in regard to the implementation of land-use planning legislation adopted in 1985. See: Jane Elizabeth Decker, "Management and Organizational Capacities for Responding to Growth in Florida's Nonmetropolitan Counties," *Journal of Urban Affairs* 9 (1987): 47–61.

19. See, generally, the discussion in Michael Lipsky, *Protest in City Politics: Rent Strikes, Housing and the Power of the Poor* (Chicago: Rand-McNally, 1970).

20. The following is based in part on data contained in: United States Bureau of the Census, *Census of Housing* (Washington, D.C.: Government Printing Office, 1980).

21. See: United States Bureau of the Census, *Indicators of Housing and Neighborhood Quality: 1975* (Washington, D.C.: Government Printing Office, 1977).

22. See: Executive Office of the President, Office of Management and Budget, *Social Indicators, 1973* (Washington, D.C.: Government Printing Office, 1973), p. 200.

23. *Building the American City*, Report of the National Commission on Urban Problems to the Congress and to the President of the United States (Washington, D.C.: Government Printing Office, 1968), p. 56.

24. See Martha R. Burt, *Over the Edge: The Growth of Homelessness in the 1980s* (New York: Urban Institute Press and the Russell Sage Foundation, November 1991); J.D. Wright, *Address Unknown: The Homeless of America* (Hawthorne, N.Y.: Aldine de Gruyter, 1989); and Cecil Bohanon, "The Economic Correlates of Homelessness in Sixty Cities," *Social Science Quarterly* 27 (December 1991): 817–825.

25. *Not in My Back Yard: Removing Barriers to Affordable Housing* (Washington, D.C.: Department of Housing and Urban Development, 1991).

26. The major federal legislation has been the McKinney Act of 1987, which created the Interagency Council for the Homeless to coordinate federal program efforts.

27. See: "Assisting the Homeless," *Intergovernmental Perspective* (Winter 1989): 31–35; and Penelope Lemov, "Cities and States Are Opening New Doors to Affordable Housing," *Governing* (November 1988): 52–58.

28. See: Howard Wolman, *Politics of Federal Housing* (New York: Dodd, Mead, 1971), pp. 28–36.

29. *Congressional Record* (5 June 1986): H3383.

30. Carol H. Hartwell, "Housing and Community Development," *Book of the States, 1985–86* (Lexington, Ky.: Council of State Governments, 1985), pp. 436–438.

31. Robert Reinhold, "Cities in North Face Reduced Federal Aid under Block Grants," *New York Times* (13 February 1977): 1, 16.

32. See: "Civil-Rights Groups Charge U.S. Grants Don't Help Living Conditions of the

Poor," *Wall Street Journal* (1 April 1976): 11. For another analysis of CDBG, see: Donald F. Kettl, *Managing Community Development in the New Federalism* (New York: Praeger, 1980).

33. See: Stephen J. Johnston and Hans B. Spiegel, "Helping to Decide Who Gets What: Evaluating Communities in Allocating Block Grant Funds," *National Civic Review* (December 1985): 521–528. A considerable amount of research, with varying results, has been done on the CDBG program. One might start with Edward T. Jennings et al., *From Nation to States: The Small Cities Community Development Block Grant Program* (Albany, N.Y.: SUNY Press, 1986). A somewhat critical account of this book, especially as it relates to the question of whether low- and moderate-income people suffered from the transition, is given by Laura L. Vertz, "Federalism and Community Conflicts, Concessions, and Compromises," review essay, *Urban Affairs Quarterly* (March 1988): 461–468. See also: David R. Morgan and Robert E. England, "The Small Cities Block Grant Program: An Assessment of Programmatic Change under State Control," *Public Administration Review* (November/December 1984): 477–482. Compare this with: Eric B. Herzik and John P. Pelissero, "Decentralization, Redistribution and Community Development: A Reassessment of the Small Cities CDBG Program," *Public Administration Review* (January/February 1986): 31–36. On variations in programs emphasized, see: Dale A. Krane, "Administering the Small Cities CDBG Program: A Federal-State Experiment," *Intergovernmental Perspective* (Summer 1988): 7–11.

34. See: Richard M. Kovak, "Urban Renewal Controversies," *Public Administration Review* 32 (July/August 1972): 362.

35. See: John H. Baker, *Urban Politics in America* (New York: Charles Scribner's Sons, 1971), pp. 318–319.

36. Under the homesteading program, the United States Department of Housing and Urban Development turns property over to cities that it acquired when the previous owner's HUD-guaranteed mortgage was foreclosed. Around forty communities now have homesteading programs.

37. See: Julian Weiss, "Enterprise Zones Are Just Part of the Answer for Reviving an Urban Economy," *Governing* (August 1988): 57–63. See also: Carla Smallwood, "Zone for Success," *American City & County* (April 1993): 30, 33.

38. On the political and other problems in implementing these programs, see: Gerry Riposa, "State Urban Enterprise Zones: Origin, Policy Content, and Administrative Constraints," *International Journal of Public Administration* (1989): 19–44. A brief account is found in David Bergman, "Enterprise Zones: A Cure for Urban America?" *National Civic Review* (Spring–Summer 1992): 186–187.

39. See, generally: "The Agony of the Commuter," *Newsweek* (18 January 1971): 44–48; Robert A. Aleshire, "The Case for Free Transit," *Nation's Cities* (October 1971): 25–28; and Wilfred Owen, *The Metropolitan Transportation Problem* (Garden City, N.Y.: Doubleday, 1966). Current information is found in: Joan C. Courtless, "Trends in Transportation," *Family Economics Review* 5 (1992): 19–26.

40. See: Bruce D. McDowell, "Reinventing Surface Transportation: New Intergovernmental Challenges," *Intergovernmental Perspective* (Winter 1992): 6–8, 18.

41. Robert W. Gage and Bruce D. McDowell, "ISTEA and the Role of MPOs in the New Transportation Environment: A Midterm Assessment," *Publius: The Journal of Federalism* 25 (Summer 1995): 133–154.

42. See: Alan Lupo, Frank Colcord, and Edmund P. Fowler, *Rites of Way: The Politics of Transportation in Boston and the U.S. City* (Boston: Little, Brown, 1971). In 1976, only four states (New York, Massachusetts, New Jersey, and Maryland) gave mass transit more than 15 percent of their budgets. See: "Cities v. States on Finances," *National Civic Review* (July 1976): 358–359.

43. United States Bureau of the Census, *Selected Characteristics of Travel to Work in 20 Metropolitan Areas: 1976* (Washington, D.C.: Government Printing Office, 1976).

44. Mayor Verna Clayton, quoted by Leslie Wollack, "House Public Works Unit Hears NLC on Surface Transportation Needs," *Nation's Cities Weekly* (7 May 1990): 6.

15

☆ ☆ ☆

THE POLITICS OF PUBLIC SAFETY

The last problem and policy area examined in this text is that of crime, police, and corrections. This chapter discusses first the nature of crime,[1] the crime problem, and the system of criminal justice (a portion of which was discussed in chapter 7). We then focus on the police, punishment, and corrections. The final section offers some observations and findings on the fight against crime.

CRIME IN THE UNITED STATES

THE NATURE OF CRIMINAL LAW

Crime, by definition, refers to behavior considered to be so deviant or dangerous that it is officially prohibited and punished.[2] Criminal law is largely developed through the legislative process and exists in the form of statutes. State legislatures enact the bulk of criminal law in this country, though the role of Congress has become more important.[3] In actual application to specific situations, what constitutes criminal activity depends on decisions made by police officers, prosecutors, and judges.

The major participants in the process of legislating criminal laws on the state level are those persons directly involved with law enforcement, such as judges, lawyers, police, and prison officials. Those most often involved are not a monolithic group. For example, there are differences of opinion between defense lawyers and prosecuting attorneys. Law enforcement groups also commonly find themselves at odds with organizations like the American Civil Liberties Union that seek to protect civil liberties and with groups concerned with certain specific causes such as prison reform.

Among legislators, some research suggests that there is a significant difference between women and men in how they view crime and prison issues—a difference akin to what we noticed in discussing male and female jurors (see chapter 7). Women appear to view crime in a broader social context, placing emphasis on prevention and early intervention strategies, while men look upon crime as a matter of individual responsibility to be dealt with by stricter sentencing and, if necessary, more prisons.[4]

Most people at least tacitly accept the decisions of the legislative process on criminal matters. Indeed, the public is unaware of many crimes and the penalties for criminal violations. But on some occasions, as shown by the widespread violation of marijuana laws, there is a wide gap between what legislators and a sizable segment of the public consider to be proper activity.

Acts such as homicide, rape, assault, and robbery are uniformly prohibited and are subject to various punishments throughout the states. Many other crimes involve activities that are not inherently dangerous except to those who commit them but are primarily violations of dominant moral codes.[5] Drunkenness, prostitution, gambling, homosexual activity between consenting adults, obscenity, and marijuana use are commonly cited as falling into this category of *victimless crimes*. Such crimes place a heavy burden on police and courts and sometimes require a degrading kind of law enforcement activity. They raise legal questions involving the right to privacy, lawful searches, and other methods of enforcement. Crimes of this nature also provide great potential for official corruption and, because of their widespread existence, disrespect for the law and injustices caused by selective enforcement (that is, going after only a few of those who violate the law).

Efforts to liberalize laws concerning most victimless crimes have made little headway in the states. Some jurisdictions, however, have made public drunkenness a medical problem rather than a crime and have established detoxification centers as alternatives to jail. Some states have also decriminalized marijuana possession laws, thereby making possession of small amounts an offense similar in seriousness to a traffic violation.

THE CRIME PROBLEM

The Uniform Crime Reports (UCR), prepared by the United States Federal Bureau of Investigation from information voluntarily submitted each year from nearly every police agency in the country, contains authoritative statistics

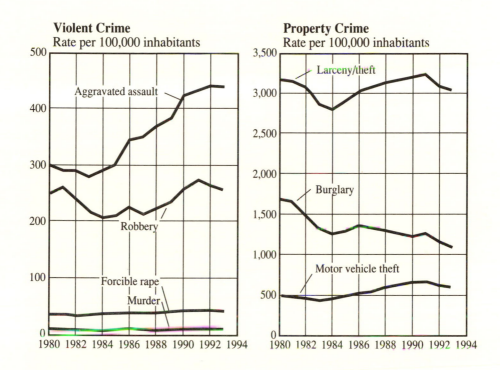

FIGURE 15–1 Violent and Property Crime Rates: 1980 to 1993

Source: Chart prepared by U.S. Bureau of the Census. Taken from *Statistical Abstract* (Washington, D.C., Government Printing Office, 1995), p. 198.

on crime in this country. The UCR covers violent crimes against individuals (murder, forcible rape, robbery, and aggravated assault) and property crimes (burglary, larceny-theft, and motor vehicle theft).[6] According to the UCR, the overall crime rate steadily increased from 1984 to 1991, before declining in 1992 and 1993. In 1993 the rate was 5,483 offenses for every 100,000 people. Figure 15–1, showing trends in the rate for particular offenses, indicates a rather steep increase in violent crimes since the mid-1980s, particularly aggravated assaults, while other crimes, such as burglary have been on the decrease. Crimes such as forcible rape, murder, and motor vehicle theft have stayed at relatively stable rates.

The usefulness of the above statistics is somewhat limited because many crimes covered by the UCR are not reported to the police and the reports of the police to the FBI may not always be accurate. Studies have found that, in any given year, only around 35 to 40 percent of all crimes are reported to the police. There is quite a variation in the rate that people report particular crimes. There are probably more than twice as many cases of simple assault, petty larceny, malicious mischief, fraud, and sex crimes than the statistics reflect. Only one out of ten cases involving consumer fraud (a crime not in the index) is reported to the police. On the other hand, auto theft is among the crimes most reported, in part because this is necessary to recover losses through insurance.[7]

Some failures to report a crime reflect a fear of retaliation. Many other failures to report are based on the belief that the matter involved was a private one. Crimes involving family members are the least likely of those covered by the FBI index to be considered police matters. Some studies suggest that a common reason given for not reporting a crime is the idea that the police could not do anything to solve the crime. Whether this reflects a rationalization for not reporting, a recognition that many crimes (like malicious mischief and burglary) are often never solved, a lack of respect for the police, or other reasons is unclear. Crime statistics may also be inaccurate because municipal officials may be eager to adjust the numbers either to reassure residents and potential tourists that crime is going down or, conversely, to convince them that more police resources are needed because crime rates are going up. The police themselves may not report all crime to the FBI out of fear that a high crime rate will reflect badly on them.

As imperfect as they are, official crime statistics do give us an indication of the location of crime and of likely offenders and victims. In recent years, the highest overall crime rates have been in the Sun Belt states of Florida, Arizona, and Texas. The rate for crimes of violence has been particularly high in Florida, New York, and California. The lowest overall rates have generally been in the lightly populated states of North Dakota, South Dakota, and West Virginia. One of the most distinctive regional variations has been the generally higher murder rate in southern states.

On the local level, the highest reported crime rates have been in the nation's largest cities (over a quarter of a million in population), though the rates vary significantly from one city to another, reflecting differences in police practices and the quality of police reporting. Crime rates are generally lowest in rural areas. Suburban crime rates generally fall between those of large cities and rural areas. In recent years, however, crime has been increasing at a faster rate in suburban and rural areas than in large cities.

Crime rates within large cities vary by neighborhoods. There is more adult and juvenile crime near the center of a large city and in deteriorated slum areas characterized by high population density, poor housing, and high unemployment. Types of crime that appear to be most concentrated in large cities include narcotics violations, gambling, and prostitution. The narcotics problem accounts for a considerable number of other crimes in large cities. Studies show that from 50 to 80 percent of the people arrested for serious offenses (burglary, grand larceny, and assault) in major cities test positive for illicit drugs.[8]

Box 15-1   Reacting to Juvenile Crime

Juvenile courts were initiated at the turn of the twentieth century in an effort to guide youngsters in trouble rather than to punish them. They served as support systems, backing up the family, in imposing discipline. As juvenile crime has increased in recent years—by 27 percent from 1980 to 1990—however, many state governments have responded by altering their juvenile justice systems. Many have lowered the age at which a juvenile can be tried as an adult, putting juveniles accused of crime on trial in adult courts. Some states have also experimented with boot camps designed to apply physical and mental discipline to straighten young people out before they become committed to a life of crime. Governmental and private agencies are experimenting with prevention and intervention programs targeted at youths in high crime areas. The long-range effects of these programs, however, are in doubt.

Sources: Donna Hunzeker, "Juvenile Crime, Grown Up Time," *State Legislatures* 21 (May 1995): 14-21; and United States General Accounting Office, *Prison Boot Camps: Short-Term Prison Costs Reduced, but Long-Term Impact Uncertain* (Washington, D.C.: Government Printing Office, April 1993).

Among the factors driving the overall crime rate reflected in the FBI's index, none is more important than the percentage of young people in the population. Crime rates have increased and are likely to increase with an increase in the number of people under nineteen. More than half of all crimes covered in the index are committed by people in this age bracket. Juvenile crimes most frequently involve larceny, burglary, and auto theft. In recent years, however, there has been a sharp increase in juvenile violent crime, a development the United States Justice Department has attributed to the increased availability of drugs and guns (see box 15–1).[9] Young people, from twelve to fifteen years old, have also had the greatest risk of being violent crime victims. This risk rate steadily declines with age.[10]

Statistics also suggest that the victims of crime usually are of the same race as the offenders. Thus, about 75 percent of white crime victims say their assailant was white and 85 percent of black victims say their assailant was black. Overall, nonwhites and those in the lower-income groups, especially in ghetto areas, are most likely to be the victims of crime. In recent years nearly half of all murder victims have been black. Homicide has become the most common cause of death for black males between the ages of fifteen and thirty-four.

Survey evidence suggests that the fear of crime and demands for crime control have been increasing in recent years.[11] Indeed, the fear of crime was growing in the 1990s, even though the official crime rate was going down.

Ironically, some of the increased fear may be due to crime awareness programs sponsored by police departments. More generally, however, fear of crime heightened with the attention the media have given to incidence of violent crime.

Generally, people see "crime" as something that happens to someone else rather than to them. Evidence of the fear of becoming a victim, however, is not difficult to find. Homes in high-crime areas commonly have bars on the windows and several locks on the doors. Over 40 percent of the residents in high-crime areas stay off the streets at night. Many people have armed themselves and/or formed neighborhood protection patrols. Women, nonwhites, and those who live in the largest communities especially fear crime in their neighborhoods. Most large cities have youthful street gangs. Los Angeles alone has more than 250 gangs roaming the streets. Some, but not all, gangs are involved in criminal activity. Unlike adult violent criminals, who usually act alone, teenagers who engage in violence usually do so as part of a group.

Many people believe that the convicted criminal gets off too easily, the police should be given more power, and steps must be taken to crack down on judges who are soft on crime. Many, if not a majority of the American people, are not interested in sociological explanations of crime (for example, its relation to unemployment or environmental conditions), but place emphasis on what are seen to be inherent personal shortcomings in criminals. The "no nonsense" and "get tough" approach is especially prevalent among whites over fifty years of age with limited formal education. People under age thirty-five, blacks, and college graduates are less likely to emphasize this approach and are more likely to be concerned with attacking the socioeconomic problems associated with crime.

From most accounts, much organized criminal activity occurs in all sections of the country—activity including gambling (especially on sports-related events), loan-sharking (loaning money above the maximum interest rate established by state law), prostitution (often taking place under the cover of massage parlors), pornography, drug trafficking, selling "protection" to businesspeople, and more sophisticated criminal activities such as land fraud, computer manipulation, and insurance irregularities.[12]

THE CRIMINAL JUSTICE SYSTEM

The system of criminal justice encompasses the activities of police, prosecutors, courts, and corrections institutions (see figure 15–2). In the mid-1990s, state and local governments were spending some $312 per capita on these activities. Close to half of the money spent on what are labeled "justice services" goes to police and about a third goes for corrections. Municipal governments pick up most of the bill for police, and state governments pay most of the costs for corrections. Generally, as one might expect, justice service expenditures are highest in the states with the highest crime rates.[13]

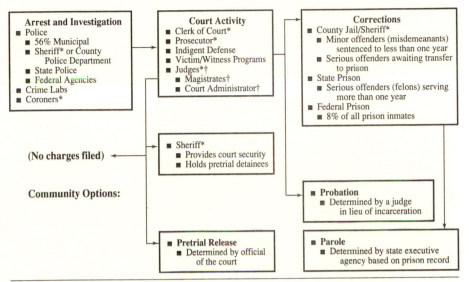

FIGURE 15-2   Criminal Justice System

Source: "The Criminal Justice Challenge: An Overview," *Intergovernmental Perspective* (Spring 1993): 12.

While problems of finance characterize debates over the criminal justice system, the amounts of money spent or proposed for spending on the system are quite small when compared to that spent on education, welfare, hospitals and health care, or highways. More controversial than the dollar amounts involved have been disputes over the performance of the system.

The criminal justice system has been described as "a nonsystem in which the police don't catch criminals, the courts don't try them, and the prisons don't reform them."[14] Not only are fewer than half of all serious crimes reported to the police but also only about 25 percent of those that are reported lead to an arrest of a suspect (crimes against property are particularly likely to remain unsolved). Moreover, only about half of all arrests lead to a conviction and about two out of three offenders who are sentenced return to a life of crime.

A great deal of discretion is exercised by public officials at every stage of the system. Decisions must be made whether or not to arrest, set bail, prosecute, convict, or release people from custody. The discretion inherent in making these decisions creates potential problems of discrimination on the basis of age, race, income, appearance, and other factors. Also of concern is the practical problem of imposing checks on this discretion through preconditioning (training) and legal corrective devices. Most important in providing at least potential legal checks have been the Fourth through Eighth Amendments to the United States Constitution. These apply either in whole or in part to state and local officials through the due process clause of the Fourteenth Amendment of the Constitution. Court-discovered violations of these civil rights may result in the banning of evidence illegally obtained and/or the freeing of a defendant found guilty.

The system of justice has functioned under great stress in recent years. Rising crime rates, disclosures about the activities of organized crime, growing drug abuse, riots, and terroristic violence have resulted in tremendous public pressure on government officials for more effective law enforcement. Most elements of the criminal justice system were designed for a far less turbulent society. Some of the most explosive problems in the criminal justice system involve race relations. Blacks have disproportionately been the victims of crime. Nearly half of all murder victims in this country are black. Blacks also are disproportionately more likely to be found guilty of crimes—about one of every five black males between fifteen and thirty-four has a criminal record.[15] The criminal justice system, on the other hand, is dominated by whites. Odds are high that a black accused of a crime will have been arrested by a white police officer, be prosecuted by a white attorney, and have a trial presided over by a white judge. Recent United States Supreme Court rulings preventing attorneys from using race as a ground for excluding potential jurors make it less likely that black defendants will be tried by juries that include blacks.

While issues involving blacks, Hispanics, and other minorities surface throughout the criminal justice system, the most explosive problems have been in the area of police-minority relations.

THE POLICE

POLICE FORCES

The police function in this country has traditionally been a local responsibility. For the most part, the police are locally recruited, trained, and paid. One result of this is that the police function in the United States is highly fragmented. There are about seventeen thousand general-purpose police departments at the local level. More than half of these have fewer than ten full-time employees. Analysts commonly regard departments with so few members as too small to do an effective job of law enforcement. While the police function remains largely local and is divided into numerous fiefdoms, much criminal activity is well organized on a national or even international basis.

Problems of fragmentation have commonly led to efforts to bring about greater cooperation among law enforcement agencies and to consolidate small departments into countywide or metropolitan police departments. Consolidation efforts, however, can be expected to encounter the types of problems discussed earlier in regard to governmental reorganization in metropolitan areas. Law enforcement is often popularly considered best performed on a decentralized rather than a centralized basis because local or neighborhood forces are more likely to be familiar with the community and to receive its support. Some evidence indicates that smaller police forces are more likely than large police forces to receive positive citizen evaluation.[16]

Formal authority over the municipal police is in the hands of a mayor, commissioner (an agent of the mayor), or city manager. In several places, the municipal reform movement resulted in the adoption of organizational arrangements intended to make it difficult for elected officials to remove the police chief. The idea, generally, was to take police work "out of politics." At the time, this meant out of the hands of corrupt political machines. Organizational arrangements adopted with this purpose in mind have been effective. In the early 1990s, for example, there was little the mayor or city council could do to dislodge Los Angeles Police Chief Daryl Gates over charges of police brutality. Removal of the chief required a finding by a five-member police board of a "good and significant cause" for removal and approval of the board's recommendation for removal by the City Board of Civil Service Commissioners.

Internally, police departments are organized in a military fashion into a "chain of command" that includes chiefs, assistant chiefs, majors, captains, sergeants, and patrolmen. The chief, or the superintendent, sets the tone of enforcement, gets personnel and money together, and seeks support for the police from other governmental officials and agencies. In practice, the chief does not have a great deal of control over subordinates, who have many opportunities to exercise their own discretion. Discretion in police work increases as one descends the organizational structure.

The number of full-time municipal police officers has increased over the years, though not as rapidly as the crime rate. In the early 1990s, the national average was 28 police officers per 10,000 people.[17] The range was from 16.3 in West Virginia to over 39 in New Jersey. Historically, averages have been highest in cities with a quarter of a million people or more, though many smaller suburbs are also particularly well protected. Some research suggests that the number of police officers increases as the proportion of the population that is nonwhite increases, regardless of the crime rate. Whites, in other words, appear to demand more protection as the black population increases, even though there may not actually be an increase in crime.[18]

Over 80 percent of the local police are white (non-Hispanic). Around 11 percent are black (non-Hispanic), and 5 percent are Hispanic. Just over 8 percent of local police are women.[19] Efforts to increase female and minority representation in city police departments have been considerably boosted by court-ordered affirmative action plans. For blacks, hirings have become more common in cities with black mayors and black police chiefs. White police officers have often resented these black gains.[20]

Though the following discussion will focus for the most part on the functions and problems of the municipal police officers, particularly in large cities, mention will be made here of other state and local law enforcement officers. In nearly all states there is an elected county sheriff, and in several states one finds an elected constable (a peace officer in towns and townships) and a county coroner whose responsibility is conducting inquests into suspicious deaths.

County sheriffs often have responsibility for enforcing laws within their entire jurisdictions. For political and economic reasons, however, they have traditionally not become involved with municipal police efforts except on request. Sheriffs typically have many other responsibilities in addition to law enforcement. They may, for example, be county court officers, jailers entrusted with the maintenance of the county jail, or even serve as tax collectors. In many of the most urbanized counties, however, the sheriff's office has become as professional as the big-city police departments, and several municipal police functions are performed by the sheriff on a contract basis with city police. In some areas, county police departments have been established independently of the sheriff's office, and the sheriff spends his or her time on nonlaw enforcement activities.

Every state but Hawaii has a state police force whose members have general police authority throughout the state. The state police departments, known as Highway Patrols, however, are largely restricted to the enforcement of highway regulations. Some of these are located in the state highway or motor vehicle departments. In some states, the governor supervises the state police through a superintendent or commissioner responsible to him or her, and the department undertakes statewide criminal investigations.

In practice, sometimes according to state law, the responsibilities of state police are restricted to unincorporated areas. However, the state police may be called in by local officials to help in riot control, to provide disaster relief, and to assist in general law enforcement. State police may provide investigations on request, hold training for local police, and have criminal laboratories open to local police. In some states, the state police may also investigate complaints against local police officers. State police have sometimes used their statewide criminal jurisdiction to enter a city and close down vice operations and other forms of illegal activity that city police have been unable or unwilling to do anything about. This type of involvement, however, is rare.

Also somewhat rare is the use of National Guard units for crime-fighting purposes such as working with United States Border Patrol agents in attempting to stem the flow of illegal drugs from Mexico.

Police Behavior and Functions

Over the years there has been a marked growth in the professionalism of police forces. This has resulted from changes that have stiffened eligibility and training requirements, shifted many noncriminal responsibilities to civilian personnel, and added new organizational or managerial controls to combat problems of corruption or incompetence and to improve departmental performance. The broad goal has been not only to improve the crime-fighting abilities of the police but also to bolster the prestige of those in the occupation.

Police do, indeed, because of their training and specialized knowledge, consider themselves "professionals." At the same time, while obviously not all police are alike, it is possible to discern certain other common police characteristics, values, and modes of behavior. Police officers, for the most part, are white, identify with the lower middle class, and are conservative in their politics. A police officer is likely to be suspicious, sparked by danger signals (for example, the way people are dressed, insolence, anyone looking out of place); to enjoy the possibility of excitement and danger; to feel he or she is not liked, respected, or supported by the community; and to be drawn particularly close to his or her colleagues, both on the job and in social life.[21] Their subculture leads police to think of themselves as part of the unappreciated "thin blue line" between civilization and barbarism.

Police officers provide general social or community services, maintain order, and enforce the law.[22] Only about one-third of all police radio calls involve criminal matters that could result in arrests. Several of the police service functions, such as animal rescue, could be performed by private enterprise but are thought to be helpful in establishing a favorable image of the police in the community.

The oldest police function is that of maintaining order. This task involves checking out suspicious conduct, getting drunks off the streets, and breaking up loitering or fights. In some areas, family disputes keep the police busier than any other activity except automobile accidents. Police officers are often injured in trying to arbitrate these disputes as one or several family members turn against the outsider. Often an arrest in one of these cases will be meaningless because charges will not be pressed. The maintenance of order is the source of many of the present-day problems of the police. It subjects a police officer to an environment of hostility, if not physical danger, because he or she must prejudge people by their appearance and may encounter community standards at odds with his or her own.

In contrast to the role of maintaining order, police may be looked on and regard themselves primarily as professional law enforcers whose job is to bring down the crime rate and enforce the laws whenever they are broken. Professional crime fighters are not apt to think highly of their performing the service functions and their emphasis on enforcing the law may actually make the job of maintaining order that much more difficult. As James Q. Wilson has pointed out, law enforcement and the maintenance of order are two different and not always compatible functions. Rigid enforcement of the laws, such as those regarding marijuana, may make the police unpopular with a segment of society and lead to disorder. Again, the police might use the law somewhat unfairly from a judge's point of view to maintain order, for example, making an arrest simply to cool things down.

Police officers on the beat have much discretion in the enforcement of the laws. In large part, this is because many of the laws, such as those against "disorderly conduct" or "disturbing the peace," are ambiguous at best. To some extent the method of enforcement is set as a departmental policy. For example, the department may emphasize the peacekeeping role, allowing patrol officers to ignore many common violations like traffic and juvenile offenses or even vice and gambling while concentrating on keeping things peaceful. Other departments see the role to be one of enforcing all laws and, indeed, each officer may have an arrest quota. Departmental policies, of course, vary over time, and not infrequently a crackdown on various activities is conducted.

In specific situations, however, patrol officers are on their own. Often they alone make the decision of who is going to enter the system of criminal justice. The mood of the individual officer, his or her prejudices, and the general demeanor of the person with whom he or she is dealing have a bearing on whether or not the law is enforced. The law is more likely to be administered against the young, nonwhite, and less affluent. The police are also more likely to dislike and punish by arrest and other means those who show attitudes of disrespect and challenge their authority.

The peacekeeping role leads to suspicion of outsiders, swift distinctions between "good guys" and "bad guys," and rather aggressive reactions to disrespect for police authority because this signifies disrespect for law and order. Respect for authority and order plays a large role in the quasi-military training of police officers and the organizational environment in which they work.

Overall, however, police underenforce the laws. They may regard less serious crimes as hardly worth the time or effort involved in making an investigation or an arrest. On some occasions, the police may pass over the violation of a law by a respectable-looking first offender in order save the offender from embarrassment. Enforcement of the law may also be waived at times to secure the support of an offender in making a more important arrest of a "higher-up."

Nonenforcement of the law, finally, may also stem from police corruption. Corruption has been particularly associated with illegal activities like gambling, prostitution, after-hours drinking in bars, and the sale of narcotics. In some cities, those who seek to engage in illegal activities are put "on the pad," that is, they are protected from arrest in exchange for monetary and other favors.[23] Police corruption may be but a part of a broader pattern of corruption that involves links between local political figures, judges, and prosecutors, as well as certain police chiefs. Police corruption may occur on a department-wide basis, within a small group workforce such as a vice squad, or in the unrelated activities of individual police officers.

Police brutality may also be a problem. This came to the forefront in 1991 with the nationwide telecast of a videotape showing Los Angeles policemen kicking and beating black motorist Rodney King. Many citizens saw the King beating as an example of a long pattern of police violence and abuse directed, in large part, against blacks and Hispanics. In the year preceding the King affair, the city paid out $8.1 million in damages to victims of excessive force.

Civil rights groups, in the aftermath of the King case, contended that a "culture of violence" directed at minorities had "swept the nation's police forces."[24] Polls indicate that a majority of Americans agree that blacks and Hispanics are the victims of much police brutality.[25] Analysts have linked the problem to several factors, including racism in police departments. Also cited are the lack of police training and discipline and the existence of fraternal pressures. The latter encourages an officer to look the other way when a fellow officer uses excessive force. Feelings of camaraderie may also make an officer cover for other officers who abuse their authority. Experts further attribute police violence to an overemphasis of military models in police organization and operations, fear of personal injury, and frustrations over the increasingly difficult task of crime fighting.[26]

Most large cities have some type of civilian board to hear and investigate complaints against police. In other cities, this function is performed by the police department itself. Though review by a citizen committee is more popular with the public, internal review systems may, in fact, be more rigorous and more severe on accused police officers.[27]

POLICE IN CONFLICT

Police values and dispositions frequently have conflicted with those of certain segments of society, other components of the system of justice (judges, prosecutors, parole boards), and elected public officials. The values of a white police officer with a working-class background can be expected to clash with those of middle-class college youths, hippies, and young members of racial minority groups. Such clashes have been particularly evident in situations involving demonstrations and riots. The police in these situations have often been provoked by militant hostility and violence toward them to respond not simply as neutral peacekeepers but as the sworn enemies of "evildoers."

Some of the most difficult and highly publicized problems of the police have been in the largely black inner-city ghetto areas. There are both positive and negative attitudes toward the police in the inner-city community. Local businesspeople would like more police protection than they now have.[28] Older members of the community seem proud of their sons and daughters who have joined the police force. At the same time, many of the young and more militant want less police intervention and look on the police as an occupying force of the white power structure that maintains order by legalized violence. Black police are likely to be seen by the more militant in the community as traitors or Uncle Toms.

Hostility between police and those in ghetto areas was cited by the Kerner Commission in the 1960s as one of the primary causes of the disorders they surveyed.[29] Specifically, blacks contended that police responded more slowly to calls from nonwhite neighborhoods and that the police harassed nonwhites far more than whites with physical and verbal abuse.[30]

Part of the problem in police-ghetto relations stems from the lack of police identity with the community. It has been difficult to find a police officer who lives in the inner-city community and shares the same conditions and culture as the people on his or her beat. Frequently, the police officer lives in a middle-class neighborhood and travels daily to the city to work. In addition to making the police officer part of the community, reformers have placed emphasis on *community policing*. This reform takes police officers out of their cars and puts them back on neighborhood streets so they can get to know the community and its problems. The police, in these types of programs, are in the neighborhood to render assistance and work with people in a nonthreatening way, rather than impose order as paramilitary units. The idea of *co-production* of police services, that is, having citizens in the neighborhood join directly in helping fight crime, has also been implemented in several communities.[31]

At times, there has been considerable tension within the system of justice between the police and the courts. On the everyday level, police frustration stems from long court delays that result in the loss of thousands of police working hours yearly and from how the courts dispose of cases. In the eyes of a police officer, an arrest is virtually tantamount to guilt. Prosecutors and judges may see the situation differently and may not (in the opinion of the police) give the offender the proper punishment. On another level, police may see judicial decisions such as the *Miranda* case (see below) as "soft on crime" and as hindering the police from doing their jobs. Similarly, police tend to be highly critical of liberal bail, probation, and parole decisions because they put arrested offenders back on the streets and may cause them to do their work all over again.

Relations between elected officials and the police also have been strained at times. This has been evident in police slowdowns and strike activity intended to secure greater material benefits and changes in local law enforcement policy. At times, the police have directly challenged civilian authority. During the urban disorders in Cleveland in the 1960s, for example, the police openly condemned the public safety director and the mayor for ordering police out of rioting areas so black leaders could restore order. Similarly, New York police strongly opposed Mayor Lindsay's proposal in the mid-1960s to add civilians to a board established to review complaints of police brutality and misconduct. The proposal immediately led to a sudden increase in the department's retirement-resignation rate and was criticized by the police commissioner, who, in turn, was replaced by the mayor. Later, however, the Patrolmen's Benevolent Association and the Conservative Party secured a referendum on the proposal and the voters gave the police a resounding victory.[32] More generally, the police, like the other local administrators who consider themselves professionals, have confidence in their own expertise and abilities and resist what they see as undue political interference in their affairs.

LEGAL CONSTRAINTS

In enforcing the laws, there are certain legal limits on the police officer's discretion. Should evidence be illegally obtained, for example, because of an illegal search or because of a forced confession growing out of prolonged police detention or brutality, it may not be used in court.

Before making an arrest, a police officer must usually secure a warrant from a magistrate by demonstrating that a crime has been committed or is likely to be committed. In an emergency, however, an officer without a warrant may make an arrest based on his or her own determination of probable cause of the need for an arrest. The police officer's judgment under these circumstances can only be questioned later in a court of law.

Technically, under the Fourth Amendment to the Constitution, a police officer must also appear before a judicial officer to secure a search warrant. The officer must demonstrate that there is probable cause that evidence (the means or result of a crime) will be found and must provide a description of the place to be searched and the evidence to be seized. As in the case of arrests, there are several situations in which a search warrant is not required. Police can make their own judgment of "probable cause" that a search is needed under emergency conditions, though again this decision may be questioned later in court. Police have the power to make searches of persons and the immediate area following an arrest to obtain weapons or to prevent the destruction of evidence. A police officer may also "stop and frisk" a suspect who appears to be dangerous or carrying a concealed weapon. Recent court rulings have also allowed the police to prove probable cause on the basis of information supplied by an unidentified informer. In most states police are allowed to enter homes unannounced. The use of "no knock" warrants has been especially aimed at preventing the destruction of evidence during drug raids. Under recent rulings, the police also may search from airplanes for marijuana growing in fenced-in private backyards without first securing a court warrant.

Under the Fifth Amendment, those accused of crime have constitutional protections against psychologically or physically coerced confessions. The Supreme Court, in *Miranda* v. *Arizona*,[33] held that the Fifth Amendment requires that following an arrest and prior to any questioning, the police warn the suspect "that he has a right to remain silent, that any statement he does make may be used as evidence against him, and that he has a right to the presence of an attorney, either retained or appointed."

Police and others immediately criticized this decision for imposing a barrier to solving crimes through confessions. Subsequent research, however, has revealed that the decision has had relatively little impact on the confession rate or on police practices. Confessions have been found essential to conviction in only a small percentage of cases, and this percentage has not decreased since *Miranda*. As before *Miranda*, most criminals, especially the experienced ones, do not make confessions or incriminating statements to the police. Research also indicates that many suspects do not take advantage of the *Miranda* decision. Those relatively few who do take advantage of *Miranda* to have their confession invalidated because it was made in violation of the procedural requirements, usually wind up convicted on other evidence.[34]

PUNISHMENT AND CORRECTIONS

SENTENCING

Penalties imposed on those convicted of a crime include probation (release under supervision for a given period), fines, short-term confinement in local jails, long-term confinement in prison, and the death sentence. The judge's discretion in passing sentence is conditioned by the sentencing code, that is, the laws prescribing penalties for each particular type of crime. These codes or laws may be inconsistent. For example, several years ago the President's Commission on Law and Administration of Justice found that in Colorado a person convicted of first-degree murder must serve at least ten years before becoming eligible for parole, whereas a person convicted of a lesser degree of murder must serve at least fifteen years. Colorado law also set the penalty for stealing a dog at a ten-year prison term, while the penalty for killing a dog was only a six-month jail sentence.[35]

The codes may carry fixed sentences and forbid the granting of probation, or they may allow a judge to choose between probation or a prison term of up to twenty-five years. Mandatory sentencing to prison is common for some types of crimes, for example, those involving violence. Otherwise, the judge may choose an alternative to prison, such as probation, a fine, or a suspended sentence. A judge may make an indeterminate sentence, "from one-to-five," and thereby allow the parole authorities to determine how long an individual will actually serve in prison.

BOX 15-2   THREE STRIKES YOU'RE OUT AND WE'RE BROKE

In response to the fear of crime, lawmakers in several states have passed "three strikes and you're out" legislation that mandates sentences from twenty-five years to life for three-time felons. While popular with the public, such laws are likely to be very expensive. Some critics have labeled them "three strikes and we're broke" laws. Research suggests, for example, that while the three-strikes law adopted in California in 1994 might reduce the crime rate by as much as 25 percent, the annual cost is likely to be about $5.5 billion. Most of the cost is for expanding the prison system. California now spends about $34,000 each year for each juvenile prisoner and $28,000 for each adult prisoner. Violent crimes are committed disproportionately by men between thirteen and twenty-three, peaking at age seventeen. Keeping them in jail all their lives dramatically increases the costs of prisons and eventually helps turn them into expensive geriatric wards. Critics also contend that the law is likely to have little effect on the amount of random violence. Those who commit such acts are apt to wind up with long prison terms in the twilight of their careers and are likely to be replaced by a new crop of youthful offenders. Critics also contend that the laws sometimes fail to distinguish between violent and nonviolent felonies and thus may be too harsh (for example, requiring a life sentence for stealing a can of beer) and are not as effective as laws aimed at particular types of crimes.

See: Peter W. Greenwood et al., *Three Strikes and You're Out: Estimated Benefits and Costs of California's New Mandatory-Sentencing Laws* (Santa Monica, Calif: Rand, 1994). See also: John H. Culver and Kimberly Thiesen, "The Impact of '3 Strikes' in California," *Comparative State Politics* (December 1995): 14-18.

Since the mid-1970s, a rising crime rate has prompted more and more states to turn from indeterminate to determinate sentencing. Under determinate sentencing, criminals are sent to prison for a specific amount of time. This practice eliminates discretionary parole and requires inmates to serve their full terms with the possible exception of time off for good behavior. Giving credit for good behavior, the law in several states requires that convicts must serve at least 85 percent of their sentences. Such laws add pressure to build or expand prison facilities and drive up the share of state budgets going to corrections. State laws concerning "three strikes and you're out" have similar effects (see box 15–2).

In addition to codes, judicial sentencing is influenced by the recommendations of prosecutors and presentence reports usually made by probation officers. Sentencing recommendations offered by prosecutors, as noted in chapter 8, are often the product of plea bargaining. Presentence reports contain basic information about the defendant, such as his or her previous criminal record and impressions of his or her attitudes based on an interview, and sentencing recommendations. Defendants or their lawyers may not be able to examine the presentence report or to offer counterevidence. Available studies indicate that judges are likely to grant probation when it is recommended. Judges, however, also appear to be less harsh in sentencing than probation officers would like. Judges often grant probation even when the presentence report calls for imprisonment.[36]

Sentences for the same crime differ greatly, not only from state to state, but also from judge to judge within the same court system. As a Committee for Economic Development study noted: "Two felons convicted of identical offenses and with comparable case histories may receive prison terms differing in length by [a ratio of] three or four to one."[37] Judges, it has been charged, often lack education on sentencing philosophy, adequate information on defendants before sentencing, and personal knowledge of prison conditions.[38] Some studies suggest that more severe sentences are given to members of minority groups (especially black males),[39] though this may not be as important as prior record in determining the harshness of the sentence. Apparently benefiting in terms of sentencing are natives or long-term local residents over newcomers or outsiders, property owners over nonproperty owners, defendants with children over those without children, and those with business suits over those wearing work clothing.[40]

CORRECTIONS

The field of corrections covers three areas of activity: imprisonment, probation, and parole. Since 1980, the number of people under correctional authority has nearly tripled. In 1994, over 5 million Americans were under the supervision of some type of correctional authority. About 1.5 million of these people were incarcerated. Federal and state prisons held about two-thirds of the total (there are about ten times as many people in state prisons as in federal prisons). The remainder of the incarcerated were in local jails. Most people under correctional authority were in the community either on probation or parole. Nearly 3 million adults were on probation and 690,000 were on parole.

Overall, the field of corrections is fragmented among the various levels of government and within levels of government. It is also characterized by debates over the purposes of corrections and between those who put emphasis on confinement and those who stress community-based rehabilitation programs.

There are more than four thousand correctional institutions in this country operated by federal, state, county, and city officials. The rate of prisoners per 100,000 population was relatively stable from the 1930s to the 1970s, but has dramatically increased since the 1980s. The rate of incarceration for prisoners sentenced to more than a year grew from 139 per 100,000 United States residents in 1980 to 387 in 1994. By the early 1990s, the United States had surpassed South Africa and the former Soviet Union for the dubious honor of having a larger share of its population behind bars than any other nation. The higher incarceration rate reflects, in large part, the higher crime rate in this country.

The prison population has swelled in response to tougher public attitudes toward crime and an increase in the number of convictions. Legislatures have added to the growth problem by extending sentences and eliminating discretionary parole. Violent offenders have contributed the most to the growth of the prison population. Better than a fourth of all inmates were convicted for a drug offense. Southern and western states have generally had proportionately more inmates. Differences among the states are due in large part to differences in crime rates and to differences in sentencing and parole policies.

Policies regarding confinement reflect several objectives. Confinement, to some, is justified as a matter of vengeance, that is, as an appropriate way to make people pay for their crimes against society. A second justification for confinement is that it is useful because it helps deter others form committing crimes. A third function of confinement is simply to protect society from dangerous people. A final view on confinement is that of reforming or rehabilitating offenders so they can become useful members of society.

State and local governments have traditionally placed emphasis on the first three of these objectives and have shunned the rehabilitative approach. In general, they have been reluctant to devote much attention or money to an effort to improve prison and jail conditions. In the absence of judicial pressure, these institutions are usually among the last to receive a piece of the tax dollar, and most of the money allocated to them is earmarked for custodial purposes. Compared to other demands on governmental resources, those of prisoners, in the absence of a well-publicized uprising, have been relatively easy for legislatures to ignore. Court decisions have been the principal factor forcing legislatures to spend more on correctional reform.[41] Expenditures per inmate in state facilities averaged $15,586 in 1993. The total cost was well over $25,000 in some states.

JAILS AND PRISONS

Jail and prison conditions around the country vary greatly, depending on financial resources and management practices.[42] Some of the greatest deficiencies continue to be found in county and city jails, which house not only those convicted of misdemeanors and serving a sentence of a year or less but also a large number of persons who have not yet been convicted of anything. Indeed, more than half of those in a typical jail may be awaiting a trial because they were unable to obtain bail or release on their own recognizance. Traditionally, city jails have also been a dumping ground for drifters, the unemployed, alcoholics, and people with severe mental problems.

City and county jails are usually operated by law enforcement personnel whose main concerns and experience usually lie in other fields. The basic job of the police or the sheriff leaves little time or expertise for the development of rehabilitation programs or jail reform. Many law enforcement officials have themselves advocated the transfer of jails to correctional control. Local jails are often poorly financed and overcrowded and lack medical, educational, and recreational facilities. As many as one-third of the nation's jails are more than fifty years old. Jails are often the scene of problems like homosexual activity, beatings of inmates and guards, drug traffic, and racial tensions. Problems of this nature are more apparent in the larger cities and more urban counties.

State prisons, though the object of much reform in recent years, generally have the same if not more pronounced problems. These problems and the need for reform were dramatically demonstrated in a series of prison riots that shook the nation in the 1970s and early 1980s. One of the most sensational of these uprisings was in 1971 at the Attica State Correctional Facility in Attica, New York. The facility, resembling others in its fortress-like structure with thirty-foot-high walls, contained twenty-two hundred prisoners, 85 percent of whom were black or Puerto Rican. The rebellion, sparked by an order that one prisoner be placed in solitary confinement, led to the prisoners' seizure of some forty guards and control of two cell blocks. The prisoners, declaring, "If we can't live like human beings, at least we can die like men,"[43] demanded a number of reforms including less cell time, freedom of religion, and better food and medical services. The rebellion ended shortly after a raiding party of state troopers opened fire, killing thirty inmates and some hostages as well. Nine years after the Attica rebellion an equally dramatic and tragic uprising occurred at the New Mexico State Penitentiary near Santa Fe in which convicts killed thirty-three other inmates. Many of the murdered convicts were "snitches" (informers to prison authorities on the activities of other prisoners). Like other prisons, the New Mexico State Penitentiary was greatly overcrowded; nearly twelve hundred prisoners lived in space designed for eight hundred.

Before the eighteenth century, prisons were used for the most part to detain people awaiting trials or punishment. Under Quaker influence, incarceration was seen as a humane substitute for punishment. The Quakers felt that the best way to reform criminals was to lock them in solitary cells so that they would have no alternative but to repent and reform themselves. Many chose suicide or went insane. Built partially on the same principles was the "Auburn System," which has had widespread influence on prison administration. The system, developed in New York's Auburn Prison, called for shaved heads, separate confinement in cells, and hard labor in utter silence in shops, fields, or quarries.

The philosophy that has traditionally governed prison administration has been essentially negative; a prisoner is expected to "do his or her time" apart from staff and other inmates. Historically, prisoners have been denied access to legal counsel and other due process protections. Since the 1960s, however, greater attention has been given to the human and civil rights of prisoners. Litigation regarding prisoners' rights has often been initiated by individual inmates and prisoner organizations. Favorable court rulings and reforms initiated by prison administrators have reduced or eliminated mail censorship and strict clothing codes in many state systems and have increased recognition of the rights of prisoners in such matters as religious practice, medical care, and working conditions. Many judges since the 1960s have based their order for prison reform on the Eighth Amendment's ban on cruel and unusual punishment.

One of the most severe problems has been overcrowding. In the mid-1990s, state prisons were operating at between 17 percent and 29 percent over capacity.[44] This problem may be attributed to not only a growth in the arrest rate but also harsher state sentencing policies. To accommodate an increase in prison population, many states have doubled up inmates in cells (commonly nine by six feet) designed for one. Some prisons are so overcrowded that judges will not commit new prisoners to them. Some states have adopted emergency early release programs to relieve overcrowded conditions. These have been accompanied by "home arrest programs" which call for close supervision of those released through electronic monitoring and other devices. Some states also confine people in local jails because of the lack of space in prison facilities.

Since the 1980s, many jurisdictions, in an effort to economize and accommodate a growing prison population, have considered contracting out for correctional services. A number of profit-making private firms, some of which are headed by former wardens, have gone into the business of building or operating correctional facilities. Critics of contracting out argue that private operation of correctional facilities need not be more economical or efficient than public operation and that, indeed, turning to private enterprise, where the goal is to maximize profits, could lead to a deterioration of conditions.

Reacting to the problem of overcrowding and court orders for reform, several states have constructed new prisons in recent years. Such facilities have generally been valued in economically depressed areas as a way of improving the local economy. Most prison authorities would rather place the new facilities near major population centers so the inmates would be closer to their families and to needed professional assistance. Few city or suburban residents, however, want a prison facility anywhere near their neighborhood and, as a consequence, state authorities are likely to find their decisions on the location of a new facility to be hotly contested.

Meanwhile, despite improvements in civil and human rights, contemporary prison conditions are generally considered to be deplorable. Prisons often mix youthful offenders with hardened ones, and homosexuals with straights. As many as 50 percent of all prisoners engage in homosexual activity at one time or another during imprisonment. Homosexual rapes are commonplace. Racial tensions are also frequent. Conflicts may occur between a prison population that is predominantly nonwhite and guards who are usually white. In other places, the prisoners themselves divide on the basis of race. There are also problems of poorly paid and trained guards, inadequate sanitary conditions, and dilapidated facilities. To a considerable extent, guards depend on the tougher convicts and gang leaders to control other inmates.

Perhaps most needed for rehabilitation are educational and vocational programs. Lack of education and a marketable skill are reasons why many wind up in prison and why many have further difficulties leading to arrest following release. Prison industries, however, have often been more concerned with making profits than with training. They do not make products that compete with private industry. Nor can prison-made goods be sold on the open market. Many prison jobs, such as license-plate making, have no direct applicability to the type of employment found on the outside and are not in great demand. Other barriers to outside employment are legal restrictions that disqualify ex-convicts from holding certain types of jobs that require licenses (barber, lawyer) and, more importantly, the prejudice of employers against hiring ex-convicts.

COMMUNITY-BASED TREATMENT

Given the high costs of incarceration, state governments have given increased consideration to probation, parole supervision, house monitoring, halfway houses, and drug treatment centers as less expensive alternatives. Some also have looked at chain gangs to save expenses and to help deter crime. Others have looked at community corrections, that is, allowing offenders to function in the community, as a way of not only saving money but giving offenders a far better chance of rehabilitation than they would have if locked up.

Common practices emphasizing the community-based approach are probation, parole, inmate furloughs, and halfway houses. Probation under a suspended sentence for a period of supervised control within the community is commonly given for less serious crimes. Supervisory authority is given to a probation officer with whom the probationer must maintain regular contact. If the rules of probation are violated, the probationer may be sentenced to jail or prison. Probation is a far more frequent penalty than confinement, particularly for juveniles and first offenders. Probation staffs in many places, however, are understaffed, untrained, and underpaid.

After serving a portion of his or her sentence, usually one-third, a prisoner may apply for parole. Parole does not come automatically. The factors considered most important by parole boards appear to be the severity of the offense, the risk to the public of granting parole, and the behavior of the convict while incarcerated.[45] Offenders given parole are subject to specified restrictions and requirements; for example, they may be forbidden to drink, drive an auto, change jobs, or marry without permission.

Inmate furloughs are largely unsupervised leaves monitored only by various types of random and formal checks. Inmates have, at times, abused such programs and in some cases, those on leave have committed serious crimes. An example of the latter is convicted killer William Horton, who raped a woman and stabbed her companion while on furlough in Massachusetts in 1987. Controversy centering on this incident and the use of similar furlough programs in forty-five other states was stimulated by George Bush's campaign against Massachusetts Governor Michael Dukakis in 1988. Despite this criticism and admitted abuses, furlough programs are defended on the grounds that they relieve overcrowding, prepare inmates for life outside prison, and reduce the rate of recidivism. Most states now limit participation in furlough programs to minimum security prisoners. Most also exclude sex offenders.

Work release programs have been used in several states, often as part of the sentencing procedure. Under these programs, selected prisoners work in the community during the day and return to confinement every night. Portions of the money earned are sent to the prisoners' families, returned to them on release, and used to pay for their lodging and board. The prisoners benefit from learning new skills and the state saves on prison costs or may even make money. The prisoners, moreover, are freed from the isolation of the prison and have a greater opportunity to live normal lives. Halfway houses have objectives similar to those of work release programs. To ease the transition from prison to community life, prisoners are sent to settlements three or four months before release. They work in the community under loose security.

The Eighth Amendment and the Death Penalty

The Eighth Amendment to the Constitution prohibits the inflicting of "cruel and unusual punishment." This ban applies to punishment that is totally inappropriate to the crime (a prison sentence for picking flowers in a public park) or that is cruel by its very nature (torture and mutilation). The standards for cruelty and unusualness are imprecise, determined by whether or not the punishment is consistent "with the evolving standards of decency that marks the progress of maturing society."[46] As it applies to corrections, the court has held that guards who use unnecessary force on prisoners may be violating the ban on cruel and unusual punishment.

Challenges to the death penalty as unconstitutional under the Eighth Amendment have thus far been unsuccessful. In 1972, however, the United States Supreme Court did invalidate all forty-one capital punishment statutes then in effect and ruled that the death penalty may not be imposed in an arbitrary or freakish manner or be applied in a discriminatory way on the basis of race. From 1930 to the early 1970s, a total of 3,859 persons had been executed under the death penalty, and 2,066 of these were black people. The impact of the Court's 1972 ruling was to remove some six hundred prisoners from death rows. State legislatures, however, were able to devise new death penalty statutes that met the Court's objections, and thirty-seven states now have such laws.

Since 1973, there has been a rapid increase in the number of persons in prison under the sentence of death. In many states, however, the death penalty seems to be of more importance as a political symbol than as a sentence intended to be carried out frequently.[47] Executions have been delayed in many states because prisoners have taken advantage of their right to pursue a series of appeals. In 1983, however, the Supreme Court made it possible for courts to speed up the time it takes to hear prisoners' appeals. In the case of *Lockhart* v. *McCree* (1986), the Court also removed a barrier to the use of the death penalty by ruling that opponents of this course of action can be barred from juries in capital punishment cases, even though the creation of "death qualified" juries increases the possibility of a conviction.

Public opinion polls suggest that Americans in the mid-1990s overwhelmingly favor the death penalty for murder, even though most agree that some people in recent years have probably been sentenced to death for crimes they did not commit.[48] Research indicates that, as one might expect, the death penalty has been more often enforced in states where conservatives are relatively prominent and in places where the murder rate has been the highest.[49]

On the individual level, however, there is considerable variation, even within the same state, as to how judges decide cases challenging the imposition of the death penalty. As one study has concluded: "Who reviews a case can quite literally mean the difference between life imprisonment and death in capital cases." Judges are more likely to uphold the death penalty when certain crimes or victims are involved, for example, murders of police officers. At the same time, to a surprising extent, one finds variation between Democratic and Republican judges on the application of the death penalty, the former being less favorably disposed. Differences also exist along the lines of age, older judges being more favorable to the death penalty, and in regard to the occupational background of judges—those with previous experience as prosecutors being more favorably disposed to the death penalty.[50]

FIGHTING CRIME

In recent years, much time, attention, and money have been given to fighting crime. However, there is little reason to believe that a mere increase in police expenditures will reduce the amount of crime. Indeed, in some places, increased expenditures have been accompanied by a higher crime rate. There is also considerable uncertainty over just what activities represent the best deployment of police personnel. Much of the time of the uniformed police officer may be wasted in riding or walking around patrolling the streets.[51] The chances of the police finding a crime being committed while they are on patrol are very slim. Some research has also indicated that police patrol activities have little, if any, impact in terms of deterring potential offenders or in giving the public a greater feeling of security.[52]

While considerable emphasis has been placed on getting tough on crime, that is, making more arrests, locking people up, and "throwing away the key," experts have suggested the need for a broader approach to crime. Municipal officials and police, for example, strongly prefer a mixture of strategies to reduce crime, rather than simply traditional law enforcement remedies. These include doing what can be done to strengthen family stability, improving the local economies and providing more jobs, and more after-school programs.[53]

In sum, there is much to be learned about what causes crime, how to protect the community against it, and how to prevent those convicted of crime from becoming repeaters.

ENDNOTES

1. This chapter is largely concerned with what is known as "common" or "street" crime. The term *white-collar crime* refers to several other activities. Among these are: (1) personal crimes such as fraud on income tax returns or insurance claims; (2) abuses of trust such as embezzlement, committed by those working within an organization against their employers; (3) business crimes such as price fixing and deceptive advertising, committed in the performance of business operations; and (4) con games such as phony contests and land frauds. See: Herbert Edelhertz, *The Nature, Impact and Prosecution of White-Collar Crimes* (Washington, D.C.: Law Enforcement Assistance Administration, 1970).

2. Herbert Jacob, *Urban Justice: Law and Order in American Cities* (Englewood Cliffs, N.J.: Prentice Hall, 1973), p. 16.

3. On the growth of the federal crime-fighting role, see: Vivian E. Watts, "Federal Anti-Crime Efforts: The Fallout on State and Local Governments," *Intergovernmental Perspective* (Winter 1992): 35–38.

4. Lyn Kathlene, "Alternative Views of Crime: Legislative Policymaking in Gendered Terms," *The Journal of Politics* 57 (August 1995): 696–723.

5. See, for example: David C. Nice, "State Deregulation of Intimate Behavior," *Social Science Quarterly* 69 (March 1988): 203–211.

6. Larceny is stealing that does not involve force or fraud. Aggravated assault is assault with intent to kill or inflict severe bodily harm.

7. Information on the estimated number of actual crimes is contained in the United States Department of Justice's annual national survey of household heads, called the National Crime Victimization Survey.

8. United States National Institute of Justice, *Drug Use Forecasting* (quarterly).

9. *Juvenile Offenders and Victims: A National Report* (Washington, D.C.: Department of Justice, 1995).

10. "Youngest Teens at Greatest Crime Risk," Department of Justice, press release (31 May 1995).

11. See more recent editions of: United States Department of Justice, *Public Opinion Regarding Crime, Criminal Justice and Related Topics* (Washington, D.C.: Government Printing Office, annual).

12. For background see, generally: National Advisory Committee on Criminal Justice Standards, *Organized Crime in America* (Washington, D.C.: Government Printing Office, 1978).

13. See: Sue A. Lundgren, "The Cost of Justice," in United States Department of Justice, Bureau of Justice Statistics, *Report to the Nation on Crime and Justice* (Washington, D.C.: Government Printing Office, 1988), pp. 120–127.

14. "Justice on Trial," *Newsweek* (8 March 1971): 16.

15. "Losing Ground," *Newsweek* (6 April 1992): 20–22. See also: Ellen Joan Pollock and Stephen J. Adler, "Justice for All?—Legal System Struggles to Reflect Diversity, but Progress Is Slow," *Wall Street Journal* article reprinted in *Congressional Record-Senate* (12 May 1992): S6514–6515.

16. See: Elinor Ostrom, Roger B. Parks, and Gordon P. Whitaker, "Do We Really Want to Consolidate Urban Police Forces? A Reappraisal of Some Old Assertions," *Public Administration Review* (September/October 1973): 423–432. See also: Elinor Ostrom and William Baugh, *Community Organization and the Provision of Police Services* (Beverly Hills, Calif.: Sage Publications, 1973). For a contrary view, see: Harry P. Pachon and Nicholas P. Lovrich Jr., "The Consolidation of Urban Public Services: A Focus on the Police," *Public Administration Review* 37 (January/February 1977): 38–47.

17. See United States Bureau of the Census, *Public Employment,* series GE, no. 1 (annual).

18. See: Thomas R. Dye, *Policy Analysis* (University: University of Alabama Press, 1976), pp. 83–88.

19. Brian A. Reaves, "State and Local Police Departments, 1990," *Bureau of Justice Statistics Bulletin* (February 1992): 1.

20. See: William G. Lewis, "Toward Representative Bureaucracy: Blacks in City Police Organizations, 1975–1985," *Public Administration Review* (May/June 1989): 257–268; Grace Hall Saltzstein, "Black Mayors and Police Policies," *The Journal of Politics* 51 (August 1989): 525–544; and report in "Battleground Chicago," *Newsweek* (3 April 1995): 26–35.

21. See: Jerome H. Skolnick, *Justice without Trial* (New York: John Wiley and Sons, 1966), pp. 42–64.

22. See, generally: James Q. Wilson, *Varieties of Police Behavior* (New York: Atheneum, 1970).

23. See: Leonard Schecter and William Phillips, *On the Pad* (New York: G. P. Putnam's Sons, 1973). See also: Lawrence W. Sherman, ed., *Police Corruption: A Sociological Perspective* (Garden City, N.Y.: Anchor Books, 1974).

24. "Brutality on the Beat," *Newsweek* (25 March 1991): 32–38, quote at 32.

25. *Ibid.*

26. For a review of the factors involved, see: Jerome H. Skolnick and James J. Fyfe, *Above the Law: Police and the Excessive Use of Force* (New York: The Free Press, 1993).

27. Douglas W. Perez, *Common Sense about Police Review* (Philadelphia: Temple University Press, 1994).

28. See: Joel D. Aberbach and Jack L. Walker, "The Attitudes of Blacks and Whites toward City Services: Implications for Public Policy," in John P. Crecine, ed., *Financing the Metropolis* (Beverly Hills, Calif.: Sage Publications, 1970), pp. 519–537; and George L. Kelling et al., *The Kansas City Prevention Patrol Experiment: A Technical Report* (Washington, D.C.: The Police Foundation, 1974).

29. See: *Report of the National Advisory Commission on Civil Disorders* (New York: Bantam Books, 1968).

30. See: Peter B. Bloch, *Equality of Distribution of Police Services: A Case Study of Washington, D.C.* (Washington, D.C.: The Urban Institute, 1974); and Peter H. Rossi, *The Roots of Urban Discontent* (New York: John Wiley and Sons, 1974).

31. Stephen L. Percy, "Citizen Involvement in Coproducing Safety and Security in the Community," *Public Productivity Review* 42 (Summer 1987): 83–93.

32. Joseph P. Viteritti, *Police, Politics and Pluralism in New York City: A Comparative Case Study* (Beverly Hills, Calif.: Sage Publications, 1973).

33. 384 U.S. 436.

34. See: David Fellman, "The Supreme Court's Changing Views of Criminal Defendants' Rights," in Barbara N. McLennan, ed., *Crime in Urban Society* (New York: Dunellen, 1970), pp. 110–113.

35. President's Commission on Law Enforcement and Administration of Justice, *The Challenge of Crime in a Free Society* (Washington, D.C.: Government Printing Office, 1967).

36. Robert M. Carter and Leslie T. Wilkins, "Some Factors in Sentencing Policy," *Journal of Criminal Law, Criminology, and Police Science* 58 (1967): 503–514.

37. *Reducing Crime and Assuring Justice* (New York: Committee for Economic Development, 1972), p. 41.

38. *Ibid.*

39. Cassia Spohn, Susan Welch, and John Gruhl, "Women Defendants in Court: The Interaction between Sex and Race in Convicting and Sentencing," *Social Science Quarterly* (1985): 176–185.

40. See: Edward Green, *Judicial Attitudes in Sentencing* (London: Macmillan, 1971), and sources cited therein.

41. Linda Harriman and Jeffrey D. Straussman, "Do Judges Determine Budget Decisions? Federal Court Decisions in Prison Reform and State Spending for Corrections," *Public Administration Review* (July/August 1983): 343–351.

42. John J. Dilulio Jr., *Governing Prisons: A Comparative Study of Correctional Management* (New York: The Free Press, 1987).

43. "Bloody Attica: Furies Unleashed," *Newsweek* (27 September 1971): 22.

44. United States Department of Justice, Office of Justice Programs, Bureau of Justice Statistics, *Prisoners in 1994* (August 1994).

45. See: Donald M. Gottfredson, "Correctional Decision-Making," in Gottfredson, ed.,

  Decision-Making in the Criminal Justice System: Reviews and Essays (Rockville, Md.: National Institute of Mental Health, 1975), pp. 82–91, and sources cited therein.

46. *Rudolph* v. *Alabama*, 375 U.S. 889, 891 (1963).

47. See: Tecia Barton and John Culver, "State Politics and the Death Penalty: Moving to a New Period of Executions?" *Comparative State Politics* 9 (December 1988): 4–9.

48. See, for example, David W. Moore, "Americans Firmly Support Death Penalty," *The Gallup Poll Monthly* (June 1995): 23–24.

49. David C. Nice, "The States and the Death Penalty," *Western Political Quarterly* (1992): 1037–1048.

50. Melinda Gann Hall and Paul Brace, "The Vicissitudes of Death by Decree: Forces Influencing Capital Punishment Decision Making in State Supreme Courts," *Social Science Quarterly* 75 (March 1994): 136–151.

51. See: Harold E. Pepinsky, "Police Decision-Making," in Gottfredson, ed., *Decision-Making in the Criminal Justice System*, pp. 21–52.

52. See: George L. Kelling et al., *The Kansas City Preventive Patrol Experiment*.

53. Randy Arndt, "Crimes, Jobs, Mandates," *Nation's Cities Weekly*, (23 January 1995): 1, 4.

INDEX

☆ ☆ ☆

ABOUT THE AUTHOR

DAVID R. BERMAN is a professor of Political Science at Arizona State University. He specializes in state and local politics, government, and public policy. He has written several books and scholarly articles in these areas and has been a regular contributor to the *Municipal Year Book*.